Y0-BQH-702

Curriculum-Based Assessment

Curriculum-Based Assessment
Testing What Is Taught

John Salvia and Charles Hughes
The Pennsylvania State University

MACMILLAN PUBLISHING COMPANY

New York

Editor: Robert Miller
Production Supervisor: Linda Greenberg
Production Manager: Sandra Moore
Text Designer: Carol Lavis
Cover Designer: Michael Jung
Cover illustration: E. Salem Krieger
Illustrations: Hadel Studio

This book was set in Electra by Huron Valley Graphics, Inc., and
printed and bound by R. R. Donnelley & Sons Company.
The cover was printed by Phoenix Color Corp.

Macmillan Publishing Company
866 Third Avenue, New York, New York 10022

Collier Macmillan Canada, Inc.

Library of Congress Cataloging-in-Publication Data

Salvia, John.
   Curriculum-based assessment : testing what is taught / John Salvia
and Charles Hughes.
      p. cm.
   Bibliography: p.
   Includes indexes.
   ISBN 0-02-405371-6
   1. Curriculum-based assessment—United States.   I. Hughes,
Charles A., 1948– . II. Title.
LB3060.32.C74S25   1990
371.2′7—dc20   89-34029
                                                    CIP

Printing: 1 2 3 4 5 6 7   Year: 1 2 3 4 5 6

This book is dedicated to

Shawn Salvia—*for your encouragement, help, and patience,*

and

Hilary Ruhl Hughes—*for your ideas and for reminding me what it's like to be a third grader.*

Preface

Curriculum-Based Assessment: Testing What Is Taught is an introduction to the assessment of learning and classroom behavior. The focus of this book is on practical classroom applications. In its preparation, we have tried to integrate useful concepts and practices from a variety of sources: applied psychometrics, applied behavioral analysis, curriculum development and evaluation, precision teaching, and current educational policy.

Curriculum-Based Assessment: Testing What Is Taught is intended for beginners, although some of the material is unavoidably technical. We have not assumed that students will bring a lot of information and experience to these chapters. Consequently, we have explained the prerequisite concepts and background information required, although these explanations lack the depth in which a student might study curriculum development and analysis, psychometric theory, or applied behavioral analysis in courses devoted to those topics. To simplify things, we have not provided statistical derivations or elaborate theoretical bases for the practices and procedures described. Where the material is technical in nature, we provide the background material that is necessary. For students unfamiliar with some basic statistical procedures, computational examples are provided in the Appendix. In addition, for interested readers, we have referenced more technical information throughout the text.

Curriculum-Based Assessment: Testing What Is Taught is designed to be user friendly and incorporates several features that should help students to learn the concepts and procedures described. At the beginning of each chapter is a list of key terms. These are important concepts to which readers should attend as they move through the chapter. Technical and supplementary information is generally dealt with in footnotes so that those interested can have such information and beginners will not be sidetracked. References are cumulative throughout the text so that students who use this text as a reference work will not have to remember the chapter in which a reference appeared. Finally, a glossary and index are provided at the end of the text.

The first chapter describes the role of assessment in a variety of educational decisions, discusses the advantages and disadvantages of various procedures that teachers might use to collect assessment information, and outlines a model for conducting systematic assessments that mirror instructional goals. The next four chapters develop each step in the model: (1) specifying the reasons for assessment (e.g., evaluating pupil progress); (2) analyzing curriculum and (3) formulating objectives; (4) developing appropriate assessment procedures; (5) collecting data; (6) summarizing data; (7) displaying data in tables and graphs; and (8) interpreting these data and making decisions. Depending on the purpose for assessment and the nature of the data collected, these steps may be combined in our discussion. For example, in discussing reliability and validity, we have combined the development of tests with the collection of data because the reliability and validity of assessment procedures are influenced by data collection procedures.

The next six chapters apply this assessment model to major elements of classroom instruction: reading, mathematics, written language, adaptive and social behavior, learning strategies, and preschool education. To the extent possible, these chapters are developed in a similar format. First, the scope (i.e., major components of the domain) and typical sequence of instruction are discussed. Next, the procedures and performance measures used to assess learning and performance are discussed. Each of these chapters concludes with one or more extended examples that demonstrate how the assessment model can be implemented within particular domains. The extended examples were carefully selected to provide a thorough coverage of the types of assessment decisions made in the schools (e.g., referral, progress monitoring), the ages of students assessed (i.e., preschool through high school), the severity of a student's problem, and the educational setting (e.g., mainstream and special-education settings). The final chapter, "Managing Curriculum-Based Assessment in the Classroom," describes a myriad of practical procedures that a teacher might use to make classroom assessment efficient and effective.

We were assisted in the preparation of this book by several individuals. First, we wish to express our appreciation to Professors Stephen Bagnato and John Neisworth, who wrote the chapter on curriculum-based assessment for preschool children, and to Professor Deborah Bott, who wrote the chapter on managing curriculum-based assessment. We also wish to acknowledge four graduate students who have assisted us in preparing various portions of this text: Delores Hartman, who prepared the glossary in addition to collaborating on the *Instructor's Manual*, Karl Fleischer and Mary Parola for their assistance in the preparation of portions of Chapter 4, and Marnie Knox Anderson, who provided suggestions on an early version of our manuscript. Also, we wish to thank Sheryl Van Dyne for several suggestions on early drafts. Finally, we wish to thank several colleagues at other universities who offered many helpful suggestions during the development of this text: Stewart Ehly, University of Iowa; Ronald Eaves, Auburn University; Anne Marie Palinscar, Michigan State University; Mark Shinn, University of Oregon; Lynn Fuchs, Vanderbilt University; Roland Good, University of Pittsburgh; Vivienne Jacobs, Purdue University; and Lori Korinek, College of William and Mary.

Most of all we wish to thank our wives, Shawn Amig Salvia and Kathy Ruhl, for their assistance, encouragement, and support throughout this project.

Contents

Contents

Chapter 3: Analysis of Curriculum and Formulation of Objectives   40

Chapter 4: Development of Appropriate Assessment Procedures; Collection and Summarization of Results   66

Chapter 8: Curriculum-Based Assessment in Written Language 184

Chapter 9: Curriculum-Based Assessment in Adaptive and Social Behavior 211

Contents

Chapter 1

Introduction to the Assessment of Achievement

Key Terms

Achievement
Attainment
Component
Criterion-referenced test
Curriculum
Diagnostic test
Group-administered test
Individually administered test

Levels
Norm-referenced test
Objective-referenced test
Probe
Rating scale
Survey test
Systematic observation

The purpose of schooling is to help students learn various concepts and behavior. Learning is usually defined as a stable change in behavior not attributable to maturation or drugs (cf. Bugelski, 1964; Travers, 1982). Thus, prior to learning a student did not do something (e.g., write correct answers to addition problems) and after learning did do something (e.g., correctly answer addition problems). Learning is inferred from the change in behavior.

Although finding out if students have learned sounds easy, three conditions must be met. First, the only way to demonstrate that learning has occurred is to demonstrate that there has been a change in behavior (although there is compelling evidence showing that latent learning occurs).[1] The changes in behavior

---

[1]Latent learning literally means hidden learning. It refers to the distinction between learning and performance: Learned behavior may not be performed. Thus, the learning is hidden until the appropriate contingencies are present.

must be observable or the consequences and products of the changes must be observable. First, to the extent that other individuals with comparable levels of training can understand and use the descriptions of the behavior, the behavior is public; all of the meanings (behaviors and products) that are intended are clearly specified. Second, objectives must be open to public scrutiny at the time the evaluation is made. Since a behavior or product is used to evaluate the attainment of an objective, evaluations are always made after the behavior has occurred or the product has been made. Also, objectives for future behavior (e.g., an objective that the student will vote regularly when 18) cannot be assessed scientifically. At best we can predict—but not know—what a student will do. Third, methods selected to assess learning must produce data that are, themselves, objective and publicly verifiable. This limitation requires that there be careful delineation of the criteria used to judge the adequacy of the behavior or product used to infer learning.[2]

What has been learned is generally termed *attainment*. Attainment represents learning regardless of where or how it has occurred. Achievement is a special type of attainment. Achievement is what has been learned as a result of a specific course of instruction (cf. Salvia & Ysseldyke, 1988, p. 9). Information about a student's attainment is useful primarily for decisions about readiness: Does Billy have the skills to begin instruction in algebra or does William have the skills to begin work as an automobile assembler? Information about achievement has more varied uses since a student's ability to learn is inferred. School personnel, parents, and students themselves use information to make a variety of decisions about students:

- *Where* students will be educated (e.g., in special education or in regular education)
- *What* students will learn (e.g., college-preparatory curricula or vocational education, algebra or business math, advanced-placement biology or general science)
- *Weaknesses* that need to be remediated (e.g., lack of mastery of basic multiplication facts or incorrect use of phonic analysis)
- *Strengths* upon which subsequent instruction can be built (e.g., relatively strong listening or reading comprehension)

Information that can be used to make these decisions comes from three general sources: observations, tests, and impressions. These sources of information are not discrete in the sense that they are qualitatively different entities. Observa-

[2]Sometimes teachers, administrators, parents, and philosophers want to develop goals for which there are no observable behaviors (e.g., the students will cooperate). In order to assess attainment of such objectives, teachers must list the objective indicators that students will evince. Thus, they must substitute for "cooperate" a list of behaviors that *in sum* they intend for the word "cooperate": for example, take turns, agree to requests made by peers, follow rules of games, use "please" and "thank you" when making requests, and comply with requests made by adults. They can perform a scientific evaluation only on those objectives that can be restated in terms of observable behaviors or products. In instances where goals for internal states or feelings cannot be recast in terms of observable behaviors, there can be no scientific assessment of attainment.

tions, tests, and impressions share many of the same attributes, but some distinctions can be made.

Observation is the most encompassing term and implies listening or watching a person as well as making judgments about that person's performance. (For example, whether Jimmy exhibited a particular behavior or wrote a particular response.) Observations can vary considerably in the degree of structure under which they occur. For example, observers may use very precise definitions of behavior to guide decision making or may not specify definitions at all; observers may use very precise schedules to guide the times observations occur or may not use schedules at all; observers may structure a situation to increase the likelihood of observing a behavior (e.g., placing particular toys in the student's environment) or may observe a student in an unprepared (i.e., natural) environment.

Tests are a way of obtaining systematic observations in a structured situation. Like other forms of systematic observation, target behaviors (i.e., correct responses) are defined. Especially important is the standardization of the procedures used in giving a test. The way in which a test is given is the same for all students: The amount of time allotted to each student is the same; the directions given to each student are the same; and the responses to requests for additional information made by any student (e.g., clarifications, hints) are the same. These procedures must be the same or neither scores earned by the same student on different tests nor the scores earned by different students on the same test can be compared meaningfully. Similarly, materials given to students are the same. Materials include such things as answer forms (e.g., multiple-choice response forms), accompanying charts, maps, figures and tables, and access to textbooks, notes, calculators, or computers.

Impressions are less structured observations or recollections. The behaviors, personal characteristics, and contexts that are to be used as well as the contribution of each are not systematized. Thus, impressions may be based on unspecified periods of contact with a student (e.g., a parent's appraisal of a student's academic progress over a school year or a teacher's observation during recess yesterday); the time when a student was observed is not specified (e.g., impressions may be based on behavior that occurred last year or today); the criteria for evaluating behavior is unspecified (e.g., parents may feel that a particular class of behavior was problematic during their child's development, or a teacher may believe that a student's classroom behavior is difficult to manage).

These three general sources of information are usually divided into finer categories. Table 1.1 contains working definitions for many of these subcategories.

It is important for educators to distinguish among categories and subcategories of information because the various types of information differ greatly in terms of the inferences that can be drawn and because different decisions require different inferences. For example, a decision about a student's eligibility for special education usually requires inferences about a student's performance compared with the performances of other students. A decision about the appropriate starting place for instruction in arithmetic requires an inference about mastery of specific arithmetic content. Information sufficient to reach a correct decision about eligibility usually is not sufficiently precise to use in locating a starting point for instruction.

3

TABLE 1.1
Common Distinctions
Among Sources of
Information

Observations

- **Systematic observations** are observations of predetermined behavior. These observations are conducted according to a strict set of procedures for defining the times of observation, the conditions of observation, and the target behaviors.

- **Critical incident observations** are observations of a restricted number of events deemed particularly important by the observer. Unlike systematic observations, the particular behavior that is observed is not specified in advance. Often, the antecedents and consequences of the behavior are also noted.

- **Anecdotal records** are quite similar to observations of critical incidents. Anecdotal records differ in that there are no restrictions on the number of observations.

- **Evaluations of permanent products** are assessments made about the outcomes of behavior. Permanent products include anything that can be inspected after it was produced. Written tests and video- or audiotapes of behavior also can be considered permanent products; however, permanent products more often refer to worksheets, essays, drawings, and so on.

Tests

- **Norm-referenced tests** are tests that compare the performance of the student with the performances of similar students (e.g., students of the same age or grade).

- **Criterion-referenced tests** are tests that compare the student's performance to an absolute standard (e.g., the student correctly adds 3 + 4).

- **Group-administered tests** are tests that can be given to more than one student at a time. Students mark their own responses, and the tester may or may not read the questions to the students. Student performance is usually reported as the number (or percent) correct or, if the test is norm referenced, in terms of relative standing (e.g., percentile rank).

- **Individually administered tests** are tests that are given to only one student at at time. Usually, the examiner reads the questions and records the student's responses. Student performance is usually reported as a number or in terms of relative standing.

- **Objective-referenced tests** are norm-referenced tests that have instructional objectives written for individual test items.

- **Probes** are timed, brief (usually 3 minutes or less) tests that are sensitive to small changes in what a student knows and that can be administered frequently. Student performance is usually reported as a rate.

- **Survey tests** are tests that contain a sufficient number of test items only to make accurate discriminations among test takers. Survey tests may assess several domains—e.g., reading, math, spelling—or several skills within a domain—e.g., addition without regrouping, addition with regrouping.

- **Diagnostic tests** are tests that have a sufficient number of test items to allow correct inferences about the type of errors a pupil makes or about a pupil's mastery of particular skills or concepts. Because they contain many more items than survey tests, diagnostic tests usually assess only one domain.

Impressions

- **Rating scales** are devices that ask parents, teachers, or others to make judgments about a student's performance or social behavior based upon the rater's experience with the student.

- **Interviews** are similar to but less structured than rating scales. In interviews, the person being interviewed is asked to make judgments about the subject of the interview. However, unlike rating scales, the interviewer often seeks to ascertain the accuracy of the judgments by requesting additional information. In some instances the interviewer simply records the judgment of the person being interviewed.
- **Clinical impressions** are professional judgments about an individual. These judgments are often working hypotheses of the professional as opposed to firm diagnoses.

Similarly, information from a diagnostic arithmetic test that allows correct inferences about where to start instruction is usually far more detailed than necessary to reach decisions about eligibility. These examples are not intended to suggest that information gathered for one purpose is useless for another purpose. They are intended to suggest that the utility of information gathered for one purpose is usually of limited usefulness for other purposes. For example, educators rely heavily on norm-referenced intelligence tests to make decisions about a student's eligibility for special educational services because direct comparisons to the intellectual functioning of other students is usually mandated in state education codes. However, norm-referenced tests of intelligence are often a source of information other than a student's IQ. Perhaps a psychologist observes perseveration or impulsive behavior during the test's administration. However, the context in which the behavior was observed precludes unqualified generalization to classroom settings. It would be better to conduct systematic observations of the student to validate the psychologist's anecdotal observation.

Teachers, especially those who work with handicapped students, are often recipients of information gathered from assessments on school-age students: intelligence quotients, descriptions of intrapsychic functioning, scores from norm-referenced survey tests, and detailed medical reports (perhaps containing discussions of chromosomal analyses or metabolic disturbances). Much of this information is of great value to other professionals working with or on behalf of the students, for example, psychologists, administrators, health-service personnel, and social workers. Information of this type may be useful in making decisions about classification and, perhaps, very long-term goals for individual pupils. However, this type of information is usually of limited value to teachers.

Teachers' primary responsibilities are instructional. They are responsible for helping the students who are placed in their classrooms to master a body of facts (e.g., addition facts, letter–sound correspondences, history, English grammar). They are responsible for helping students to become proficient in various processes—concept attainment, critical thinking, problem solving, scientific method, logical deduction, organization of information, and so on. They are responsible for helping students to develop appropriate methods of behaving toward adults and other students. Finally, they are held responsible by many parents and school boards for the development of certain attitudes—patriotism, worthwhile use of leisure time, respect for authority, and so on. In short, teachers are responsible for changing students in several ways.

Assessment is an integral part of the instructional process. It can provide teachers with information about what their students know and do not know. This information, together with information about what the teachers are actually teaching, can lead to correct inferences about how well their students are learning, in what areas their students are having difficulties, where added instruction is necessary, and how well the the teachers themselves are teaching.

The information that is needed by teachers concerns how well the students are, in fact, learning the individual components of the curriculum—the objectives—and how rapidly they are progressing through the curriculum. Moreover, to plan and evaluate effective educational programs, teachers need assessment information gathered frequently, accurately, quickly, and painlessly (certainly for the students and preferably for the teachers themselves).

Use of Observations

Observation is the preferred method of assessing social behavior as well as many types of academic behavior. By observation we mean watching (or listening to) behavior that is occurring or examining the permanent products of behavior. (Permanent products include transcripts or tapes of the behavior as well as the other indices of the results of the behavior—e.g., a student's worksheet, graffiti on a wall.)[3] There are two general types of observations: systematic and unsystematic. Both have advantages and disadvantages.

In systematic observations the observer sets out to evaluate predetermined behavior using carefully developed definitions of the behavior to be observed, a plan for the times at which the behavior is to be observed, and a plan for the number of observations that are to be made. The primary advantage of systematic observations are their precision and accuracy. However, they can be time consuming.

In unsystematic observation, the observer simply watches (or listens) and notes behaviors that seem important. The advantage of this type of observation is that it allows the observer to reach a general conclusion about a student or a situation quite efficiently. When properly used, unsystematic observations can be used to generate target behaviors for systematic observations. There are two major disadvantages in the use of unsystematic observations. First, they are often inaccurate because unrepresentative behavior may be observed.

- The period of time in which the observation occurs may not be representative. For example, a high school English teacher may note that Jimmy often seems tired and sleeps in class. Yet the teacher may see Jimmy only after basketball practice.

[3]We cannot observe things that have not yet occurred. Some might exclude Jean Dixon, the Delphi Oracle, tarot readers, and spiritualists from this generalization. However, except in certain religious and parapsychological circles, this principle is widely accepted.

- The context in which the behavior occurs may not be representative. For example, the high school English teacher notes that Jimmy sleeps in class. However, that teacher only sees Jimmy in English where *Beowulf* is being studied. Jimmy may be a lively participant in social studies, where he finds the content more interesting and relevant.

Second, unsystematic observations may be inaccurate because the personal definitions of behavior used by the observer may not be precise or stable. For example, Jimmy's teacher may think Jimmy is sleeping because he has his eyes closed. However, the teacher's definition of sleeping does not distinguish between daydreaming—or even listening—with closed eyes. Third, as nonsystematic observations become more subjective, they become more susceptible to bias (but more on this point when we deal with impressions).

In addition, we generally distinguish between unsystematic observations of past and current behavior. Retrospective observation—the recall of behavior or events that have occurred in the past—is usually not as accurate as current observations. For example, eyewitness accounts of crime are not terribly reliable even though the behavior observed has high social importance.

Observational assessments usually should combine unsystematic and systematic observations. Teachers generally watch their students and note atypical behavior—both positive and negative. If they observe behavior that is disturbing to them, they develop more systematic procedures to verify that behavior.

Use of Tests

Two general types of tests can be distinguished: published and teacher-made[4] tests. These two types of test differ in several important ways: how the content of the test is developed, what type of interpretations can be made from the scores, and how appropriate the tests are for making various educational decisions.

Published Achievement Tests

Two types of published achievement tests are available: tests published with norms and tests published without norms. These two types of tests are quite different in terms of underlying assumptions and usefulness.

Published Tests, with Norms

Published norm-referenced achievement tests presumably offer a host of advantages (Thorndike & Hagen, 1978)[5] about which there is little controversy:

- *Carefully prepared items.* Preparation of test questions is time consuming and fairly difficult. Moreover, it would be unusual if the first version of a test con-

---

[4]We use the term *teacher-made* generically throughout this text to refer to tests constructed by an educator, including psychologists, speech and language specialists, and others.

[5]See the Glossary for more complete definitions of these concepts and Chapter 4 for a discussion.

tained nothing but good questions—questions that contained no tip-offs to the correct answer, that used appropriate vocabulary, and so on. More often, test questions go through several revisions before all of them can be considered good.

- *Items of known difficulty and scores of known reliability.* These two bits of information are useful in interpreting student performance. Item difficulty refers to the number of students who answer the test question correctly; reliability refers to the accuracy with which one can generalize from a particular sample of questions (i.e., the test) to all similar questions. Both indices require that the test be given and statistics be calculated.[6]

- *National norms.* Knowing how other students across the nation perform on test questions provides a generalized frame of reference for evaluating pupil attainment, the effectiveness of a teacher's curriculum in developing the knowledge assessed on the test, and perhaps the effectiveness of instruction.

The fundamental problem with using published tests is the test's content. If the content of a test—even content prepared by experts—does not match the content that is taught, the test is useless for evaluating what a student has learned from school instruction. To measure achievement, as opposed to attainment or academic aptitude, the content of the achievement test should closely resemble the content of the curriculum. Thus, when one gives a published *achievement* test, one assumes that students taking the test have been exposed to its content and that the test measures the more important aspects of the curriculum. Moreover, published achievement tests are achievement tests (as opposed to aptitude or attainment tests) *only when the content of the achievement test matches the content of instruction.* The scores that pupils earn when an "achievement" test does not match instruction will more likely reflect their intellectual ability rather than their true achievement (Good, 1981).

The research literature that deals with curriculum–test match is quite clear: Commercially prepared published achievement tests vary considerably in the degree to which there is a match. To illustrate, consider this simple example. Suppose that Ms. Roscoe, a special-education teacher, was stressing sight vocabulary with her educable mentally retarded (EMR) students. Further, suppose that she decided to teach the American Heritage word list—1,000 of the most commonly used words in American English prose—for word recognition and spelling. (The American Heritage list contains words from the Dolch list and more than 800 sight words from the first three grades of the Bank Street reading series.) Ms. Roscoe's instruction was effective. After one year, all of her students could recognize and spell all of the words she taught, but none of the variants. If they knew "cat," they would not be able to recognize or spell "cats" or "bat." Thus, the students learned exactly what they had been taught but nothing more. Finally, suppose that Ms. Goodnight, the school psychologist, tested the reading recognition and spelling of each pupil with the Wide Range Achievement Test (WRAT) and the Peabody Individual Achievement Test (PIAT). When given the reading subtest on the WRAT the students would know 21 words: *cat, see, red, to, big, work, book, eat, was, him, how, then,*

---

[6]This material is discussed in some detail in Chapter 4.

	PIAT	WRAT
Reading Recognition	< 65	78
Spelling	77[a]	83

TABLE 1.2
Standard Scores for
Ms. Roscoe's Pupils on
Four Subtests

[a]If basal and ceiling rules were ignored, the raw score correct would be 25, and the standard score would be 102.

open, letter, deep, even, size, weather, should, felt, and *huge.* On WRAT spelling, the students would be able to spell 19 words: *go, cat, in, boy, and, will, make, him, say, cut, light, must, reach, order, watch, enter, explain, edge,* and *result.* When given the PIAT, the students would recognize the following words on the reading recognition subtest: *run, play,* and *round.* On the spelling subtest of the PIAT, the students would be able to spell 13 words: *me, go, man, good, has, when, time, girls, brother, last, sentence, science,* and *business.*

If the basal and ceiling rules[7] were applied during testing and if it is assumed that the students are between the ages of 7 and 7 years, 5 months, standard scores (mean = 100, S = 15) can be found for Ms. Roscoe's pupils on the four subtests (see Table 1.2). Several things should be noted. The two tests do not produce the same estimates in either reading or spelling. On neither of the tests do the students earn scores of 100, the average of students that age. In this particular instance, neither the WRAT nor the PIAT is measuring achievement since they both are assessing material that has not been taught.

The procedures used in the preceding example are very similar to those used by Jenkins and Pany (1978) in their comparison of several measures of reading achievement with several basal reading series. Table 1.3 contains the essential findings from their study. These results are more dramatic because they have found substantial differences using reading programs and a number of tests that are widely used.

The conditions imposed in our example (i.e., Ms. Roscoe) and the study by Jenkins and Pany are very restrictive, and two major issues could be raised about the relevance of such restrictive examples. *First,* teachers often supplement basal series so that actual instruction consists of more than what is contained in a basal reading series. Some researchers (Leinhardt & Seewald, 1981; Leinhardt, Zigmond, & Cooley, 1981) have examined this broader issue of instruction–test overlap. The results of these studies indicate that, even taking into account what is taught beyond what is contained in a text series, there is still not a strong relationship between test content and what is taught.

Second, students sometimes generalize (or transfer) what they learn so that their actual achievement may be greater than what is contained in the curriculum. While it is obvious that many students generalize what they have learned, the research literature on spontaneous generalization by handicapped students is far

[7]Basal and ceiling rules are rules for scoring tests. A basal is the highest score below which the students gets all items correct. The ceiling is the lowest score above which a student gets all items wrong. Use of basal and ceiling rules allow the tester not to give all the test items.

			Word	Word		
TABLE 1.3	Curriculum	PIAT	Knowledge	Analysis	SDRT	WRAT
Comparison of Five						
Reading Programs with	Bank Street Reading Series					
the Peabody Individual	Grade 1	1.5	1.0	1.1	1.8	2.0
Achievement Test	Grade 2	2.8	2.5	1.2	2.0	2.7
(PIAT), Word	Keys to Reading					
Knowledge and Word	Grade 1	2.0	1.4	1.2	2.2	2.2
Analysis from the	Grade 2	3.3	1.9	1.0	3.0	3.0
Metropolitan	Reading 360					
Achievement Test, the	Grade 1	1.5	1.0	1.0	1.4	1.7
Stanford Diagnostic	Grade 2	2.2	2.1	1.0	2.7	2.3
Achievement Test	SRA Reading Program					
(SDRT), and Wide	Grade 1	1.5	1.2	1.3	1.0	2.1
Range Achievement	Grade 2	3.1	2.5	1.4	2.9	3.5
Test (WRAT), after	Sullivan Associates					
Jenkins and Pany	Programmed Reading					
(1978)	Grade 1	1.8	1.4	1.2	1.1	2.0
	Grade 2	2.2	2.4	1.1	2.5	2.5

From "Standardized achievement tests: How useful for special education?" by J. Jenkins and D. Pany, *Exceptional Children*, 44, 1978, page 450. Copyright 1978 by The Council for Exceptional Children.

from encouraging. It has been repeatedly demonstrated that students with cognitive and learning handicaps often have marked problems generalizing without careful and systematic instruction and practice (Borkowski & Cavanaugh, 1979; Stokes, Baer, & Jackson, 1974). One direct test of generalization from instructional content to test content was made by Good and Salvia (1988). They found that the scores earned on various achievement tests by normal students were substantially related to the match between test and curricular content. Thus, although curriculum includes more than the content of commercially prepared materials and although student performance does not correspond solely to the content contained in the curriculum, the essential conclusion remains unchanged: The performances of students in different curricula are assessed with differential accuracy by different achievement tests.

There are at least five reasons test content and curricular content do not correspond. These reasons are related, as are their consequences.

1. There is no national or state curriculum that all students are expected to master. Within fairly broad guidelines, local districts can teach the content they wish by methods they choose. In practice, curricula vary substantially— even arithmetic curricula (Shriner & Salvia, 1988). Not only do curricula vary in content, they vary in quality: Some curricula are better than others.[8]

[8]One might argue that, to safeguard students against poor curricula, tests should be developed independently so as not to reflect poor curricula. While we oppose poor curricula, our view is that students should not be doubly penalized by poor curricula and tests that do not reflect what they have been taught.

2. The number of items contained in both survey and diagnostic tests is very limited. The cost of educational and psychological testing is in direct proportion to the amount of time it takes to administer and score a test. Authors and publishers of tests try to minimize testing time, in part by using the fewest number of test questions that will produce accurate results. For norm-referenced tests—and even for diagnostic tests—"accurate results" are equated with discriminations among students. For example, one of the most widely used diagnostic tests of arithmetic is the KeyMath Test. Careful inspection of its content indicates that at the second-grade level[9] there are only 5 items that assess addition facts: "1+3," "5+4," "47 + 2," "7+9," and "66+4."

3. Since only a few items are included, test items are selected to have the widest appeal—to assess content widely used in curricula.[10] In the best of cases, test items are selected to represent popular curricula; for example, the items on the Test of Written Spelling -2 (Larsen & Hammill, 1986) were selected to correspond to 10 spelling curricula. In the worst of cases, test items are selected solely on the basis of their psychometric properties;[11] for example, the items on the Peabody Individual Achievement Test (Dunn & Markwardt, 1970) were selected primarily because of their difficulty levels.

4. When only items with broad appeal are selected, idiosyncratic elements of a curriculum are neglected. For example, some elementary curricula might teach identification of geometric shapes. Because many curricula do not teach these concepts, tests of mathematics are less likely to assess recognition of triangles, squares, and rectangles because they are not relevant for most students.

5. While the content of a test and a curriculum might match in general, the sequences in which the contents are presented may not correspond. Curricular content is seldom lockstepped; it can be taught at different times in elementary or secondary schools. Test authors place a skill or concept within their test according to the performance of the standardization sample. If a student is enrolled in a curriculum that differs substantially in terms of when a topic is taught, that student's performance can be adversely affected.[12] For example, if telling time is taught much later in Curriculum A than it is in most other curricula, then it is likely that children enrolled in Curriculum A will be tested before they are taught the material, even though telling time will eventually be taught.

It should be noted that the principle of matching test content to curriculum content holds for the behavioral and social domains. When self-help skills or

---

[9]Here, "second-grade level" means raw scores (number correct) corresponding to grade equivalents between 1.0 and 3.1.

[10]Devices with broad appeal sell many copies and make profits for all concerned.

[11]Two psychometric properties are often used to select items. First, items that have moderate to high correlations with total scores are incorporated because such items tend to produce homogeneous content; tests that contain homogeneous items tend to be reliable. Second, items that are passed by 40% to 60% of test takers are selected because such items tend to produce distributions of total scores that are normal and to allow higher item–total correlations (see Chapter 4).

[12]Ceiling rules exacerbate the problems when tests and curricula are not in the same sequence. Students may not get the opportunity to respond to items they could answer if those items are above a false ceiling.

various interpersonal behaviors are taught as part of a school curriculum, the appropriate use of published rating scales and observation guides requires that assessment match the curriculum.

There are several important consequences when tests lack content validity. First, mismatched test–curriculum content can lead to incorrect decisions about eligibility and placement of students in special educational programs. For example, suppose that Lucky, a first-grader with normal intelligence, had learned everything taught in his reading curriculum (the Bank Street Reading Series). Also, suppose Lucky was referred for evaluation because of attention problems. As the data in Table 1.3 suggest, if Lucky were tested with the Metropolitan Achievement Test, his reading scores are likely to indicate a significant discrepancy between his ability (i.e., intelligence) and his achievement because the content of the test does not correspond to the reading series. Thus, he might be found eligible for special educational services as a learning disabled student based on this discrepancy. If, on the other hand, he were tested with the Wide Range Achievement Test, he would quite likely earn a higher score because of the closer correspondence of test and curriculum content. Thus, it is less likely that a significant discrepancy between his intelligence and achievement scores would be noted and that he would be found eligible for special education.

Second, tests with too few items cannot be used for making decisions about goal selection, appropriate progress toward instructional goals, or instructional revision. Tests with too few items can be used only for gross approximation for placement within an instructional sequence; tests with too few items are insensitive to small, but real, progress through a curriculum. For example, since KeyMath has only five items appropriate for second-graders, it should not be used to place students in instructional sequences or to monitor their progress on particular objectives. Finally, error analyses cannot be conducted on a test with too few items.[13]

In conclusion, the use of published tests to assess achievement is very limited at this time. While published tests offer a number of potentially useful features, they do not match curricula closely enough for use in instructional or programming decisions. Their primary uses lie in the areas of estimating attainment and, perhaps, *very tentatively* estimating achievement.

Published Tests, without Norms

There are several varieties of tests published without norms: unit and review tests that accompany text series, criterion-referenced tests, and probes. These tests can save teachers significant amounts of time in test construction. However, their uncritical adoption presents many of the same problems inherent in the use of published norm-referenced tests. Specifically, banks of criterion-referenced test items and stacks of probes may not match curriculum or contain enough

---

[13]Error analysis is a technique in which the teacher tries to find a pattern in a student's errors. See Chapter 3 for a discussion.

test items to allow reasonable conclusions about student performance. This is true even of chapter tests that accompany curricular materials.

Teacher-Made Tests

Teacher-made tests offer four potential advantages in providing information about achievement. First, teachers can match exactly the curriculum being taught. Second, teachers can create multiple and interchangeable forms of their tests. Third, teachers can create assessment devices that are sensitive to small changes in student performance. Fourth, teachers can use their own tests flexibly to conform to their current needs and schedule.

Moreover, three of the supposed advantages of commercially available, norm-referenced devices (estimated reliability, known item difficulties, and appropriate normative data to which to compare a student's performance) can be equaled in teacher-made tests.

- *Known item difficulties* (also called *p*-values) presents little challenge to classroom teachers since *p*-values are easily calculated. However, what is desirable in a norm-referenced test is quite different from what is desirable in a teacher-made test. In order to discriminate among test takers with just a few test items, norm-referenced tests usually have items that 40% to 60% of the test takers pass—about half of the sample does not answer each question correctly. Since the purpose of classroom instruction is for *all* students to learn everything that is taught, test items that assess what has been carefully taught should not be so difficult.

- *Known reliability* is not much of a problem either because teachers can (and do) estimate the reliability of their tests. Moreover, several researchers (Deno, Mirkin, & Chiang, 1982; Deno, Mirkin, Lowry, & Kuehnle, 1980; Fuchs, 1986; Marston, Tindal, & Deno, 1984) have demonstrated that one of the most useful types of teacher-made tests—timed probes—provides reliable assessment of student achievement in reading (when students read orally vocabulary words or from a basal text), in written expression (when students write for 3 minutes in response to a story starter or a topic sentence), in math (when students compute a sample of math problems taken from their texts), and in spelling (when students write words from dictation).

- *Appropriate normative data* can be obtained by developing local norms based on students working through specific curricula. While national comparisons may be very interesting to administrators who would like to compare the performances of students in their school district to the performances of students in other districts,[14] local norms are more useful in establishing the appropriateness of goals and objectives and in comparing the progress of individual students to that of their instructional peers, both within a classroom and district-wide. Several sources describe how local norms can be developed (e.g., Shinn, 1988).

[14]National normative comparisons also provide a partial check on the appropriateness of the curriculum adopted in a district since published norm-referenced tests assess what are believed to be the most important and common curricular elements.

The other attributes of commercially prepared tests (i.e., carefully prepared and empirically tested items) are advantages only if teachers do not prepare their test items carefully or do not revise poor items.

Use of Impressions

Impressions refer to beliefs or insights based upon nonsystematically collected data (or no data at all) or undefined criteria for reaching a conclusion about a person. Impressions can be useful in the earliest stages of assessment. Professionals may have tentative conclusions, hunches, or insights about a student or a situation. These nebulous beliefs can act as a starting place for the collection of more systematic forms of data and refined hypotheses.

However, some professionals use only their impressions rather than other forms of information. For example, many teachers prefer to use informal observation and impressions to assess student progress and believe they are accurate in doing so (Fuchs, Fuchs, & Warren, 1982; Salmon-Cox, 1981). For example, Fuchs et al. surveyed special education teachers about how they made judgments about pupil progress and found informal impressions to be the preferred assessment. Unfortunately, a follow-up analysis of the accuracy of these teachers' impressions of student progress within the curriculum was less than encouraging. In addition, they found that students of teachers who made instructional decisions based upon impressions did not progress as rapidly as students whose teachers made data-based decisions. Thus, despite an occasional brilliant insight, the use of impressions by most educators typically does not result in good decision making, probably because the decisions they must make about pupils and learning are quite complex and do not lend themselves to simplistic impressions.

Moreover, the research literature is filled with reports about how impressions and judgments can be biased by irrelevant information. Teachers have been influenced by such things as a pupil's first name (Harari & McDavid, 1973), a pupil's speech accent (Crowl & MacGinitie, 1974), how a pupil's sibling performed in school (Seaver, 1977), the social class of a pupil's parents (Lenkowski & Blackman, 1969; Miller, McLaughlin, Haddon, & Chansky, 1968), a pupil's facial attractiveness (Ross & Salvia, 1975; Salvia, Algozzine, & Sheare, 1977), the diagnostic label given to a student (Foster & Salvia, 1977; Foster, Ysseldyke, & Reese, 1978; Siperstein & Bak, 1978), and probably several other variables. To the extent that these factors affect teacher impressions, students may receive faulty assessments that result in inappropriate treatments.

Choosing Among Procedures

Each procedure for gathering information has advantages and disadvantages. We believe that student learning and behavior are the most important criteria on which to base educational decisions and that the most accurate evaluations of learning and behavior are made on the basis of how students are, in fact, learning and behaving. These criteria are quite different from those typically used in the schools, and their implementation is not as simple as it may sound. In theory, impressions could accurately reflect a pupil's instructional progress; in practice, impressions are simply too imprecise to be used by educators in reaching decisions about students. In theory, published tests could reflect pupils' instructional progress; in practice, only one or two tests actually do. Therefore, in their present form, published tests are not appropriate to use to evaluate learning. In theory, systematic observations and teacher-made tests have the potential to mirror academic and social learning. In practice, teacher-made tests and observational procedures often lack precision.

The tasks confronting educators are how to develop and to apply accurate and appropriate assessment procedures that can be used to monitor and to summarize student learning. Given the current state of affairs, we believe that teacher-made tests and systematic observations have the greatest potential utility because their limitations can be overcome. Over the years, several authors have written cogently about developing teacher-made assessment procedures that offer high accuracy and validity (e.g., Gronlund, 1985; Gronlund, 1982). More recently, several models for developing assessment procedures that closely follow classroom curricula have been reported in the professional and scientific literature (Blankenship, 1985; Deno, 1985; Gickling & Thompson, 1985; Howell & Morehead, 1987; Idol-Maestas, 1983). These recent models have used the term "curriculum-based" to describe their evaluation procedures. The models share a common attribute—assessment precisely based on what a student has been taught within a curriculum—although they differ in underlying views about how assessments are to be conducted and the names given the models (see Shinn, Tindal, & Stein, 1988).

A Model for Curriculum-Based Assessment

In developing the model of educational assessment used in this text, we have been influenced by literature from several areas—applied behavioral analysis, curriculum analysis, curriculum-based assessment (CBA), mastery learning, precision teaching, and test construction theory. Based on these perspectives, appropriate educational assessment must have six capabilities:

- *Curricular match.* Assessment of pupil achievement must reflect what a student has been taught. Educators must know what is being taught before they can determine if students have profited from instruction.

- *Direct measurement of pupil performance.* The behavior assessed should be a measure of the behavior taught. Many educational goals can be translated directly into pupil performance. For example, goals for spelling can be translated directly into writing correctly spelled words; goals for oral reading can be translated directly into the number of words correctly read aloud. Other goals cannot be measured directly, and pupil progress on such goals must be inferred. For example, reading comprehension cannot be measured directly because it is an internal process that cannot be observed; reading comprehension is inferred from direct measures such as answering questions about the text. Whenever possible, direct measures should be used. When goals of education are associated with internal processes, inferences should be minimized.

- *Evaluation of progress on specific objectives as well as more general goals.* Two general paradigms of instruction (or combinations of the two) are used in schools—equal opportunity to learn and mastery learning. In *equal opportunity to learn* paradigms, all students are given equal exposure to material, and levels of mastery are allowed to vary. For example, all students observe the same explanation of material and are given the same amount of practice; differences in pupil mastery are expected. In *mastery* learning, all students are expected to learn the same objectives to the same levels of proficiency, and the time and procedures required to attain mastery are allowed to vary. For example, all students are expected to be able to read passages containing a basic vocabulary. However, the rates at which they learn and the sequences through which they proceed instructionally are allowed to vary while the level of mastery is consistent across students. We believe that a distinguishing feature of special, remedial, and compensatory education should be individualization of instruction whereby students master material at different rates.[15] Consequently, assessments should be capable of yielding data about pupil mastery of important instructional objectives.

- *Frequent administration.* Because we stress mastery of objectives rather than equal exposure to material, repeated assessments are often required. Teachers cannot know that students have mastered objectives until the students demonstrate mastery. Thus, assessments are repeated. In addition, since retention (i.e., maintenance) is an important dimension of learning, material that is mastered is systematically retested occasionally. For these reasons, assessment procedures must have the potential for frequent administration. This requirement means that assessments must be efficient—they should yield accurate information with the minimum investment of time. The time a student is in school is finite. Thus, time spent in assessment takes away from time spent teaching and practicing. Obviously, time spent gathering inaccurate, useless data is more inefficient than spending a bit more time collecting accurate data.

- *Provision of valid inferences about instructional modification.* When students are not mastering instructional objectives, teachers modify instructional programs. Assessment procedures that yield inferences about instructional modifications are more useful than assessment procedures that do not yield such inferences.

- *Reliability.* Assessments should yield information that can be generalized from one set of assessment materials to another, from one observer to another, and from one time to another.

- *Sensitivity to small but important changes in pupil performance.* Progress from one instructional objective to the next often represents relatively small changes in student performance. These changes are important and require assessment for the reasons previously noted. Consequently, assessment procedures must be capable of identifying these changes.

---

[15]It also implies that different sequences of instruction or algorithms may be used.

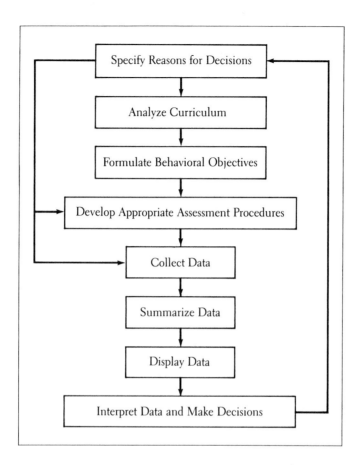

Figure 1.1.
Model for Curriculum-
based assessment.

The foregoing six capabilities must be built into a model for educational assessment. However, these considerations alone do not guarantee appropriate assessment. The assessment procedure must also provide information about student achievement that can be used to answer the variety of questions that prompted assessment in the first place, and must be interpreted correctly. The model for curriculum-based assessment offered in this text (see Figure 1.1) is designed to systematize assessment so that it will be more likely that the assessment information will be useful. The eight steps in this model are interactive; decisions at each step affect decisions at the other steps. These steps are also dynamic; decisions made at each step can be modified as decisions are made at other steps and as instruction and assessment proceed.

1. Specify Reasons for Assessment

Data-based teaching decisions rely on two types of assessment data, which have been called formative and summative (Bloom, Hastings, & Madaus, 1971). Formative data are collected during the process of instruction and are useful for decisions about how to teach and what to teach. Summative data are collected at the end of an instructional sequence. These data are used to make evaluations about student learning (e.g., for grading) that are useful in deciding what to teach and where to teach.

Teachers do not assess just to assess; they should always assess for a reason. Teachers should specify, in advance, the reasons for assessment since different data are used for different purposes. Thus, the first step in the model is to specify the reasons for conducting a curriculum-based assessment. CBAs can generate data that can be used to decide what to teach, how to teach, and where to teach.

What to Teach?

Good achievement data are used to formulate instructional objectives, place students within curricula, and monitor progress through curricula. Teachers need a clear and precise understanding of their educational goals and objectives for each pupil they are teaching. Precise goals and objectives can be combined with precise assessment of achievement so that teachers can specify the skills, information, and behaviors a pupil currently has in relation to the skills, information, and behaviors that are to be learned. The differences between what should be known (goals and objectives) and what is known (attainment) form the instructional goals and objectives.

Teachers also routinely collect achievement data to see how their students are progressing. Are the students learning the particular objectives? If not, the material will have to be retaught or revised and retaught. Are the students progressing through the objectives at an appropriate rate? If not, the instructional program or the expected rate of progress (or both) will have to be revised.

How to Teach?

Assessment data can be used to alter instructional methods; pupil performance should be used as the basis for altering how teachers teach. Mastery of curriculum by students is a clear signal that the instructional program is adequate: Enough of the teaching methods have worked, the curriculum is broken down into satisfactorily sized objectives, and so on. Repeated student failure indicates that something is wrong. Often a pupil's performance will give the teacher a pretty good idea of how to alter instruction to make it more effective. For example, inconsistent performances during extended practice sessions (after an objective has been learned) indicates that the reinforcer[16] may not be effective; this conclusion suggests altering the reinforcer.

Where to Teach?

Assessment data are used to make decisions about referral, classification, and placement. For example, Harry's reading achievement may be so poor that he needs additional instruction outside the classroom by a remedial-reading special-

---

[16]A reinforcer is a consequence of behavior that increases the likelihood that the behavior will recur. For example, if Ms. Li comments, "Good work, Harry" when she notices Harry concentrating on a worksheet and if her comment has the effect of increasing Harry's diligent efforts, "Good work, Harry" is a reinforcer.

ist. In referral, achievement data are used in two ways. First, achievement data can be used to compare a particular pupil with other pupils in a classroom to show that the pupil is so far behind that he or she is instructionally isolated. Second, many states require that teachers document that they have attempted one or more interventions without success before a student can be referred for special services.

In classification decisions, achievement data are used to make decisions about whether a pupil is exceptional and, if so, what is the nature of the exceptionality. Gifted students should have very high achievement. Mentally retarded individuals should have achievement commensurate with their limited intellectual abilities. Learning disabled and emotionally disturbed students should have achievement that is significantly below that predicted by their intellectual abilities.

In placement decisions, achievement data also are used to make decisions about the location and grouping in which instruction will occur. For example, if a handicapped student's achievement in reading and writing is as good as most of the students in Ms. Li's regular class, the handicapped student might be integrated into her class for instruction in these areas. On the other hand, a student's reading and writing skills may not be commensurate with those of most children in any regular educational classroom. If it can be documented that several attempts have been made to improve achievement in these areas and that these attempts were unsuccessful, instruction in reading and writing might be conducted in a special education classroom until achievement is high enough to allow instructional integration.

2. Analyze Curriculum

The next step in the CBA model is analyzing the curricular content that a student is learning. To assess what the student should learn or how well a student has learned, it is, of course, necessary to know what will be taught or has been taught. Thus, a precise curriculum analysis must be conducted. This analysis usually occurs prior to instruction, when teachers decide what to teach; in this case, teachers merely confirm that the material has been presented as planned. Here, curriculum is broadly defined as anything that a teacher intends to teach and have students learn. Thus, curriculum includes both academic subjects as well as such nonacademic objectives as learning how to behave in class, learning self-help skills, and learning how to get along with peers. In conducting a curriculum analysis, teachers pay attention to the levels and components of the curriculum. *Levels* refer to the extent to which mastery occurs and include both cognitive (e.g., knowledge, comprehension, and application) and behavioral levels (e.g., acquisition, fluency, generalization, and maintenance). *Components* are parts of the curriculum. "Component" is used throughout this text as a generic term that can refer to domains (e.g., reading), strands (e.g., sight vocabulary, decoding, or comprehension), or finer subdivisions (e.g., all sounds of the letter *a*). The term is vague because what constitutes a part of a curriculum cannot be defined precisely. For example, writing one's name might appear to be a very simple objective. However, writing one's name consists of smaller parts—writing the individual letters, maintaining proportionality among the letters, and spacing between the letters. Even writing individual letters can be broken down into finer gradations—strokes and parts of strokes. The process of analyzing a curriculum into its components regresses infinitely.

3. Formulate Behavioral Objectives

Behavioral objectives are statements about what students will do to demonstrate they have learned a particular curricular component. Thus, behavioral objectives focus on student performance rather than teacher performance. Behavioral objectives consist of the behavior the student will demonstrate, the conditions under which that behavior will be demonstrated, and the criteria for evaluating the adequacy of the student's performance.

4. Develop Appropriate Assessment Procedures

The fourth step in the model is developing the assessment procedures. A teacher decides how and when learning and performance will be measured and develops (or finds) an appropriate assessment tool. Teachers have several options when deciding how to assess: They can evaluate students' performances from tests, probes, and systematic observations of student performance. They can assess in highly structured situations (e.g., testing time, chalkboard activities, oral recitations) and less structured situations (e.g., seatwork, discussion groups, activities within a learning center).

Decisions about the final form an assessment will take depend on four considerations. First, the purpose for which the assessment data will be used must be considered. Decisions about referral and eligibility for special-education services usually require data that allow for direct comparisons of student performances. For example, those who are eligible for services for learning-disabled students should have substantially lower achievement than students with the same intellectual ability and opportunity to learn.[17] Decisions about instructional goals and the adequacy of pupil progress require data that provide direct measurement of student acquisition of information or behavior. Second, the way in which criterion statements in instructional objectives are conceptualized determine the performance measure to be used. For example, if a criterion is stated as a rate of correct responses per minute, the assessment procedure should permit the calculation rates (i.e., the assessment must be timed, there must be more problems than can be completed in the time period, and so on). Third, direct measures of student performance[18] are more accurate than indirect measures.[19] Thus, direct measures

---

[17]Determination of what constitutes a substantial deficit can be a fairly complicated statistical procedure that compares a student's actual achievement to the achievement predicted from his or her score on an intelligence test. The interested reader might refer to Salvia and Ysseldyke (1988).

[18]A direct measure requires a student to do a task in such a way that the performance can be observed. For example, writing answers to addition problems is a direct measure of addition.

[19]An indirect measure is a measure from which student performance is inferred. For example, reading comprehension cannot be directly observed but is inferred from answered questions about what was read.

should be used whenever possible. Finally, it may be important to consider several student characteristics when developing assessment procedures. Sensory and motor disabilities are easily confounded with achievement when teachers require the use of the impaired capacity. For example, if blind students are required to read printed test materials to assess their understanding of history, estimates of the knowledge of history are hopelessly confounded with their inability to see the test materials. Another example is the student who writes very slowly due to a motor impairment. A teacher who assesses mastery of addition facts by assessing rate of correct answers written per minute confounds hand speed with addition.[20] Less obvious characteristics are also important: stamina, attentiveness, language ability, and so on. Although we will not dwell on pupil characteristics in this text, teachers are urged to consider relevant student characteristics in the development of tests. A guiding principle should be to assess content and not a pupil's characteristics or handicaps.

Once the final form of the assessment has been decided and if a teacher must develop the assessment procedure, careful attention must be paid to developing reliable and valid measures. First, the scoring of student performance should be accurate and replicable. Second, if what is assessed is a sample of a larger domain of content or behavior that might be assessed, the sample should be representative of the domain. Third, student performance should be stable across times. Fourth, student performance should reflect accurately the attainment of instructional goals.[21]

5. Collect Data

Assessment data are collected carefully. First, data must be collected systematically. For example, if the rate of oral reading observed in reading groups is used to monitor pupil progress, then a teacher must plan to have each pupil read a sufficient amount aloud at one time as well as enough times during the week. If a teacher plans to use a paper-and-pencil test to assess arithmetic skills, the test must be administered with sufficient time and supervision to ensure independent work.

Second, data collection should be standardized. Because pupil performance will be compared to some type of standard—the performance of other students, their own earlier performance, an absolute standard of performance (e.g., 90% correct), or some combination—pupil performance must be collected in the same way for all students. Thus, students will be allowed to have the same materials (e.g., tests or stimulus materials), the same accessories (e.g., calculators or dictionaries), the same directions, and the same amount of time. In addition, each student should get the same hints or help during data collection. For example, if a student asks that a word on a test be defined, all students should be given the definition of that word.

Finally, teachers should also consider several practical aspects in collecting

---

[20]Rate of correct answers (or digits) per minute is generally a good measure of mastery. However, in this example oral responses are preferred.

[21]These concepts are more involved than what is presented here. They are treated in detail in Chapter 4.

assessment data. Factors such as the amount of time one wishes to spend in assessment are very important. For example, suppose a special-education teacher had 18 pupils and wished to give a 2-minute reading comprehension test to each pupil every day. The teacher might spend 36 minutes per day individually assessing students, or students might be paired and assess each other, in which case the assessment would take 4 minutes.[22]

6. Summarize Data

Teachers must next put the data into usable form; raw data are converted to some type of performance measure (e.g., number correct, percent correct, or number of correct responses per minute). The types of score to be used generally are stated explicitly in the behavioral objectives. The computations used to make the conversions should be double-checked to ensure accuracy, even when calculators are used.

Finally, the converted data are assembled and stored in an orderly fashion. For example, a teacher can record the data in a grade book or computer file. The two basic options are assembly and storage by student or by task. Data stored by student are useful for making decisions about individual students. Data stored by task are useful for making decisions about a teacher's effectiveness in teaching the skill or behavior across students.

7. Display Data

Pupil performance is usually displayed in tables or graphs. Tables are useful when making summative decisions about performance: Did most of the students master the objective? Which objectives did Harry master?

Graphic display of pupil performance is highly recommended when making decisions about an individual student's progress toward an instructional goal. Numerous researchers have demonstrated that the acts of graphing data and providing graphic feedback to pupils significantly improves learning (Brandstetter & Merz, 1978; Fuchs, Fuchs, & Warren, 1982). Teachers can choose among several options for graphing; the primary consideration is clarity in communicating results to themselves, pupils, parents, or administrators.

8. Interpret Data and Make Decisions

The first step is verification that the data collected are appropriate for making the decision. If they are not, a terrible and expensive mistake has been made; new data will need to be collected. Next, the criteria for decision making are reviewed. If they are no longer appropriate, they are revised. When the criteria are appropriate, they are applied to the data to make the decision that initially prompted the assessment. Data are interpreted in terms of the criterion established to make decisions. Making decisions leads a teacher back to other steps in the model. After

---

[22]Each student in a pair of students would read for 2 minutes; the pair would read for a total of 4 minutes.

the original decisions have been reached, teachers may wish to specify new reasons for assessment, to revise their analysis of the curriculum, or to revise their plan for collecting data.

Implementation of the Model

This model is generic. It can be applied in a number of ways that depend on the specific situation. Different reasons for assessment lead to different implementations. For example, if a student transfers to a teacher's class in November, that teacher would probably assess the student to place him or her within the curriculum. Such an assessment most likely would use a *top-down* format. The teacher would analyze the curriculum in terms of major goals in the instructional sequence, develop a quick screening device to assess mastery of each goal, and assess in depth only those goals not mastered. On the other hand, if a teacher were monitoring progress toward a particular instructional goal, the assessment more likely would include mastery of each component objective (a *bottom-up* format).

Differences in curricula can lead to different implementations. Some curricula are carefully analyzed by someone other than the teacher (e.g., the curriculum author). In such cases, curriculum analysis is as simple as referring to the curriculum's teachers' manual. Teachers may have already developed a complete and well-sequenced set of behavioral objectives. Finally, special-education teachers may have complete and sequenced objectives from their students' Individual Educational Plans (IEPs).[23] In such cases, there is no need for that teacher to formulate initial objectives, although they may need to be revised occasionally for particular students.

Development of appropriate assessment procedures may vary as well. Sometimes the development process may be very simple. Teachers often maintain test files that contain questions that match their curriculum and that have been used and found to be effective. In such cases, a teacher need only select test questions, not develop them. Similarly, if a teacher wants to make an initial placement for instruction in oral reading, test development would be simple. That teacher could simply have the student read passages aloud from the beginning, middle, and end of texts in the reading series until the student's rate of correct and incorrect reading indicated instructional level performance. In other situations, the development of appropriate assessment procedures could be time consuming.

Finally, differences in the collection, summarization, and display of data can vary considerably as a function of local resources and administrative policies. For example, the availability of personal computers and appropriate software[24] can alter the steps in the model. Collection might be automatically accomplished by computer-administered tests. Summarization and display might be accomplished

---

[23]P.L. 94–142 requires that each student receiving special-education services have an Individual Educational Plan that specifies, among other things, long-term goals and short-term objectives.

[24]See Chapter 12.

by the testing program or by inputting unsummarized data. Similarly, the availability of teacher aides, parent volunteers, or peer tutors can modify the specifics of our model.

The next four chapters provide a detailed discussion to elaborate on the general considerations at each step in the model. These chapters stress not only *what* should be done and *why* it should be done, but they also provide the general principles of *how* to do it. The next six chapters apply these general principles to major curricular areas—reading, math, and so on. Each of these chapters has one or two extended examples in which the model for CBA is applied. In their application, some steps may be combined because they tend to be combined in real life. The last chapter returns to a level of general presentation. In that chapter, general procedures for efficiently implementing and managing a program of assessment are provided.

Summary

Educators are responsible for facilitating pupil learning and development. We believe that the only way to know if learning and development have occurred is to assess them systematically and regularly. Educators have a number of options by which these assessments can be accomplished—different types of observations, different types of tests, and impressions. Of these options, teacher-made tests and systematic observations have greater potential of providing accurate and useful information. To reach this potential, these assessment procedures must be developed carefully within the context of the purposes for assessment and the curriculum that students are expected to master. Once assessment data are gathered, they must be put into usable form and actually used to make decisions. While there are general principles to guide educators through the assessment process, specific options and implementations are embedded in each educator's particular situation.

Chapter 2

Specify Reasons for Assessment

Key Terms

Classification
Evaluation of pupil progress
Instructional modification

Placement
Prereferral decision
Referral

The assessment process starts with decision making because different decisions require different types of information. Every day teachers make important decisions for and about their students. Some decisions require information, but systematic data collection is not needed—for example, it's raining so there will be indoor recess today; or, Harry and Ralph are fighting, and the scuffle must be stopped. Our concern is for the many educational decisions that require not only information but also the collection of information. These decisions can be prompted by nonsystematic observations and impressions (e.g., Henry doesn't seem to be doing very well lately) or by a classroom management plan that schedules specific times for decision making (e.g., every Friday decide if each student's progress in math is satisfactory). In either case, systematic assessment begins with a decision that needs to be made and that can be made better on the basis of information.

Five types of decisions are particularly important: decisions about instructional planning, decisions about pupil progress, decisions about referral, decisions about eligibility, and decisions about placement. Each type of decision can be better made when systematic information about pupil achievement and behavior is gathered. Indeed, pupil performance data should be the basis of each of these types of decisions.

Decisions about Instructional Planning

Three instructional planning questions are asked routinely: What should a student be taught? How should a student be taught? Should instruction be modified? The answers to these questions—the decisions that are made—require different information and, therefore, different assessment procedures.

What Should a Student Be Taught?

Achievement within particular curricula is regularly assessed so that teachers can find out what should be taught. Information from a careful assessment of a student's current achievement is a necessary but insufficient condition for planning instruction. Teachers must have achievement information, but this type of information alone is not enough to plan instruction. Teachers also must know the curriculum that they intend to teach to their students. Thus, if they know precisely what they intend their students to learn and if they know what their students already know, where to start in a sequence of objectives is obvious—start where students' knowledge ends.

The procedures for ascertaining what to teach vary according to the circumstances. Teachers are assigned new students regularly. At the beginning of the year (or semester) or any time that students transfer into their classrooms, teachers must decide where to begin instruction and/or into what group to place the students. Generally, new students are given a test (or tests) to survey their mastery of curricular content—prerequisite skills, beginning skills and concepts, and more advanced material. These tests should contain enough questions per content area to allow a reasonably accurate decision about student mastery of the content.[1] Moreover, as part of the assessment for new students, it is often a good idea to make sure that they understand the format in which the questions are asked. For example, students may have learned division facts using slightly different stimuli (e.g., $3\sqrt{15}$, 15/3, or 15 ÷ 3), and may not, as yet, understand that there are different ways to ask the same question.

Results from such surveys can be used in two ways. First, they can be used for initial placement within a curriculum. By examining a student's performance on each major content area, teachers can locate where a student's knowledge of the curriculum ends or mastery is emerging; this marks the place in the curriculum where instruction begins. Second, when results suggest that prerequisites may not have been mastered, more precise assessments are given to pinpoint the prerequisite skills and concepts that must be taught in addition to the next material in the curriculum. Thus, teachers often find it necessary to design brief sequences of instruction to cover important material that others in the class already know.

As the teacher becomes familiar with the student, assessments of student progress guide the decision-making process. As content is mastered, new objectives

---

[1]When a survey test is used, three to five questions for each major skill are often sufficient. Teachers can also use the same multiple-skill probes they use to monitor pupil progress during instruction. Probes are explained in Chapter 4. An example of this type of test is described in the extended example in Chapter 7.

are selected. Also, through the process of error analysis, teachers can generate very specific instructional objectives to correct student mistakes. Finally, teachers participate in the annual preparation of Individualized Educational Plans for students in special education. Knowledge of a pupil's previous progress is essential in developing both short-term and long-term educational objectives. The short-term objectives represent learning the next curricular objective. Long-term goals (i.e., goals for a semester or school year) are based upon both a student's current achievement and rate of progress within the curriculum. Since the time a student spends in school each year is fixed, how fast a pupil masters behavioral and instructional objectives suggests how far a student can proceed in a semester or year.

How Should a Student Be Taught?

Teachers have several choices about instructional methods and materials. Once again, the procedures used in reaching the decision vary according to the circumstances. When confronted with a new student, the decision about how to teach is usually based on what is generally successful: Teachers rely on those techniques that have worked in the past with other, similar students. In addition, teachers might assess students directly in an effort to find out how to teach. For example, students might be asked to select their own rewards, often from a list called a *reinforcer menu*. Teachers also can request information about a pupil's learning preferences. Figure 2.1 lists a variety of instructional preferences about which teachers might gain information.

As that teacher becomes more experienced with the student, decisions about how to teach should be based on data derived from ongoing evaluations of pupil progress. For example, when a pupil performs erratically on review and drill work, the teacher should consider the pupil's motivation because the erratic

---

Environmental Preferences

> Lighting (bright vs. dim; brightly lit room vs. lighted work area only)
>
> Noise (silence vs. background music; TV and so on vs. white noise)
>
> Temperature (warm vs. cool)
>
> Seating (front/middle/rear of classroom; near friends; and so on)

Learning Preferences

> Testing (objective formats vs. essays)
>
> Information Presentation (verbal vs. visual or mathematical; reading vs. listening; inductive vs. deductive)
>
> Cooperation (independent vs. cooperative vs. competitive)
>
> Level of Challenge (easy vs. difficult material)
>
> Rewards (primary vs. social and so on)

FIGURE 2.1.
Instructional preferences of some students.

performance indicates that the student can do the work but does not always do it. Increasing incentives for fast and accurate performance might eliminate the problem. Chapter 5 considers in some detail how teachers can use pupil performance data to modify instruction.

Should Instruction Be Modified?

Logically, one question, "Was instruction actually delivered?" precedes questions about instructional modification. Sometimes teachers intend to teach curricular content or behavior but may not for various reasons—teacher or student absence, modification of school schedule (e.g., assemblies, fire drills), absentmindedness. If the material was not taught, questions about instructional modification are premature.

However, if instruction was provided, teachers can use data from ongoing evaluations of pupil progress to decide if program modification is necessary for an individual student, for an instructional group, or for an entire class. Instruction should be modified when student progress is slower than predicted or necessary to reach the instructional goals in the amount of time available. Teachers answer this question by modifying instruction and observing the effect on pupil progress.

Modifications for an Individual Student

Depending on the particular skills or concepts being taught, inadequate progress by individual students is judged on the basis of two interrelated performance characteristics—too few desirable responses or too many undesirable responses. Desirable responses include such things as correct answers on a test, quick oral responses to questions, prosocial behavior (e.g., using polite words such as please and thanks), behavior that complies with classroom routines (e.g., hand raising), and so forth. Undesirable responses include such things as inaccurate and/or slow responses, antisocial behavior, and noncompliant behavior.

When teachers decide that a program should be modified, they have two sources of inspiration for the specifics of the modification. First, they may get hints about specific modifications from student performance. For example, suppose Mike was learning his addition facts at an acceptable rate but was not remembering them once practice and drill activities were stopped. His performance suggests that more drill and practice may be necessary for retention or that more effective drill and practice activities should be used.

Second, even when the nature of a student's performance does not give any hints about how to modify instruction, teachers can rely on several well-defined instructional practices that are known to be effective with most, if not all, students. While the primary consideration is to provide sufficient time for teaching and learning, time alone does not guarantee results. Students must be—in today's jargon—engaged (i.e., paying attention, trying, and responding correctly). If a student is paying attention, teachers can do several things to enhance learning and retention.

- Use more prompts (i.e., manual guidance) and cues (stimuli added to a task to provide information about the correct response) to elicit correct responses.

- Provide more meaningful rehearsal (i.e., purposeful practice) to facilitate recall.

- Provide knowledge of results (including positive and corrective feedback) to maintain responding and increase accuracy.

- Break down complex tasks into smaller sequential steps to facilitate acquisition.

- Plan for integrating steps or components in learning through shaping and chaining.

- Provide more consistent consequences for student behavior to increase desired responses and to decrease undesired responses (i.e., positive consequences—as interpreted by a student—increase the chance of a behavior recurring while aversives decrease the chance of repetition).

- Plan for more systematic and meaningful practice to increase the likelihood of retention.

- Plan instruction to increase the likelihood of generalization.

These practices are implemented in different ways with different students. For example, while it is a good idea to plan opportunities for rehearsal of any learning task, individuals vary in how much practice and what type of practice will be effective. Some students will require more rehearsal than other students; some students may recall better when using visualization strategies, while others may do better with mnemonic devices. However, teachers should not waste their time searching for the very *best* way to teach particular children. The best way is very elusive and is neither stable (it probably varies over time) nor constant across subject matter. (There is no reason to believe that Jimmy's most effective rehearsal strategy in math and language arts would be the same.) Teachers should look for *adequate* matches when they manipulate instructional principles. Unfortunately, what is an adequate way is seldom known *a priori*. Usually, teachers know only if their instruction was effective after they have taught and a student has performed successfully. If student progress accelerates, the modification was effective. If progress remains unacceptable, further modification is necessary.

Modifications for a Group or Class

When small or large group instruction is used, it is generally a good idea to examine the collective performances of the students to ascertain if enough students are making adequate progress to warrant the continued use of instructional materials and procedures. For example, Ms. Li has summarized her class's performance on each objective in a brief teaching unit. Inspection of Figure 2.2 indicates that objective 3 was mastered by only 3 of 17 students in the class. First, Ms. Li should reconsider how, in general, to teach that material to her class; second, the unmastered material should be retaught. In addition to consistently poor performance by a large percentage of students on particular objectives, several other characteristics of student performance might tip off a teacher that group instruction should be modified.

Objectives	Students																
	BA	CA	JB	RB	AC	CC	WC	JF	JG	CH	TJ	LM	RP	JS	CT	HT	DW
Obj. 1: add. facts (0–9)	+	+	+	+	+	+	+	+	+	+	+	+	+	+	+	+	+
Obj. 2: add. facts (10–18)	+	+	+	+	+	+		+	+	+	+	+	+	+		+	+
Obj. 3: sums 1− + 2− digit# no Regrouping					+				+					+			
Obj. 4: Subtr. facts (minuends 2–9)	+		+	+	+		+	+	+	+	+	+	+	+		+	+
Obj. 5: differences, 2-digits less 1-digit, Regrouping																	
	BA	CA	JB	RB	AC	CC	WC	JF	JG	CH	TJ	LM	RP	JS	CT	HT	DW

FIGURE 2.2. Mastery of math objectives by students in Ms. Li's class.

- The time to modify group instruction is less than the time required to adjust the programs of individual students. It is simply more efficient to modify instruction once (for the group) than it is to modify instruction several times (for individual students).

- A number of students are making the same type of error. This pattern of performance suggests where (and sometimes how) modifications should be made. Modifications should be made quickly so that students do not practice their mistakes.

- The better students in the group are not making the type of progress that they usually make. (One might expect that relatively good students would progress in spite of mediocre instruction.)

Instructional modifications might occur in any of the major components of group instruction—demonstration, guided practice, or independent practice. As was the case with instructional programs for individuals, analysis of student error patterns can often provide hints for specific instructional modifications for groups of students. In the absence of such hints, teachers might modify demonstrations by breaking instruction into smaller steps, providing more examples, providing examples that are more concrete, and pointing out common errors (and why they are errors). They might modify guided and independent practice by providing more cues in the beginning stages, incorporating learning strategies,[2] making what is to be practiced more explicit, increasing incentives for good practicing, and giving quicker feedback.

[2]See Chapter 10.

Decisions about Referral

The basic questions asked in making a referral decision is, "Are student behavior and/or academic progress so atypical that another instructional arrangement should be considered?" Questions about the adequacy of an instructional situation are typically initiated from two[3] different sources—parents or school personnel.

Referrals from Parents

Parents of students new to a school district may already know that their children require extra services or special instructional arrangements because their children have been receiving them elsewhere. A youngster may have been identified previously as handicapped by a physician, a preschool program, or former school. When parents agree with the need for services that have been provided elsewhere, they are apt to make their children's needs known when they enroll their children in a new school.

Parents of students without a history of receiving special services also refer their children. Sometimes parents are the first to recognize that there are problems at school. Parents may be alarmed by changes in their children.

- Changes in report cards (e.g., a student going from A's to C's).
- Changes in study habits (e.g., no longer doing homework or crying while doing homework).
- Changes in feelings about school or their teachers (e.g., a student who once liked school now hates school).
- Changes in school-related behavior (e.g., regularly missing the bus or feigning illness to avoid attendance).

In such cases a parent might contact the teacher, guidance counselor, or principal and inquire about the desirability of an educational change.

Referrals from School Personnel

Teacher referrals may be initiated out of concern for the general welfare of a student or because a student's in-school behavior requires more attention than can be given. In the first case, a teacher might refer a child because physical appearance or behavior suggests child abuse or neglect. Figure 2.3 contains clues that might indicate potential problems.

Most of the time, students are referred for negatively atypical achievement and behavior, although students are also referred for positively atypical achievement (i.e., gifted students). When a teacher refers a student, the teacher is indicating the belief that appropriate instruction cannot or should not be pro-

[3]It is also possible for students to self-refer. However, our impression is that self-referral is rare in elementary schools and infrequent in secondary schools.

FIGURE 2.3.
Conditions and
behavior indicative of
potential physical
problems.

Eyes

- red or crusted eyes
- squinting, rubbing the eyes, and unusual posturing of the head or body in relation to the material being looked at
- complaints about headaches, visual fatigue, blurred vision, and difficulties seeing material that is far or near
- nastagmus or amblyopia

Ears

- discharges from the ear canal
- rubbing the ears and unusual posturing of the head or body in relation to the sound
- complaints about inability to hear, ringing in the ears, or not understanding what is heard
- difficulty hearing in noisy situations, unusually frequent requests to have statements repeated
- inconsistent responses or lack of responsiveness to oral directions or signals
- poor articulation

Appearance

- cuts, burns, or bruises
- tired, listless appearance

Other Indicators

- distractibility
- impulsivity
- lack of risk taking
- lack of self-confidence
- indifference
- lack of coordination, extreme clumsiness
- seizures
- diskinetic movements

vided in the current classroom. A teacher's inability to provide appropriate instruction may be caused by three factors. First, a teacher might be unwilling to try other instructional procedures. Second, a teacher might lack information about other instructional procedures. Third, a teacher might be unskilled in using alternate instructional procedures. We can also think of three reasons why teachers may not believe services should be provided in their classrooms. First, other specially trained educators provide the services needed by the student in

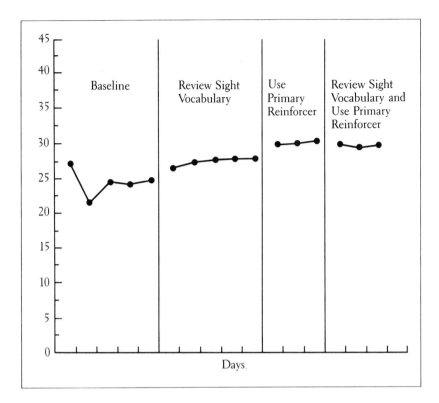

Figure 2.4.
Effects of various
interventions on
Martin's rate of oral
reading.

question. Second, the student in question presents a danger to other students. Third, the instructional modifications required to bring the student in question up to satisfactory performance are so extensive that their implementation would jeopardize the instruction of the other students.

Prior to seeking outside help, teachers should do more than simply note that a student has not progressed at acceptable rates. They are also expected to have attempted several appropriate interventions and to have monitored pupil performances during these interventions. For example, in Mr. Albans's class the students in the lowest reading group read orally at a rate of about 85 words per minute. Martin read at rate that was considerably slower—so slow that Mr. Albans would either have to increase Martin's performance substantially or provide separate materials and instruction for him. Mr. Albans first tried to improve Martin's performance. Figure 2.4 illustrates several unsuccessful interventions. Note that Martin's rate of oral reading was about 25 words per minute in the lowest reading group. When his teacher reviewed the sight vocabulary in each reading lesson prior to oral reading, Martin's rate went to about 27 words per minute. When Mr. Albans told Martin he would give him a Hershey chocolate bar if he read about 35 words per minute for 2 days in a row, Martin's performance went to about 29 words per minute. When Mr. Albans paired flash-card drill with the promise of a Hershey bar, Martin's performance stayed at about 29 words per minute. Mr. Albans tried three interventions with Martin that were unsuccessful. Moreover, Mr. Albans could document that the other students in the lowest reading group and the other students in his classroom were reading the material with better speed and accuracy.

When teachers are ready to seek additional help in solving classroom problems, they always have the option of talking informally with other teachers or supervisors. Should these informal discussions not lead to resolution of the problem, teachers then turn to a more formal means—referral.

Currently, many school systems are approaching the referral process more formally and systematically than in the past. Consequently, teachers may be required to complete a referral form to document the nature of the problem and interventions that have been tried. (Figure 2.5 contains a minimal referral form.) Generally, referral forms or requests should make explicit comparisons between the performance of the student in question and the rest of the class or the lowest acceptable performance. Summary scores (e.g., totals, averages) or examples of inadequate performances should be included with a completed referral form.

Referrals go to administrators or committees (often called "alternative programming committees" or "child study teams"). These teams typically include a psychologist, a guidance counselor, and a school administrator. They may also include teachers from a regular class, from special education, or from remedial programs. A child study team reviews the nature of a student's problem, the program modifications tried by a teacher, and the effectiveness of the teacher's program modifications in altering student learning and/or behavior. At that point the team might decide that more information should be gathered to clarify the nature and severity of the student's problem or to assist in providing suggestions to the teacher about possible interventions.

When there is sufficient information, the team decides one of three things. First, it might decide that a student's problems are not severe enough to warrant the provisions of additional services. However, this decision might also include recommendations that:

- The student be placed with another teacher whose style and methods are more compatible
- The student might be retained and placed with a different teacher
- The student be seen by an agency outside of the schools
- The parents become involved through frequent contacts with the teacher or a home–school cooperative[4] agreement
- The parents seek assistance from an agency outside of the schools

Second, the team might decide that a student's needs are so great that they cannot be met in the regular classroom without the provision of additional services by specially trained professionals who work within the school system. Thus,

---

[4]A home–school contract is an agreement that calls for parents and teachers to act in concert to modify a student's behavior. For example, parents might positively reinforce at home a student's progress in school or parents might tutor their children on skills specified by the teacher.

Referral Questionnaire

FIGURE 2.5.
A referral form.

Directions: Please complete this questionnaire. Attach additional pages if necessary. Give the completed form to your building principal.

Student _____   Grade _____
Teacher _____   Date _____

1. For what problem(s) are you referring this student?

_____

_____

_____

2. What curriculum is being followed in the problem areas?

_____

_____

_____

3. List three behaviors/circumstances most indicative of the problem.

_____

_____

_____

4. Have these behaviors/circumstances been documented? Please describe.

_____

_____

_____

5. What modifications in curricular or classroom management have been made to ameliorate the problem? List all modifications separately. How effective were these modifications?

_____

_____

_____

_____

_____

they might decide that, in addition to instruction by the regular classroom teacher, the student receive extra instruction from a remedial specialist and/or additional services from other school specialists (e.g., the school counselor). The team might also decide to provide the parents with additional services (e.g., direct instruction or family counseling).

Finally, the team might decide that a student might be exceptional.[5] In this case, the student is referred to one (or more) specialists to gather information pertinent to that student's eligibility for special-education services. Different states have different rules for determining eligibility, so determination of the appropriate specialist varies. Usually, speech and language specialists receive referrals dealing with speech and language problems; school psychologists receive referrals dealing with learning and behavioral problems; medical specialists receive referrals dealing with sensory handicaps (i.e., hearing and vision), chronic health problems (e.g., muscular dystrophy), and neurological impairment.

Decisions about Eligibility

Public Law 94-142 requires that multidisciplinary teams (MDTs) decide eligibility for special education. When all of the additional assessments have been completed, MDTs meet and discuss all of the pertinent information about a student—school history, reasons for referral, efficacy of remedial interventions designed to obviate the need for referral, and the results of the assessments by the school psychologist or other specialist. The team compares the information that has been collected to the state's legal stipulations about eligibility.

Eligibility decisions generally rely on norm-referenced comparisons (i.e., how a particular student compares to other students). Indeed, many states specify that a student must be in the bottom X percent of students on particular kinds of tests to be eligible for special-education services.[6] If a student meets the criteria established in the state's education code, he or she is eligible for special-education services. Finally, as shown in Table 2.1, many federal definitions of exceptionality require documentation of inadequate learning before a student can be classified.

Even though a student's eligibility for services as a handicapped student requires a determination of a pupil's *learning*, data from direct assessments of learning are seldom used in eligibility decisions, although there are a few notable exceptions. Rather, MDTs still rely on scores from general achievement tests. As noted in Chapter 1, published achievement tests are inadequate to assess learning because they seldom reflect the curriculum that teachers have taught: There is no guarantee that a pupil has been exposed to the content that is being tested. Even if published achievement tests did match a curriculum, valid inferences about a

---

[5]The results of several studies (e.g., Graden, Casey, & Bonstrom, 1985; Gutkin, Henning-Stout, & Piersel, 1988; Ponti, Zins, & Graden, 1988; Ritter, 1978) suggest that when school systems use systematic programs for systematic prereferral intervention the number of students tested and placed in special education decreases substantitally.

[6]With the exception of age and grade equivalents, any norm-referenced score can be converted to the percentage of students scoring higher or lower.

Mentally retarded students must demonstrate inadequate adaptive behavior. For school-age individuals, inadequate learning is often sufficient to demonstrate inadequate adaptive behavior (Grossman, 1983). **Learning-disabled students** are classified on the basis of having great difficulty learning written or oral language, reading, writing, spelling, or mathematical calculations (USOE, 1977). **Emotionally disturbed students** must demonstrate "an inability to learn which cannot be explained by intellectual, sensory, or health factors" (USOE, 1977).	TABLE 2.1 Role of Achievement in Definitions of Handicaps

particular student's achievement would still not be possible unless the test matched the curricula of students in the norm group. Only when the contents of a test and curriculum are appropriately matched for the student being evaluated *and* for students in the norm group can appropriate inferences about relative learning be made. Therefore, teachers are in a better position to provide other MDT members valuable information about

- How much of the everyday academic content a pupil has learned
- How adequate a pupil's current performances are when compared with the performances of other students in class or in the district
- How adequate progress is toward educational goals

Such information is of the utmost importance to multidisciplinary teams that are entrusted with evaluating students' achievement and making classification decisions.

Decisions about Placement

When a student is found eligible for special-education services, another professional will be assigned to share or take over responsibility for the student. Decisions about the degree of shared responsibility are called "placement" decisions. The degree to which responsibility can be shared can vary considerably.

- A regular classroom teacher might retain responsibility for all of the direct instruction of a handicapped student with a special educator consulting with that teacher about methods and materials that could be used.
- A regular educator might retain primary instructional responsibility with a special educator assuming some responsibility for instruction in particular content areas.
- A special educator might assume most of the responsibility for instruction with a regular classroom teacher retaining responsibility for instruction in some content areas.
- A special educator might assume all of the responsibility.

Federal regulations require that handicapped students be educated with nonhandicapped students to the maximum extent that is appropriate. While standards for making these decisions are as yet unclear, it seems to be a matter of common sense to place handicapped students in academic and social situations where there is a reasonable expectation for them to succeed. Thus, students to be integrated should possess sufficient academic skills to function in at least the lowest groups in a regular classroom if provided with some support; students should possess sufficient social and study skills to meet the nonacademic demands of the classroom if provided with some support.

Classroom teachers should possess detailed information about their students. This information can be very useful to MDTs when they recommend actual placements and to administrators when they select the actual classrooms in which to enroll a handicapped student. Teachers know the relative effectiveness of particular types of instruction that they have used in the classroom with a student. This knowledge can help an MDT match a student to appropriate instructional situations. If a student can read the social studies materials used in Ms. Li's classroom but not those used by Mr. Wright, there is an obvious advantage in placing the student with Ms. Li for social studies. Similarly, if a student behaves unacceptably in open classrooms but can behave acceptably in highly structured situations, integration of the student should begin in structured situations.

Summary

Assessment does not occur without a purpose; indeed, the need to have information about a student drives the entire assesssment process. Classroom teachers are concerned primarily with five questions: (1) How well are students achieving instructional goals? This goal entails both questions of level of proficiency and rate of acquisition. (2) Should instruction be modified to help students attain their instructional goals? Teachers have two general options in modifying instruction: (a) they can modify the content of what is being taught (e.g., perform task analyses and teach smaller slices of an objective) and (b) they can modify how they are teaching (e.g., provide more opportunities for purposeful rehearsal). (3) Should a student be referred for special services? When a student's achievement or behavior cannot be successfully managed in a classroom and when a teacher has tried, unsuccessfully, several ways to accommodate a student, it may be appropriate to seek advice or assistance from other professionals. (4) Is a student eligible for special education? When a student's problems are so severe that a teacher is unable to provide appropriate instruction in a regular educational setting and when those problems meet state criteria for special education, a student may be classified as handicapped. (5) If a student is classified as exceptional, what administrative arrangements (i.e., placement) would be the least restrictive and appropriate? Because a student is handicapped does not mean automatically that the student should be enrolled in a self-contained classroom for exceptional students. Often, relatively unobtrusive programs can be implemented that allow a student to remain in the regular educational stream. For example, a special educator might provide a regular classroom teacher with special materials or strategies that the regular educator can use, or the special educator might provide a few hours of specialized instruction outside of the regular classroom with the regular classroom teacher retaining the bulk of the responsibility for the student's education.

Regardless of the decision that is reached, the decision-making process should be data driven. Moreover, the most relevant data typically quantify pupil achievement of important educational goals.

Chapter 3

Analysis of Curriculum and Formulation of Objectives

Key Terms

Amplitude

Application

Comprehension

Duration

Extinction

Frequency

Goal Component

Instructional objective

Knowledge

Latency

Long-term objective

Punishment

Quality

Reinforcement

Sequential objective

Short-term objective

Strand

After purposes for assessment have been determined, curricula must be analyzed. Without a thorough curricular analysis, appropriate assessment procedures cannot be developed. Sometimes teachers already have at their disposal carefully prepared analyses. In such cases, teachers need only confirm that the analysis is still appropriate. Some purposes for assessment (e.g., monitoring pupil progress) require that behavioral objectives be prepared. This chapter is intended for those situations in which teachers need to perform curricular analyses and preparation of objectives.

General Considerations

The purposes and functions of education have interested many notable philosophers (e.g., Plato and Dewey). General intentions about education abound. For example, the *Seven New Cardinal Principles of Education* are health, command of fundamental processes, worthy home membership, vocation, civic education, worthy use of leisure, and ethical character (Gross, 1978). A curriculum translates instructional intentions into more precise goals that provide a general direction for educators.

By curriculum we mean a complete and precise statement of instructional objectives for a student or group of students, whether stated formally and written down or merely encouraged by boards of education or teachers. Curricula are integrated, hierarchical, and sequenced statements about instructional intentions.

In the United States, no national curriculum exists. Education is under state control, and the states delegate much of their authority to local school districts. Children in different states and commonwealths learn different curricula. Commercial publishers go so far as to prepare different curricula for different regions of the country. Curricula can vary in several ways.

- Content of instruction. For example, some curricula cover metric measurement, others cover imperial measurement, others cover both imperial and metric but do not cover converting from one system to the other, and still others cover conversion between the two systems.

- Level of instruction. For example, some curricula stress memory of basic concepts while others stress an understanding of these concepts.

- Sequence of content. For example, some reading curricula begin with basic rules of phonics while others begin with a basic sight vocabulary that is phonetically regular and then introduce basic rules of phonics.

- Pace of instruction. For example, curricula intended for students in *slower* tracks move very slowly and give extended practice of concepts; other curricula move quickly from one component to the next.

- Levels of abstraction. For example, some curricula present concepts deductively while others present concepts inductively.

Even within the same school district, groups of students receive different curricula. High-achieving students may take advanced academic courses while the less talented students are offered curricula more in keeping with their abilities. Tracking of students in regular education, especially at the upper elementary and secondary levels, is a fact of life. Of course, special education often offers curricula that are distinctly different from the regular tracks or streams. Moreover, there are also considerable differences in the curricula offered to different types of exceptional students. The curricula followed for visually impaired students contains unique strands and components, as do the curricula for hearing-impaired students. Emotionally disturbed students often receive curricula that stress appropriate behavior and the development of interpersonal skills and relationships. Mildly retarded and learning-disabled students receive curricula stressing basic academics. Moderately and severely retarded students receive curricula stressing daily living skills. Within tracks and special educational groups, individual classes of students may receive fairly unique curricula; within classrooms, teachers may individualize instruction or form smaller, more homogeneous instructional groups.

Parent groups are often consulted about general curricular goals for their sons and daughters, and special-interest groups may press for including their points of view into the school curriculum. P.L. 94-142, the Education of All Handicapped Act, guarantees parents of handicapped students the legal right to be consulted and to approve a general curriculum—educational goals and objectives—for their children by giving parents the right to approve or disapprove the individual educational plan proposed by school officials.

Educational goals can be subdivided into academic and social goals. Academic goals are derived from general instructional intentions in two ways. First, general intentions are expanded to indicate the skills, abilities, and attitudes that are encompassed by the more general intention. Thus, *command of fundamental processes* is restated as content areas of reading, oral and written language, mathematics, and so forth. Second, terminal proficiency in each content area—the level of performance expected at adulthood—is analyzed to elucidate the hierarchy of attainment. In general terms, these aspirations for students as adults determine many of the skills, concepts, and behaviors that must be acquired during the school years. If eight-year-old Mike wants to become a teacher, he will have to complete the college-level coursework that the state, commonwealth, or province requires for certification. Completion of coursework in college requires admission to an accredited college. Admission requires high-school graduation with certain courses completed—so many credits of English, certain competence in math (e.g., one unit of algebra and one unit of geometry), foreign language, and so forth. Thus, becoming a teacher means that Mike will have to pass algebra and geometry in high school. Schools translate goals such as satisfactory knowledge of algebra or geometry into curricula.

Social goals are also derived from instructional intentions. However, in addition to expanding social goals to indicate the skills, abilities, and attitudes encompassed, social goals also include a nonspecific goal: Do not annoy or disturb the adults in the school. Since there are literally thousands of ways to disturb teachers, secretaries, administrators, nurses, custodians, bus drivers, and others, only some of the prohibited behaviors are specified precisely—for example, dress codes, truancy, use of chemical substances (alcohol, tobacco, marijuana), safety regulations, and use of profanity. Even so, there are no exhaustive lists of the words students cannot say in school or the substances that cannot be ingested.

Moreover, teachers have particular rules for their classrooms—for example, no chewing gum, food, or drinks, only speaking with permission, and punctuality for assignments. In the same way, all of the prohibited behavior is not specified. However, teachers establish goals to alter, decrease, or eliminate behavior that is antisocial, disruptive, annoying, harmful, or otherwise disturbing. The goal, in effect, becomes "the student will stop doing it."

Analysis of Curriculum

There really is no single way to analyze a curriculum. For academic content, teachers are concerned with curricular strands and levels of mastery; for social and academic processes, teachers are concerned with the antecedents and consequences of those behaviors. In addition, the various characteristics of the target pupils affect the way in which curricula are analyzed. Generally, the lower the level of functioning of the students, the more detailed the analysis. Within special education, teachers often must analyze the instructional goals, formulate behavioral objectives that translate those goals into observable outcomes, and perform task analyses to break behavioral objectives into bits of behavior that can be mastered by handicapped learners.

Curricular analysis requires three steps:

1. The content of the curriculum must be specified.

2. The level of proficiency at which each component of the curriculum must be learned must be specified.

3. The relative importance of each component-by-level combination must be quantified.

Each of these steps is discussed in this chapter, and a general explanation of how teachers might do each of these steps is provided. Since academic and social curricula are analyzed differently, they are treated in separate sections.

Academic Curricula

Specification of Content

Content consists of domains such as arithmetic, reading, and social sciences. Within domains are strands, and within strands are components.[1] For example, within the domain of arithmetic are strands for operations, measurement, geometry, and so forth. Within the strand for operations are components of addition, subtraction, multiplication, division, and so forth.

There are several ways to analyze the content of academic curriculum. Often a text series will provide a teacher's edition that provides a "scope and sequence" chart that usually contains the strands, components, and subcomponents. If no "scope and sequence" chart is available, teachers will have to develop their own. The analysis of one's own curriculum requires a thorough familiarity with the content area and one's own instructional intentions. Teachers should begin by identifying the major components of a domain. For example, a writing curriculum could contain as major components:

- Fluency (number of words written)
- Organization (paragraph usage, sequencing of ideas)
- Mechanics
- Spelling
- Handwriting
- Content (e.g., the number of independent thoughts)

---

[1]Further subdivisions are common in multifaceted curricula. Thus, within components are subcomponents, and within subcomponents are subsubcomponents.

Then teachers would identify the major subcomponents within each component. For example, mechanics might contain as major subcomponents:

- Punctuation
- Capitalization
- Indentation of paragraphs
- Grammar

Finally, teachers identify major subsubcomponents within each subcomponent. For example, capitalization might include using capital letters for the first word in a sentence, proper names, and names of days and months.

Specification of Level of Proficiency

"Level of proficiency" refers to the degree of mastery that students are expected to exhibit following instruction. Mastery is conceptualized in different ways depending on the content area. Bloom, Hastings, and Madaus (1971) developed a taxonomy that is useful for content areas consisting of facts and concepts. A range of understanding and manipulation of information—from simple knowledge to high-level evaluation—can be attained for many objectives. Bloom, Hastings, and Madaus described six types of cognitive demand:

- *Knowledge* requires that students learn to recognize and produce factual information or specifically taught behavior. For example, a student might be required to learn that the Declaration of Independence was signed in 1776.
- *Comprehension* requires that a student go beyond recognition and recall. Comprehension objectives require translation of information (putting content into the "student's own words"), interpretation, and/or extrapolation (i.e., foreseeing likely outcomes). For example, a student might have to explain, in his own words, what the Declaration of Independence is.
- *Application* requires that a student go beyond comprehension. Application objectives require that a student use the information or behavior in a context or situation in which it was not learned or previously practiced. For example, Mike might be asked to write an essay on the origins of the Bill of Rights to the U.S. Constitution. If he includes information about the Declaration of Independence without being prompted to do so, he has exhibited application. Objectives written at these levels are extremely demanding and are seldom used in special education.
- *Analysis* requires that a student break down the information or performance in a way that has not been taught in order to gain additional information about the relationship among the parts of the information or performance. If Mike wrote a paper analyzing the social forces leading colonists to declare their independence from England and if his analysis was original, he would have demonstrated learning at the level of analysis.

- *Synthesis* requires a student to combine information and/or performances into a new (at least for the student) whole. For example, if Mike wrote an essay showing how various economic factors interacted to produce sufficient social pressure to lead colonists to declare their independence from England and if his synthesis of economic factors was original, he would have demonstrated learning at the level of synthesis.

- *Evaluation* requires a student to select and apply evaluative criteria to information, concepts, and performances in order to make judgments about their worth. As a final example, suppose that Mike wrote a paper discussing various causes of the U.S. Revolutionary War and, in that paper, developed criteria for selecting among conflicting interpretations. Finally, suppose that Mike's paper concluded with a judgment about which hypothetical causes were likely causes. Mike would have demonstrated learning at the level of evaluation.

A different hierarchy of mastery is used by behaviorists who are more likely to be concerned with types of performance.[2] Within this framework as many as five types or levels of functional skill use have been identified: acquisition, fluency, maintenance, generalization, and adaptation.

- *Acquisition* refers to learning a fact, skill, or complex behavioral chain. Acquisition implies going from knowing little or performing poorly to a high level of accuracy, usually 80% or more correct.

- *Fluency* (also called proficiency) refers to a behavior that is not only performed accurately but also rapidly and/or with a brief latency. Fluent behavior can be characterized as smooth, confident, and automatic.

- *Maintenance* refers to continued performance of the behavior or skill in the absence of instructional prompts or cues and in the absence of artificial contingencies.

- *Generalization* (also called transfer) refers to both response and stimulus generalization. In response generalization, a student's trained response to a stimulus is generalized to a similar but untrained response. For example, a child who learns to say "hello" in response to a greeting from another person; saying "Hi" or "What's happenin'?" or "Hey" is generalizing the response to a greeting. There are three types of stimulus generalization. First, a student's response can spread from a trained stimulus to similar, but untrained, stimuli. For example, a child learns that a particular color is red; calling other very similar colors red is generalizing from the trained stimulus. Second, a student's response can generalize from the setting in which the behavior was trained to a setting in which no training occurred. For example, a student can learn to estimate addition sums in the classroom and then generalize that learning to the supermarket. Third, a student's response can generalize from the trainer to another person who did not train the student. For example, a student learns to say "hello" to his teacher and then generalizes that greeting to other persons who did not train the greeting.

[2]Although these five types have been discussed, they may grouped in fewer categories (cf. Alberto & Troutman, 1986).

- *Adaptation* refers to a person's modification of an acquired response when confronted with new situations. Thus, a person who has learned a skill to the level of adaptation can use that skill in a flexible manner depending on the characteristics of the task. For example, a student who learns a study strategy for memorizing lists of facts for a multiple-choice test spontaneously uses portions of that strategy to study for an essay test covering more conceptual material.

To analyze the levels of proficiency of a curriculum that has a scope and sequence chart, a teacher inspects the activities that students perform and judges the level of proficiency required. Of course, components and subcomponents may be taught at several levels in one grade level. Therefore, teachers must note each level at which the particular content is taught. For example, students might be taught the recognition of words as sight vocabulary (i.e., knowledge level), be taught primary and secondary meanings of those words (i.e., comprehension level), and be encouraged to use those words in their writing (i.e., application level). In the absence of a scope and sequence chart, teachers will need to inspect their own taxonomies and ascertain the levels of the content.

Quantification of a Curricular Analysis

Once the components and levels have been specified, it is useful to display them in a figure, as shown in Figure 3.1. The intersection of subcomponents and levels forms a cell. Curriculum analysis is quantified by computing the amount of instructional effort devoted to each cell. Since any one instructional component need not be taught at all levels, some cells may contain zeros or be left blank.

Teachers can estimate instructional effort in several ways, the choice of which depends on the nature of the curriculum and their own preferences. There are essentially three ways to quantify:

- *Teacher time.* Often, teachers' editions of text series provide guidelines for instructional effort. Sometimes these manuals suggest an amount of time a teacher should devote to teaching the subcomponent (e.g., how many days or weeks to be spent); sometimes a teacher's lesson plans specify the number of hours provided in class for direct instruction and practice. The numbers in the cell of Figure 3.1 indicate the percent of effort devoted by Mr. Wright. As shown in that figure, 45% (i.e., 25% + 20% +0%) of Mr. Wright's teaching activities in arithmetic is devoted to addition of single digits without regrouping, 10% to the addition of single-digit problems with regrouping, 25% to addition of multiple digits without regrouping, and 20% to subtraction facts. Seventy

FIGURE 3.1. Mr. Wright's instructional effort in arithmetic.		Add single-digit no regrouping	Add single-digit regrouping	Add multiple-digits no regrouping	Subtract facts	Subtract multiple-digits no regrouping
	Knowledge	25%	00%	25%	20%	00%
	Comprehension	20%	10%	00%	00%	00%

percent of his instruction occurs at the knowledge level since he is stressing computation; 30% of his effort is at the comprehension level.

- *Student Time.* Student effort forms a different basis for quantifying the curriculum. For example, the number of hours of practice in class and at home or the number of problems assigned can also be used. Teachers can use the number of pages in the text as very rough approximations of instructional effort.

- *Number of subobjectives.* Teachers can also use the number of subobjectives to be taught in the domain. To do so requires the assumption that all objectives are of equal importance. Thus, the objective (and not teacher or student effort) is tabulated. To quantify on this basis, teachers simply note the most precise level into which a taxonomy is organized (for example, subsubsubcomponents) and count their number in each cell.

Social Curricula

Specification of Content

Instruction aimed at developing, eliminating, or maintaining social behavior is analyzed by examining the behavior itself, the conditions under which the behavior occurs, and the consequences of that behavior.

Behavior is often categorized as *prosocial* or *disturbing*. Prosocial refers to desirable behavior that promotes the student's personal and social development—behaviors that allow his repertoire of behavior to expand. Disturbing behavior annoys adults (e.g., teachers, bus drivers) or other students. Regardless of whether the behavior is prosocial or disturbing, what constitutes a class of behavior must be delineated. For example, cooperative behavior and unacceptable vocal behavior are classes of behavior that are too imprecise. Teachers must specify what they mean by cooperation and unacceptable vocal behavior. *Cooperative* behavior might include

- Turn taking
- Using polite language (e.g, saying "please" and "thank you")
- Helping peers in play activities (e.g., pushing a peer on a swing)
- Helping adults (e.g., handing out treats)

Unacceptable vocal behavior might include

- Humming
- Talking out
- Whispering to a neighbor
- Shouting obscenities

When social goals are stated in very general terms (e.g., students will learn to cooperate), the first step in the analysis is to specify what behaviors are meant within each goal (e.g., cooperation equals turn taking). Next, the context in which the behavior occurs is described in terms of three aspects: (1) the conditions under which each of the specific behaviors occur, (2) the antecedents of the specific behavior, and (3) the consequences of the specific behavior.

- *The conditions under which the specific behavior occurs.* Teachers must determine if there are particular settings in which the behavior occurs. These settings give us insight into the *whys* and *hows* of the behavior. Often, behavior only occurs in the presence of certain stimuli (called discriminative stimuli). If Martin hits other children only in the presence of female teachers, perhaps male and female teachers are a signal that hitting is acceptable; perhaps Martin has learned that hitting is punished when men are present but unpunished (or even rewarded) when women are present. Similarly, perhaps Howard only swears and curses during gym and recess. He might have learned that such language was "outside" talk. In each of the preceding examples, a person or place has set the stage for the performance. Knowing the conditions under which behavior occurs is useful in changing the behavior.

- *The antecedents of the specific behavior.* What immediately precedes the behavior is often the stimulus for the student's behavior. For example, Hector may hit other children whenever they make an ethnic slur. If Mr. Clayburg knows what triggers a behavior, he may be able to stop the behavior by removing its cause or by teaching the student to substitute a response that has greater social acceptability.

- *The consequences of the specific behavior.* The events that follow a behavior are very important in terms of the probability of its future occurrence. Some consequences (i.e., reinforcers[3]) maintain or promote behavior—even when that behavior is undesirable. Other consequences (i.e., extinction[4] and punishment[5]) reduce the likelihood that the undesirable behavior will occur again.

---

[3]A reinforcer can be one of two types. Positive reinforcers are events that, by their introduction, increase the likelihood that a behavior will occur. Thus, if a teacher gives a student a "happy face" sticker on a good paper and subsequently that student completes more good papers, then "happy faces" were positive reinforcers of the student's behavior. Negative reinforcers are events that, by their removal, increase the likelihood that a behavior will occur. For example, suppose that 15-year-old Joey jogs around the track during his P.E. class. His teacher, Mr. Dennis, wants his students to run (not jog) and yells at those who are not moving fast enough (e.g., "Get the lead out, Joey" "You're too slow, Joey"). Mr. Dennis does not yell when Joey is running. If Joey runs faster to avoid the yelling, not yelling (i.e., removal of an aversive stimulus) is a negative reinforcer for running fast.

[4]Extinction is the removal of a reinforcer following an event that had been previously reinforced. For example, suppose that infant George often cried when he was put to bed, that his mother then picked him up, and that instances of crying at bedtime increased to the point that it happened every night. (Crying was positively reinforced by picking up.) Then suppose that mother stops picking up George when he cries at bedtime and that crying at bedtime then ceases. The crying has been extinguished by removing its reinforcement.

[5]Punishing events are of two types also. Positive punishers are events that, by their introduction, decrease the likelihood that a behavior will occur. Thus, if Joey misbehaves in class, Mr. Dennis follows his behavior by making Joey run five laps around the track. If the misbehavior decreases, running laps is a punishment. Negative punishers are events that, by their removal, decrease the likelihood that a behavior will occur. Thus, if Mr. Dennis had not allowed Joey to play in Saturday's junior varsity football game because of his misbehavior in P.E. class, and if subsequently Joey's misbehavior decreased, withdrawing the opportunity to play football was a punisher.

	Saying "Please"	Taking turns	Handing out supplies	Tidying up area	Getting into line
Fluency	X	X	X		
Maintenance	X	X			
Generalization	X				

FIGURE 3.2. Table of specifications for some social behaviors.

Specification of Level of Proficiency

Like academic content, social content can be taught at acquisition, fluency, maintenance, generalization, and adaptation. Therefore, teachers must note each level at which they intervene on the particular social behavior. Teachers will need to inspect their own analyses of behavior and ascertain the levels of performance expected.

Quantification of a Curricular Analysis

Once the specific social behaviors, their contexts, and levels have been specified, it is useful to display them in a figure, as shown in Figure 3.2. Specific social behaviors are treated as components, and contexts provide subcomponents. The intersection of subcomponents and levels forms a cell, in the same way that cells are formed in the analysis of academic behavior. As shown in Figure 3.2, three of the social behaviors are to be learned only to fluency; two, only to a level of maintenance; and one to a level of generalization.

Teachers can estimate instructional effort to expend in developing prosocial behavior or eliminating disturbing behavior by using a table of specifications to tabulate the number of subcomponents (behavior within contexts) and the level of proficiency at which the behavior is to be performed. Two thirds of the teacher's efforts are devoted to cooperation.

Sequence of Curriculum

When analyzing a curriculum, attention must also be directed to mastery of enabling skills, concepts, and behavior. Well-sequenced curricula prepare students for new instructional goals by developing an instructional base upon which new learning can rest. In addition to enabling skills, sequencing consists of three aspects:

- The order in which goals are taught
- The order in which levels of proficiency increase
- The way in which goals are combined

Usually the order in which goals are taught is understood as the sequence of a curriculum or curriculum strand. For example, letter identification might precede letter–sound correspondence, which precedes sound blends and diphthongs, and so forth. Expectations for increased proficiency are also sequential, however. Instruction in factual material often proceeds from a knowledge level to an application level; instruction in more behavioral strands often proceeds from acquisition to fluency or even maintenance and generalization. Thus, an analysis of a curriculum's sequence might reveal discontinuity in expected levels of proficiency. For example, a teacher might incorrectly jump from acquisition to generalization without considering fluency and maintenance.

Especially with lower functioning students, teachers must explicitly plan and instruct students in combining new information and skills with previously acquired facts and skills. Teachers should not expect students to integrate information spontaneously and independently—even in college. Two general methods have emerged for combining instructional goals: integrated instruction of two or more goals and isolated instruction of separate goals with an additional step of integration. Suppose Ms. Hopkins wanted to teach her preschoolers two colors (e.g., red and blue). In the first general method (integrated instruction), she would teach the students red and blue on alternate trials. She might show a red star to the class and say, "This star is red; what color is it, class? That's right, the star is red." Then she would show a blue star and say, "This star is blue; what color is it, class? That's right. This star is blue." After one or two demonstrations, Ms. Hopkins might stop prompting the answer but continue practicing and providing immediate feedback. Red and blue stimuli would be varied randomly. Thus, students would learn the correct association of word and color, and they would learn to discriminate red from blue within the same general instructional sequence.

In the second method, Ms. Hopkins would teach red to mastery; then she would teach blue to mastery. Then she would teach students to discriminate between red and blue, in much the same way as might be done under method one. There is limited research on which method of integration is superior; what does exist suggests that the second method (teaching each component before teaching the integration) is much faster (Sniezek, 1983).

Formulation of Behavioral Objectives

As philosophic intentions are translated into curricular goals, so curricular goals are translated into more precise and objective statements. A behavioral objective is a way to state the performance that a student must demonstrate so that others (e.g., parents, teachers, and other professionals) can be sure the student has met the instructional goal. Teachers cannot know when a student gets there if they do not know where the student is going.

Components of Behavioral Objectives

Behavioral objectives provide teachers with a method of specifying exactly what is meant by an instructional goal that is expressed in a curriculum, under exactly what conditions and constraints that instructional goal will be performed, and exactly what a student will have to do to demonstrate attainment of that instructional goal. Thus, behavioral objectives have three components: the specific behavior to be demonstrated, the conditions under which the performance will be demonstrated, and the criterion for a successful performance (Mager, 1961).

Specific Behavior and Products

In order to get a correct representation of behavior and skills, we specify what the student will do when the instructional goal has been met. Thus, teachers who want Suzy "to read" will specify what exactly they mean by read—"say the word represented by a sequence of letters," "answer comprehension questions," "use word attack skills," and so forth. Fuzzy or imprecise descriptions are replaced by observable and measurable behavior.

Conditions of Performance

After developing a careful description of the behavior or skill to be acquired by the learner, it is also necessary to delineate the conditions under which the behavior or skill is to be demonstrated. By conditions, we mean three things:

- What the student will be allowed to use
- What the student will not be allowed to use
- The circumstances (what, when, or where) of performance

The first two criteria are readily understood. For example, "given the use of a calculator and formula sheets" or "without the use of calculator and formula sheets," the student will write the answer to four problems that require the computation of the area of a circle. The two different sets of conditions produce quite different demands. In the first condition, the student only must choose the correct formula for the area of a circle, substitute into the formula, and multiply correctly. In the second condition the student must recall the formula for the area of a circle, substitute into that formula, and multiply correctly.

The circumstances of performance constrain the performance by specifying the conditions under which the performance will occur. For example, "*After reading two pages about the causes of the American Civil War, the student will state three causes, . . .*" sets the conditions for the student's performance. Figure 3.3 contains several conditions for various types of performance.

Criteria for Successful Performance

Objectives also include minimum standards for acceptable performance. These standards or criteria allow a teacher to measure *how well* a student performs the behavior or skill after instruction has been completed. There are two facets to criteria for behavioral objectives. First, teachers select the characteristic of the behavior they will use in the criterion statement. Second, they use a level of performance that will be satisfactory.

FIGURE 3.3.
Examples of conditions
of performance in
behavioral objectives.

Given a map with the 50 states of the United States outlined but unnamed,[1] the student will write the names of the states on the map. . . .

After viewing a film on dam building by beavers, the student will answer factual questions. . . .

Upon the teacher's request, the student will line up. . . .

With compass and protractor, the student will construct an equilateral triangle. . . .

When shown flashcards with single-digit addition facts that do not require regrouping, the student will say the sums. . . .

Without reference to programming manuals, the student will write a computer program to alphabetize entries. . . .

When playing a board game with other students, the student will take turns. . . .

[1]Italics illustrate conditions; criteria for performance have been omitted.

1. Characteristics of Behavior

Behavior can be characterized along several dimensions: amplitude, duration and latency, quality, and frequency and rate. Each of these dimensions is discussed below.

Amplitude

When strength of a response is of interest, amplitude may be used in the criterion of a behavioral objective. In laboratory settings, amplitude can be measured easily—mechanically or electronically. However, in classrooms its measurement is less precise and is usually evaluated more subjectively through ratings. For example, William may speak too softly in class, and his teacher may want to increase his volume.

Duration and Latency

Duration and latency, while different, are both used to assess the length of time associated with a response or performance. Duration refers to how long a behavior lasts once it begins. For example, a teacher may be interested in decreasing the length of time undesirable responses occur (e.g., temper tantrums) or in increasing the length of time desirable responses occur (e.g., working independently). Latency refers to the amount of time elapsed between the time a stimulus is presented and the onset of a student's response. Many teachers try to shorten the latency of responses (e.g., "Answer before I count to three") or lengthen the latency (e.g., "Think before you answer").

Determining optimal latency or duration is not as straightforward as determining some of the other criterion measures. In the absence of empirically verified standards for latency and duration, the expectations and preferences of individual teachers dictate criteria. Three factors should be taken into account when establishing latency and duration criteria: (1) length of the task, (2) time allocated to the task, and (3) characteristics of the student. For example, students with poor motor skills should not be expected to take the same amount of time to complete a motor-involved task as would a nonhandicapped peer.

To set reasonable criteria, teachers should select students whom they perceive to be performing the target skill adequately and use the median of their performances as criteria for all students. For example, Ms. Li may observe Suzy and Peter (e.g., "typical" students) for a few days and record how long they take to respond to directions; Ms. Li could then use the median latency for these two students over several days as the criterion for her behavioral objectives for "beginning work."

Quality

Quality criteria are used appropriately to evaluate departures from the ideal performances in complex tasks. Criteria for a quality performance will vary with each type of performance or product. For example, if a child is asked to draw a diamond, the acceptable performance can be specified by four criteria that are illustrated in Figure 3.4. First, the alignment of the vertical angles must be correct: Lines connecting the vertical and horizontal angles (lines *a* and *b* in Figure 3.4) must be within 10 degrees of perpendicular—a right or 90° angle. Second, the sides of the diamond must be of approximately equal length: no side may be more than 20% longer than any other side. Third, the sides of the diamond must not be too bowed: No side may be more than 10% of the length of the line from a straight line connecting the two ends of the side. Fourth, the sides must meet to form an angle: The sides must actually touch; crossing is allowed. Figure 3.4 contains illustrations for each of these types; simple behavior and conditions are used for convenience.

Frequency and Rate

Frequency and rate are closely related; rates are based on frequencies. Frequency (i.e., the number of times an event occurs) can be used for any discrete behavior—a behavior that has a definite beginning and end. Often, teachers are interested in increasing the frequency of positive social and academic behavior and in decreasing the frequency of undesired social and academic behavior. While the frequency of behavior is important, simple frequencies are often difficult to interpret since they are a function of the opportunity that a student has to perform. For example, a teacher could expect more turn-taking on the playground in a semester than in a morning.

Frequencies are more often expressed as a rate, and two types of rates are regularly used in schools—percentages and frequency per minute. Percentages are an expression of the frequency multiplied by 100 with the product divided by the opportunity for performance. Thus, if Marcie correctly calculates 15 math problems on a 20-item test, her score is 75%. Percentage correct is useful when

1. **Alignment of vertical angles.**
   Drawing must have 4 angles. Connect top to bottom angle and left to right angles with straight lines. Angle formed by the crossing of these lines should be perpendicular (within 10 degrees).

   Acceptable: Unacceptable:

2. **Sides of equal length.**
   The size of the diamond is not important. Find the longest and shortest side; the longest side cannot be more than 20% longer than the shorter.

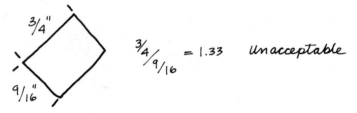

3. **Sides of straight lines.**
   Draw lines to connect the angles. For each side, draw a line that is perpendicular to the line you drew to connect the angles. The perpendicular cannot be more than 10% of the line that connects the angles.

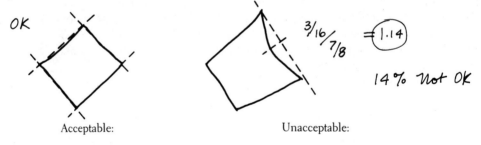

   Acceptable: Unacceptable:

4. **Formation of angles.**
   Sides must meet but may not extend more than ¼ inch past the angle.

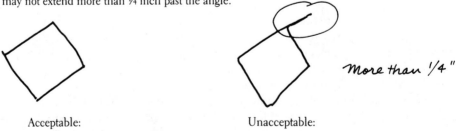

   Acceptable: Unacceptable:

Figure 3.4.   Criteria for judging the quality of a diamond.

54

the speed of performance is not controlled by the student (e.g., a group spelling test on which a teacher dictates the words to be spelled and, therefore, controls the speed). It is also an appropriate criterion to use for nondiscrete[6] and complex skills or when more than one skill is being assessed (e.g., a mathematics test on which both addition and subtraction are tested).

There are four concerns about the use of percentage as a performance measure. First, it does not indicate the fluency or rate at which the skill is performed. Second, a percentage statement does not distinguish omissions (no attempt to solve a problem) from errors; such information is important for planning instruction. Third, percentages, by themselves, do not indicate how many problems or behaviors the student has completed. Fourth, percentages may not be sensitive to small changes in behavior.

Frequency of correct responses per minute (rate[7]) is often preferred over percentage correct for several reasons. Rate is sensitive to small changes in behavior. Rate also provides information about both accuracy and speed of performance and can discriminate among students who are accurate but slow and those who are fluent (accurate and fast) in their performances. This distinction is important for several reasons. First, fluency may be a discriminating factor between skill acquisition and proficient use of a skill (Eaton, 1978). A common example used to illustrate this is the case of two students, both of whom score 100% on a math test of 50 problems. Bernice takes 4 minutes to complete the test while Beatrice takes 50 minutes. Both students have acquired the skill but Bernice is a much more proficient user of the skill. Additionally, as White and Haring (1980) suggest, fluency is significant because it is a good indicator of student ability to maintain and generalize a skill and, in some instances, can positively affect how fast a subsequent related skill can be learned. For example, a student who is fluent at addition facts 0 to 9 will learn addition facts 10 to 18 faster than a slower student. Finally, rate offers the advantage of being a constant unit of measurement (i.e., it is a measure of performance that can be compared across tasks with unequal numbers of trials or items).

Rate is an appropriate measure when behaviors being assessed are discrete, repeatable, and when speed or fluency is of concern. Fluency in a skill may be important (1) because of time expectations in classrooms (e.g., a teacher may only allot a certain time period for completion of a task), (2) because of the functional value of being able to perform a task at a particular rate (e.g., typing 90 words per minute), or (3) because the outcome of the task is dependent upon the speed with which it was done (e.g., pouring concrete, laying bricks).

Usually expressed as rate per minute (e.g., 30 words read correctly per minute), rate is calculated by dividing the frequency of a behavior by the number of minutes it was performed or observed. For example, if Lucy read a passage from

---

[6]Discrete-trial learning refers to learning activities that have clear-cut beginnings and endings. For example, if James is shown a flashcard and asked to say the answer to "5 × 7", the beginning of the trial is when the multiplication fact is requested; the end of the trial is when James answers (or a predetermined time without answer). Nondiscrete trials are simply trials that have no clear-cut beginning and end.

[7]While we recognize that both percentage correct and frequency per minute are rates, frequency per minute is commonly termed "rate."

her text for 3 minutes and read 150 words correctly, her reading rate would be 50 words per minute (i.e., 50 words per minute = 150 words/3 minutes). Rate of error also is included when assessing and recording performance. For example, if Lucy made 15 errors during the 3 minutes she read, her error rate would be 5 words per minute. Knowledge of error rate is important in assessing whether a student is performing an objective consistently and/or in a careful manner.

Choosing the Appropriate Characteristic

Teachers have several choices when it comes to what characteristic of behavior (singly or in combination) to which to direct their attention. However, there are some guidelines that can help teachers make the right decision.

Select percentage correct

- If the objective is written at the acquisition level
- If accuracy is of primary importance
- If it is not possible to obtain a free operant

Select rate

- If the objective is written at the fluency level
- If speed is a critical element of task performance
- If obtaining information about the rate of correct and incorrect behavior is important

Select quality

- If the topography of the behavior is of primary concern; quality is often used for objectives involving physical actions (e.g., performing a forward roll) or the permanent product of a physical act (e.g., correct formation of a letter)

Select duration or latency

- If time is of primary concern

2. Level of Satisfactory Performance

Several methods exist for establishing minimal rate standards for acceptable performance. As with other proficiency standards, those used currently for rate are not thoroughly validated and should be viewed as tentative guidelines. Five methods to establish criteria have been suggested: (1) expert opinion, (2) peer performance, (3) previous performance, (4) performance in tool skills, and (5) long-range goal setting.

- *Expert opinion.* Little in the way of general guidance can be offered for amplitude, latency, duration, and quality criteria. These characteristics of performance are quite task specific. For percentage criteria, Stephens, Hartman, and Lucas (1978) have offered three levels of criteria: mastery (90 to 100%), instructional (70 to 90%), and frustration (0 to 70%). They point out that determining the criterion for a particular task depends on the task itself. For example, a student will need to learn the alphabet and sound–symbol relationships to 100% mastery in order to perform subsequent skills. Common sense also dictates percentage aims for other skills—a teacher's goal for looking both ways before crossing the street should *not* be 85%. Mercer, Mercer, and Evans (1982) reviewed literature on efforts to establish rate standards on basic academic skills typically found in a variety of curricula. These rates are reported in later chapters in this text.[8] There does appear to be consensus about typical error rates, however: Two or fewer errors per minute is considered acceptable.

- *Peer performance.* Standards for acceptable performance often come from the performance of age or grade peers (cf. Deno & Mirkin, 1977; Howell & Kaplan, 1980). Especially in the case of developing skills or behavior—when less than perfect performance is expected of normally developing students, an appropriate comparison can be made to the average performance of classroom peers. Such standards also rest on the assumption that it is appropriate for a particular student to perform the task at the same rate as nonhandicapped peers. To obtain proficiency criteria in this manner, a teacher can administer a CBA of a particular skill(s) to the class (or an entire school or school district may collect data on a broader sample of students) and use the median rate of performance to establish the criteria. If more stringent criteria are desired, the median rate of the top 10% of the class may be used.

- *Previous performance.* Teachers have routinely used impressions of individual differences to set performance criteria for individual students. For example, Joey might need twice as many repetitions as Suzy to remember how to spell a word; students who learn slowly generally require higher criteria for retention (cf. Underwood, 1954). Eaton (1978) has suggested a more precise variant— using a student's previous performance on similar tasks to select appropriate standards for performance on new but related tasks. For example, if a student reached an oral reading rate of 100 words per minute with no errors on his last reading unit, it is reasonable to use the same criterion for the next unit. Blankenship and Lilly (1981) recommend a systematic approach—varying performance criteria and observing subsequent student performance.

- *Performance on tool skills.* Tool skills are basic skills necessary to perform more complex or advanced skills. For example, writing numbers is a tool skill for solving written math facts. Other tool skills include writing letters in isolation, saying the alphabet or phonic sounds, or counting out loud. How fast a student performs these basic skills will affect the performance rate of the related skill. For example, if Lionel cannot perform the tool skill of writing letters at a high

---

[8]Additional information may be obtained by contacting existing programs that emphasize the use of rate data: Precision Teaching Project, Skyline Center, 3300 Third St. N.E., Great Falls, MT 59404; Regional Resource Center Diagnostic Inventories, Clinical Services Building, University of Oregon, Eugene, OR 97403; and SIMS Reading and Spelling Program, Minneapolis Public Schools, 807 N.E. Broadway, Minneapolis, MN 55413.

rate (in comparison with peers), his expected rate for related skills such as copying from the board or taking dictation would be lowered. A general rule for using skill rate to set instructional standards is to compute the average tool-skill rate per minute and multiply this rate by one half or two thirds to arrive at the instructional standard. Thus, if Lionel's rate of writing single digits (i.e., 0 to 9) were 50 digits per minute, an appropriate rate aim or criterion for computing addition facts would range from 25 to 33 digits per minute. If a student's tool-skill rate is much lower than the suggested rate for beginning instruction, a teacher may wish to work on tool-skill fluency before beginning instruction on other skills.

- *Long-range goal setting.* Wesson (1989) describes a method for establishing rate criteria used in writing a long-range goal or objective (i.e., how well a student will perform the skill at the end of the year) for students with mild handicaps. Three steps are used: (1) administer several (i.e., 4 to 5) baseline probes and determine the median rate of performance, (2) multiply the number of instructional weeks left in the school year by two, and (3) add the product obtained in step two to the median rate obtained in step one. For example, if the median baseline rate for words read per minute from a passage taken from a basal reader is 50 words per minute and there are 22 instructional weeks left in the year, the criterion is 94 words per minute (i.e., $2 \times 22 = 44 + 50 = 94$). Wesson adds that it may be advisable to modify this method for students labeled educably mentally retarded by multiplying the number of instructional weeks by 1.5 instead of 2.

There is growing evidence (e.g., Ivarie, 1986) that setting stringent (i.e., higher) criteria may increase student performance more than lower criteria. Exactly how high a teacher should set criteria depends on the nature of the objective and the student. For short-term objectives that will be incorporated into a chain of skills, criteria can be set at fairly low levels since students will have ample opportunity to continue to perfect the objective as part of the longer instructional chain. For example, sight vocabulary in a basal reading series will be encountered over and over again as students read new passages. Teachers are more likely to teach stand-alone skills (i.e., a skill that is not practiced as part of a skill sequence, such as telling time) to mastery because they cannot control continued practice of that skill. Finally, skills that are necessary for survival are taught to a higher criterion.

Sources of Individualized Behavioral Objectives

The totality of behavioral objectives that are held for a student constitute that student's curriculum. In this sense curriculum is totally individualized, although there may be almost complete correspondence among curricula for students with similar abilities and aspirations.

A difficulty that teachers (and textbook writers) encounter when dealing with curriculum analysis is that curriculum is not static until after it has been completed by a student. A student's performance interacts with curriculum so that behavioral objectives may be revised and additional objectives formulated. The ultimate curriculum that a student receives comes from four sources: the intial general curriculum, task analysis of specific behavioral objectives, analysis of student errors, and observation of a student's performance during learning.

1. Behavioral Objectives Derived from a General Curriculum

The first task of a teacher (or committee of teachers) is to translate general statements of educational goals into precise behavioral objectives. This process entails specifying the components and subcomponents of a general goal and deciding the relative complexity of behavior to be taught. Then these precise objectives may be further refined for individual students. For example, it may be necessary to alter the conditions under which the behavior is to be demonstrated; thus, Jimmy might be allowed to use his calculator although other students may not.

Specifying Components of the Goal

Writing objectives in terms of behavior and products is necessary, but it takes more time. Teachers should specify all important aspects or *components* of the target behavior or domain. Thus, if we were developing an objective dealing with aggressive behavior, we would expect that all of the intended component behaviors of aggression (e.g., hitting, threatening, shoving) would be included in the definition. If we were developing an objective for addition and subtraction of single-digit integers, we would expect that all of the intended components of this domain (i.e., each combination) would be included in the definition. Figure 3.5 contains two examples of components of a domain: the major components of "cooperative" behavior for preschoolers and the major components of "use of the comma" for seniors in high school.

Specifying the Size of an Objective

Teachers must still decide the relative size of the objective to be taught. For example, there are several different ways that an objective for writing the numeral 3 might be developed, and exactly how an objective is written depends upon the student for whom that objective is written. A teacher might prepare a simple objective for an average student:

- Given a pencil and paper, the student will write the numbers 0 to 9 from dictation with 100% accuracy on three consecutive days.

For other, lower performing students such an objective is too complex. The teacher would need to specify less complex behavior in the objective. Perhaps two behavioral objectives would be substituted for writing the numeral 3.

- Given a pencil and paper, the student will write the number 3 correctly when requested to do so by the teacher on five consecutive trials on three consecutive days. To be correct, the numeral must be in the correct orientation (i.e., closed portions of the numeral on the right), the top portion of the numeral must be formed with straight lines and the top line must be horizontal (within 10

FIGURE 3.5.
Examples of
components within a
social and academic
domain.

PART I: COOPERATION

	taking turns	using polite words	following game rules	complying with teacher requests	complying with peer requests
Acquisition					
Maintenance					
Generalization					

PART II: USE OF THE COMMA

	dates	series	direct address	appositives	compound sentences	letter salutations
Knowledge						
Comprehension						
Application						
Analysis						
Synthesis						
Evaluation						

degrees) to the bottom of the paper, the bottom portion of the numeral must be generally circular with the opening no less than one-half of the vertical diameter, and the bottom must be larger but no more than twice as large as the top portion of the numeral (see Figure 3.6).

- Given the numeral 3 written on a 3 × 5 flashcard and asked, "What number is this?" the student will answer "3" on five consecutive trials on three consecutive days.

Such objectives could be too complex for some students. In this instance, a teacher could specify an even simpler behavior in the objective. Perhaps the first objective would be reformulated into four objectives.

- Without physical guidance by the teacher and given worksheets with the numeral 3 outlined by 15 dots (as shown in part 1 of Figure 3.6), the student will trace the dots to form the numeral correctly five times in a row on five consecutive days. "Correctly" means the student will use one continuous line and that the line will fall within one sixteenth of an inch of every dot without an obvious change in direction to cover the dot.

Part I: Highly cued writing of "3"   Part II: Moderately cued writing of "3"   Part III: Slightly cued writing of "3"

Figure 3.6.   Breaking down an objective into simpler subobjectives.

- Without physical guidance by the teacher and given worksheets with the numeral 3 outlined by 10 dots (as shown in part 2 of Figure 3.6), the student will trace the dots to form the numeral correctly five times in a row on five consecutive days. "Correctly" means the student will use one continuous line, that the line will fall within one sixteenth of an inch of every dot without an obvious change in direction to cover the dot, and that the line will maintain within one half inch the configuration traced in the preceding exercise.

- Without physical guidance by the teacher and given worksheets with the numeral 3 outlined by 5 dots (as shown in part 3 of Figure 3.6), the student will trace the dots to form the numeral correctly five times in a row on five consecutive days. "Correctly" means the student will use one continuous line, that the line will fall within one-sixteenth of an inch of every dot without an obvious change in direction to cover the dot, and that the line will maintain within one-half inch the configuration traced in the preceding exercise.

- Given a pencil and a blank sheet of paper, the student will write the numeral 3 correctly when requested to do so by the teacher on five consecutive trials on three consecutive days. To be correct, the numeral must meet the same criteria used in the second set of objectives.

2. Task Analysis

Often a behavioral objective is too complex to be mastered by a student. In such instances teachers break down complex behavioral objectives into discrete subobjectives. This process is termed *task analysis*. Anderson and Faust (1973, p. 82) have given a widely accepted definition:

> A task analysis describes the subskills and subconcepts a student must acquire in order to master a complex skill or an interrelated set of concepts and principles. Such an analysis should be complete, presented in the proper amount of detail, with relationships among component skills and concepts clearly specified. It should identify when and under what circumstances each component skill is to be performed. In short, the task analysis provides a blueprint of the things a student must master if he is to reach the objectives that have been set.

The number of steps and the degree of proficiency will depend on the pupil; bright, capable students require fewer steps and attain higher proficiency than pupils with learning problems.

Goes into

Cumulative Subtraction

Button-Button

$$3\overline{)21} \begin{array}{r} 7 \\ \hline \end{array}$$
$$\begin{array}{r} 21 \\ \hline 0 \end{array}$$

$$\begin{array}{r} 21 \\ 1 \; -3 \\ \hline 18 \\ 1 \; -3 \\ \hline 15 \\ 1 \; -3 \\ \hline 12 \end{array} \quad \begin{array}{r} 12 \\ 1 \; -3 \\ \hline 9 \\ 1 \; -3 \\ \hline 6 \\ 1 \; -3 \\ \hline 3 \end{array} \quad \begin{array}{r} 3 \\ 1 \; -3 \\ \hline 0 \end{array}$$

Count tallies (7)

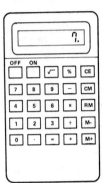

Figure 3.7.   Different algorithms for teaching division.

A complete task analysis requires that the algorithm of instruction be specified. For example, there are several ways to teach simple division, as shown in Figure 3.7. The first method, sometimes called the *goes into* method by youngsters, is the way most learn to divide: 5 goes into 15 exactly 3 times. A second method occasionally used in special classes is cumulative subtraction. Subtract 5 from 15, and 10 is left; subtract 5 from 10, and 5 is left; subtract 5 from 5 and none are left. Three fives were subtracted. Thus, 15 divided by 5 is 3. The last algorithm for teaching division is the *button to button* paradigm. Here the student learns to use a hand calculator to solve division problems by pushing the correct sequence of calculator buttons. Each algorithm leads to a different task analysis and different behaviors that distinguish the novice from the competent performer.

3. Error Analysis

Additional instruction objectives often come from systematic analysis of student errors. Called *error analysis*, this is the process whereby a teacher analyzes a pupil's incorrect responses on a test or other permanent product in order to generate and test hypotheses about the nature of the student's mistakes. For example, Figure 3.8 depicts George's responses to a weekly multiplication quiz. Inspection of his responses indicates that problems 4, 13, 19, 21, 23, 25, 27, 29, 31, 34, and 36 are incorrect. All require George to multiply by 8. However, further inspection of problems 18, 20, 22, 24, 26, 28, 30, 32, 33, and 35 shows that George sometimes does, in fact, multiply correctly by 8. How might this difference be reconciled? George correctly multiplies "8 × 1," "8 × 2," "8 × 3," "8 × 4," and "8 × 5." He incorrectly multiplies "8 × 6" through "8 × 9," giving all of these facts as "54." Analysis of George's errors on the weekly quiz suggests that he does not know half of his "8 facts."

Sometimes students learn a rule or principle incorrectly, and they apply their incorrect rule scrupulously. Error analysis can help the teacher discover these incorrect "rules." For example, in Figure 3.9, Lucy's essay indicates several grammatical errors. All of her plurals end in *s* even when they should not. It

Name George

1) 7 ×1	2) 7 ×9	3) 7 ×2	4) 7 ×8	5) 7 ×3	6) 7 ×7	7) 7 ×4	8) 7 ×6
7	63	14	54	21	49	29	42
9) 5 ×7	10) 4 ×7	11) 6 ×7	12) 3 ×7	13) 8 ×7	14) 2 ×7	15) 9 ×7	16) 1 ×7
35	28	42	21	54	14	63	7
17) 7 ×5	18) 8 ×4	19) 8 ×6	20) 8 ×3	21) 8 ×7	22) 8 ×2	23) 8 ×8	24) 8 ×1
35	32	54	24	54	16	54	8
25) 7 ×8	26 1 ×8	27) 8 ×8	28) 2 ×8	29) 7 ×8	30) 3 ×8	31) 6 ×8	32) 5 ×8
54	8	54	16	54	24	54	40
33) 8 ×5	34) 8 ×9	35) 4 ×8	36) 9 ×8				
40	54	32	54				

FIGURE 3.8.
George's responses to multiplication quiz.

Figure 3.9.
Error analysis of Lucy's essay.

lots of
My fren, Sally, has lotsa pets. She has dogs,
pl S–V
kittens, and white (mouses). The pets is friendly.
S–V pl
The dogs licks my hands and (feets). They tikle me.

seems that she is using this rule: To make all plurals, add *s*. However, this conclusion is *only an hypothesis*. A relatively simple way to verify that a student is using a particular rule is to ask students about their responses. In this case the teacher might ask Lucy about why several words end in *s*. Both correctly and incorrectly formed plurals should be queried to verify that, indeed, Lucy is using the rule that she appears to be using.

Often an incorrect response can have more than one potential cause. For example, a child who reads *dab* for *bad* may have trouble discriminating *b* from *d,* may have trouble with left-to-right sequencing, or may have trouble recalling the sound that is associated with each symbol. Very different psychological processes are involved, and very different interventions are required to ameliorate the problem—one, discrimination training; the other, strategies for associating symbol and sound. Further assessment is required to ascertain which problem should be addressed.

Sometimes error analysis does not lead to direct interventions. First, problems left unanswered or answered "I don't know" or "That's too hard" provide no information about incorrect processes or facts that the student is using. Second, the interventions required for some types of errors may not be derived from the error made. For example, if a pupil has difficulty answering comprehension questions that follow a reading passage, a good intervention is to increase the pupil's reading rate since improvement in rate is associated with improvements in comprehension; the nature of the comprehension questions missed may be irrelevant to the intervention. Third, mistakes that are the result of random errors (e.g., misreading directions) are unanalyzable, except of course when impulsive responding or failure to attend to directions are the problems. Fourth, sometimes students use unusual strategies that may not be recognized as consistent errors. Suppose Johnny has twice missed problems involving "8 × 7," but twice he correctly answered problems involving "8 × 7." The pattern appears inconsistent. However, suppose Johnny's teacher asked him about it and he responded: "Hey, I couldn't remember what "8 × 7" was. It's 54 or 56. I figured that I could get them all right if I guessed right or all wrong if I guessed wrong. So I figured, 'Why take a chance?' I guessed 54 on half the problems and 56 on the other half. That way I'd only miss half the ones I didn't know."

4. Student's Approach to Task

Observation of students while they are working can generate instructional objectives that relate directly to how a student learns. Some students work impulsively, not listening to directions, not paying attention to written directions (including arithmetic operators), beginning a response without getting all the necessary information (e.g., not reading the entire problem), working carelessly, and so forth. Some students do not persevere; they do not maintain attention to the task, they give up easily, allow interruptions to terminate their efforts, and so forth. Feuerstein and Rand (1979) have noted other inadequate problem-solving strategies that characterize handicapped students: failure to recognize errors, failure to sequence, failure to discriminate relevant from irrelevant details, failure to relate events, and failure to make comparisons. Teachers who observe *how* their students solve problems may generate additional behavioral objectives to remediate inadequate problem solving.

Summary

In this chapter the second and third steps ("analyze the curriculum" and "formulate objectives") of the CBA model are described. Curriculum is defined in the simplest terms—what students are expected to learn. Curricula may be commercially prepared and include scope and sequence charts, be developed at the state or local level, or, in the case of many students receiving special education services, be specified by the objectives included on an individualized education plan (IEP). The purpose of curricular analysis is to identify exactly what will be taught, how well each curricular component is to be learned, and how much student and teacher time and effort will be required. Curriculum analysis also requires attention to the sequence in which components and subcomponents are taught. A sequence must be logical and special care must be taken to ensure students have the prerequisite/enabling behaviors needed to progress through the curriculum in the specified sequence.

Once a curriculum has been analyzed, general goals are formulated into specific objectives. An appropriate objective contains three components: the behavior, the conditions under which the behavior is performed, and the criteria for successful performance of the behavior. While behaviors are constrained by the skills identified during the curricular analysis, the teacher has a variety of options from which to select the conditions and criteria.

At this point curricular expectation and sequence are precisely outlined. The teacher is then in an excellent position to develop appropriate assessment procedures that clearly reflect what is, or will be, taught.

Chapter 4

Development of Appropriate Assessment Procedures; Collection and Summarization of Results

Key Terms

Content validity
Duration recording
Event recording
Halo effect
Interscorer reliability
Interval recording
Keys
Momentary time sample

Partial interval recording
Performance measure
Reliability
Stability
Standard error of measurement
Table of specifications
Whole-interval recording

Once the purpose of assessment has been decided and the curriculum has been analyzed, assessment procedures are developed (or selected). Then data are collected, and the results of the assessment are summarized. In Chapter 1, the conclusion was reached that educator-made tests and systematic observations had the greatest potential utility because they had the potential to match curricular content and because their technical limitations could be overcome. The development and use of appropriate assessment procedures require a basic understanding of reliability and validity, as well as their specific applications to the development of tests, observations, and probes.

Reliability

Reliability refers to the extent to which we can generalize to a domain from a sample. Three domains are of interest: test items (i.e., all potential test items that might be asked); time (i.e., all potential times that questions might be asked or that observations might be made); and observers (i.e., all potential observers or testers). The actual test questions or behaviors to be observed, the actual times when tests are given or observations are made, and the actual testers or observers are the samples from which these generalizations are made to domains. Thus, reliability refers to generalizations from a student's performance at one time and with one set of materials or circumstances to performance at other times with similar (but different) materials or situations.

Two indices of reliability are usually reported—the reliability coefficient and the standard error of measurement. The reliability coefficient is a special case of a correlation[1] coefficient and ranges from .00 to 1.00. The higher the value, the more reliable is the test. How large a reliability coefficient should be depends on the generalization a teacher wishes to make, as well as the importance of the decision. While there are no established guidelines for teacher-made tests, a reliability of .80 or greater is probably sufficient for generalizations to other test items and times of testing when content is tested frequently; when testing is infrequent, a minimum reliability of .90 is desirable. A reliability of .90 or greater is usually sufficient for generalizations to other observers or testers.

The standard error of measurement (SEM) is a bit more complicated. An SEM is the standard deviation[2] of a person's actual (obtained) scores around that person's true score. Suppose that Ms. Li wanted to assess her students' addition of single-digit facts. Because her students are young, she did not want to test the entire domain—all 90 of the possible combinations of addition facts. She would rather sample some of the facts and infer pupil knowledge about all of the facts. If she decided to give a 10-fact test, she has an almost infinite choice among possible 10-fact tests from which to choose. However, only students who had learned all of the facts or none of the facts would earn the same score on each of the possible tests. It turns out that if we could give students all of the possible tests, these test scores should form a normal (bell-shaped) distribution, except for the

---

[1]Correlation is a statistical procedure used to estimate the degree of relationship between two or more variables. The computation of a correlation coefficient is demonstrated in the Appendix. Throughout this text, correlation is used synonymously with simple linear (Pearson product–moment) correlation although there are several types of correlations. Explanation of the other types of correlation and demonstration of their computation are beyond the scope of this text.

[2]The standard deviation, the square root of the variance, is a descriptive statistic used to describe the relationship of each score to the mean (arithmetic average) of the scores. The computation of variance and standard deviation is demonstrated in the Appendix.

scores earned by students who knew all (or almost all) or none (or almost none) of the facts.[3]

If we scored every 10-point test, we could compute an average test score for each student. This average for all of the possible tests for one student on the domain is called that student's *true score*. The standard deviation of that student's distribution of 10-point test scores is the standard error of measurement.[4] The error implied by this term is the 10-item test's inability to estimate a student's true score exactly. The error is the discrepancy between a student's score on a quiz and that student's true score. Thus, any test score consists of at least two components—true score and error.

Item Consistency

Item consistency refers to the interchangeability of tests selected from the same domain.[5] Test makers usually are interested in large domains and have a choice of which questions to ask. Moreover, a student's performance on a particular test is usually of less interest than that student's performance on the entire domain.

Two methods are used to estimate item consistency: correlations between alternate test forms and correlations among test items. The first method, usually called *alternate-form reliability*, requires that the scores earned by several students on one form of test be correlated with scores earned by those students on the other form of the test. When multiple forms of a test are not available, reliability also can be estimated directly from the test items. After a test has been given to a number of students and scored, it is divided into two halves. The two halves are correlated.[6] There are, however, several ways that a test could be halved (e.g., odd-numbered items and even-numbered items), and these different ways produce different estimates. A statistic called *coefficient alpha* provides the average correlation among all of the possible halves. The computation of this statistic is illustrated in the Appendix. Although the statistical methods used to estimate item consistency appear different, it turns out they are conceptually and mathematically very similar.

---

[3]For students who knew all or none of the facts, there would be no distribution of scores since those students would earn the same score. For students who knew almost all or almost no facts, the distribution of obtained scores would be skewed—asymmetrical.

[4]We shall see shortly that three different standard errors of measurement can be obtained since there are three generalizations that are subsumed under the term reliability—one related to the consistency of test questions, one related to stability, and one related to consistency among observers.

[5]To avoid redundancy, only the consistency of test items is discussed. However, the principles discussed in this section apply equally to observations. For example, an observer may select particular behaviors to represent an entire class of behavior (e.g., hitting and spitting to represent aggressive behavior) or specific definitions to represent less restrictive conditions.

[6]The correlation coefficient is corrected because it is based on only half of the test items and, therefore, systematically underestimates reliability. The formula for calculating the corrected correlation, called the Spearman–Brown formula, is given in the following equation: $2 \cdot r/(1 + r)$. (r is the correlation between the two halves.)

Stability

The second type of reliability, called *stability* or *test–retest reliability*, refers to the degree to which observations or test scores obtained at one time can be generalized to observations made at any other appropriate time. For example, suppose that Mr. Wright was concerned about Martin's aggressive behavior. Further suppose that Mr. Wright decided to observe him 10 times for 10 minutes per observation. Further suppose that any time during a particular 5-day week was appropriate for observing. Assuming a 5.5-hour day, he would have a choice of 1,550 10-minute periods in which to observe. If Mr. Wright observed Martin for the entire day, it would be possible to obtain behavior rates for Martin during each of those overlapping time periods. The rates from all of the 10-minute observations should form a normal distribution. The mean of the student's distribution would be the true rate of aggressive behavior over time; the standard deviation of the student's distribution also would be called a standard error of measurement. Thus, reliability can also refer to the degree to which we can infer a student's performance from a sample of observation times to all times.

Stability is traditionally estimated by repeated measurement with the same test or observation procedures. The most commonly used method for estimating a test's stability is to test a group of students, wait a period of time (usually two weeks), and test that group of students again. The scores from the first administration are correlated with scores from the second administration. The resulting coefficient is a stability coefficient. This procedure is quite suitable for systematic observation of behavior and probes where repeated measurement with the same (or equivalent) procedures or devices is common. A standard error of measurement based on stability also can be calculated, and its interpretation is much the same as the standard error of measurement associated with item consistency. An SEM based on stability is the standard deviation of obtained scores around the true score, and the error implied is the difference between a score obtained at one time and a student's true score across time.

However, teachers seldom have the time or inclination to assess the stability of tests although they are interested in the stability of information. Thus, they are more likely to assess stability through maintenance (or retention) checks in which information is reexamined periodically. Done consistently, maintenance checks should lead to the same conclusions about stability.

Observer Consistency

The third type of reliability, observer consistency, usually is called interobserver, interscorer, or interrater reliability or agreement. This type of reliability refers to the degree to which we can generalize observations to all possible qualified observers. Suppose Mr. Wright wanted to observe Martin's aggressive behavior during recess. Further, suppose he got every teacher and teacher's aide to observe Martin during recess. Each observer's score could be computed and these scores would form a distribution of scores. Martin's true score across observers would be the mean of this distribution. The standard deviation of this distribution would be the SEM for observers. Thus, reliability also refers to the degree to which we can infer a student's performance from a sample of observers to all observers.

Two general approaches are taken in estimating interobserver reliability—correlational and percentage agreement. These two approaches rest on different assumptions, yield different estimates, and rely upon different computational procedures.

Correlational Approach

Generalization to other observers can be estimated by having two judges observe a number of students. The paired data for the group are correlated, and the resulting coefficient estimates reliability for observers. A correlational approach is generally favored by individuals with a psychometric orientation since its computational procedures and interpretations are interchangeable with the procedures and interpretations used to estimate item consistency and stability.

Percentage Agreement Approach

Although there are several ways to estimate percentage agreement, only three methods are commonly used: simple agreement, point-to-point agreement, and agreement of occurrence. These three methods differ in how they are calculated and interpreted as well as when they can be used appropriately.

1. *Simple agreement.* Simple agreement is useful for estimating the reliability of latency, duration, and amplitude. However, when used to estimate frequency, one must assume that the smaller number is a subset of (i.e., is completely contained within) the larger number. If the smaller number is not a subset of the larger, then percentage of simple agreement cannot be interpreted correctly.

As its name implies, simple agreement is the easiest way to calculate percentage agreement. Suppose Ms. Jenkins and Mr. Clayburg were observing Julius to see how long he took to begin working after he was requested to do so. Further suppose that Ms. Jenkins estimated that Julius took 12 seconds, while Mr. Clayburg estimated he took 10 seconds. To compute simple agreement, one divides the smaller number (10) by the larger number (12) and multiplies the quotient by 100. In the preceding example, simple agreement is 83.33%.

$$\% \text{ simple agreement} = (100)(\text{smaller number/larger number})$$
$$= 100 \, (10/12)$$
$$= 83.33\%$$

2. *Point-to-point agreement.* Point-to-point agreement is used to estimate the reliability of frequency data. As its name implies, this index uses agreement for each observational instance. Suppose two teachers (Mr. Clayburg and Ms. Jenkins) observed Marcie on the playground to see how well she took turns with other students. They synchronize their watches and agree to check Marcie every 30 seconds for 12.5 minutes and to note whether she is engaged in cooperative behavior. The results of their observations appear in Part 1 of Table 4.1; their responses are summarized in Part 2 of that table. Mr. Clayburg observed 19

Part I				Part II			
Word Read					*Clayburg*		
	Clayburg	Jenkins			(−)	(+)	(Total)
1	+	+					
2	−	+		(+)	1	16	17
3	+	+					
4	+	+					
5	−	−					
6	+	−		*Jenkins*			
7	+	+		(−)	5	13	8
8	+	+					
9	−	−					
10	+	+		(Total)	6	19	
11	+	+					
12	+	+					
13	+	+					
14	+	+					
15	−	−					
16	+	−					
17	+	+					
18	+	+					
19	+	+					
20	−	−					
21	+	+					
22	−	−					
23	+	+					
24	+	+					
25	+	−					
Totals	19	17					

TABLE 4.1
Marcie's Cooperative Behavior, As Observed By Two Teachers.

instances of cooperation, while Ms. Jenkins observed 17. They agreed on 16 of the 25 observations that Marcie was cooperating and on 5 of the 25 observations that she was not cooperating. They disagreed on 4 observations: On 1 observation, Ms. Jenkins rated Marcie's behavior as cooperative but Mr. Clayburg did not; on 3 observations, Mr. Clayburg rated Marcie's behavior as cooperative but Ms. Jenkins did not. Point-to-point agreement for the data in Table 4.1 is computed by dividing the number of agreements of occurrence plus the number of agreements of nonoccurrence (i.e., 16 and 5) by the total number of observations (i.e., 25) and multiplying the quotient by 100:

$$\% \text{ point-to-point agreement} = \frac{(100)(\#\text{agreement of occurrence} + \#\text{agreement of nonoccurence})}{\#\text{observations}}$$
$$= (100)[(16 + 5)/25]$$
$$= 84\%$$

3. *Agreement of occurrence.* Like point-to-point agreement, agreement for occurrence is also used for frequency data. When there is a substantial discrepancy between agreement about occurrence and agreement about nonoccurrence, point-to-point agreement tends to overestimate reliability. Therefore, a more conservative procedure, agreement for occurrence, may be used to estimate agreement. The calculation of percent agreement for occurrence is similar to the calculation of point-to-point agreement: Divide the number of observations that both observers agree occurred (i.e., 16) by the total number of observations less agreements on nonoccurrence (i.e., $25 - 5 = 20$) and multiply the quotient by 100. For the data in Table 4.1, the percentage agreement for occurrence is .80.

$$\begin{aligned}
\frac{\% \text{ agreement}}{\text{of occurence}} &= \frac{(100)(\#\text{agreements of occurrence})}{\#\text{observations} - \#\text{agreements of nonoccurrence}} \\
&= \frac{(100)(16)}{25 - 5} \\
&= 80\%
\end{aligned}$$

Which Estimate of Reliability Should Be Used?

The three types of reliability are not interchangeable. For example, a teacher cannot use item consistency to estimate stability or interobserver reliability to estimate item consistency (even when correlational procedures are used to estimate interobserver agreement). Thus, teachers should use the estimate for the generalization they wish to make. The good news is that the errors estimated by the three types of reliability are additive, and any combination of reliabilities can be estimated. To estimate all three sources of error, teachers must use different test items (or observation guides), different times of assessment, and different observers. Whenever highly objective assessments are used, teachers correctly expect high levels of interscorer or interobserver agreement; thus, estimating this type of reliability may not be necessary. Whenever teachers assess an entire domain (e.g., all of the letters of the alphabet or all of the addition facts), estimating item consistency is not necessary.

Validity

Validity refers to the extent to which a test or other assessment procedure measures what it was intended to measure. In traditional measurement texts, several types of validity are usually discussed: content validity, construct validity, concurrent validity, predictive validity, factoral validity, and so forth. For classroom purposes, the overriding concern is for an assessment's content validity. The content validity of tests "is established by examining three factors: the appropriateness of the types of items included, the completeness of the item sample, and the way in which the items assess the content" (Salvia & Ysseldyke, 1985, p. 131).

This definition also applies to forms that guide systematic observations and that are used to assess permanent products (e.g., drawings, essays).

Content Appropriateness

Every item on a test and every behavior on an observation guide should "belong." For tests, there are two aspects to content appropriateness: (1) the behavior, skill, or fact itself and (2) the level of proficiency demanded during the assessment. For observations, usually only the former is considered.

The Behavior, Skill, or Fact

Teachers must be able to answer affirmatively, "Is the behavior, skill, or fact part of the domain[7] being assessed?" If a teacher can demonstrate that every piece of an assessment procedure is appropriate, this portion of content validity is satisfied.

Level of Proficiency

The level of proficiency at which content is assessed should match the level of proficiency at which the content was taught. As discussed in Chapter 3, material can be taught at several levels: knowledge, comprehension, application, analysis, synthesis, and evaluation (Bloom, Hasting, and Madaus, 1975). Material should not be assessed at higher levels than at which it is taught. Thus, if the instructional objectives are taught at the knowledge level, teachers should neither test nor expect students—especially students with learning handicaps—to know the material at a comprehension (or higher) level. The principle holds true for performance. If a teacher has not expected fluency during instruction, fluency should not be required during assessment.

Content Completeness

The assessment procedure either must assess all of the domain or use a logical and systematic procedure to sample from the domain. For example, a test of single-digit addition facts that asked only "What are 5 and 5?" would lack content validity because it is so incomplete and because there is no logical reason to believe that "5 + 5" in any way represents the entire domain. Similarly, an observation schedule that allowed for only one 5-second period to observe or an observation schedule that defined aggression as only "spitting" would lack content validity.

Method of Content Measurement

The actual performances that are required of a student to demonstrate learning also must be appropriate. Of particular concern are response capabilities, stimulus capabilities, and enabling behaviors that are required for a student to demonstrate learning.

---

[7]A domain is all of the items that could appear on a test or all of the behaviors that define a class of behaviors, such as "attention."

Students must be physically capable of making the response that is demanded by the assessment procedures. Otherwise, a student's response incapacity and not the target behavior or fact is assessed. For example, timed oral reading should not be used as a measure of a stutterer's decoding (reading) skill; written essay questions should not be used to evaluate a quadriplegic's knowledge of American history; word problems, written in English, should not be used to evaluate the mathematical skills of non–English-speaking students.

Students must be capable of understanding what is expected of them. They must be able to see the written directions and hear the spoken directions. There are several variations of these abilities: discriminating colors when materials are color coded, having olfactory integrity when the sense of smell is required, having sufficient neurological organization when balance and coordination are involved, and so forth.

Finally, students must have in their repertoires the behaviors and knowledge presupposed by the assessment procedures. For example, when a teacher uses a machine-scored test, students must know how to use a multiple-choice answer sheet, as well as know the content being tested; if a term paper is assigned, a student must have certain minimum library skills (e.g., use of card catalog or use of the library's computer). Finally, a student must have acquired the language skills to understand what is demanded by a teacher. Language skills are especially important for students in special education since a disproportionate number of handicapped students come from linguistic minorities.

Developing Appropriate Assessment Procedures

There are five actions teachers can take to develop good assessment procedures. Some of these apply to all assessment procedures; others apply more specifically to tests, observations, or probes.

1. Allocate Time

When allocating time, teachers must consider the time it takes to develop or find an appropriate assessment procedure, the time needed to administer the assessment, and the time to score and record student performance. Whatever the purpose, assessment should be efficient and come close to the minimum time necessary. However, we recommend that one err on the side of giving too much time to assessment rather than too little. To monitor ongoing instruction, teachers should plan on spending at least 10% of their time in assessment activities, although some of that time can serve double purposes—monitoring drill, seatwork, and homework.

Pupil progress should be assessed regularly and frequently to plan and evaluate the effectiveness of instruction. Daily measurement of fundamental skills (i.e., reading, writing, arithmetic) is certainly preferable, but in certain circumstances (e.g., mainstream classrooms[8]) that may not be possible. Collecting brief samples of performance two to three times a week is probably adequate for making decisions about pupil progress and teaching effectiveness in these content areas (Fuchs, 1986; Ysseldyke et al., 1983). Teachers may choose to evaluate the acquisition of more complex skills and the maintenance of more basic facts less often—weekly or biweekly. These evaluations will of necessity cover much more material less thoroughly.

Tests

Teachers generally fit tests to the classroom time allocated for testing. The time needed to administer a test depends on the age and maturity of the students. Generally, older students can be tested in longer sessions—for 30 to 60 minutes; younger students and students with shorter attention spans should be tested in briefer sessions. Teachers then fit the questions to the time allowed for students to take an exam. The conceptual demands of the test questions affect the number of questions that can be used. Knowledge and relatively easy comprehension questions can be answered quickly. Therefore, students can answer relatively more of these than more difficult questions—higher-level comprehension, application, analysis, synthesis, or evaluation.

Teacher time for administration and scoring are closely related. The general rule of thumb is that the easier and faster a test is to develop, the harder and slower it is to score. Essay tests can be constructed relatively quickly, but student responses take a considerable amount of time to score because they are very slow to evaluate; objective tests require a lot of time to construct, but student responses can be scored very quickly.

Observations

Except in contrived observational situations, no additional student time is required. However, a teacher's time for development can vary considerably. The forms on which observations are tallied (i.e., observation guides) generally can be developed quickly when target behaviors are few and unambiguous. However, a considerable amount of time may be required to operationalize fuzzy concepts (e.g., cooperation) into observable behavior. Moreover, if someone other than the teacher collects the observational data, then that person will have to be trained. Training can take a lot of time. A teacher provides a definition of target behaviors as well as examples and nonexamples of their occurrence. Then the observer is given practice that begins with fairly clear instances of every delimiting condition and then proceeds to less clear and more difficult instances. The adequacy of training should be evaluated in situations that are at least as difficult as those the observer will encounter during real observations.

---

[8]"Mainstream" is a term borrowed from the British. In American usage, mainstream refers to the "normal" tracks in elementary and secondary schools. The concept of the mainstream is closely tied to the implementation of P.L. 94-142, especially with its requirement to educate handicapped students in the least restrictive environment. It also should be noted that "mainstream" is also used as a verb that means to enroll students in classes and programs that are or that approximate regular/normal tracks and curricula in the schools.

Probes

When teachers develop their own probes, time for deciding what items to include is minimal since usually probes directly assess acquisition, fluency, and maintenance on specific objectives by having students fill in answers. However, formatting and typing time will usually be longer than for tests given in the same amount of time because probes contain so many more items than tests.

Probes are usually administered in very brief periods of time, usually lasting from 1 to 3 minutes. Therefore, a student's investment in time is minimal. However, teacher time for administering probes may be considerable because they are administered frequently (at least once a week or more frequently if possible) and may be administered individually.

2. Select Appropriate Assessment Procedure

Theoretically, teachers have a choice among a variety of assessment procedures. In practice, teachers correctly rely almost exclusively on tests, observations, and probes to gather information. Often, any of the three procedures could be used to obtain information about learning and performance data to make a particular decision. More often, one procedure is better suited than the other two. Two criteria guide most decisions about which procedure to select.

The Nature of the Performance to Be Evaluated

Tests are well suited for assessing a student's comprehension, analysis, synthesis, and evaluation of information. For example, if Mr. Albans wished to assess his students' interpretation of the American Revolutionary War, a test could provide the information he wanted. Observations are well suited for the direct assessment of processes and behavior. Thus, observations are the desired method of assessing social behavior, compliance, strategy usage, and so forth. For example, if Ms. Clayburg wished to assess how well Henry complied with teacher requests, direct observation would be a better assessment procedure than a test on classroom procedures. Probes are well suited for direct and frequent assessments of student knowledge and fluency. For example, if Mr. Albans was monitoring progress in oral reading twice each week, a 2-minute oral reading probe would provide him with the information he needed.

The Efficiency of the Procedure

Time (both student's and teacher's) and money are fixed resources, and teachers should always try to use them wisely. When two or three different procedures can produce satisfactory information, the fastest and easiest procedure is preferred. For example, suppose a new boy transferred to a school district in mid-semester and his resource-room teacher wanted to assess his knowledge of math to select appropriate educational objectives for him. The teacher would have a choice among giving him a fairly lengthy survey test, administering tests that covered the content of several teaching units, and administering multiple-skill probes that covered the content of the same teaching units. If the probes were made and the tests were not, it would be inefficient to construct tests.

Select Formats			FIGURE 4.1.
Stem	Options	Key	Example questions
Multiple-Choice	*What 5 letters are always vowels?*		using select formats.
	a) a,b,c,d,e	b	
	b) a,e,i,o,u		
	c) h,c,o,w,y		
	d) v,w,x,y,z		
True-False	*The letter,* y, *is sometimes a vowel.*		
	True	True	
	False		
Matching	*Write the letter of the invention to the*		
	left of the person who invented it.		
	___1. Bell a) Cotton gin	(d)	
	___2. Edison b) Incandescent bulb	(b)	
	___3. Land c) Self-developing film	(c)	
	___4. Whitney d) Telephone	(d)	

3. Select Appropriate Performance Measure

Teachers have choices among performance measures—things a student does to demonstrate learning. The primary consideration is that the performance measure reflect the intended educational outcomes in the domain without distortion.

Tests

Teacher-made tests are generally classified on the basis of scoring and response formats. Scoring formats range from total objectivity to total subjectivity. Completely objective formats are those in which the criteria for correct answers, called *keyed* responses, are specified prior to scoring, and all responses are scored with the same criteria. At the other end of the continuum are completely subjective scoring formats. Subjective tests do not have predetermined criteria for correct responses; consequently, scoring criteria may be applied inconsistently from student to student. Some scoring formats fall between complete objectivity and complete subjectivity; such formats have scoring *guidelines* intended to reduce subjectivity.

The two response formats are select and supply. Select formats (i.e., multiple choice, true–false, and matching questions) can be efficient and effective in evaluating a student's mastery of educational objectives prepared at the knowledge, comprehension, and application levels. Questions prepared in this format are usually objective. The answer that has been determined to be correct by the test maker is called the key.[9] Figure 4.1 contains examples of each select format with each component of the question labeled. Multiple-choice questions are

[9]Students sometimes write justifications for their selections. When a teacher considers these justifications, and especially when a teacher alters the key for a student as a result of the written justifications, scoring becomes subjective.

made up of two parts. The stem makes the demands upon the test taker and contains all of the common relevant information. The response bank contains the options from which a student selects an answer. True–false tests are a special type of multiple choice. In this type of question, the stem is composed of a statement, but there are only two options: The statement is true, or the statement is false. Matching tests are also variants of multiple-choice tests. However, instead of presenting a student with one stem at a time, several stems are presented with the same options; the response bank is the same for all items. Different types of matching questions allow each option to be used only once, each option to be used more than once, and more than one option to be used with each stem (sometimes called *multiple matching*).

Supply-format questions require a student to produce (orally or in writing) the correct answer. These formats are used on tests of educational objectives prepared at the levels of analysis, synthesis, and evaluation because students are expected to produce novel answers. There are three general types of supply questions (see Figure 4.2). *Fill-in* questions—most useful for knowledge-level questions—require a student to give a word or number in response to a question; a variant of this format presents a student with a sentence with more than one word missing, and the missing words (or synonyms) must be supplied by the student. Fill-in questions can be quite objective if a teacher lists acceptable responses (often called a response bank) in advance; should an unanticipated correct response be encountered, it can be added to the response bank, and previously scored items can be

---

FIGURE 4.2.
Examples of supply questions.

Fill-in Questions

Stem

$14 - 8 =$ _____

Columbus's fleet was made up of the Nina, the Pinta, and the

_____.

What is the term for a U.S. Senator?

Restricted-response Questions

State three powers reserved to the U.S. Congress.

What are the three components of behavioral objectives?

What freedom(s) are guaranteed by the First Amendment to the U.S. Constitution?

Extended Essay

Discuss the social and economic conditions that led to the French Revolution.

Compare and contrast colonial revolutions and class revolutions.

How was the British-American War in 1812 related to Napoleon Bonaparte?

---

rescored with the modified response bank. *Restricted-response* questions—useful for questions prepared at knowledge, comprehension, and application levels—place limits on what a student is required to produce, and responses may consist of a few words or a few sentences. *Extended-answer* formats—most useful for questions prepared at analysis, synthesis, and evaluation levels—require a student to produce a detailed response consisting of a paragraph to several pages. Tests prepared in restricted-response and extended-answer formats are likely to be scored subjectively.

The primary disadvantage of select and fill-in questions is the time required to prepare them. This disadvantage is more than offset by their five advantages: (1) Highly objective scoring can be attained readily; as a result, interscorer reliability is usually very good. (2) Scoring is fast and simple; only when there are numerous erasures or indecipherable writing is scoring tedious. (3) Teachers can sample exactly the objectives they wish to assess, and they can sample a larger number of objectives at appropriate levels of understanding. Thus, content reliability is increased. (4) By limiting the responses a student might produce, students cannot avoid unknown information or bluff their way through a question; moreover, various unwanted influences (e.g., handwriting and spelling) are readily controlled. (5) Since relatively more questions can be asked, students are required to study extensively.[10]

In addition to allowing students to hone their writing skills, questions prepared in the formats of restricted response and extended answer have three advantages: (1) Fewer questions need to be prepared for an examination since response time for each question is significantly longer than that required in other formats. (2) Preparation of these types of questions is substantially easier since plausible, but incorrect, options are not prepared. (3) Successful answers to these types of questions require students to organize and integrate large chunks of course content.

These advantages are offset, at least partially, by four disadvantages: (1) Scoring is time consuming and more subjective; thus, interscorer reliability should be lower than with more objective tests. (2) Content is sampled poorly since few questions can be asked in any examination period; thus, reliability (item consistency) should be lower than with other types of questions. (3) Opportunities for bluffing and evasion are increased; students can form their answers to be intentionally ambiguous and incomplete, and they can structure their responses so that unknown information is not obvious. (4) Assessment of knowledge and comprehension objectives is inefficient.

Observations[11]

Four basic types of measure can be obtained by systematic observation—frequency, duration, latency, and amplitude. Of these four types, amplitude is the most difficult to measure directly in classroom situations. Here, amplitude is

---

[10]Especially in the case of multiple-choice questions, examination preparation is not restricted to studying isolated facts and details; multiple-choice questions are well suited to higher-level questions.

[11]We wish to thank Karl Fleischer and Mary Parola for their assistance in the preparation of this section.

usually estimated through various rating schemes (e.g., Likert-type scales[12]). Latency is always measured in seconds.

By far the most commonly used measures are frequency and duration recording. In *frequency recording*, one selects the time during which observations are to occur. For example, hitting may be observed during recess or lunch periods or during academic instruction, or between 2:00 and 2:30 P.M. regardless of the activity. The observer simply counts the number of target events or behaviors that occur during that time. Generally frequency recording is used for behavior only when that behavior is frequent and discrete (i.e., has a discernible beginning and ending). In *duration recording*, a period for observation is selected and an observer records the time that a discrete event or behavior lasts, generally by noting the time at the start of the event and at its conclusion. Duration recording is appropriate when one is interested in the latency[13] of response as well as duration.

Moreover, these two types of measure can be obtained in two ways— continuous and discontinuous observation. *Continuous observations* are made by observing and recording each event as it occurs throughout an entire period of observation (Rojahn & Kanoy, 1985; Springer, Brown, & Duncan, 1981). *Discontinuous observation* estimates events from samples taken within specified time intervals (Arrington, 1943; Powell, Martindale, Kulp, Martindale, & Bauman, 1977; Repp, Roberts, Slack, Repp, & Berkler, 1976). *Discontinuous observations* are used when continuous observations are neither possible nor practical, as in often the case in the classroom (Green, McCoy, Burns, & Smith, 1982).

Historically, three methods of discontinuous sampling have been used: whole interval, partial interval, and momentary time sampling. For all three types, observers first establish a schedule for observation. For example, an observation schedule might call for 10 seconds to observe, 5 seconds to record, 10 seconds to observe, and so on within the observation session. In whole-interval recording, the event must last for the entire interval in order to be considered an instance of occurrence. Thus, a behavior that starts or ends inside the interval will not be considered an instance of occurrence. In partial-interval recording, the event is recorded if it occurs within any part (or all) of the interval. Thus, if a behavior started or ended within the interval, it would be considered an instance of occurrence if partial-interval recording were being used. In momentary time sampling, the recording interval is only a brief moment (e.g., 0.5 seconds). This moment is usually signaled. For example, the observer may buy or prepare an audiotape that gives a pure tone signal every so many seconds.

In the last two decades, a number of studies have been carried out to learn which discontinuous recording technique provides the more accurate estimate of actual behavior (behavior observed continuously) and to ascertain the effect of the length of observation interval on the accuracy of observation (Ary &

---

[12]Likert scales are usually constructed with a statement (e.g., "Jim talks too loudly") and four response options—strongly agree, agree, disagree, and strongly disagree. Midpoints (e.g., "neither agree nor disagree") are generally not used to force the respondent to one direction or another. Variants of Likert-type scales might use options such as "always," "often," "seldom," and "never."

[13]Latency refers to the period of time between a signal for a behavior to begin (e.g., John, take your seat) and when the behavior actually starts (e.g., John sits).

Suen, 1984; Barton, 1981; Brulle, 1981; Brulle & Repp, 1984; Dunbar, 1976; Powell et al., 1975; Powell et al., 1977; Powell & Rockinson, 1978; Repp et al., 1976; Sanson-Fisher, Poole, & Dunn, 1980). The results of these studies indicate that:

- Both whole-interval and partial-interval sampling generally provide inaccurate estimates of behavior.

- Momentary time sampling provides generally acceptable estimates of both frequency and duration of behavior.

- Momentary time sampling is affected by the length of the observation interval, the rate at which the behavior is produced, and the consistency with which the behavior is produced (i.e., whether the behavior occurs in bursts or is spaced evenly throughout the observation session).

Determining the appropriate interval for momentary time sampling is a bit time consuming as well as imprecise. A teacher should observe the behavior continuously before selecting the sampling technique to ascertain the rate at which the behavior occurs and if it occurs in bursts. The appropriate observation interval is determined by the characteristics of the behavior—its frequency or duration and its consistency throughout the observation intervals. If the behavior is of relatively low frequency or of short duration, shorter observation intervals (e.g., 30 seconds) and more observations should be used because accurate measurement is a function of the number of observations in which the behavior is observed. If the behavior occurs in bursts, both smaller intervals (e.g., 30 seconds or shorter) and more frequent observations should be used. If the behavior is relatively consistent and occurs frequently (e.g., 25 to 75% of the time), larger intervals (e.g., 60 or 120 seconds) can be used, provided that there is a sufficient number of intervals (for example, 35 or more) in which the behavior occurs.

For example, suppose Mr. Clayburg wanted to reduce Hector's wandering about the classroom during seatwork. He asks his aide, Ms. Freeman, to observe Hector's behavior for a couple of days and note the times when seatwork begins and ends as well as the times when Hector leaves and returns to his seat. From this data, Mr. Clayburg computes the duration of Hector's out-of-seat behavior and notes if it occurs continuously or in bursts. Table 4.2 contains the data collected by Ms. Freeman. From these data, Mr. Clayburg notes that the overall out-of-seat behavior lasted about 17% of the time during which Hector was observed. However, the behavior lasted longer during the morning (i.e., about 24% of the time) than in the afternoon (i.e., less than 10% of the time). Given these characteristics of the behavior and if Mr. Clayburg wished to use momentary time sampling, observation intervals of 30 seconds or shorter would be needed to produce accurate estimates of Hector's behavior in the morning, and intervals of 5 seconds would probably be necessary in the afternoon. To simplify the observation schedule, Mr. Clayburg decides to use the same interval—5 seconds—during the morning and afternoon. Therefore, he prepares an audio

TABLE 4.2 Hector's Out-of-Seat Behavior	Beginning/Ending Times for Seatwork		Beginning/Ending Times Hector Is Out of Seat	
Day One				
	8:45	9:15	8:55	9:00
	10:45	11:10	11:00	11:07
	11:45	12:00	11:55	12:00
	1:30	2:00	1:35	1:38
	——	——	1:50	1:52
	——	——		
	——	——		
Day Two				
	8:45	9:15	9:05	9:10
	10:45	11:10	11:00	11:07
	11:45	12:00	11:55	12:00
	1:30	2:00	1:40	1:41
	2:20	2:45	2:21	2:24
	——	——	——	——

cassette tape with beeps every 5 seconds and a simple recording form (see Figure 4.3). Ms. Freeman would play the cassette in her Walkman (with an earphone). Whenever she hears the beep, she looks up and notes whether Hector is in his seat or out of his seat by placing a tally mark in the appropriate spot on the recording form.

Probes

Since probes are used to assess skill fluency, the performance measures most often used are rates of correct and incorrect responses supplied per minute. However, frequency, percent correct, or even duration are also appropriate performance measures.

Start Time:	Start Time:	Start Time:	Start Time:	Start Time:	Start Time:
———	———	———	———	———	———
———	———	———	———	———	———
———	———	———	———	———	———
———	———	———	———	———	———
———	———	———	———	———	———
———	———	———	———	———	———
———	———	———	———	———	———
———	———	———	———	———	———
———	———	———	———	———	———
———	———	———	———	———	———
———	———	———	———	———	———
———	———	———	———	———	———
———	———	———	———	———	———
———	———	———	———	———	———
———	———	———	———	———	———
———	———	———	———	———	———
———	———	———	———	———	———
———	———	———	———	———	———
Stop Time	Stop Time	Stop Time	Stop Time	Stop Time	Stop Time

FIGURE 4.3.
A simple recording form for Ms. Freeman.

4. Ensure Reliability

Teachers can take several steps to ensure the item consistency, stability, and scorer reliability of their assessment procedures. For tests, observations, and probes, longer assessments tend to be more reliable than shorter assessments because longer assessments usually produce better (more representative) samples of the domain being assessed. For example, if Ms. Li wanted to assess her students' recognition of upper- and lowercase letters in three different type styles, there are 156 different elements in the domain. With other things being equal, there is more of a chance to get a biased sample of 25 items than there would be if there were 50 or 75 items assessed.

Tests

Item Consistency

The development of reliable tests requires that test items consistently assess the same domain.[14] Developing tests with consistent items usually requires ongoing test revision and development, and it may take several semesters before a test's content is highly reliable. Three steps are involved.

Step 1. Carefully prepare original items and score. Guidelines for the preparation of test items can be found throughout this chapter. Commercial test developers usually try out items prior to standardization. Teachers seldom have this luxury; they are more likely to treat each administration of the test with their classes as a tryout and revise items for subsequent administrations. Therefore, it is generally a good idea to prepare more items than are desired in the final test. Bad items can be dropped and the test can be rescored. (Criteria and procedures for doing this are discussed in the next section.) If the number of items is so large that student fatigue is a concern, give the test in two or more sessions.

Step 2. Conduct item analyses. The guiding principle in item analysis is that students with high total scores should generally do better on an item than students with low total test scores. Application of this principle results in consistent tests.

To conduct item analyses, teachers record student scores on each item as well as the total score on the test. On objective and fill-in tests, a student's performance on each item is scored *1* if the item is passed and *0* if the item is failed, while on essay questions any item will have a larger range of potential values. Next, the mean and variance[15] for each item is calculated. If the test items are scored *1* and *0*, these calculations are very simple (e.g., the variance equals the product of the proportion correct and the proportion incorrect). Items with relatively high means are items on which most students did well. Items with relatively low means are items on which most students did poorly. These may be poorly constructed items, or they may indicate insufficient learning. Unfortunately, the numerical value does not indicate to a teacher which is the case.

Items that discriminate between students with high total scores and students with low total scores are retained; other items are dropped or revised. (However, a teacher may decide to retain items that all or almost all of the students answered correctly even though these items will discriminate poorly; retention of such items

---

[14]We recognize that many domains may be factorally complex. However, preparation of reliable tests in such domains requires knowledge of factor analysis and, perhaps, multidimensional scaling—topics better left to professional test authors.

[15]See the Appendix.

has little effect on the reliability but does raise total scores.) Decisions about which items to drop can be reached through two statistical procedures. The more accurate but more complicated procedure is to correlate[16] each item with the total score. An easier procedure is to compute, for each item, the *index of discriminating power* by dividing the students into two groups—those who are in the top half of the group and those in the bottom half. Then the scores on the item earned by students in the upper half (X_u) are compared to the scores on the item earned by students in the lower half (X_L) using the formula below,[17] where T equals the number of points on the test. When the index is positive, students in the upper half do better on the item than students in the lower half; negative indices indicate that students in lower half of the class do better than students in the upper half.

$$\text{Discriminating power} = \frac{X_u - X_L}{\frac{1}{2} T}$$

Items that discriminate poorly[18] are usually dropped. Then the remaining items are re-added to get a new total score, and coefficient alpha as well as item–total correlations or indices of item discrimination are calculated to make sure that the test is reliable and that the remaining items still discriminate. If these indices still look good,[19] the retained items are compared to curricular content. If the items still reflect the curriculum as initially intended, a teacher's work is done. It is more likely, however, that more items will be needed, and the best place to look for new items is discarded items that can be revised.

Item revision requires an examination of student errors. For multiple-choice and matching tests, error analysis means inspecting student selection of distractors. Generally, there is no need to examine the performance of an entire class; a teacher can usually compare the performance of the top and bottom quarters (based on total score). The number of students selecting each option is tallied. Then the patterns of response for the two groups are inspected. As shown in Figure 4.4, some patterns may suggest plausible hypotheses about why an item did not discriminate and where a teacher might make revisions.

For supply questions, error analysis is more qualitative although teachers still compare the errors of students who do well on the test to those who do poorly. Error patterns may suggest a need to revise scoring criteria, the wording of questions, and/or directions.

---

[16]Classroom computers make this a relatively quick task. Numerous statistical programs are available to perform these calculations in a second or two. Teachers without computers can perform the calculations by hand. A shortcut procedure for item–total correlations is given in the Appendix.

[17]This formula can be simplified when test questions are scored dichotomously (i.e., 1 or 0). In this case, X_u equals the number of students in the top half who pass the item, X_L equals the number of students in the bottom half who pass the item, and T equals the number of questions.

[18]While there are no absolute standards by which to decide that an item discriminates poorly, item–total correlations and item discrimination indices less than .40 suggest poor discrimination.

[19]It is possible that when total scores are recalculated, one or two items will no longer discriminate well enough to be retained. If that happens, those items will need to be dropped, total scores recalculated, and the statistics recomputed before coefficient alpha can be calculated.

Options	A*	B	C	D	Omitted
FIGURE 4.4. Patterns of student errors on multiple-choice tests.		Item Is Too Easy			
Upper quarter	12	1	0	0	0
Bottom quarter	11	1	0	1	0
		Item Is Too Difficult			
Upper quarter	3	3	3	4	0
Bottom quarter	3	3	3	3	1
		Wrong Option Is Keyed			
Upper quarter	1	1	11	0	0
Bottom quarter	2	2	6	2	1
		More Than One Distractor May Be Correct			
Upper quarter	5	0	7	1	0
Bottom quarter	5	2	3	2	1
*Keyed answer.					

The preceding steps are repeated until a consistent test is developed. Often two or more administrations of a test are required before there are enough items to make a reliable test.

Step 3. Maintain test files. Since no one automatically prepares a test with all effective items on the first attempt, teachers should maintain files of effective items for future use. It is a good idea to cross reference questions to instructional objectives and to keep the data from item analysis with the question. Teachers without access to a computer can use separate 3 × 5 index cards for each exam question. The cards can be grouped so questions assessing the same objective are placed together.

Stability

Once mastered and fluent, facts and concepts tend to be stable. Therefore, if instruction continues to fluency, assessments should be stable.

Scorer Reliability

The simplest way to achieve high levels of interscorer agreement is to use objective tests (i.e., tests with items that require a student to select or to fill in). If teachers use essay questions, it is better to use two or three restricted-response essays rather than one extended essay. For either type of essay question, scoring guidelines should be developed, and these guidelines should be made explicit to the students. Kubiszyn and Borich (1984) have offered several guidelines; these have been modified somewhat and appear in Figure 4.5.

There is a tendency for scoring standards to change over time. Teachers can do four things to reduce this tendency:

- *Score all answers to the same questions before scoring answers to the next question.* A particularly good or poor answer by a student may influence a teacher's evaluation of that student's next answer. For example, Marcie may give an absolutely

Content. Score the essay for both the presence and accuracy of factual information.

Organization. Score the essay for the presence and consistency of factual and logical support for recommendations, inferences, and conclusions. Score sequence of ideas and points.

Mechanics. Decide if errors in spelling and grammar will be scored as well as their relative importance.

Process. In responses to analysis, synthesis, and evaluation questions, score the logic, coherence, and factual accuracy of the student's conclusions and judgments.

Completeness. Score the extent to which the responses deal with the problem or question presented as well as the adequacy and accuracy of factual support.

Originality or Creativity. Credit unusual and unexpected solutions when appropriate.

FIGURE 4.5.
Scoring guidelines for extended essays (based on Kubiszyn & Borich, 1984).

brilliant answer to the first question but try to bluff her way through the second. Because her first answer was so good, her teacher might give her the benefit of the doubt on her second answer. Teachers can lessen, if not eliminate, this tendency by grading all responses to one question before grading the next.

- *Avoid fatigue.* When answers to examination questions are long or when there are a large number of examinations to score, teachers should consider scoring examinations over several sessions rather than in one marathon session. If this is done, scoring criteria should be reviewed prior to each session.

- *Spot check the consistency.* After each question has been scored, teachers should cluster the examinations by scores—for example, put all of the A's together. Then the responses should be spot checked to make sure that they are consistent within clusters (e.g., the responses receiving A's are comparable) and that papers within higher-rated clusters are indeed superior to the papers within lower-rated clusters.

- *Maintain student anonymity.* Generally, teachers should not know whose paper they are grading since there is a tendency for teachers' general feelings about a student to influence scoring. For example, Harry is a difficult student who is always in trouble and seldom completes homework. Harry's teacher might unintentionally allow impressions about Harry's classroom behavior to influence the grading of his essay. One way to lessen this possibility is by having students put their names on the back of their exams or use their social security numbers, matriculation numbers, or special codes rather than their names.

Observations

Item Consistency

The consistency of the particular behaviors systematically observed is of concern only when the observer wishes to generalize to related behavior in the same domain. For example, if Ms. Li observed Julie's hitting, kicking, and spitting and wanted to drawn an inference about other aggressive behaviors, calculation of item consistency would be appropriate. In this case, the procedures that are used to develop consistent objective tests are used to develop consistent observation guides. Most often, however, teachers are interested only in the particular behavior—e.g., hitting, kicking, and spitting. In this case, no generalizations are intended, and estimation of item consistency should not be made.

Stability

Stability of systematic observations is of particular concern for observations made prior to intervention (i.e., during baseline). Like tests, performance measures (e.g., rate or duration of response) based on a large number of observations are more likely to be stable than indices based on a few observations. Stability also can be enhanced by conducting observations in highly similar circumstances since behavior is likely to change as a function of the environment (e.g., setting, demands, people). A related concern is the presence of an observer. If a stranger or someone not regularly associated with the classroom suddenly appears and begins to conduct systematic observations, that observer's presence may distort the situation. For example, many children will not bully other students when an adult can observe the situation. When novel observers will be conducting the observations, it is generally better to let the students get used to their presence before conducting observations. Finally, stability can be enhanced by restricting the total length of time in which observations are conducted. Observations over a five-day period are more likely to be stable than observations over a five-month period since there is less chance that the target behavior will be modified systematically over a shorter period of time.

Observer Reliability

Although teachers may not always assess interobserver agreement, there are five things they can do to increase the reliability of their observations. The first, and most important, consideration in making reliable observations is to define the target behavior precisely and completely. The more carefully teachers delineate the characteristics of the behavior, the more likely it becomes that teachers (or anyone else with similar training) can observe and score the response accurately.

Second, teachers should avoid unnecessary complexity in their observations. The more complex observations become, the greater the chances of error. There are two elements to complexity. The first is the functional number of behaviors to be observed. While the number of potential categories or types of behavior to be observed (i.e., the number of behaviors appearing on the recording form) is important, of greater importance is the actual number of categories used. For example, if we were observing antisocial behavior, we might include categories of murder, arson, extortion, and armed robbery as well as swearing, threatening, hitting, and shoving. It is unlikely that we would observe many instances of murder. The functional categories (i.e., categories with frequencies of behavior greater than zero) would more likely be swearing, threatening, shoving, and hitting. Of course, observers should note additional behaviors of great importance but low frequency. For example, if observers witness a murder or robbery they should note it on the observation form in space for anecdotal observations. The second element in complexity is the number of students that will be observed during the observation session. The greater the number of students, the more complex is the task.

Third, teachers can make spot checks for the accuracy of their observations. There is a tendency for observers and test correctors to alter their definitions over time—to become systematically more lenient or more stringent in the applications of behavioral definitions. Observers who know that they will be checked at random intervals are more accurate in their observations (Smith, 1978).

Fourth, fatigue often interferes with accurate assessment. Allow rest periods when conducting systematic observations and scoring tests. It is a good idea not to work (e.g., conduct observations) from a position that requires you to strain to hear or to see.

Fifth, as part of the assessment process, teachers can develop permanent products (e.g., video- or audiotapes) and assess these if probes or observations do not result in permanent products. For example, if Jim is reading a passage out loud, Ms. Li can use a "follow along" sheet (a probe that is identical to the student's) and will record any errors on the sheet as Jim reads. Additionally, Ms. Li can note the type of errors[20] made (e.g., mispronunciations and omissions of words).

Probes

Item Consistency

Improving the consistency of items on probes can be done in two ways. First, probes should be constructed in such a way that they are interchangeable; probes for the same objective should assess the same content in the same ways. However, probes for the same objective should *not* present the items in the same order. If a single-skill probe is used to assess learning on a narrow objective, the same items should be rearranged. On multiple-skill probes and probes designed to assess rule usage, different items in different orders should be used. It is very important to vary the order in which skills on a multiple-skill probe are assessed. Unless skills are spread throughout a probe, students might never get a chance to respond to items assessing some skills.

Stability

Stable performance is desirable during baseline and maintenance. Stability during baseline usually can be attained by desensitizing students to the observational procedures, by using consistent definitions, and by applying the observational procedures consistently across sessions.

---

[20]For a more complete discussion of error analysis and oral reading, see Chapter 6.

Scorer Reliability

Since written probes almost always use fill-in responses, there should be little problem with interscorer agreement if scoring criteria are specified clearly prior to scoring and revised should unanticipated, but correct, responses be given. For probes using oral responses, teachers can tape record a student's performance and replay responses that are difficult to score. Use of recorded performances also allows the direct estimation and spot checking of interscorer reliability.

5. Ensure Content Validity

Four primary considerations in ensuring content validity are to guarantee that (1) important learning outcomes and performances are assessed rather than trivial (but easily assessed) outcomes, (2) objectives taught for acquisition, fluency, maintenance, knowledge, and comprehension are evaluated in the manner in which they were taught and practiced, (3) objectives for generalization, adaptation, application, analysis, synthesis, and evaluation are evaluated in ways that have not been taught or practiced, and (4) intended learning and performance are assessed rather than unintended information, skills, or student abilities.[21]

Tests

Preparation of effective test items takes a lot of thought and improves with experience. Whether select or supply questions are used, there are nine general principles that should guide preparation of test items (Gronlund, 1982).

1. *Sample the content appropriately.* Sampling the domain appropriately means making a table of specifications. Such a table is a blueprint of the curricular area to be assessed; it delineates the components of the curriculum that are taught and the levels of performance that are expected for each component. Each *cell* in the table (each intersection of component and performance level) represents potential instruction. However, as discussed in Chapter 3, not all cells must be used. Often, teachers choose different performance levels for different components. In Figure 4.6 we see that component "a" is taught at both knowledge and comprehension levels, component "b" is taught only at a knowledge level, and component "c" is taught at a knowledge, comprehension, and application level.

2. *Use clear presentations.* Examinations should be typed because they are easier to read than handwritten examinations. Type size should be no smaller than that used in regular reading material, and type face should be clear and easily read. Top, bottom, and side margins should be generous—1 to 1.5 inches.

3. *Use clear and precise directions.* Whenever possible tell the student what is to be done (e.g., compare and contrast, circle the correct option).

4. *Keep sentence structure simple.* Unless a teacher intends to assess a student's ability to understand complex sentences, the structure of the language used in directions, given information, and response options should be simple enough for all students to understand readily.

---

[21]One of the loudest student complaints occurs when teachers fail to test material that was stressed in class or homework; students are apt to call such tests "unfair," although the technical term is invalid.

Components				FIGURE 4.6.
Performance				Generalized table of
Levels				specifications.
	(a)	(b)	(c)	
Knowledge	X	X	X	
Comprehension	X		X	
Application			X	

5. *Keep the vocabulary simple and nontechnical.* Unless a teacher is assessing technical vocabulary or jargon, the simpler the vocabulary the better.

6. *Keep reference illustrations clear.* If a teacher uses graphs, charts, pictures, and so forth, they should not be confusing and they should contain the information intended.

7. *Avoid ethnocentric or sexist language.* Teachers should not use "he" or "his" to refer to unspecified individuals; when possible use plurals (e.g., they) or examples (e.g., "suppose John wanted to have his way" rather than "suppose *a student* wanted *his* way"). Also, avoid stereotypic sex roles (e.g., making all teachers women and all principals men). Racial and ethnic slurs are inappropriate, even if accidental or intended to be humorous. One way to avoid slurs is never to use identifiable ethnic groups—no identifiable photographs or names. Unfortunately, this leads to a different form of discrimination—an absence of ethnic groups represented in assessment materials. Thus, teachers should try to balance ethnic groups (and sexes) among desirable (and undesirable if necessary) statuses, traits, and so forth.

8. *Prepare enough questions.* During question preparation teachers must consider the learning outcomes to be assessed (as summarized by a table of specifications), the number of questions to assess each learning outcome, the time needed to answer each question, and the amount of time available for testing. A decision about one factor influences the options for the remaining factors. In deciding on the learning outcomes to be assessed, teachers need not evaluate all cells in the table of specifications; relatively unimportant cells may not be assessed at all if there are pronounced time constraints. Moreover, if cells have the same order of difficulty for most students, a teacher may want to assess only the more difficult cells under the presumption that, if students can answer relatively difficult questions, they also can answer easier ones. (Of course this procedure would not be appropriate for assigning grades or planning instruction.) If all cells are to be evaluated, teachers may extend the total amount of time devoted to assessment or restrict the amount of time devoted to assessing each cell. For example, select questions could be used rather than restricted essays since several select questions can be asked in the time required for a student to answer one essay.

9. *Other considerations.* There are also considerations specific to student characteristics. Students with reading problems should be tested orally; students with difficulty writing should be given select rather than supply tests. Finally, there are considerations specific to the types of questions used on tests. Generally the

considerations for fill-in questions and select questions are the same, while they are different for restricted- and extended-essay questions.

Supply Questions

Essay questions require that students understand the material being tested to answer the question. Typically, there are some code words that communicate precisely to students how they should answer a question.

- *Compare.* Students should look for and describe similarities among concepts, events, and so forth. For example, "Compare the treatment of Loyalists in the American and French Revolutions."
- *Contrast.* Students should look for and describe differences among concepts, events, and so on. For example, "Contrast the treatment of native Americans in Spanish and English colonies."
- *Define.* Students should give the meaning of a term or concept. For example, "Define 'psychotropic drug.'"
- *Evaluate.* Students should tell or compare the worth, value, or importance of a concept, impact, work, and so forth against stated or self-selected criteria. For example, "Evaluate the adequacy prophesies based on astrology using scientific models of prediction."
- *List.* Students should list without explanation the things requested. For example, "List the 20 powers of Congress."

Terms such as *describe* or *explain* require additional elaboration before a student can be sure of the desired response. For example, if a teacher asked students to describe the sinking of the U.S.S. *Maine*, one student might correctly write, "There was an explosion. The ship filled with water and went to the bottom of the ocean." Another student might explain why the *Maine* was in Havana harbor, the controversy surrounding who was responsible for her sinking, and the consequences of her sinking to U.S. foreign policy in both the Caribbean and Pacific. Therefore, directions to describe or to explain should specify the form the description or explanation should take.

Select Questions

In addition to the general considerations described at the beginning of this section, teachers can do three things to improve the effectiveness of select questions.

1. Use common misconceptions and errors. When students work through a question or problem and do not find their answers among the options, they might well suspect their answer is not correct. However, if teachers are aware of common mistakes and misunderstandings, these errors can be included among the response options. Thus, students will find an answer that matches theirs and will be less likely to suspect that their own answer is incorrect. Therefore, effective distractors are based on common mistakes. Although most teachers would not use multiple-choice tests to assess multiplication problems, such a format provides an easy illustration of this principle. Suppose a teacher used "63 × 7" as the stem of a multiple-choice question. The correct answer, 441, would of course be one of the response options. However, other effective response options might include 4221 (a failure to regroup), 432 (carrying the wrong number), 421 (failure to carry), 423 (left to right multiplication), 561 (recombining before multiplication), or none of the above (other errors including those in basic facts).

2. *Use clear formats.* The format of select items should make test taking easy and increase the likelihood of valid assessment.

- Avoid tricky wording (e.g., double negatives).
- Put as much information as possible into the stem (as opposed to the options).
- Emphasize critical words (e.g., underline *not* when it is used in the stem of a multiple-choice question).
- Use double spacing between questions and single spacing within questions (including response options).
- Present options horizontally and allow student to mark their answers directly on the test. (Transferring answers to a separate answer sheet may significantly increase the chances of error because students can forget the letter they wished to mark, lose their place on either the test or the answer sheet, and spend extra time double checking their recording.)

3. *Avoid tip-offs.* A tip-off is information that a teacher unintentionally provides and that helps a student answer the question on a basis other than knowledge of the content. There are several types of tip-offs.

- Avoid specific determiners. Specific determiners are adjectives and adverbs such as all, never, and none.
- Avoid grammatical hints. Things to watch for include subject–verb agreement and gender agreement.
- Avoid comical or implausible—even absurd—incorrect options.
- Do not state the correct answer as an exact quotation from the text.
- Keep response options about the same length. Teachers especially should avoid the tendency to make the keyed response the longest option.
- Avoid response sets. In multiple-choice tests, keep the number of keyed options approximately the same (e.g., equal numbers of "a", "b"). Avoid alternating (e.g., a, b, d, c, a, b, d, c).
- Avoid giving two options that are highly similar and both wrong.

Figure 4.7 contains examples of items containing tip-offs and items that are better constructed.

FIGURE 4.7.
Examples of items
containing tip-offs and
that item rewritten to
avoid the tip-off.

Grammatical Hint:

Tipped

The vice presidential candidate whose husband had some business notoriety
was

    a) George Bush
    b) Geraldine Ferraro
    c) Lyndon LaRouche
    d) John Glenn

Rewritten

Someone in the immediate family of one of the 1984 vice presidential
candidates received some business notoriety. Who was the candidate?

    a) George Bush
    b) Geraldine Ferraro
    c) Lyndon LaRouche
    d) John Glenn

Comment

The use of "husband" in the stem restricts the answer to a woman. Since
there is only one woman in the set of options, the answer must be that
woman. The use of "husband" would have been okay if all of the options
had been women.

Implausible Options

Tipped

In 1898 the United States went to war with _____

    a) the Masters of the Universe
    b) the NFL
    c) Spain
    d) the USSR

Rewritten

In 1898 the United States went to war with _____

    a) Germany
    b) Mexico
    c) Spain
    d) Japan

Comment

All options except Spain are implausible, in varying degrees. Masters of the
Universe are toys; the NFL is a sports league that is very familiar to almost

any North American; the USSR did not exist in 1898. The rewritten question is better since there are no implausible or absurd options: The United States did go to war with all countries listed, some before Spain and some after.

Key Is Too Long

Tipped

Which of the following is a way for a U.S. president to stop a bill from becoming a law?

    a) urge friends not to pass the bill
    b) declare war
    c) use a pocket veto so that the president need not veto the bill directly but cannot act on it for 10 days
    d) tell Congress the bill is unacceptable

Rewritten

Which of the following is a way for a U.S. president to stop a bill from becoming a law?

    a) urge friends not to pass the bill
    b) declare war
    c) use a pocket veto
    d) tell Congress the bill is unacceptable

Comment

In the tipped question, the correct answer is longer than all of the options. It is usually unnecessary to define a term in options. However, if one term must be defined, try to define all of them.

Two Highly Similar (and Wrong) Options

Tipped

James Bond regularly drank _____

    a) vodka martinis
    b) fruit juice
    c) lemonade
    d) milk

Rewritten

James Bond regularly drank _____

    a) vodka martinis
    b) Jack Daniels
    c) Cognac
    d) beer   *(continued)*

FIGURE 4.7
(continued)

Comment

Lemonade is a fruit juice, and both cannot be correct so neither is correct. Similarly, orangeade and lemonade would likely both be incorrect. Milk is implausible, as any James Bond fan knows. The rewritten item contains beverages that James might drink, but he prefers vodka martinis (shaken, not stirred).

Observations

Ensuring the validity of systematic observations requires that the target behavior be defined in generally credible ways; a definition of behavior cannot be so restricted or unusual that people will not accept it. For example, "hitting" might be defined as striking another's nose with a closed fist and with sufficient amplitude that the nose bleeds. While no one would question that this definition describes hitting, "hitting" is a far broader concept than its definition implies. "Hitting" includes targets other than a nose and amplitudes less than those that produce bleeding. Similarly, the contexts in which the target behavior is observed should not be so restrictive or unusual that people will not accept it. For example, out-of-seat behavior would not, usually, be observed during recess but would, typically, be observed during lunch in the cafeteria, during instruction in various academic areas, and during seatwork. Beyond these general considerations, teachers can also take two steps to increase the validity of their observations.

1. *Avoid halo effects.* Although precise and systematic observations are much less susceptible to halo effects than nonsystematic observations and impressions, expectations can, nonetheless, have an influence. For example, if a teacher has implemented a behavioral intervention to decrease an undesired behavior and if that teacher believes the intervention is likely to be effective, there is a possibility for observations to be colored in favor of seeing a reduction in the unwanted behavior. Whenever feasible, teachers should enlist "blind" observers. (In professional jargon, blind observers are observers who are unaware of the reasons for the observations.) If observations are recorded on video- or audiotapes, segments can be organized randomly to avoid earlier behavior influencing the scoring of later behavior.

2. *Avoid reactivity.* The presence of an observer or intrusive equipment for observation can alter the situation and affect student and teacher behavior. Two strategies are important for minimizing reactivity. First, teachers should discount data taken during the first observation sessions. Wait until the students are accustomed to being observed and their behavior returns to what is typical for them. Second, use procedures that are unobtrusive: Sit behind or at the side of students being observed (unless, of course, the behavior being observed can only be seen from the front); avoid intrusive procedures such as using high-intensity lights and whirring cameras to catch *candid* moments.

Probes

While many of the preceding suggestions and constraints apply to probes, there is one special technical consideration—the number of opportunities to which a student can respond. Since performance is stated in terms of rate, there must be more problems, words, letters, and so forth than a student can complete during the probe period.[22] If a student answers all possible problems before the time is up, the teacher cannot assess that student's fluency[23] because an artificial ceiling has been created. Usually teachers should include about 50% more items than the rate criterion (e.g., if the criterion was 50 digits per minute, the probe should include the opportunity for 75 digits).

Probe sheets that provide permanent products often contain spaces to note several other bits of information:

- Class and student and teacher names
- Date and time (or class period) when the probe was administered
- Rate per minute of correct and incorrect responses
- Curriculum material being assessed (e.g., the title of the text, chapter number, or section number or title)
- Objectives[24] or skills being assessed
- Scoring aids (i.e., the number of possible correct responses in each row and a cumulative count written in the right margin to assist in tabulating)

Figure 4.8 contains an example of a math probe sheet that incorporates these features.

Collection of Data

Once the assessment procedures are in place, teachers use them to obtain data on student performance. There are three general considerations in the collection of assessment data—standardizing of procedures, giving directions, and preventing cheating.

Standardizing Procedures

It is not enough to design good assessment and scoring procedures; assessments must be carried out correctly—that is, assessments must be standardized. *Standardized* means conducting the assessment consistently and with the directions, materials, and conditions intended by the teacher. Consistency among students assessed with the same procedure allows a teacher to compare student performances. Consistency over time allows a teacher to compare students' performances with their previous performances. Comparisons over time additionally

---

[22]Technically, when assessing the rate of a behavior, it cannot be constrained; this is known as having a *free operant*.

[23]Although it is more efficient to limit the amount of time a student has to take a probe, rate of performance could be computed also by allowing a student unlimited time to complete a probe and then dividing the number of correct responses by the time it took to complete the probe.

[24]Precision teachers advocate stating skills ("pinpoints") in terms of learning channels: input and output. For example, a behavior—copying words from the chalkboard—is stated as see (input)-write (output) words from the board. Other examples are see–say words from text (oral reading), hear–write words (spelling), and think–write (written expression).

FIGURE 4.8.
Example of a math
probe.

Date _____

Teacher _____

2-digit + 2-digit, no regrouping

Student _____

Text _____

(digits)

11	20	72	13	23	21	11	82	10	35
+48	+44	+15	+25	+26	+66	+16	+14	+29	+22

(20)

10	29	35	40	34	24	40	23	20	87
+38	+60	+53	+18	+23	+35	+59	+51	+12	+12

(40)

32	41	50	34	41	30	26	50	50	75
+62	+26	+22	+44	+12	+28	+63	+21	+15	+12

(60)

60	32	34	20	10	23	62	11	48	35
+37	+34	+14	+63	+16	+76	+27	+67	+31	+44

(80)

57	10	51	33	20	19	45	11	23	22
+41	+35	+16	+62	+63	+80	+21	+51	+72	+76

(100)

41	50	19	45	87	20	11	10	13	11
+26	+22	+80	+21	+12	+12	+67	+16	+25	+48

(120)

Digits per minute correct _____   Digits per minute incorrect _____

Teacher: "I want you to read the words on this sheet. Starting with the top row, read from left to right. When you finish the first row, go on to the next row and so on until I say it is time to stop.

   I want you to read these words as fast as you can, but not so fast that you make careless errors.

   Do you have any questions?

FIGURE 4.9
Example of directions
for an oral reading
probe.

---

require that student performance is summarized in the same units of measurement (e.g., number of correct responses per minute) and that the behaviors assessed have comparable difficulty and meaning.

Giving Directions for Tests and Probes[25]

Directions should be clear, simple, and to the point. When administering tests, teachers should be matter of fact in their manner. Students should be told the major parameters of the situation, including:

- How much time they will be allowed
- If they will be penalized for guessing
- How much each correct response is worth if questions are of different values
- How many problems they will be asked
- Whether the results will count on their grade

Since probes are given frequently, students become accustomed to taking them quickly. Thus, simple directions are usually sufficient. (Figure 4.9 contains directions that could be used for a timed probe in oral reading.) Initially, however, some students may be anxious and agitated when they are asked to complete a probe as quickly as possible or when there are more problems than they can complete in the time allowed. Usually, administering a probe a few times in an untimed condition and encouraging students to beat previous rates will desensitize them. If students are upset by the fact that they cannot complete all of the problems, a teacher can explain that students are not expected to finish all problems and that the test contains more problems than *any* student can complete.

Preventing Cheating

Moral issues aside, cheating is unacceptable because it systematically alters the accuracy of generalization. If students cheat on an assessment and earn scores much higher than their true abilities, any generalization based on those inflated scores will be inaccurate.

---

[25]Seldom are directions provided for observations. When they are provided, they usually take the form of "Don't pay any attention to the observer; just act as you usually do."

Teachers can take several steps to reduce the likelihood that students will cheat on tests. First, teachers can communicate to their students what constitutes cheating. Definitions of cheating vary with the age, ability of students, and beliefs of the teacher. Most would consider copying from another student, using notes on closed-book tests, or obtaining copies of a test before it is given to be types of cheating. Plagiarism and asking other students who previously have taken the test may or may not be considered cheating. Second, teachers can communicate that cheaters will be punished if caught. For example, Professor Smith might tell her classes that when she gets the same term paper from two (or more) college students, she grades the paper and divides the points by the number of authors. So, if the paper earns a a grade of 90% and three people have handed it in, each person gets a grade of 30%. Third, teachers can give the impression that they are actively trying to prevent cheating. They can

- Circulate around the room during testing or take a position at the back of the room
- Prepare multiple copies of tests
- Give the impression that there are multiple test forms by having three stacks of tests and giving students in rows one and four tests from the first stack, students in rows two and five tests from the second stack, and so forth
- Require alternate seating

Summarize Results

Summarizing assessment results is the simplest step. Teachers assemble the basic information (e.g., number of correct responses, the duration of observations) for each student and calculate their appropriate derived scores (e.g., percent correct, number of errors per minute, average duration of behavior). The data for individual students are then entered into a permanent record (e.g., grade book, computer file). For some purposes of assessment (e.g., referral, evaluating teaching), group statistics also might be computed.

Summary

Good assessment procedures are reliable and valid. Reliability refers to three types of generalization: generalization to other similar items (i.e., item consistency), to other times (i.e., stability), and to other appropriately trained individuals (i.e., interscorer or interobserver reliability). Numerous but somewhat different steps can be taken by teachers to ensure the reliability of tests, observations, and probes. In validity, teachers are primarily concerned with content validity: content appropriateness, content completeness, and how content is assessed. Development of appropriate assessment procedures requires somewhat different methods for select and supply tests, observations, and select and supply probes, although three general considerations apply to each type of procedure: allocation of time, selection of the appropriate assessment procedure, and selection of an appropriate performance measure.

There are three major considerations in the collection of assessment data. First, procedures should be standardized so that the data are interpretable. Second, clear and precise directions should be given to students so they know exactly what they are expected to do. Third, teachers should prevent cheating. Arraying assessment results, calculating of appropriate student scores, and entering data into a permanent record should be routine chores if the development of assessment tools and the collection of data have been well planned.

Chapter 5

Display Data, Interpret Data, and Make Decisions

Key Terms

Abscissa	Ordinate
Aimline	Phase change
Celeration	Quarter-intersect
Data point	Semilogarithmic graph
Equal-interval chart	Split-middle method
Formative evaluation	Trend
Learning picture	Visual inspection

After teachers have identified the purpose for assessment, analyzed their curriculum, developed appropriate assessment procedures, and collected the assessment data, they will have lots of numbers—rates, percents, frequencies, and so on. In and of themselves these data have limited use. To make sense of these data and to use them effectively it is necessary to (1) display the data in an organized fashion, (2) interpret the data, and (3) make appropriate educational decisions based on what the data imply.

Displaying Data

How assessment data are displayed and interpreted depends, in large part, on the purpose of assessment. Will the data be used for screening, referral, and placement within a curriculum or for continuous monitoring of student progress on curricular objectives? In education, data are usually systematized and displayed in one of two formats, either tables or graphs.

Tables, also referred to as record sheets, are used to organize and summarize students' performance data. They can be used with individuals or with whole classes. Figure 5.1 provides an illustration of an individual record sheet used to keep track of a student's performance on one objective. Well suited for keeping track of progress on a single objective, record sheets are also the preferred way to display data for making decisions about referral.

1. Referral

As noted in Chapter 2, screening is a procedure used to identify students performing differently enough from classroom peers that they may require specialized treatment and, therefore, referral for special services. When CBA is used as a screening and referral tool, criteria must be adopted to determine which (and when) differences are significant enough to warrant further assessment.

One effective method is to develop school- or district-wide norms using a three-step procedure. First, randomly select a large number of students from each grade level. One hundred students per grade is a desirable minimum because this number allows the establishment of percentile norms. (Norms based on substantially fewer students should be interpreted carefully, and normative comparisons should be buttressed with other data.) Second, administer a CBA for each academic area during the first few weeks of the fall and spring semesters and at the end of the spring semester. Third, establish cut-off scores. Cut-offs are always rather arbitrary and usually are based upon the percentage of students for whom a district is willing to provide additional services. Overall, 15% is a reasonable number.[1]

When district-wide or school-wide norms cannot be established, classroom norms can be used tentatively if supported by other data (e.g., results from prereferral interventions). The results of these CBAs are then displayed in tabular form and the median performance computed for each academic area at each time of testing.[2] Once results are displayed, a 2× (i.e., two times) criterion of discrepancy is used to decide which students require further assessment.[3] Bursuck and

---

[1] This percentage should approximate the number of students receiving services in programs for slow learners and mildly handicapped students. If a district has a substantial number of students who need special services, the cut-off can be raised. The converse is also true: If a district has an unusually small percentage of students that require specialized services, the cut-off can be lowered.

[2] The median is a descriptive statistic that divides the top 50% of the group from the bottom 50%. When the number of students in the group is an odd number, a student will earn the median; when the number of students in the group is even, the mean will fall between two scores unless several students who perform at the median earn the same score.

[3] The discrepancy is calculated by dividing the score of a student who is performing below average into the class or group median. For example, suppose the median score of Ms. Li's class on a reading passage is 100 words correctly read per minute, and Harvey reads 50 words per minute. The discrepancy would equal 100 divided by 50; the discrepancy would equal 2. Thus, Harvey's performance meets the 2× criterion. If a student is 2× or more in one or more academic areas, that student is a strong candidate for referral. To increase the reliability of the assessment, the CBA should be given several times (three is a nice number) and median performance used. This method can also screen for students who may be performing significantly (i.e., 2×) higher than their peers and may therefore be in need of enrichment services. These students are identified by dividing the score by the median of their peer group (e.g., 200/100 = 2) (Bursuck & Lessen, 1987).

FIGURE 5.1.
Record sheet for an
individual student.

Student _____   Skill _____

Objective _____

Date	# of problems	# correct	# wrong	% correct	comments

Lessen (1987) described how this system was used in one Illinois school district and suggested displaying CBA results on a record sheet similar to the one shown in Figure 5.2. Median scores in each of the academic subjects taught in the curriculum are shown for each student. Scores that are circled indicate the stu-

Student	Oral Reading (Text)	Add. Facts (0–9)	Subt. Facts (1–5)	Spelling (Text)	Upper/Lower Case (Dictated)
Mary	105	45	42	28	35
Fred	(48)	40	32	27	36
George	120	68	60	40	65
Rita	115	70	45	39	60
Kathy	(21)	(15)	(10)	(4)	32
Lou	(19)	(20)	(9)	(8)	34
Chuck	100	48	43	38	61
Alan	75	62	41	41	70
Todd	125	70	48	45	72
Rene	95	45	40	44	80
Leslie	78	50	38	(15)	37
Fred L.	100	52	42	(19)	38
Sam	110	60	55	43	68
Jennifer	102	50	(19)	32	60
MEDIAN:	100	50	42	38	60
	words per min.	digits per min.	digits per min.	letters per min.	letters per min.

Class _1st (Ms. George)_   Dates of Assessment _9/7; 9/11; 9/15_

○ = 2 × below class median

FIGURE 5.2.
Table displaying CBA screening results for an elementary class.

dent is functioning at least two times below the median score of his peers. In this example, Kathy and Lou are definite candidates for follow-up assessment for possible eligibility for special education services since they are 2× discrepant in several academic areas. At a minimum these two students need additional support within the regular class (e.g., material modification, individual tutoring). Other students (e.g., Fred) are discrepant only in one area—in Fred's case, orally reading a passage taken from his text. Other factors need to be taken into account before referral is considered. In this example, Fred is relatively close to the median in other academic areas so some additional support within his current placement may be sufficient to bring up his performance. In Jennifer's case, low performance may not be due to lack of response to instruction in subtraction facts but rather to lack of exposure to instruction. Obviously, further investigation into student history and analysis of curriculum and instruction should take place when using the 2× rule.

2. Placement and Progress in the Curriculum

Tables are useful for displaying scores from CBAs designed to locate appropriate instructional objectives in a curriculum for students and for keeping records of achievement of specific curricular objectives. CBAs for placement in a curriculum should be administered over three sessions to increase reliability, and the median used to make the placement decision. Deciding where to start an assessment is usually done by making a best guess based on available information (e.g., formal assessment results, teacher reports, records of previous year-end performance). Testing should then continue until reaching a level or objective that

Student Jason H.		Curriculum	GINN 700	Objective	able to read a 100-word passage at 90 words correct per minute with 2 or fewer errors
		Words read per minute (100-word passage)	Errors per minute	% correct on comprehension questions	Error analysis
L E	Session 1 pp. 2–3	90	2	100	2 substitutions
V E	Session 2 pp. 26–27	92	0	90	
L	Session 3 pp. 48–50	93	1	90	1 substitution
I	Average	92	1.5	93	1.5
L E	Session 1 pp. 1–2	65	10	70	8 omissions 2 substitutions
V E	Session 2 pp. 27–28	62	8	70	5 omissions 1 substitution
II	Session 3 pp. 51–52	63	7	65	2 reversals 6 omissions 1 substitution
	Average	63	8	68	8

FIGURE 5.3. Record sheet for placement in curriculum.

cannot be performed consistently over several trials. Figure 5.3 is an example of a suitable record sheet. In this example, Jason was administered a CBA in order to determine in which level of the Ginn Reading Series he should be placed. Given three 100-word passages (taken from the beginning, middle, and end of the text) to read from level one and related comprehension questions, Jason met the following criterion: 90 or more words read per minute, 2 or fewer errors, and 80% or more of the comprehension questions answered correctly averaged over the three trials. Mr. Clayburg then administered a CBA for the next level and found that over three sessions, Jason's average performance was less than the criterion. Therefore, he placed Jason in level two for instruction.

When used to display curricular objectives mastered by students, the purpose

Class (Period) ———————————————— Grade/Level/Book ————————————————

Math Curriculum (Text) ———————————————— (Checks (√) indicate mastery)

Skill	Gerry	Diane	Louise	Brad	James	Tanya	Fred	Les	Dave	Bert	Ernie	Sam
Sums to 6												
Missing Addends												
Subtraction to 6												
Sums to 10												
Subtraction to 10												
Counting by 2s												
Counting by 5s												
Time (hour)												
Time (half-hour)												
Identify coins												
Sums to 18												
Subtraction to 18												

FIGURE 5.4.   Record sheet for math objectives mastered.

of tables is essentially record keeping. This record permits quick noting and quantification of how many objectives have been met over time. This record also provides information needed for analysis of student progress on IEP objectives and overall program effectiveness. Figure 5.4 contains an example of a record-keeping form for objectives met in a math sequence.

Graphs

When large amounts of data are collected over extended periods of time (i.e., time-series data), it is desirable to display the data on a graph (frequently called a chart). Graphs are more appropriately used when teachers want to monitor progress over time, either on a single objective or over an entire instructional sequence. While tables or record sheets are sometimes used to summarize progress data (such as in Figure 5.1), they are not well suited for this purpose. Record sheets can organize this type of data, but progress is not readily discernible nor can it be communicated easily to others (Kerr & Nelson, 1983). Moreover, in their analysis on progress evaluation, Fuchs and Fuchs (1986a) found that student achievement increased when data were graphed rather than displayed on record sheets.

Graphing allows a teacher to display what a student scored on any CBA and how well—at what rate—that student is progressing on a particular skill or set of objectives. Because progress is readily seen when performance is charted, a teacher can communicate student accomplishment more easily to others (e.g., parents, teachers, administrators, and the students themselves).

While graphing and analyzing data may be more time consuming[4] than merely recording them in tabular form, the practice appears to help students significantly. Also, as discussed in Chapter 11, computer software is available to assist in graphing and analyzing student progress (e.g., Fuchs, Deno, & Mirkin, 1983; Hasselbring & Hamlett, 1983).

1. Graphing Conventions

Different graphs available for use by teachers share several common characteristics. The vertical (y) axis of the graph (called the *ordinate*) is plotted on the left and contains the number, frequency, or rate. The scale for the ordinate goes from zero to beyond the largest number that will be plotted. The horizontal (x) axis of the graph (called the *abscissa*) is plotted near the bottom and reflects relevant intervals (e.g., calendar days or observation sessions if more than one observation per day is made).[5] If there is insufficient room to plot the entire range, the ordinate or abscissa is broken with two slashes ("//"). Zero on the ordinate is plotted above the abscissa, and zero on the abscissa is plotted to the right of the ordinate. *Data points* (the dots where points on the ordinate and abscissa intersect) that require elaboration or explanation are circled. Figure 5.5 contains an illustration of these graphing conventions.

Data are plotted on the graph by finding the time on the abscissa and the proper value on the ordinate. The intersection between the vertical line from the denoted point on the abscissa and horizontal line from the denoted point on the ordinate is then located. For example, in Figure 5.5, on day three Louise correctly completed 9 arithmetic problems per minute during her daily seatwork assignment. This fact is represented by the dot at the intersection of day three (on the abscissa) and 9 problems per minute (on the ordinate). Data points representing a student's performance on CBAs are connected with a straight line. When a data point is missing because of absence, the adjacent points are connected; absences are indicated by marking the estimated data point with the notation "abs" or "NC" (i.e., no chance) although some teachers simply ignore absences.

---

[4]One method to decrease the amount of time spent by a teacher in charting activities is to teach students to chart their own progress. Procedures for doing this are found in Chapter 12.

[5]Calendar days are typically recommended over observation sessions as the metric for the abscissa since the calendar format shows exactly when the data were collected. Too, if absences, holidays, and weekends are not shown (as when observation sessions are used) information about variability of performance may be unclear (e.g., after long absences or holidays, the students' accuracy or rate usually decreases).

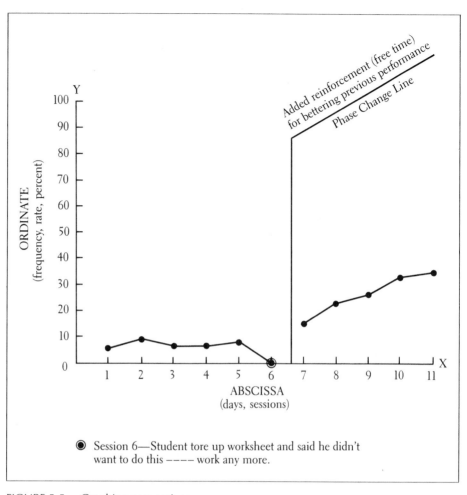

FIGURE 5.5.   Graphing conventions.

If rate data are used, two types of points are plotted; the rate of correct responses and rate of incorrect responses. Rate of incorrect responses are plotted as an *x*.

Breaks in the connected lines occur when teachers change their educational programs (types of intervention used). These changes are called *phase changes* and are indicated by heavy vertical lines. A short but clear description of the intervention change should be written on the chart at or near the line, placed as far as possible from the data points so as not to confuse visual inspection (Schloss, Halle, & Sindelar, 1984).

2. Types of Graphs

Two types of graphs are routinely used in education, *equal-interval* and *semilogarithmic* graphs. The equal-interval graph is used most commonly and is easily understood by teachers, students, and parents. Since the vertical axis is segmented equally (the distance between consecutive values is the same), equal-interval charts display an *absolute* rate of growth. Figure 5.5 is an example of formative data plotted on an equal-interval graph.

A second type of graph, the semilogarithmic (or ratio) graph, has similar conventions as the equal-interval chart except for one critical difference. The vertical axis is a ratio scale and displays *proportional* change in rate of behavior. The graph displayed in Figure 5.6 is called a standard behavior chart and was developed originally by Lindsley (see Pennypacker, Koenig, & Lindsley, 1972). This type of graph is especially useful for many classroom and social behaviors that occur less than once per minute or for behaviors that occur frequently and for which the observation period is long (e.g., a whole school day) resulting in a very high number. Figure 5.6 contains Louise's progress data on a math objective regraphed on a ratio chart. Notice how the rates on the ordinate get closer together as the rates get greater. Also, notice how proportion of change remains the same. Going from 3 problems completed to 6 problems completed per minute is a 100% increase; going from 15 problems completed per minute to 30 problems per minute is also a 100% increase. The proportion increase is the same for each and *looks* the same on a semilogarithmic chart.

Another form of this type of chart is shown in Figure 5.7. This chart, called the AC-4 (Berquam, 1979), is similar to the standard behavior chart in that it has a proportional scale but differs in that the range of rates is reduced: It does not go below zero or above 500 movements (behaviors) per minute. It also includes a place to record raw data. The AC-4 is appropriate for use when administering timed probes when rates will be more than 1 response per minute.

Advocates of semilogarithmic graphs (e.g., White, 1986) state that proportional changes more accurately reflect student effort and the effects of instruction in addition to being able to display larger ranges of behavior. Also, since the standard behavior chart (as well as other forms of ratio charts) is used for all behaviors, time is saved since a teacher does not have to draw and label a chart for each student and behavior. Advocates of equal-interval graphs believe that these charts are simpler to use and more effective in interpreting and projecting growth. For example, Marston (1988) found teachers were more accurate in predicting student performance for goals in reading and written expression when they used equal-interval graphs than when semilogarithmic graphs were used. While each type of graph has its proponents and advantages, the criteria for choosing between them remains unclear. What is clear, however, is that graphing formative data is better than not graphing it (Brandstetter & Merz, 1978; Fuchs & Fuchs, 1986a).

Interpretation of Graphed Data

As discussed in Chapter 1, traditional assessment devices and procedures are usually summative in nature, generally providing information on the relative standing on one student in comparison to a national sample. This type of assessment does not provide precise information about students' continuing rates of learning on particular curricular objectives and therefore has limited use for

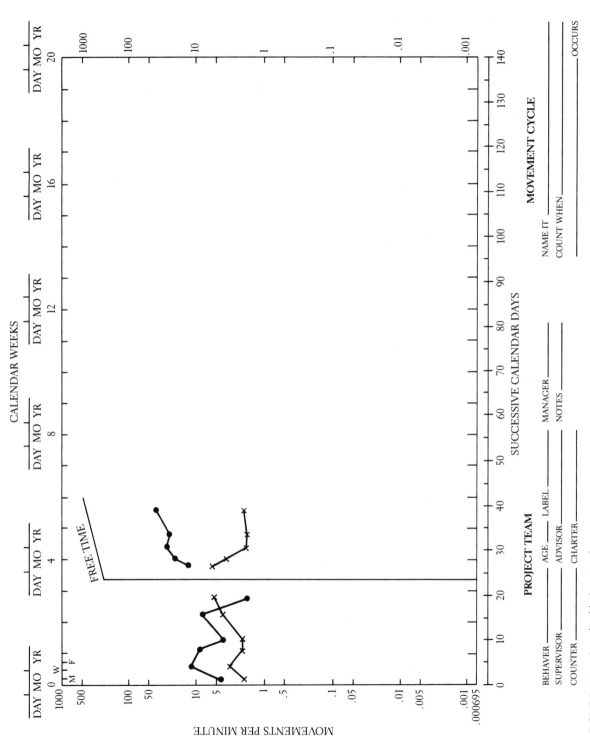

FIGURE 5.6. Standard behavior chart.

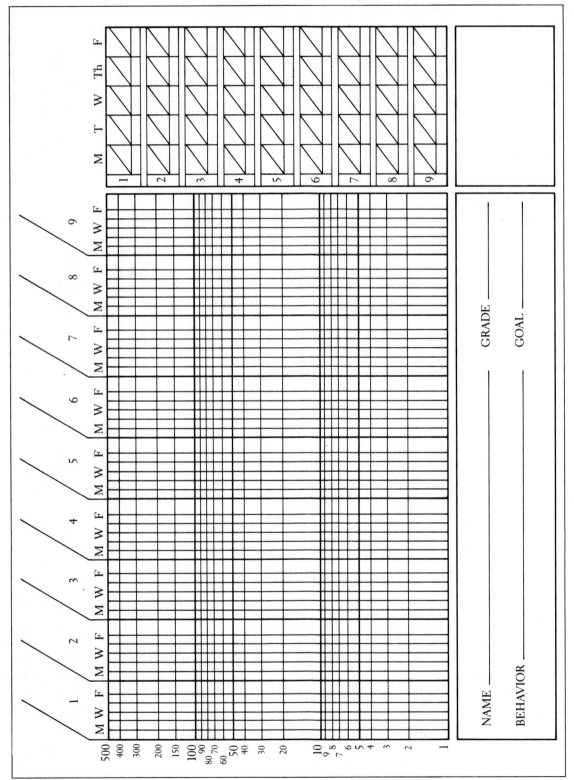

FIGURE 5.7. AC-4 semilogarithmic chart. (Copyright by Eugene M. Berquam, Performance Data Co., P.O. Box 13289, Gainesville, FL. 32604, used by permission.)

monitoring student progress. In reaction to the limitations of summative assessment procedures, especially published norm-referenced tests, movement to a more direct and continuous formative measurement has been promoted (Deno & Mirkin, 1977; White & Haring, 1980). Formative data are best displayed graphically. Once the data are displayed, they require interpretation to make decisions regarding the impact of instruction.

Trend is of greatest interest to a teacher for deciding if learning is taking place.[6] "Trend" refers to the amount and direction (increasing or decreasing) of change. When trend is determined, graphed data provide a visual record of progress, sometimes called a *"learning picture."* There are three general types of pictures—improving, maintaining, and worsening. Since it has been recommended that error rates be plotted concurrently with rate of correct responses on a CBA of a curricular objective, there are in fact two elements of a learning picture. *Improving pictures* are generally characterized by increase in rate of correct responses accompanied by decreases in errors. *Maintaining pictures* show flat trends (neither increasing nor decreasing) in both correct responses and errors. *Worsening progress pictures* are distinguished by correct responses decreasing and/or errors increasing. Primary pictures of improving and worsening data and their variants are displayed in Figure 5.8. Visual analysis of these trends allows teachers to make early decisions about student progress and instructional efficacy.

Estimating Trend through Visual Inspection

The most common method for interpreting charted time-series data is through *visual inspection* (Skiba, Marston, Wesson, Sevcik, & Deno, 1983). Visual inspection, in its simplest form, requires looking at charted data and making a decision about whether change is occurring and whether it is occurring at an acceptable rate. Often, trend is obvious from simple visual inspection of the data—especially if a student is making steady progress.

Calculating Trend

In some cases, however, student progress may not be so obvious. For example, Figure 5.9 shows markedly variable performance. While it appears the student is improving in ability to compute math facts correctly and fluently, it is not clear how much (i.e., at what rate) improvement is occurring; there is a resultant lack of information crucial to making instructional decisions. To measure student growth more precisely it is a good idea to estimate trend by calculating and using *trend lines* or *lines of progress*. Using trend lines also increases agreement about the degree of student progress when time series-data are interpreted (Bailey, 1984). Four methods can be used to calculate trend.

---

[6]Evaluating learning trends requires repeated testing with the same (or equivalent) assessment device.

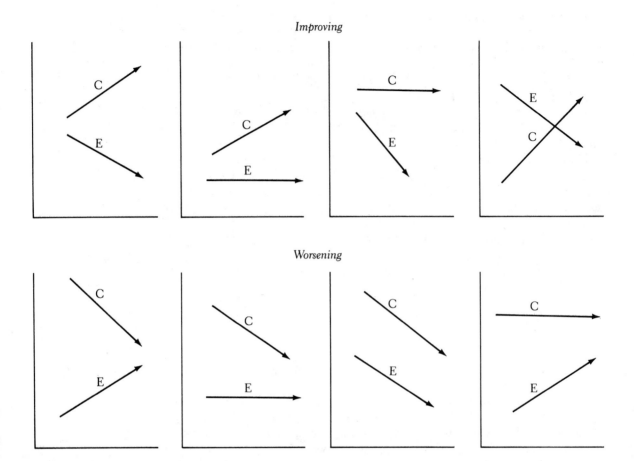

Key: C = correct; E = errors

FIGURE 5.8.   Learning pictures of improving and worsening data.

Quarter-Intersect Method

Trend or progress lines can be drawn using the quarter-intersect method (White & Haring, 1980; White & Liberty, 1976). Figure 5.9 contains an example of how this method is used to draw a trend line following the steps below.

1.   Divide the data in half by drawing a vertical line (1) through the middle of the phase. If there is an odd number of data points, as in Figure 5.9, the line will pass through one of the points (e.g., if there are 11 points, the line will pass through the sixth data point). If there is an even number of points, the line will pass half way between 2 data points; for example, if there are 12 points, the line will pass between the sixth and seventh.

2.   Draw lines (2), (3) through the mid-dates of the two halves of the phase created by the first line. Then find the mid-performance for each half phase and draw horizontal lines (4), (5) intersecting the mid-date lines. As with the first step, if

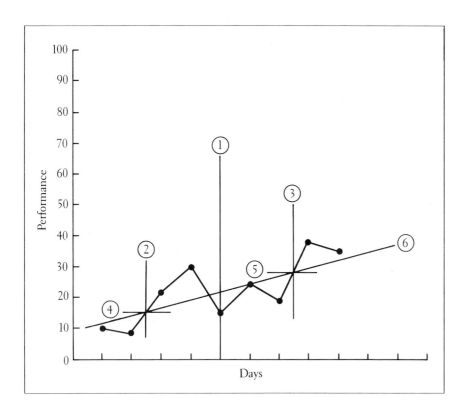

FIGURE 5.9.
Finding the line of
progress using the
quarter-intersect
method.

the mid-session or mid-performance consists of odd numbers, the lines are drawn through data points; if there are even numbers, the lines are drawn between points. (As shown in Figure 5.9, it is possible for several points to fall on the mid-performance line.)

3. Once the mid-performance–mid-session intersections are drawn on both halves of the chart, draw a line (6) connecting them. This line is the trend line.

Split-Middle Method

The split-middle method (White & Haring, 1980) takes the quarter-intersect method one additional step farther to provide an even better estimate of trend. The split-middle method uses the quarter-intersect line of progress (Figure 5.9). However, a teacher moves the trend line, keeping it parallel with the original trend line, until the same number of data points are above and below it.

Celeration Rate

Another way to analyze time-series data is to calculate a *celeration* value or rate.[7] This value indicates the extent or magnitude of student learning over time (Evans, Evans, & Mercer, 1986). White and Haring (1980) offer a method for

---

[7]Celeration is a precision teaching term. While not a "real" word, this term is the root of the words accelerate and decelerate. Therefore, celeration describes the upward or downward trend of graphed data.

calculating a celeration value. Using two weeks of data, the median rate for each week is found. The smaller median is divided into the larger. If the smaller median occurs in the first week, use a mulitplication sign (×); use a division sign if the larger median occurs in the first week. In Figure 5.10, the data trend has a celeration value of ×1.8. This quantification of learning rate can be used to make decisions about progress.[8]

Aimlines

Yet another method for analyzing student performance data is referred to as an *aimline*. Its purpose is not to describe existing data but rather to indicate the rate of progress (or celeration) the student must make in order to reach criteria by a certain time. Figure 5.11 contains a graph that includes an aimline. Aimlines are drawn using three steps. First, find the intersection of the median date and median rate for three to five days of baseline data and mark it with a small *x*. Next, draw a star at the intersection of the desired criteria (e.g., rate) for the behavior and the date at which the criteria is expected to be reached. This date can be based on necessary progress (e.g., student must master content before the end of the semester to be mainstreamed), past performance on similar objectives, instructional time available, and so forth. It is better to set higher expectations (i.e., how soon the student will reach criteria) than lower ones. Remember, the aimline can be adjusted if rate toward criteria turns out to be unreasonable. Third, draw a line connecting the intersection described in step 1 and the star described in step 2.

Once the line is drawn, it is used to make decisions about student progress and the efficacy of instruction. For example, Haring, Liberty, and White (1980) promote making a program change if data for three consecutive days/sessions fall below the aimline.

The above methods are used to aid teachers in making sense of charted data. Once teachers have an idea whether progress is occurring, they need to make decisions based on their interpretation of the data.

Decision Making

Making decisions about students (what to teach them, how to teach them, where to teach them) is a difficult but a very important part of the teacher's job. We have already discussed some decision rules based on CBA results, rules based on analysis of relatively infrequent assessment—screening/referral, where to place a student in a curriculum, and overall program evaluation. The following section focuses on how decisions are made about effectiveness of day-to-day instruction made from analysis of frequent measures of progress on curricular objectives.

Several researchers (Fuchs, Deno, & Mirkin, 1983; Fuchs & Fuchs, 1986a; Wesson, Skiba, Sevcik, King, & Deno, 1984; White & Haring, 1980) have

---

[8]A rule of thumb for minimum progress is a celeration rate of 1.50.

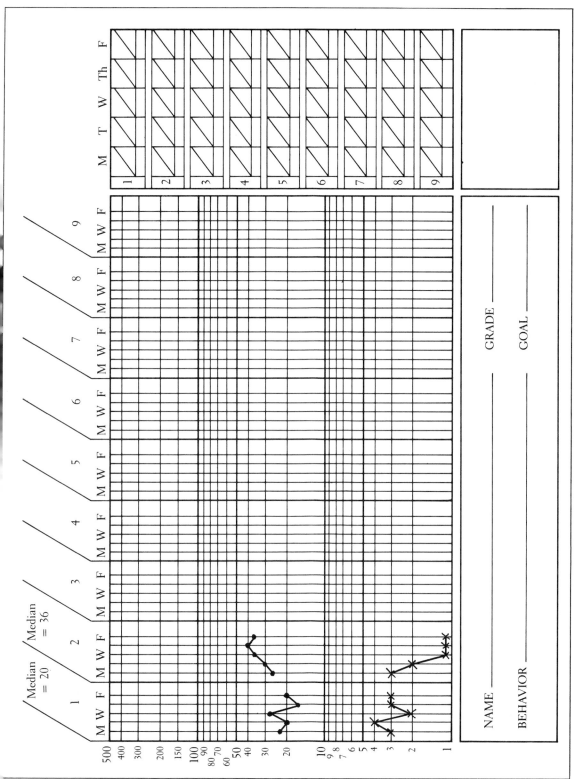

FIGURE 5.10. Two weeks of data used to calculate acceleration value. (Copyright by Eugene M. Berquam, Performance Data Co., P.O. Box 13289 Gainesville, FL. 32604. Used by permission.)

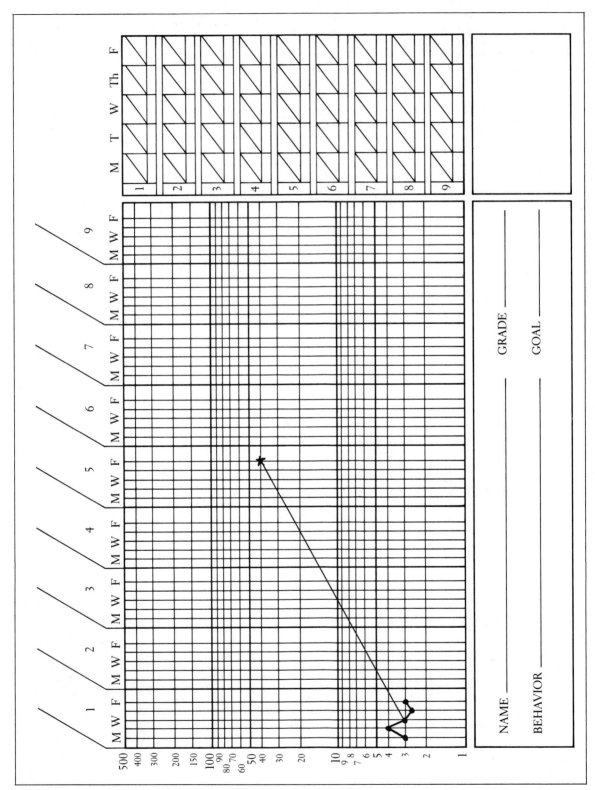

FIGURE 5.11. Drawing an aimline. (Copyright by Eugene Berquam, Performance Data Co., P.O. Box 13289, Gainesville, FL 32604. Used by permission.)

reported that students of teachers who systematically applied decision-making rules (along with other elements of CBA) showed better growth. While no specific guidelines have been validated for how often decisions should be made, general suggestions have been offered. Fuchs, Deno, & Mirkin (1983) recommend decisions should be made every 7 to 10 data points, while Howell and McCollum-Gahley (1986) suggest every two weeks. However, common sense may dictate earlier decision making. For example, if a student has not made any progress or data are worsening for three days in a row, it is a good indication that something needs to be changed. The timing of decisions is a complicated issue, and it is currently left up to the teacher to decide when to interpret data and to make data-based decisions. This decision should be based on consideration of several variables, including the type of objective and intervention as well as prior student performance. With some objectives, interventions, and/or students, teachers may have to give more (or less) time to judge an intervention's impact.

There are four basic decisions teachers can make based on analysis of formative data: (1) to maintain the instructional program currently in use, (2) to change the current program, (3) to begin instruction on a new level of the objective, and (4) to begin instruction on a new objective. Teachers need to interpret performance, make a hypothesis about why a student is performing as he or she is, and decide what, if any, changes need to be made.

1. Maintain Current Program

One of the more gratifying decisions a teacher can make is to continue with the existing program of intervention. This decision is made when a student has not reached the instructional aim (criterion for mastery) but is making satisfactory progress. Deciding whether satisfactory progress is occurring depends upon how the data are interpreted. For example, if visual analysis is used, an improving learning picture such as that in Figure 5.12 assures a teacher that an obvious increase in accuracy with concomitant decrease in errors is occurring. If celeration values are used to quantify progress and a student is maintaining a rate of celeration above minimum ($\times 1.50$), a teacher may assume adequate progress if this minimum is appropriate for the student. If an aimline is used, no change is indicated if data points remain at or very close to the aimline.

2. Change Current Program

When students are not progressing satisfactorily, teachers need to make program changes. The tasks at this point are to decide when to make changes and what changes to make. Some attention has been paid to identifying types of decisions and types of performance trends and data patterns that signal a change is needed (e.g., Fuchs, Deno, & Mirkin, 1983; Fuchs, Fuchs, & Hamlett, in press; Haring, Liberty, & White, 1980; Howell & McCollum-Gahley, 1986; White & Haring, 1980; White & Liberty, 1976). Types of program changes include:

- Increasing the slope of the aimline by setting an earlier-than-expected date for reaching criterion

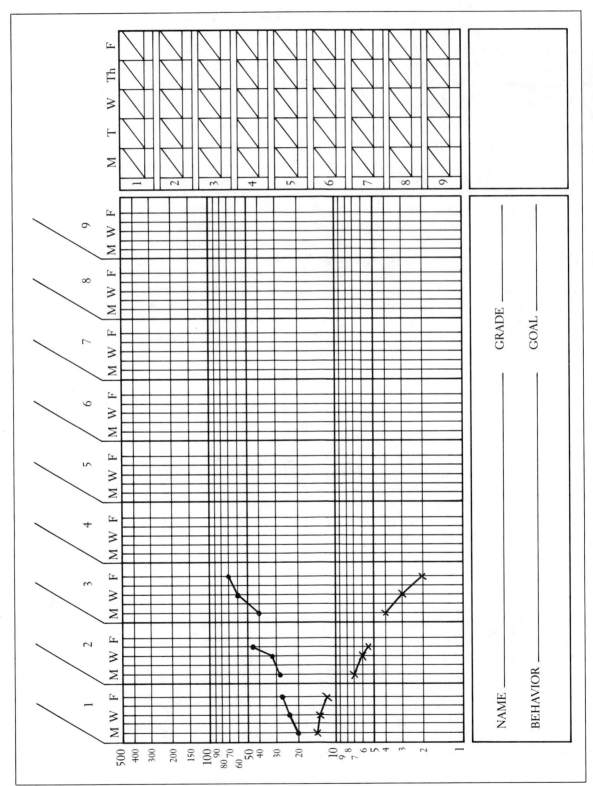

FIGURE 5.12.　Improving learning picture. (Copyright by Eugene M. Berquam, Performance Data Co., P.O. Box 13289, Gainesville, FL 32604. Used by permission.)

- Increasing the aim (i.e., criterion)
- Decreasing the slope of the aimline by extending the expected date for reaching criterion
- Teaching a smaller "slice" of the objective
- Moving back to a different objective that is prerequisite to the original objective
- Changing instructional procedures (i.e., how and under what conditions the skill is taught)

It is important to keep in mind that each student is unique and that these decisions are in fact hypotheses that can only be confirmed by analyzing performance *after* a change in the program has been made. Teachers continue to collect, display, and interpret data after decisions are made. With this caution in mind, several patterns signaling a need for making decisions about program change are discussed below:

Signal for change: correct responses exceeding anticipated progress. When a student's performance proceeds at a higher rate than projected, teachers have at least two options (in addition to celebrating). First, teachers can set a more ambitious goal (i.e., adjusting the criteria upward and leaving the aim date unchanged). Fuchs, Fuchs, & Hamlett (in press) found that students of teachers who used this decision rule outperformed students whose teachers did not use these rules. Second, teachers can set an earlier aim date based upon the student's current rate of progress. This change allows a teacher to move to another level of the current objective or to a new objective sooner than anticipated.

Signal for change: few or no correct responses. For example, visual analysis of Harry's data shows he is unable to read consonant-vowel-consonant (C-V-C) words taken from his basal reading text. With this type of performance, a likely hypothesis is that the skill is too difficult for Harry at this time. An appropriate program change for Harry would be to move back to a prerequisite behavior. Since Harry cannot read C-V-C words, a less difficult, but prerequisite objective, would be pronouncing short-vowel sounds in isolation. If Harry's objective had been addition of single-digit facts with sums from 0 to 18, slicing back to facts with smaller sums (e.g., 0–9) might be indicated if error analysis had shown the student to be able to solve problems with lower sums.

Signal for change: correct responses but too many errors. If Deborah's performance on a handwriting objective indicates she is increasing her rate of copying letters but with a high rate of errors, her teacher may try any of the following instructional procedures: (1) make an error analysis to aid in planning corrective instruction; (2) teach the skill using modeling and prompting procedures; or (3) provide more closely monitored practice combined with corrective feedback. Too, if Deborah is not ready for emphasis on speed (e.g., acts confused or frustrated), acquisition (accuracy) may need to be stressed first.

Signal for change: accurate but slow. If students consistently perform a skill accurately, but with speed of completion so slow that they are hindered, the following program changes can be made. First, encourage speed. Sometimes merely telling a student, "I want you to work faster" may be enough. Second, providing incentives to "beat" previous rates is often effective. Third, giving more frequent timings, such as after each drill and practice session, can be effective.

Signal for change: consistent performance below aimline. When students are improving but performing below the aimline for three consecutive days or sessions, teachers should give serious consideration to altering instruction. Teachers have several changes available to them: (1) Vary the format of the lesson (Howell & McCollum-Gahley, 1986). (2) Adjust the aimline. If it has been decided that the objective is appropriate and motivation is not a problem, it may be necessary to decrease the slope of the aimline by extending the expected date for the completion of the objective. (3) Adjust the criteria for mastery. If the objective is appropriate and the student is motivated, the teacher may have an unrealistic expectation for the level of pupil performance. The teacher should check the level of performance expected against able members of the class or make sure the student in question is physically capable of producing the desired level of performance.

Signal for change: correct responses flattening or worsening. Figure 5.11 shows that Walter was improving adequately over several sessions but then his performance worsened. Walter's teacher may ask him why he is not doing as well or may try one of the following procedures: (1) Evaluate whether the student is bored and needs additional motivation. Increasing the strength or amount of reinforcement may be needed to provide a boost to the student. (2) Vary drill and practice formats. If the same old worksheet is interfering with motivation to improve, provide practice using instructional games, self-correcting materials, or peer assistance. (3) Involve the student. Discussing the rationale for learning the skill may give more meaning to the task. (4) Increase instructional time or time on task.

3. Begin Instruction on a New Level of the Objective

If skill acquisition (e.g., the student can perform the skill with 90% accuracy) has been obtained, a new objective stressing fluency is indicated. After the student can perform the skill both accurately and quickly, an objective written at the generalization level may be appropriate.

4. Begin Instruction on a New Objective

The decision rule for when to begin instruction of a new objective occurs when a student performs at or above the accuracy and fluency aim for two out of three days. However, this does not mean that a teacher can no longer be concerned about the skill. Rather, at this point a teacher makes another decision—to start maintenance procedures. Maintenance usually consists of periodic skill review and intermittent assessment. Too, if the curriculum is sequential the student will have opportunity to practice the skill in the context of other problems (e.g., will need to add when multiplying).

Summary

In order to make optimal use of information collected on student performance, teachers organize it (display it), make sense of it (interpret it), and act on it (make decisions). Depending on the original purpose of assessment, several options are available for displaying data. Tables are useful for displaying information when the purpose of assessment is screening, referral, deciding on a starting point for instruction, or keeping track of mastered objectives. Graphs are most appropriate for monitoring progress of students on specific objectives or skills.

Once CBA data have been collected and graphically displayed, interpretation is necessary. The purpose of this interpretation is to determine whether change is occurring and whether it is occurring at an acceptable rate. Several methods can be used to interpret formative data: visual inspection, calculation of a celeration value, judging performance in relation to a trend line, or judging performance in relation to an aimline.

Using graphed data and criteria for what is acceptable growth, a teacher makes decisions about what program modifications, if any, need to be made. While general guidelines are provided on what changes may be indicated, program modification should be seen as hypothesis testing: A teacher makes a best guess as to why the student is performing in a certain manner, modifies the program based on that hypothesis, and continues to monitor performance closely to see if the modification has worked. If not, the process is repeated.

Chapter 6

CBA in Reading

Key Terms

Aid
Cloze Procedure
Consonant blends
Developmental curricula
Digraph
Diphthong
Disregard of punctuation
Functional curriculum
Graded passages
Insertion
Inversion
Miscue analysis

Mispronunciation
Phonics
Phonogram
Reading comprehension
Repetition
Reversal
Script implicit questions
Structural analysis
Substitution
Text explicit question
Text implicit question
Word recognition

Functional reading skills are recognized as a goal of education by every organization that has promulgated comprehensive goals for education. They are generally considered the most important curricular area in education.

Reading is the process of translating written symbols into words and obtaining meaning from the sequence of those words. Overall academic performance is largely dependent on mastering reading skills beginning in the elementary grades, where instruction in reading starts. Reading becomes even more important at the secondary level where success in subject matter areas depends on ability to decode and comprehend large amounts of information written at up to a college reading level. Beyond school, reading proficiency has an impact on the ability to function in society in many ways. Inability to read and use information included in maps, menus, manuals, and magazines restricts an individual's ability to function in transportation, leisure, social, and vocational situations. For example, job opportunities for nonreaders are usually restricted to unskilled labor that pays nominal wages (Wilson & Cleland, 1985).

Many diverse (and occasionally contradictory) approaches to reading have been advocated. For example, some educators believe a phonics approach is the most efficient method, while others suggest that whole-word methods are better. Still others promote a meaning-based approach and state that decoding skills will follow spontaneously through "discovery" learning. While it is not the purpose of this chapter to present a comprehensive discussion of the nature of reading or the best approach to teaching it, the reader should be aware that one's orientation (or that of the author who wrote the curriculum being used) dictates the form taken by a curriculum. This in turn guides the curriculum-based assessment procedures used.

Reading is an interactive process and isolating skills is somewhat artificial. Nonetheless, in this chapter, general reading curricula are divided into three major strands: word attack, word recognition, and reading comprehension. In the following sections, scope and sequence, performance measures, level of assessment, and error analysis are discussed for each strand.

Word Attack

Scope and Sequence

Most publishers of reading curricula include scope and sequence charts intended to provide teachers with an overview of the skills taught in each grade level. As with scope and sequence charts in other academic areas, the skills included and the sequence of instruction reflect the beliefs of the author(s) or "expert" opinion rather than empirical validation. Moreover, since children do not learn in the same manner and bring different combinations of skills to the classroom (Bartel, 1986), they do not need to proceed through the curriculum in the same sequence. Thus, teachers need to use scope and sequence charts flexibly—and somewhat skeptically—while taking the needs of individual students into consideration.

Word-Attack Skills

Word-attack skills, sometimes referred to as decoding or word-analysis skills, allow students to decode words by associating sounds with letters or groups of letters. Typical approaches to word attack are *phonics* and *structural analysis*.

Phonics deal with sound–symbol relationships, and students are required to remember and produce the sounds of individual vowels and consonants as well as groups of letters. There are two components in phonics instruction: recognition of sounds and blending sounds. Phonics systems are based on the premise that the letter–sound relationships of the English language are consistent. However, this is not the case. To work around phonetic irregularities in reading materials,

TABLE 6.1 Phonics Teaching Sequence[1]	Simple Consonants
	b, p, m, w, h, d, t, n, hard **g** (gate), **k,** hard **c** (cake), **y** (yet), **f**

Simple Consonants
b, p, m, w, h, d, t, n, hard **g** (gate), **k,** hard **c** (cake), **y** (yet), **f**

More Difficult Consonants
v, l, z (zoo), **s** (sat), **r,** soft **c** (cent), **q, x, j,** soft **g** (engine), **s** (as)

Consonant Blends and Digraphs
ck, ng, th (the), **zh, sh, th** (thin), **wh, ch**

Simple Consonants with l, r, p, or t (**bl ,pl, gr, br, sp, st, tr, thr, str,** etc.)

Short Vowels
a (back), **e** (get), **i** (sit), **o** (top), **u** (cup), and **y** (happy)

Long Vowels
a (cake), **e** (be), **i** (five), **o** (old), **u** (mule), and **y** (cry)

Silent Letters
k (knife), **w** (write), **l** (talk), **t** (catch), **g** (gnat), **c** (lack), **h** (hour)

Vowel Digraphs
ai (pail), **ea** (each), **oa** (boat), **ee** (bee), **ay** (say), **ea** (dead)

Vowel Diphthongs
au (auto), **aw** (awful), **oo** (moon), **ow** (cow), **ou** (out), **oi** (oil), **oy** (boy), **ow** (low)

Vowels with r, l, w
a (car), **e** (her), **i** (bird), **o** (corn), **u** (burn)

Phonograms
ail, ain, all, and, ate, ay, con, eep, ell, en, ent, er, est, ick, ight, ill, in, ing, ock, ter, tion

Alternates: ake, ide, ile, ine, it, ite, le, re, ble

[1]Adapted from G. D. Spache and E. B. Spache, *Reading in the elementary school*, 4th ed., 1977. Boston: Allyn and Bacon. Used by permission.

phonics-based curricula use passages containing only words that have regular letter–sound relationships (Lerner, 1985). Irregular words are introduced later to avoid confusing beginning readers.

Table 6.1 contains a teaching sequence recommended by Spache and Spache (1977) for phonics skills and includes the majority of skills included in commercial scope and sequence charts. Consonant sounds are taught first, then students are taught consonant blends. (Consonant blends are two- or three-letter combinations in which each consonant retains its separate sound when it is blended— e.g., *bl, sm, str.*) Next, students are taught consonant digraphs. (Consonant digraphs are two-letter combinations that create a single sound, such as *gh, ph*). Long and short vowel sounds are then introduced. When these are mastered, vowel digraphs and diphthongs are taught. [Vowel digraphs are letter combinations that, when said together, make a single sound (e.g., *ea* in heat), vowel diphthongs are two vowels that are both heard in making a compound sound (e.g., *oi* in soil).] Finally, vowels combined with *r* and groups of letters commonly

TABLE 6.2
Phonic Rules[1]

Consonants
1. When **c** is frequently follwed by **e, i,** or **y,** it has the sound of **s** (e.g., city or race); otherwise **c** has the sound of **k** (come).
2. **G** followed by **e, i,** or **y** is soft (gem); otherwise, **g** is hard (gone).
3. When **c** and **h** are adjacent, they make only one sound, and **ch** is usually pronounced as it is in kitchen.
4. When a word ends in **ck, ck** sounds **k** (cock).
5. When consonants are double, only one is sounded (butter).
6. Sometimes **s** sounds as **z** (music).
7. **X** has the sound of **ks** or **k** and **s** (box or taxi).

Vowels
8. When a consonant and **y** are the last letters in a one-syllable word, **y** has the long **i** sound (cry); in longer words, **y** has the long **e** sound (baby).
9. The **r** gives the preceding vowel a sound that is neither long nor short (far, fir); the letters **l** and **w** have the same effect.

Vowel Digraphs and Diphthongs
10. With **oa, ay, ai,** and **ee,** the first vowel is usually long and the second is silent (boat).
11. In **ea** the first letter may be long and the second silent (beat) or it may have a short **e** sound (bread).
12. **Ou** has two sounds: long **o** (bought) and **ou** (round).
13. **Au, oi, oy** blend into a single sound (author, oily, and coy).
14. **Oo** has two sounds, as in moon and wood.

[1]Adapted from G. D. Spache and E. B. Spache, *Reading in the elementary school,* 4th ed., 1977. Boston: Allyn and Bacon. Used by permission.

used as word endings (e.g., *-ing*) are taught. (These endings are sometimes called phonograms.) While this sequence includes elements of common scope and sequences, many curricula break some of the phonics skills down into finer categories, such as initial, final, and medial digraphs, and recommend teaching them in that sequence.

Additionally, since students are also expected to learn and apply phonetic rules, these rules can be tested. Table 6.2 contains commonly taught rules.

Structural analysis, sometimes referred to as morphology, is a word-attack approach whereby unfamiliar words are decoded by subdividing them into meaningful parts or units (e.g., root words, prefixes, and suffixes). Instruction in structural analysis resembles both phonics and sight-word approaches. As in phonics, students are taught to break words into parts and then put the parts back together when pronouncing the word. Additionally, these parts or units are presented in isolation so that students recognize them immediately on sight. Finally, students are also taught the meanings of units; specifically, prefixes and suffixes. An examination of frequently used curricula shows that structural analysis is not a major emphasis of reading curricula but is usually taught in conjunction with phonics. Accordingly, there does not seem to be a widely accepted scope and sequence for this approach. However, several components appear frequently in reading curricula: identify root words, decode and state meanings of prefixes and

suffixes, recognize words in compound words, pronounce contractions and identify both words represented by the contraction, and break words into syllables
using syllabication rules.

Performance Measures

Performance measures follow a sequence that begins with assessing a student's
ability to pronounce letters and groups of letters in isolation and ends with
pronouncing words in passages taken from student readers. These performance
measures reflect skills taught in most curricula; however, their content and use
should be dictated by the specific curriculum used and the purpose of assessment.

All of the measures stress both accuracy and speed since a major goal for most
academic skills is fluency. However, teachers may want to consider adding rate
criteria after the student has demonstrated accuracy since some students may
become confused or frustrated when asked to do something quickly before they
have mastered a skill. Mercer and Mercer (1985) report a range of suggested rates
that they derived from several sources. The following are approximate median
rates for three reading skills:

- Isolated sounds—70 per minute with 2 or fewer errors
- Words in a list—80 per minute with 2 or fewer errors
- Words in text—100 per minute with 2 or fewer errors

A teacher should use suggested rates flexibly and make adjustments based on
individual student performance and the age/grade level of the student. (Rates tend
to increase as students get older.) When setting rate criteria for word-attack skills,
teachers may also use a variety of methods, such as establishing local norms,
using previous performance on similar skills, or suggested rates (see Chapter 3), to
establish criteria for reading and error rates.

Performance Measure 1: Fluency in saying sounds in isolation. Some curricula
teach in isolation the sounds of letters or letter combinations. When sounds are
taught in isolation, they should be assessed at least initially in isolation. A student
would be requested to say all sounds of a letter (e.g., the hard and soft sound of *c*)
if they have been taught. A teacher can also add an initial or ending letter or
combinations of letters by telling a student the sound of the added letter and
instructing the student to add this sound to the sound of the other letters. Probes
are an efficient way to assess fluency of sounds in isolation. Probe content can
vary depending on the number of phonic skills being assessed and the purpose of
assessment. For example, if several digraphs are taught together and the purpose
of assessment is to evaluate the effectiveness of instruction on these skills, the
probe would include all of them; if the purpose of assessment is to survey student
ability for purposes of placing them within a curriculum, all skills to be taught at a
particular level would be included. Figure 6.1 is an example of a probe sheet used
to assess a student's ability to say the sound of both vowels and consonants. If
untimed probes are used, the criterion for successful performance should be set at
90% or more correct.

Student _____ Skill: *Saying sounds in isolation* FIGURE 6.1.
A probe to assess
Total Number Correct _____ Total Errors _____ saying consonants and
vowels in isolation.

Long Vowels Correct _____ Long Vowel Errors _____

Short Vowels Correct _____ Short Vowel Errors _____

Hard Consonants Correct _____ Hard Consonant Errors _____

Soft Consonants Correct _____ Soft Consonant Errors _____

n	s	z	p	m	r	v	b	k	e	(10)
t	c	d	i	f	o	h	a	y	g	(20)
w	l	u	n	s	p	z	r	u	d	(30)
e	f	b	a	o	m	c	y	v	k	(40)
l	i	h	t	g	j	w	u	t	w	(50)
e	s	n	k	j	f	r	c	h	l	(60)
d	p	o	i	a	v	m	b	g	y	(70)
z	o	m	z	n	k	y	r	v	w	(80)
h	b	g	p	a	e	t	i	c	j	(90)
i	d	u	s	f	y	f	l	a	r	(100)

Performance measure 2: Fluency in saying nonsense words. Since curricula typically do not include or teach nonsense words, assessing student ability to read them may seem to violate a main tenet of CBA—testing what is taught. However, if the skill being measured is ability to apply phonics skills or rules within the context of other letters, problems may arise if real words are used. Students may, through prior exposure, know the word on sight. If this is the case, word recognition is assessed rather than phonetic analysis and blending. In developing a probe of this kind, nonsense words should be similar to real words. For example, if probing for student ability to say the long sound of *a* in the context of a consonant–vowel–consonant–*e* word, the nonsense word might be *tave* instead of *gave*. It is good practice to tell the students that these are not real words in order to avoid possible confusion.

Performance measure 3: Fluency in saying phonetically regular words. If a teacher wishes to sample a student's ability to apply phonetic skills and rules to actual words, a probe sheet containing words in isolation can be constructed. Commercially prepared, graded word lists are available and usually sample 20 to 25 words typically taught for each grade level. However, to develop a test reflecting the curriculum used, teachers can select words from the glossary provided in

FIGURE 6.2.
A probe to assess
saying consonants and
vowels in words.

Student _____   Skill: _____

Total Number Correct ____   Total Errors ____

   Long Vowels Correct ____   Long Vowel Errors ____

   Short Vowels Correct ____   Short Vowel Errors ____

   Diphthongs Correct ____   Diphthong Errors ____

   Digraphs Correct ____   Digraph Errors ____

groan	sprain	seal	throw	foam	speech	toast	wheat	foe	(9)
paid	croak	faint	soap	owe	gain	hoe	flown	pray	(18)
peel	coal	teach	pay	leap	clay	hail	crow	peak	(27)
toe	seem	stray	sweet	blow	pail	doe	least	sheet	(36)
say	float	day	bowl	sweep	heal	play	teeth	need	(45)
toad	creep	train	treat	sway	claim	peep	braid	peak	(54)
foam	sheet	braid	need	peel	stray	pail	train	sway	(63)
foe	speech	leap	pay	bowl	creep	croak	sweet	claim	(72)
play	blow	teeth	paid	clay	soap	hoe	flown	pray	(81)
least	sprain	hail	say	faint	crow	peep	groan	toe	(90)
heal	throw	toast	wheat	day	teach	float	toad	sweep	(99)
seem	treat	doe	gain	coal	woe	seal	toe	least	(108)
sweet	teeth	sweep	foe*	need	speech	play	hail	foam	(117)

the teacher's edition of most published curricula. Some curricula, such as the Macmillan Reading Program, list words in several ways: by story, by phonic skill taught in a unit, and cumulatively. If the total number of words available is too large to be assessed by a single probe, a representative sample of words can be selected. When scoring student responses, teachers may wish to record only if a word was pronounced correctly. However, if the goal is to measure phonetic skills, teachers may wish to score only whether the *sounds/blends* in question were pronounced correctly. Figure 6.2 is an example of a probe for words in isolation; several consonant rules are sampled. Note several opportunities to respond to each rule are provided.

Performance measure 4: Oral reading accuracy and rate on passages from text. In the absence of evidence indicating comprehension problems, teachers often use accuracy or fluency of word-attack skills to place students within a reading curriculum and to measure progress within the curriculum.[1] Teachers select passages from the reading text that range from 50 to 250 words, depending on the age or grade level of the student (e.g., 50 words for first graders and 250 words for students at the secondary level). Since the purpose is for placement within a curriculum, passages must be selected from several levels. Passages are typed, and copies are made for both the student and teacher. The student reads the selection aloud, and the teacher follows along and notes the number and type of errors made. (The teacher also has the option of having the student read the passage into a tape recorder and scoring it at a more convenient time.) After scoring the number of words read correctly and calculating the percentage of words read correctly, the teacher identifies the students' independent reading level (e.g., 95%+), instructional level (e.g., 85%–95%), and frustration level (e.g., below 85%) and places the student in reading materials at the instructional level. If reading rate (fluency) is also being measured the student usually reads from 1 to 3 minutes. Usually a student is told to skip over any difficult words and to read as fast as possible without making careless errors. Scoring is done by counting the number of words read correctly and incorrectly and dividing the totals by the number of minutes the student read. This results in a score stated as words read correctly/incorrectly per minute.

Performance measure 5: Fluency in saying prefixes and suffixes in isolation. When structural analysis is used to teach word recognition, instruction often begins with a presentation of prefixes and suffixes in isolation since they— unlike other structural analysis units (i.e., noun/verb/adjective endings, compound words, and contractions)—lend themselves readily to initial instruction in isolation. Figure 6.3 is an example of a probe sheet that assesses saying prefixes in isolation.[2] Content of probes varies according to the purpose of instruction. If a teacher wishes to identify those prefixes and suffixes a student can pronounce, all types included in the curricular level to be taught are included.[3] If formative evaluation of recently taught prefixes and/or suffixes is the purpose of assessment, then only those are included. In the latter case there may not be a sufficient number to allow for a free operant unless the prefixes/suffixes are repeated on the probe.

Performance measure 6: Fluency in saying endings, prefixes, and suffixes with nonsense root words. Teachers wishing to control for word familiarity when assessing a student's skill in structural analyses may use nonsense words (as was done in measure 2 above). For example, students might be told the pronunciation of the

---

[1]This measure in all likelihood is assessing word recognition skills since, if students are reading fluently, they are not sounding out individual words. Many assessment and reading texts refer to the use of graded passages to assess reading accuracy, fluency, and comprehension as an informal reading inventory (IRI). Procedures for developing this type of measure are discussed in the performance measures section for both word recognition and reading comprehension.

[2]In many curricula the *meanings* of prefixes and suffixes are taught (e.g., the prefix *pre* can mean before, in front of, or superior) concurrently with their pronunciation. However, this is a comprehension skill that is not the focus of this discussion.

[3]A comprehensive list of prefixes and suffixes and their meanings can be found in Ekwall (1981).

FIGURE 6.3 A probe to assess saying prefixes in isolation.	Student _____				Skill: _____			
	Total Number Correct ____				Total Errors ____			
	ab	de	extra	hyper	kilo	out	per	post	(8)
	poly	auto	dis	for	in	mis	phono	re	(16)
	pre	pro	bi	en	fore	iner	mono	semi	(24)
	sur	tele	sub	com	ex	geo	intra	multi	(32)
	under	extra	un	tri	con	hemi	intro	non	(40)
	post	re	semi	multi	non	per	phono	mono	(48)
	out	mis	inter	geo	hemi	kilo	hyper	for	(56)
	en	com	tri	multi	extra	dis	bi	sub	(64)
	un	semi	de	auto	pro	tele	extra	re	(72)
	ab	poly	pre	sur	under	post	inter	con	(80)

nonsense root word, "grob," and then given a probe sheet with different prefixes and/or suffixes used with grob (e.g., regrob, grobable, regrobable).

Performance measure 7: Fluency in saying words that can be analyzed structurally. If a teacher wishes to sample a student's ability to "break apart" words and then blend them, probe sheets are developed. These probes would contain words that can be analyzed structurally and that come from student readers (or words that have been taught if a commercial curriculum is not being used). Figure 6.4 contains an example of a probe to assess both prefixes and suffixes in actual words. There are two measurement options in administering this type of probe. First, the teacher may just ask students to read the words as quickly as they can for a specified period of time and score incorrect and correct responses—either for pronouncing the whole word or just the prefix or suffix. Second, the teacher may ask students to say the parts of the word (e.g., prefix, root, and suffix) and then blend them. This procedure more closely approximates the actual process of attacking an unfamiliar word using structural analysis. If the latter method is used, words on the probe should be unfamiliar to the student.

Level of Assessment

The levels of assessment for word-attack skills are the knowledge and application levels. At the knowledge level, students must associate letters and sounds, recognize prefixes and suffixes, and so forth. At the application level, students must apply various rules in decoding unfamiliar words.

Student _____ Skill: _____

FIGURE 6.4.
A probe to assess
saying prefixes and
suffixes in context.

Total Number Correct _____ Total Errors _____

cautious	experiment	loudly	excuse	unwash	shortness	fearless	(7)
management	smoother	report	healthy	expert	reuse	prefer	(14)
thirsty	disable	until	imprint	income	leadership	fifth	(21)
demand	mistreat	expert	vacation	thankful	increase	tricky	(28)
engrain	sixth	cupful	uncook	harmful	careful	kindness	(35)
helpless	impose	sinkable	deform	prejudge	marvelous	quickly	(42)
information	burnable	misstep	engulf	frighten	disorder	soften	(49)
readable	battleship	expert	engulf	demand	leadership	deform	(56)
sinkable	income	helpless	shortness	impose	until	misstep	(63)
tricky	disable	burnable	soften	kindness	experiment	report	(70)
vacation	healthy	report	frighten	cupful	cautious	disorder	(77)
readable	increase	fifth	sixth	quickly	smoother	thirsty	(84)
expert	information	fearless	harmful	uncook	battleship	loudly	(91)

Error Analysis

In order to establish what types of mistakes readers make and how often they make them, assessment of reading usually includes an error analysis.[4] Information from an error analysis is used to hypothesize causes of particular errors and ways to remediate them. Three general approaches to the analysis of word-attack skills have been developed. The first two, topological analysis and miscue analysis, are quite general and have yet to have their utility validated. The third type, analysis of word-attack errors, is far more precise.

Topological Analysis

In topological analysis, students read orally from graded passages as their teachers follow along on their own copies and note the type of errors that are made. Teachers are concerned with how well students reproduce the text exactly. When

---

[4]The premise for evaluating oral reading is that students read in the same manner when reading silently—the most natural way of reading. However, this assumption may not be valid; errors made during oral reading may be different from errors made during silent reading. When students are asked to read orally they are typically asked to read each word correctly. However, when students read silently, they read for comprehension; word calling is deemphasized, and words can be deduced from context instead of being sounded out. Moreover, they can adjust their reading rates depending on whether a section of the passage contains new information and/or difficult words. Therefore, some "errors" made when reading silently may have little effect on how well the student understands what is read.

teachers are pressed for time, they can have students read into a tape recorder and analyze their reading at a more convenient time. Below are noted commonly made errors of oral reading, possible reasons for them, and notations used to mark the errors on a teacher's copy when they occur (Ekwall, 1981).[5]

- **Omissions:** A student skips over parts of words, whole words, or groups of words. Errors may result from carelessness or poor word-recognition and/or word-analysis skills. *Notation:* Circle omitted material.

- **Insertions:** A student inserts word endings and/or one or more words not present in the text. Errors may result from a lack of comprehension, carelessness, or oral language that exceeds reading ability. *Notation:* Place a caret, "^" at the point of insertion, and write the inserted words above the sentence.

- **Substitutions:** A student substitutes a word in a passage with one not in the passage. This error may indicate carelessness, lack of word recognition and/or word-analysis skills, or dialectic differences. *Notation:* Draw a line through the word, and write the substituted word above it.

- **Mispronunciations:** The "word" the student says is not recognizable. This may be an indication of poor word-analysis or recognition skills. *Notation:* Draw a line through the word mispronounced and write the mispronunciation above it.

- **Inversions or reversals:** A student reverses part or all of a word. For example, Jim might read *deb* for *bed*. The cause of this type of error is unknown, but neurological problems are sometimes postulated as an underlying cause. Another hypothesized cause is student failure to realize the importance of letter order. *Notation:* Draw a line through the word, and write the inversion above it.

- **Repetitions:** A student repeats words or phrases. This error may indicate poor reading habits (e.g., attention problems), poor sight vocabulary, and/or difficulties in word analysis. *Notation:* Underline repeated material with wavy lines.

- **Disregard of punctuation:** A student does not pause for commas or periods, change inflection for questions and exclamations, and so forth. A student may not know the meaning of a particular punctuation mark or may be distracted by difficult reading material. *Notation:* Circle the punctuation mark.

- **Aid:** A student asks for help or waits so long (e.g., more than 10 seconds) that the teacher has to supply the word. This may indicate difficulty in word-attack/ recognition skills. *Notation:* Place a bracket, "[ ]," around the word.

When summarizing student reading errors with these procedures, a teacher notes how often each type of error is made in order to identify the most frequently made type(s). When adding up the number of errors of each type, teachers should avoid inflating the error by counting the same error twice. For example, if the same word was mispronounced several times it should only be counted once.

[5]For a detailed discussion of error types, hypothesized causes, and recommended teaching activities based on those hypotheses, the reader is directed to Ekwall, 1981.

Miscue Analysis

Errors that distort or change the meaning of a passage are more important than errors that do not, and topological analyses do not address this aspect of error. To overcome this shortcoming, another method has been developed—*miscue analysis* (e.g., Goodman, 1969; Goodman & Burke, 1972). Here, a teacher is concerned with the relationship of the substitution to the word in the text, both semantically (meaning) and syntactically (grammar). This analysis is based on a psycholinguistic theory that reading errors are due to underlying language competence. Miscue analysis focuses on both word analysis and comprehension; emphasis is placed on the type of error rather than how many errors are made. For example, a student may say the word "lady" instead of "woman." In this case one word is substituted for another. However, it is likely that the meaning of the passage is unchanged and the teacher would note this. An example of an error that does not violate grammar is substitution of one word for a word that is the same part of speech. For example, "however" (a conjunction) might be substituted for "but" (also a conjunction). Goodman (1969) proposes 28 different types of miscues, while Goodman and Burke (1972) present a simpler system in which nine types of miscues are analyzed: intonation shift, dialect, graphic and sound similarity, grammatical and semantic acceptability, grammatical function, correction, and meaning change.

Miscue analysis is not without criticism, however. Currently, we know little about the reliability and validity of miscue analysis. Moreover, we lack developmental (normative) data for student errors. Finally, there is little evidence to suggest that miscue analysis allows teachers to establish instructional reading levels (Spache, 1981). These concerns, combined with the elaborate and somewhat time-consuming scoring and interpretation, make miscue analysis of limited use for the classroom teacher.

Analysis of Word-Attack Errors

The two preceding methods of error analysis yield general information about students' oral reading. When the purpose of error analysis is to zero in on word-attack skills, a more specific approach is needed. For example, some errors are related directly to word-attack skills: faulty vowel and consonant usage (e.g., "run" as "ran"), the insertions of sounds (e.g., "pig" as "prig"), or problems with initial, medial, or final sounds (Algozzine, Siders, Siders, & Beattie, 1980). The type of word missed (e.g., C-V-C,[6] C-V-C-V, C-V-C-C, words with prefixes) also can be recorded. However, a teacher should note exactly where the error occurred in order to obtain precise information. For example, if the student missed a prefix word although the prefix was read correctly, a teacher should note this. Since the error was not associated with identifying the prefix, remediation would not be directed to the prefix, but to the root. Similarly, if a C-V-C word is missed, it should be noted whether the student mispronounced the vowel, inserted a different vowel, or made an error by substituting a wrong initial or final consonant sound.

---

[6]"C" stands for consonant; "V" stands for vowel.

FIGURE 6.5. Sample passage used for analyzing errors in word-attack skills.	"Oh you <u>poor creature</u>," Leslie said when she saw the bird. "Do you think it will be able to <u>fly again</u>?" Ralph asked. Leslie picked up the bird carefully. "Let's take it <u>home</u> and read about sick birds," suggested Leslie. When they got <u>home</u>, Ralph <u>took out</u> the <u>book</u>. Ralph noticed Leslie was <u>about</u> to <u>cry</u> and asked her, "<u>Would</u> you <u>like</u> to <u>read</u> it?"

As the student reads, the teacher checks underlined words missed and notes if the mispronunciation was related to the word-analysis skill rule in question.

When conducting an error analysis on specific word-attack skills, the reading materials that are used for oral reading are important. There should be several opportunities to use the skills that have just been taught. It is a good idea for teachers to mark the skills of concern on their own copies. For example, in Figure 6.5, a teacher has selected a passage from a reader and has underlined the words that reflect the following skills and rules: "silent e" (i.e., home, like,), -y endings (i.e., fly, cry), vowel digraphs (i.e., creature, again, read), and vowel diphthongs (i.e., about, would, out, book, poor, growing).

Word Recognition[7]

Scope and Sequence

Word recognition, usually called "sight vocabulary," refers to a student's ability to treat a sequence of letters that form a word as a single unit. To be within a student's sight vocabulary, a word must be recognized without hesitation (usually within 1 second) and without the use of word-analysis skills (e.g., phonics).

The scope of sight words included in a curriculum varies according to the type of curriculum used—developmental or functional. *Developmental curricula* are sequenced according to the typical progression that students follow throughout their school careers. Sight vocabulary in developmental curricula can come from several sources: vocabulary lists derived from a student's reading series, graded word lists (which make up the majority of words used in elementary texts and organized by grade level), lists of high-frequency words that make up the majority of written American English,[8] and lists of phonetically irregular words. Many of these word lists are commercially available or included in preservice methods texts (e.g., Carnine & Silbert, 1979; Dolch, 1950; Ekwall & Shanker, 1983).

[7]Some reading curricula treat sight vocabulary as the highest level of word analysis. After a student decodes a word several times, it becomes readily recognized and read automatically (i.e., without reliance upon decoding skills). Other curricula do not teach decoding skills. Rather, they introduce whole words to students, and the students are repeatedly drilled until the word can be said automatically. Yet other curricula use a combination of whole-word methods and decoding. For example, a sight vocabulary that is phonically regular is introduced and mastered before phonic rules are taught, then phonic rules are applied to new reading vocabulary.

[8]For example, Ekwall and Shanker's New Instant Word List contains 300 words that they purport includes 65% of words used in common basal series.

Several concerns exist about the use of word lists as the primary source for teaching word recognition within developmental curricula. First, since the student is only required to say the correct pronunciation of the word on the list, word meaning is neither taught nor assessed. Moreover, many words included in these lists have multiple meanings (Weiderholt & Bryant, 1987). Second, these lists do not include many of the words frequently included in children's literature; their exclusion may hamper a student's ability to read these materials. Since reading for enjoyment is a typical goal for reading instruction, this becomes a serious concern (Eeds, 1985). Finally, high-frequency word lists are limited to reading vocabulary used in the elementary grades; such lists should be extended to the secondary school (Bachor & Crealock, 1986). For example, Summers has provided a list that includes words used in high school subjects such as science and social studies (cited by Bachor & Crealock, 1986).

Functional curricula differ from developmental curricula in that they are designed for students who have not benefited from exposure to typical curricula and have fallen behind to the extent that it is unreasonable to expect them to catch up. These students, often classified as exceptional, are taught to recognize functional or high-utility words that are assumed to be critical to independence in everyday life. Word lists of this type include safety words (e.g., danger, keep out, poison, traffic signs), vocationally related words (i.e., words used frequently on job applications), and other environmental words (e.g., bathroom signs, exit and entrance signs). While instruction—and therefore assessment—for generalization is important for all students, it is critical for students with significant learning problems. Instruction and measurement of student ability to recognize functional words need to go beyond recognizing these words on a list or flashcard. Students should be able to recognize these words in their actual form (e.g., provided with a picture of a stop sign, within an actual job application) and in the actual setting where they occur. Additionally, students should be able to recognize words written in different ways (e.g., manuscript and cursive, capital and lower case) and variations. For example, words identifying the appropriate public restroom to use include men and women, boys and girls, and bouys and gulls at seafood restaurants. Finally, students should be taught to understand the meaning of these words as well as how to say them.

Performance Measures

When assessing word recognition, the general purposes are (1) to identify specific words that a student does not recognize or cannot say fluenty and (2) to obtain a measure of overall reading fluency. Therefore, two measures are used—*latency* and *rate*. Since automaticity is the primary goal of word recognition, how long (latency) it takes a student to say a word is of as much importance as accuracy. A latency measure is used when the purpose of assessment is to identify specific words that a student can or cannot say without hesitation—typically within one-half to one second. Reading rate is used when overall fluency in reading words is of concern. Words taught as sight words can be tested either in isolation or in context.

FIGURE 6.6
Probe for recognizing words in isolation taken from a basal story.

Student _____				Skill: _____			
Total Number Correct _____				Total Errors _____			
apart	basketball	breath	dinnertime	forgetting	grinned	hour	(7)
knocking	lets	popped	somebody	tagging	wouldn't	basket	(14)
cake	breath	forgets	apart	gives	basketball	grinning	(21)
dinnertime	hugged	hour	learning	knocking	maybe	lets	(28)
seventeen	popped	stuck	somebody	works	tagging	wouldn't	(35)
apart	dinnertime	cake	hour	maybe	learning	knocking	(42)
forgetting	seventeen	gives	grinning	hour	popped	basketball	(49)
breath	grinned	knocking	lets	somebody	tagging	wouldn't	(56)
basket	cake	breath	forgets	apart	gives	basketball	(63)
grinning	grinned	lets	somebody	wouldn't	cake	gives	(70)
weeks	breath	knocking	tagging	grinned	forgetting	seventeen	(77)
somebody	grinning	seventeen	dinnertime	popped	basket	forgets	(84)
dinnertime	hugged	learning	maybe	breathe	cake	hugged	(91)

Performance measure 1: Latency of words read in isolation. The most common method[9] of assessing the latency of words read in isolation is to use flashcards since a teacher controls the rate of presentation. Scoring of words said with or without hesitation is done through the "two pile" method, whereby words correctly said within one-half second are placed in one pile and the remaining words are placed in the other.

Performance measure 2: Rate of saying words in isolation. When measuring rate of word recognition in isolation, timed probes are appropriate. (The flashcards and tachistoscopic methods do not allow for a free operant.) Probe sheets are developed from either the word list used (e.g., Dolch list) or words from the basal reader. When developing probes of this nature, a teacher should consider several things. To ensure a free operant, the probe sheet should contain more responses than the criterion of mastery; for example, if the criterion for mastery was set at 80 words per minute, a 2-minute period probe should contain more than 160 words. Also, each word should be included two or three times on each probe to ascertain whether a student consistently reads it. Therefore, only 20 to 25 different words should be included per probe. Figure 6.6 is an example of a probe sheet based on words from a basal story.

Performance measure 3: Oral reading rate on passages in text. Procedures for

[9]Another method for measuring latency is through the use of a tachistoscope, whereby words from a list can be exposed at a controlled rate.

selecting the passage to be read are the same as those described in performance measure 4 for word attack; they are also discussed in greater detail later in this chapter in the discussion of reading comprehension measures. A teacher instructs a student to read at a fast pace for a specified, brief period of time (i.e., 1 to 5 minutes). If the student hesitates on a word, the teacher supplies the word, checks it on the teacher copy, and tells the student to continue if necessary. At the end of the time period, the teacher calculates the reading rate (i.e., words per minute) and makes a list of words not fluently read.

Level of Assessment

Cognitively, the level of assessment is recognition—students must only associate the sequence of symbols with a word. Behaviorally, the level of assessment is automaticity—students must recognize the sequence of letters automatically.

Error Analysis

First, error analysis is appropriate only for words that are missed more than once. (All readers have occasional lapses.) Teachers have several options for conducting error analyses. We believe the best option is the one that allows a teacher to distinguish between words that a student can read without time constraints and words a student cannot read at all. (Often students are able to recognize—or decode—words that could not be recognized within one-half or one second; thus, students may know the word but have not attained fluency with it.) This distinction is important since there are different teaching procedures for increasing fluency of words already known and teaching unknown words. Therefore, it can be helpful to retest the words that were not read fluently.

A teacher can have the option of conducting a topographical analysis of reading recognition errors. However, some types of errors presented are not very important, while others are critical. Errors of importance include *hesitations* and *aid*—since fluency is critical—as well as *substitutions, mispronunciations*, and *omissions. Reversals* are important if the student reversed letters within the words as opposed to reversing two words but saying each correctly.

Reading Comprehension

Scope and Sequence

Reading comprehension is a common strand in all reading curricula. Whether one advocates *word attack* or *word recognition* to translate visual symbols into sounds and words, these methods of decoding are means[10] to the terminal goal of understanding and using what is read. Reading comprehension can be defined as

[10]It is possible for some disabled readers to pronounce words correctly but not understand what they read. Indeed, it is possible for good readers to correctly pronounce words in a reading selection and not comprehend the material if the grammatical structure is extremely complex or if many technical words with which the reader is unfamiliar are included.

FIGURE 6.7.	Literal	Inferential	Critical
Components and subcomponents of reading comprehension.	*recall details	*infer main idea and details	*identify author's purpose and viewpoint
	*recognize sequence of events	*predict outcomes	*fact vs. opinion
		*infer cause and effect	*fact vs. fantasy
		*draw conclusions	*compare and contrast
		*paraphrase	*make value judgments about content
		*summarize	*identify propaganda/bias
			*judge adequacy/worth of a selection
			*apply ideas presented to solve problems

the ability to obtain meaning from the printed word. It encompasses skills required to understand, to remember, and to apply information contained in phrases, sentences, paragraphs, and entire passages. Therefore, students must be able to choose the correct meanings of words[11] and to understand the meaning of word sequences.

Defining reading comprehension and identifying the scope of skills contained within this reading strand is a more involved (and confusing) process than defining the other reading strands. The reader should be aware that the complex nature of reading comprehension has lead to disagreements among professionals as to the components and subcomponents. This notwithstanding, comprehension is typically broken into components or levels including literal, inferential, and critical. *Literal comprehension* requires a reader to recognize, locate, or recall information explicitly stated within a reading passage. *Inferential comprehension* requires a reader to use information from a passage to make inferences, hypotheses, or extrapolations that go beyond what is explicitly stated in the text. *Critical comprehension* requires a reader to make judgments about different aspects of the reading selection (e.g., fact or fiction, the author's intent). Moreover, each of the three components include several subcomponents, as shown in Figure 6.7.

Even less research and expert consensus exists about the sequence to be followed in teaching comprehension skills. For example, Rosenshine (1980) found no data-based studies about the best sequence for teaching reading comprehension. He also analyzed five frequently used primary reading curricula and found no specific order for presentation of these skills; many of the skills are introduced about the same time. Too, these skills are reintroduced at various points in the curriculum. Only one sequence of skill introduction was common to several of the curricula; locating the main idea was typically introduced later than the other skills (Rosenshine, 1980).

[11]Readers often run across words with multiple (and occasionally contradictory) meanings. Often these words cause no problem in oral communication because they are pronounced differently (e.g., *present* as in "We will *present* a project in class" and "I was *present* when roll was called"). Sometimes they are pronounced in the same way (e.g., *roll* as in "It was the gambler's turn to *roll* the dice" and "That is butter on my *roll*").

As a final introductory point, Ekwall (1981) notes that comprehension is frequently assessed but seldom taught. About the only times students are required to use comprehension skills is when they are tested. If this observation is correct, students—especially those with reading problems—are not provided with enough instruction and supervised practice. This violates a basic tenet of CBA: If you don't teach it, don't test it.

Performance Measures[12]

Like silent reading but unlike oral reading, *comprehension* cannot be measured directly. Comprehension is inferred from a student's responses. Moreover, the difficulties in assessing reading comprehension go beyond those associated with measuring inferred processes. Much of what passes for reading comprehension is more accurately termed language, cognition, memory, literary skills, or prior knowledge.

- *Language.* Most fundamentally, reading comprehension requires understanding the surface structure of language communication—both vocabulary (semantics) and grammar (syntax). Students must understand the core meaning of the words that they read, and the match between the language used by text and by the learner must not be significantly disparate. Reading comprehension cannot exceed general language competence.[13]

- *Cognition/reasoning.* Some measures of reading comprehension require prediction or extrapolation. For prediction, students are asked to go beyond information presented in the reading passage and to anticipate what could logically result. For example, if students read the nursery rhyme "Jack and Jill" they might be asked, "What do you suppose Jack's mother said when he got home with a broken crown?" For extrapolation, students are asked to go beyond information presented in the reading passage and to provide unstated conclusions. For example, students might be asked, "How do you think Jack felt when he went up the hill?" Finally, students may be asked to use high-level study and/or logical skills to demonstrate their comprehension. For example, they may be asked to summarize what they have read, to identify cause-and-effect relationships, or to analyze or synthesize what they have read.

- *Memory.* Memory is also involved in many reading comprehension tasks. After students have read a passage, they may be asked to retell, to recall, or to recognize details and main ideas of a passage.

- *Literary skills.* Literary skills are often taught in conjunction with reading comprehension. Thus, students may be asked to recognize irony, satire, and sarcasm; to recognize and interpret similes, metaphors, or other literary devices; or to interpret poetry.

---

[12]The reader should note that these techniques also can be used to *teach* comprehension as well as measure it.

[13]However, certain handicaps (e.g., deafness) could result in reading comprehension scores that are relatively higher than listening comprehension scores.

- *Prior knowledge.* Another variable that is often, and inadvertently, measured and that can affect comprehension scores is prior knowledge of the content covered in a reading selection. Some students may be considered to have excellent comprehension skills but when presented material with which they have no experience their scores may be atypically low.

Since the assessment of reading comprehension is affected by other skills and abilities, effective performance measures for reading compehension can only minimize the influence that these other skills and abilities can have. Five principles should guide the selection and use of performance measures.

- Measures of reading comprehension should not use vocabulary and sentence structures that are more difficult than those contained in the reading passage.
- Measures of reading comprehension should contain reading comprehension questions at the levels of knowledge and comprehension; teachers should not require responses above comprehension (i.e., analysis, synthesis, and evaluation).
- Measures of reading comprehension should use literal comprehension and translation; teachers should avoid using prediction and extrapolation—as well as the interpretation of irony and various other literary devices.
- Measures of reading comprehension should make available to a student the reading passage that is to be comprehended; teachers should avoid requiring recall/memory.
- When measuring reading comprehension and prior knowledge is suspected to have a possible effect on student performance—as opposed to problems in decoding, basic language skills, and so forth—teachers should assess prior knowledge by asking general questions about the topic. If necessary, the student should be provided relevant background information.

Given this analysis of reading comprehension, teachers have a choice between three performance measures: (1) a sentence verification test, (2) retelling (in students' own words) of information contained in the reading passage, and (3) timed oral reading from a passage.

Performance measure 1: Sentence verification test. The sentence verification test (SVT) has been developed to establish whether a reader has retained the meaning of text read and can recognize whether information in a sentence has the same or different meaning as the original text (Rasool & Royer, 1986; Royer & Cunningham, 1981; Royer, Hastings, & Hook, 1979). Typically, a student is presented with a paragraph of approximately 12 sentences; this length is sufficient to assess comprehension but short enough to be remembered. Without the paragraph present, a student next reads four sentences written by the teacher and indicates which ones means the same as the sentence in the passage (old) and which ones are different in meaning (new). There are four types of test sentences based on each sentence.

1. *Original sentences* are exact copies of sentences in the text.

2. *Paraphrased sentences* have basically the same meaning as the sentence in the text. Original words may be replaced with synonyms, or the ideas from two sentences may be combined. In constructing paraphrased sentences, teachers should avoid using substituting pronouns when their antecedents do not appear in the paraphrased sentence.

3. *Sentences with meaning changes* are sentences that include many of the original words in the sentence, but the overall meaning of the sentence is changed.

4. *Distractor sentences* are sentences about the general topic of the passage and are similar in length and grammar to the original sentence; however, meaning is changed. Generally, it is a good idea to avoid inserting the word *not* into original sentences; it is better to add new, but related, information.

Figure 6.8 contains an example of how a sentence verification test might be constructed for a passage. Each sentence is coded as *OS* for original sentences, *PS* for paraphrased sentences, *MC* for sentences with meaning changes, and *DS* for distractor sentences. (These codes do not, of course, appear on a test, but are included in the example to clarify the procedure.)

Directions:
I want you to read this paragraph to yourself. Tell me when you have finished.

Passage:
Jack and Jill climbed Goose Hill to get some water from the spring in the pine grove at the top. They each carried two empty containers that clanked as they climbed. When they reached the grove and found the spring, they filled their pails and drank their fill. Then they headed back down. It was hot, and Jack stumbled and fell. He rolled head over heels. The water spilled and the now-empty pails clanged. Jack struck his head on a sharp rock. Jill, turning to see what was the commotion, herself tripped and went sprawling. She, however, was unhurt.

Directions:
I want you now to read each sentence below. Next to each sentence, write "old" if there was a sentence in the passage that meant the same thing; old sentences may use different words but they will mean the same thing. Write "new" next to the sentence if this information was not in the paragraph.

Sentence Verification Test:
OS for original sentences, PS for paraphrased sentences, MC for sentences with meaning changes, and DS for distractor sentences.

_____ Jack and Jill went up the hill to bring back some water. (*PS*)
_____ They filled their pails and drank their fill. (*OS*)
_____ The water was cool, and they were refreshed. (*DS*)
_____ It was hot and Jack decided to roll down the hill. (*MC*)

FIGURE 6.8.
An example of a sentence verification test.

Performance criteria used to decide placement in a reading curriculum (e.g., which level or book) have been suggested but at present lack empirical validation. Suggested average performance is 75% correct, and a score of 85% or more indicates the material is too easy, while a score less than 65% indicates the material is too hard. A teacher may also decide to set criteria using a local norming method by administering several SVTs to several students considered to have good comprehension scores and use their mean scores to establish a basis for comparison (i.e., plus or minus 10% of the average would indicate appropriate placement level).

Performance measure 2: Percentage correct paraphrasing or retelling. When using paraphrasing as a performance measure for reading comprehension, students are required to retell, in their own words, what the story is about. Students could be asked to paraphrase paragraphs as they read or wait and paraphrase an entire passage. A combination of both procedures allows a teacher to assess comprehension for both. Teachers have several choices in selecting the criteria that will be used to score a student's retell or paraphrase: the percentage of main ideas, the percentage of supporting details, or the percentage of words. Teachers also can choose to count only verbatim retells, only paraphrased retells, or any retell that contains correct information. Theoretically, paraphrasing is more desirable than retelling because recall may not be the same as understanding. However, the more simple the material is, the more difficult it is to paraphrase. For example, to paraphrase "Sally pulled the red wagon" would require the substitution of more advanced vocabulary and grammar to avoid retelling (e.g., "The crimson cart was towed by Sally"). Therefore, before using paraphrasing, a teacher should ensure that students have appropriate language skills since they will need a fairly large repertoire of synonyms and syntactic structures in order to rephrase textual material. Two relatively simple scoring procedures have been described by Fuchs, Fuchs, & Maxwell (1988) and appear to be valid.[14] The first procedure requires the teacher to tally the words retold, while the second procedure requires calculating the percentage of content words retold. Either scoring procedure should provide comparable estimates of reading comprehension so teachers may wish to use the first measure because it is easier and less time consuming since the teacher does not have to verify whether words retold are correct in terms of the actual passage content. However, the second scoring method should be used periodically because it allows the teacher to ascertain if the retell content is based on the passage. Finally, teachers can choose between oral or written retelling or paraphrasing although written retelling is more highly associated with other measures of comprehension than is oral retelling (Fuchs, Fuchs, & Maxwell, 1988) even though many students with reading difficulties also have problems in written expression.

Performance measure 3: Oral reading rate on passages from text. Fluency in reading passages from text has been mentioned earlier in this chapter as a performance measure for both word recognition and word attack. Interestingly, the number of words read correctly during timed oral reading from text passages is

---

[14]An example of another scoring procedure for paraphrasing is outlined in Chapter 9.

also closely related to comprehension (Deno, 1985; Deno et al, 1982; Fuchs, Fuchs, & Maxwell, 1988). Oral reading rate on passages taken from student readers can be used for both placement in existing curricular materials and as a measure for monitoring a student's general reading progress.

1. *Passage selection*. The criteria for selecting the actual reading passages depend on the purpose of assessment. When assessment data are used for placement within a curriculum, testing should occur over several levels and days to increase reliability.[15] Equivalent passages should be selected from the basal text or the primary curricular material, and the passages should span several levels. Passage lengths should vary according to the age and grade of the student— from 50 words for primary students to 400 words for students at the secondary level. The reading selection should make sense as an independent passage and, therefore, should not start in the middle of an idea or topic. Moreover, the passage should be one the student has not read before. Finally, when the text is from a basal series, passages should be taken from the middle of the text because the beginning and end often contain review material. When using text from content areas (e.g., science or social studies), selections can be taken from any part of the book.[16] If oral reading is used to monitor pupil progress, the passages come from the students' instructional level rather than over several levels. Otherwise, the same criteria for passage selection are used.

2. *Passage preparation*. The passage should be clear and legible with the starting and ending points clearly marked. If teachers wish to conduct error analyses, they should have their own copies to follow along, so it is generally more convenient to have photocopies of the passages. Otherwise, teachers can type the passages or use the actual text.

3. *Provide directions*. Teachers should tell students to read the passage aloud as quickly as they can without making careless errors for a specified period of time (usually from 1 to 5 minutes). If a student hesitates on a word for more than 2 seconds, the teacher should say the word and tell the student to continue.

[15]Typically, assessment continues until the frustration level is found. However, one assessment may not provide reliable data. For example, Fuchs, Fuchs, and Deno (1983) found that, for half the students they tested, the instructional level indicated by a second assessment was above the frustration level indicated on their first test. Therefore, good practice requires sampling reading behavior over several days with several attempts over the same levels. Average performance over these trials can then be used to decide in which text to place a student.

[16]One should not assume that writers and publishers of basal series have controlled for reading level within and between each book and that the reading level follows a sequence of difficulty. Because there is some evidence indicating variability of reading levels within texts (Bradley & Ames, 1978; Fitzgerald, 1980), random selection of passages may not ensure representativeness of the reading level. Moreover, using a readability formula to establish reading level may not help for two reasons. First, the factors used to decide readability such as word length and sentence length do not take into account syntax and the logical flow of the prose (cf. Kemper, 1983). Second, different formulas result in different readability levels when applied to the same passage. For example, Fuchs, Fuchs, and Deno (1983) used six different formulas and found little agreement between them. It appears that teachers are left somewhat to their own devices when selecting passages.

Student performance is scored by counting the number of errors made and the total number of words read correctly. The number of words read correctly is then converted to rate per minute.

While the three preceding performance measures have the advantage of controlling to some extent the impact of other skills (e.g., memory and cognition), other valid and commonly promoted measures exist and are used frequently in classrooms. While these measures provide information about reading skills, teachers should keep in mind that poor performance does not necessarily mean students cannot understand what they read but could have problems related to memory, prior knowledge, and so forth.

Performance measure 4: Cloze procedure. The cloze procedure is used to measure how well contextual clues are used to identify words that have been omitted from text. Student performance on this measure is typically used to place the student in the appropriate reading text/level. Figure 6.9 provides an example of a cloze test. Four steps commonly are used in developing a cloze procedure.

1. Select passage(s) of about 250 words from several levels in the reading curriculum. Ekwall and Shanker (1983) recommend a range of 200 to 300 words and suggest that the smaller number of words should be used with younger students and the larger number with older students.

2. Type the passage, omitting every fifth word; the first and last sentences should be left intact. In place of omitted words, type a blank. The blanks should be of equal length to avoid giving students clues about the length of the missing word. (Passages can be laminated with clear plastic or a plastic overlay can be used so that the test can be used again.)

3. Provide the students with explicit instructions for completing the test. Explain to the students that you want them to read the passage orally—or silently if testing a group of students—and to write the missing words in the blanks. If spelling is not a concern and if the test is individually administered, students may say the missing word. To ensure students understand the task, teachers should demonstrate the procedure and/or allow students to practice with several easy sentences.

4. Score the test and decide reading placement. It is generally suggested that the student must provide the exact missing word in order for the response to be correct. The major reason for this criterion is that it makes scoring easy and reliable. However, if the teacher is primarily concerned with a student's com-

---

FIGURE 6.9.
An example of a cloze procedure using the material from Figure 6.8.

Jack and Jill climbed Goose Hill to get some water from the spring in the pine grove at the top. They each carried two _____ containers that clanked as _____ climbed. When they reached _____ grove and found the _____, they filled their pails _____ drank their fill. Then _____ headed back down. It _____ hot, and Jack stumbled _____ fell. He rolled head _____ heels. The water spilled _____ the now-empty pails _____. Jack struck his head _____ a sharp rock. Jill, _____ to see what was _____ commotion, herself tripped and _____ sprawling. She, however, was _____.

prehension of a passage, synonyms that do not change the meaning of the sentence may be accepted. Additionally, misspellings are not counted as incorrect if the word is identifiable. Reading level is determined from the percentage correct: 57% or higher is considered an independent reading level; 44% to 56% is considered an instructional level; and less than 43% is the frustration level (Ekwall, 1981).

There are four variations of the cloze procedure. First, teachers can choose to delete specific types of words or parts of speech instead of every fifth word. For example, if usage of pronoun referents is of concern, only these words could be deleted. Second, some younger readers may require cues to complete the task. In this case the teacher can provide the first letter (or the first two letters) of the deleted word. Third, a variation of the cloze method called the "maze procedure" is sometimes suggested. With this procedure a student is provided with several words and asked to select the correct one to fill the blank. This mulitple-choice format may be more of a measure of word recognition, language, or prior knowledge than the cloze so caution should be used when interpreting the results. Finally, since one of the problems in using the cloze procedure as a comprehension measure is that it does not assess ability to synthesize or make inferences from the whole passage, a procedure called macro cloze may be used (Whaley, 1981). When using macro cloze, whole-story categories such as setting are deleted and the student reads the passage and provides the missing information.

Performance measure 5: Answering questions based on text. Answering questions based on material included in a reading selection is a frequently used, informal measure of reading comprehension. These questions, typically prepared in select formats (e.g., mulitple-choice questions), are sometimes included with textbooks and basal readers or may be developed by teachers. If the teacher prepares the test, the passage should be preread and important content (i.e., main ideas and relevant details) should be noted. What is selected as *important* content should be consistent with what students have been taught to recognize as important. A teacher should prepare 5 or 10 comprehension questions for each passage (using the general guidelines described in Chapter 4) at the same reading difficulty as the passage. Questions that can be answered "yes" or "no" should be avoided. Types of questions have been suggested by Pearson and Johnson (1979) and include text explicit, text implicit, and script implicit. *Text explicit* questions are about information that is stated directly in the material and are factual in nature (e.g., What happend next? Who took the bus to the store? Where did Bob and Ray go?). *Text implicit* questions require inference on a student's part (e.g., Why did Fred go to the store? What caused the party to break up?). Questions that cannot be answered unless the student has prior knowledge or experience about the topic or material are *script implicit*. For example, a passage may simply describe a forest as green, but a student might be asked, "What makes the leaves green?" The expected answer, chlorophyll, would not be included in the text.

A teacher should tell a student to read (orally or silently) the passage and explain that questions will be asked—orally or in writing—about what has been read. If the teacher wishes to control for memory, the student can be allowed access to the passage when answering. The teacher then scores the student's responses and estimates comprehension level as independent, instructional, or frustration. Commonly used criteria for deciding levels are 90% or greater for independent reading, 75% to 89% for instructional reading, and below 75% for frustration.

Level of Assessment

Literal, inferential, and critical comprehension obviously represent different levels of understanding, and these levels of understanding require different levels of assessment. For beginning students, reading comprehension is best assessed at the literal level. Here, the recognition or recall of main ideas and important details is stressed. With students who are learning more advanced topics (literature, history, and so forth), however, teachers may be interested in other types of comprehension. Inferential comprehension requires a student to analyze and/or synthesize information in order to draw appropriate conclusions. Critical comprehension requires a student to evaluate what is read and make judgments about worth.

Error Analysis

For literal comprehension, the most important potential errors are related to vocabulary and grammar. Teachers should ascertain if a student's errors in literal comprehension can be attributed to ignorance of the meaning of the words used in a passage or to ignorance of the grammatical structure used. For example, many readers have difficulty understanding the message of William F. Buckley's prose because of his arcane and esoteric lexicon. More practically, deaf readers often have trouble understanding relatively simple grammatic transformations (Power & Quigley, 1973). For example, a large proportion of these students use word position within sentences to gain meaning. Thus, a sentence such as "The girl was hit by the boy," would be understood as the girl hit the boy. While problems of semantics and syntax should be considered language problems, they are often addressed within reading curricula. Thus, systematic instruction to overcome weaknesses in these areas can be initiated.

When students understand the vocabulary and grammar within their reading passages but still do not understand what they have read, several possible errors should be investigated. First, students might be reading so slowly—or devoting so much attention to decoding—that they lose their trains of thought. In such cases, increasing reading speed can significantly improve their comprehension. Second, if students are reading at satisfactory rates, they may have trouble grasping the main idea or relevant details within a passage. Paraphrasing and summarizing strategies can be useful in improving performance (Brown, 1978; Palinscar, 1986).

Summary

In this chapter reading curricula are broken into three major strands: word attack, word recognition, and reading comprehension. Word attack, or decoding, is typically taught through phonics and structural analysis. In essence, students are taught to memorize the sounds of letters and groups of letters along with numerous phonic rules and to use this knowledge to sound out unfamiliar words. Measures of student ability to use word-attack skills range from saying isolated sounds to reading words in passages taken from student readers. Error analysis can help the teacher identify general types of reading errors as well as zero in on errors related to particular phonic skills.

Curricula stressing word recognition require students to memorize whole words. Often, curricula of this type take the form of word lists consisting of commonly used words found in basal readers or functional words necessary for independent living in a variety of settings or environments. Performance measures for assessing student ability in this strand include identification of specific words as well as overall reading fluency. When conducting an analysis of word recognition errors teachers are typically concerned with substitutions, hesitations, mispronunciations, and omissions.

Reading comprehension, the ability to understand what is read at a variety of levels (e.g., literal, inferential, and critical), is difficult to measure since comprehension can only be inferred rather than directly measured. Additionally, common reading comprehension measures sample a variety of skills (e.g., memory, prior knowledge about the information contained in a reading selection, interest in the topic). Several measures that minimize the influence of skills other than comprehension were discussed along with other commonly used reading comprehension assessment procedures.

One measure common to all three strands is the rate of oral reading. While somewhat tentative, rate of correct words read per minute from a passage taken from a student's reading material appears to be a valid, overall measure of reading ability. This measure also has the advantage of taking little time to develop, administer, and score. It may be more realistic, in terms of time constraints, for teachers to use this measure for formative purposes and periodically to use the other measures mentioned in this chapter to identify specific types of problems or errors a student may be experiencing.

Extended Example 1

Scenario

Tom is a sixth-grader with above average intelligence. He was diagnosed as having a learning disability in reading, and he was placed in a part-time special-education resource room. His decoding skills were deficient: On a nationally standardized reading achievement test, he scored equal to or better than about 12% of students in his grade; using his peers in Mr. Wright's class, he could not read the materials used by the slowest students. His approach to oral reading could be characterized as slow and word-by-word; in fourth-grade material his rate of reading is less than 80 words per minute with an error rate of about 4 words per minute. Both his reading and listening comprehension were excellent. While Tom had some difficulties in content areas, the multidisciplinary team attributed them to his reading problems. His math skills were excellent.

Since Tom had completed six years of reading instruction and his progress had been so limited, it was decided to abandon systematic instruction in word-attack skills. Instead, Mr. Wright decided to concentrate on increasing both his sight vocabulary and his reading speed.

Step 1: Specify Reasons for Assessment

Regular assessments were conducted to monitor Tom's progress in reading. Data from these assessments could be used to alter his resource-room program should it prove ineffective.

Step 2: Analyze the Curriculum

The three sources of sight vocabulary were the American Heritage word list,[17] Tom's spelling lists, and words from his previous reading series that had not been mastered. Mastery of the American Heritage list would significantly improve Tom's ability to read in school and in his everyday life. Mastery of previously assigned reading and spelling vocabulary should fit directly into his future curricula.

Since Tom's IEP specified that he receive assistance only in reading, Mr. Wright devoted all of his efforts to the area. During the first week of the year, Mr. Wright, with the able assistance of his aide, conducted an extensive evaluation of Tom's sight vocabulary. Through grade five reading materials, there were 356 words that could not be read fluently. Tom could not read an additional 461 words from his spelling texts. Finally, Tom did not know 47 words from the American Heritage word list. Thus, Tom would need to learn 864 words in addition to any new words that might be assigned during the year. Mr. Wright decided to try to teach all of the words in the 35 weeks that remained in the school year. If Tom could learn 25 words each week, he could meet his goal. To develop the pool of words for each week, Mr. Wright first selected unknown words from Tom's reading passage. These words were taught first. To the words from the week's reading passages, Mr. Wright added words from previous readers and spelling lists that Tom had not mastered. When Tom mastered these previously unlearned words, words from the American Heritage list were added.

Step 3: Formulate Objectives

First, behavioral objectives were developed for the acquisition and maintenance of sight vocabulary. In addition, since emphasis was placed on Tom's rate of oral reading, a third objective addressed his oral reading speed.

Behavioral Objective 1: Given a flashcard with a previously unknown word, Tom will say the word within 1 second on two consecutive days.[18]

Behavioral Objective 2: Given a flashcard with a recently learned word, Tom will say the word within 1 second.

[17]The first 500 words in this list comprise about 90% of all written English.

[18]Mr. Wright wanted to increase the chances of Tom retaining the words he learned so he decided to have Tom met the 1-second latency criterion on two consecutive days.

Behavioral Objective 3: Given a reading passage for which Tom could read each word fluently, Tom will read the passage orally at a rate of at least 100 words per minute.

Step 4: Develop Appropriate Assessment Procedures

Mr. Wright developed a simple assessment procedure for each objective. To assess ascquisition and maintenance of sight vocabulary. Mr. Wright decided to have his aide handle most of the daily testing using the "two-pile" method. To assess oral reading, Mr. Wright used a stopwatch to see how long Tom took to read a passage of at least 300 words. Mr. Wright followed along with Tom and circled any words that Tom missed.

Steps 5 and 6: Collect and Summarize Data

Collection

For testing Tom's acquisition of new words, Mr. Wright or his aide initially used the following directions.

> Tom, we're going to check this week's words now. I'll show you the word, and you say it as quickly as you can. If you say the word in 1 second or less, it will go into your pile. If you take more than 1 second or say it incorrectly, it will go into my pile.

Later, the directions were shortened: "Tom, it's time to check you on this week's words."

To assess maintenance of newly acquired words, Mr. Wright also used the flashcard method for twice-weekly probes. For the first few maintenance probes, Tom was told:

> We're going to see if you remember some of the words that you learned so far this year. We'll do this the same way we always do. I'll show you the word, and you say it as quickly as you can. If you say the word in a second, it goes in your pile. If you've forgotten the word, we'll add it to this week's list so you can practice it some more.

When Tom got used to maintenance testing, the directions were shortened: "Tom, it's time to check you on the words you've learned."

The directions used to test Tom's rate of oral reading were a bit more involved. The first time Tom was tested, he was told:

> Tom, I want you to read at least 100 words per minute in your texts. This [pointing to the passage] is from one of your books. Read it as fast as you can, but not so fast that you make careless errors. I'll time you. Any questions?

If Tom reads at a rate of less than 100 wpm, he is told his rate and that he will have to reread the passage because his rate was less than 100 wpm.

Summarization

Sight Vocabulary. Since the instructional objective required correct responses on two consecutive days, Mr. Wright developed a coding system for the flashcard. When Tom finished the words, the back of each flashcard in the known pile was marked with a "+". On subsequent tests, flashcards in the known pile that had a plus were removed; if a card in the unknown pile had a plus, the plus was crossed out. As words are learned, Mr. Wright deletes them from his master list of words Tom has acquired. Also, Mr. Wright enters the number of words Tom learns each week in his gradebook.

    Reading Rate. After administering each oral reading probe, Mr. Wright tabulates Tom's rate (i.e., wpm and errors per 100 words). These are also entered in his gradebook.

Steps 7 and 8: Display Data; Interpret Data, and Make Decisions

Mr. Wright used two different graphs to display Tom's performances. On the first graph he displayed the percentage of words Tom has learned and recalled each week. As shown in Figure 6.10, Tom did very well, learning between 95% and 100% of each week's words. Moreover, his recall was quite good. Mr. Wright did

FIGURE 6.10.
Percent of words learned and recalled by Tom.

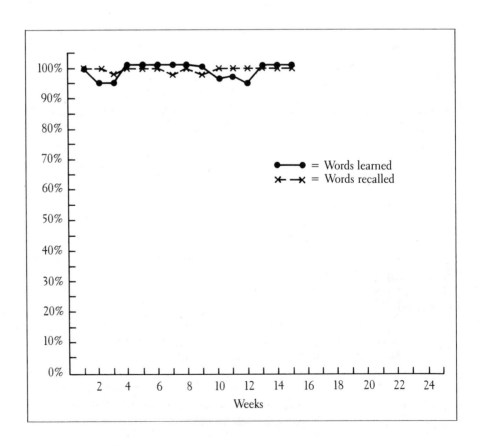

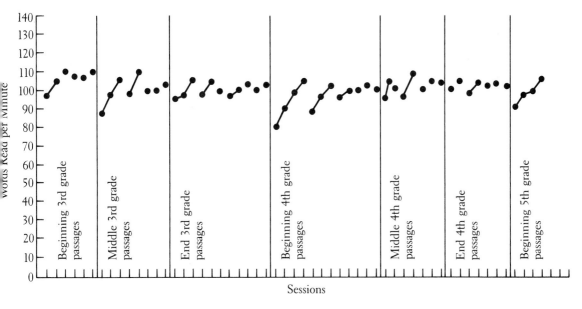

Note: Connect points indicate reread material.

FIGURE 6.11.   Tom's reading (and rereading) rates.

not consider increasing the number of words Tom should learn each week because Tom would catch up by the end of the year.

On the second graph, Mr. Wright plotted Tom's rate of oral reading. Rates for the same passage are connected, and vertical lines separate passages from different reading levels. As shown in Figure 6.11, Tom started reading materials written at beginning third grade. After four passages, Tom's rate regularly exceeded 100 words per minute on the first reading. Along the way, Mr. Wright decided that when Tom could read three consecutive passages above the target rate, he would move Tom up a third of a grade level. As shown in Figure 6.11, Tom advanced rapidly until fifth-grade material, where his progress slowed considerably. Mr. Wright thought that Tom's slowdown was predictable—Tom should make the greatest progress on the easiest material. Therefore, he continued the intervention.

Summary

Mr. Wright decided to stop instruction in word-attack skills and concentrate on sight vocabulary and rate of oral reading. First, he assembled a sight vocabulary curriculum from several sources. He then developed systematic instructional procedures. Tom was assessed frequently to monitor his acquisition and maintenance of the sight vocabulary. Mr. Wright also required Tom to read orally each day, and Tom's daily performance was graphed. Tom progressed rapidly and really enjoyed the charts. He did get bored occasionally, but with a bit of encouragement he would renew his effort.

Extended Example 2

Scenario

Mike and his family just moved into the school district, and he has been in Mr. Borkowski's resource room. The fourth-grade class into which Mike will be mainstreamed is using a Ginn reading series. Mike's parents report that reading has been his major difficulty in school, but that is all the information Mr. Borkowski has received about Mike.

Step 1: Specify Reason for Assessment

Mr. Borkowski decides to assess Mike's oral reading to ascertain a starting place for instruction in that strand. Specifically, he wants to determine Mike's rates of oral reading and errors in materials of varying degrees of difficulty. He will then use rate and accuracy to make his initial placement within the reading curriculum.

Step 2: Analyze the Curriculum

Mr. Borkowski plans to use a skip-and-drill procedure (Lovitt & Hansen, 1976) to help Mike get to grade level in the Ginn series as quickly as possible. Since this series is graded in terms of grammatical, lexical, and conceptual difficulty, gradations correspond to passages at the beginning, middle, and end of levels. At this stage of assessment, Mr. Borkowski is interested only in reading fluency and comprehension.

Step 3: Formulate Behavioral Objectives

Since the purpose is to locate the reading level where instruction should begin, objectives will not be formulated until after the initial assessment.

Steps 4, 5, 6, and 7: Develop Good Assessment Procedures; Collect, Summarize, and Display Data

Mr. Borkowski assembles the primary readers through grade six to develop reading probes that are representative of the beginning, middle, and end of each reading level. He selects passages that meet the following criteria.

- The passage forms a logical unit. The selection always starts at a new paragraph and comprehension does not depend on preceding, unread material.
- The passage contains between 150 and 200 words.
- The sight vocabulary is generally representative of the reading level in the series.

Mr. Borkowski makes two photocopies of each passage—one for Mike and one for himself. On his own copy, he wrote the cumulative number of words at the end of each line of text.

While the other students are occupied with seatwork, Mr. Borkowski and Mike go to a quiet corner of the room where Mike is given the following instructions.

Mike, I want to see how you read so I know what I should be working on with you. We may do things a little differently in this class than the last class you were in. In here, we want you to read as quickly as you can without making errors. If there is a word you don't know, ask me and I'll tell you what it is. To see how quickly you can read, I'm going to time you. Do you have any questions?

Mike responded that he did not like to read out loud, but that he understood the task. Mr. Borkowski assured him that many students in the class had reading problems when they arrived, that he would try to help Mike become a better reader as he had helped other students in the class, and that no one was allowed to comment on anyone else's reading. Mike then agreed to read for him.

Because Mike was a still a bit nervous and had a history of reading difficulties, Mr. Borkowski began probing with the beginning first-grade material. He gave Mike the first passage, told him to begin at the beginning of the passage, and started his stop watch when Mike began. As Mike read, his teacher underlined mispronounced and unknown words and wrote in any words that his student inserted. When Mike had read for 3 minutes, Mr. Borkowski put a slash on his own copy after the last word read. He then asked Mike literal comprehension questions on the material he had read and noted both the number of questions asked and the number of questions answered correctly. Mike was commended for his effort, and then the probe was quickly scored. Mr. Borkowski tallied the number of reading errors and divided the number of words read by 3. He then entered these data in a summary table (see Table 6.3). Testing was terminated when Mike's rate fell below 30 words per minute.

Step 8: Interpret Data and Make Decisions

After testing was completed and Mike had rejoined the class, Mr. Borkowski looked at the data in the summary table. Mike handled beginning and mid-first-grade work well. His reading and error rates were acceptable, as was his comprehension. By the end of first-grade material, his comprehension was still good, but his rates for oral reading and making errors indicated he could not read these materials independently. Beginning second-grade material was at the frustration level.

Based on these findings, Mr. Borkowski would begin skip-and-drill activities with the end of first-grade passages. Also, since Mike could not read grade level materials, Mr. Borkowski arranged for Mike to borrow taped versions of the texts used in content areas so that Mike could keep up with his peers in mainstream settings. Finally, Mr. Borkowski knew that taking written tests would be difficult for Mike. Therefore, he met with Mike's regular classroom teacher (Ms. Smythe), explained that Mike should be tested orally since he did not read well, and volunteered to test Mike when he was in the resource room. Ms. Smythe said she understood that Mike had problems reading, but that it would not be fair to

TABLE 6.3 Summary of Oral Reading	Student _Mike Rogers_		Date Tested: _10/19/1988_
Reading Material/Level	WPM	No. Errors	Compre-hension Checks (No. Correct/ No. Asked)
Ginn 1^1	_63_	_1_	_3/3_
Ginn 1^2	_68_	_1_	_3/3_
Ginn 1^3	_32_	_7_	_3/3_
Ginn 2^1	_17_	_13_	_1/3_

the other students to give him special consideration on tests. Mr. Borkowski pressed his point, but to no avail. He left the meeting expecting that, even if he got Mike up to grade level in reading by the end of the year, he would probably fail in his content areas.

Summary

Mr. Borkowski got a new student with reading difficulties. He developed a set of curriculum-based probes in about 30 minutes. With an additional 15 minutes of effort, he located the starting point for reading instruction.

Chapter 7

Curriculum-Based Assessment in Mathematics

Key Terms

Abstract level	Operations
Algorithm	Problem solving
Concrete level	Semiconcrete level
Materials	

Mathematics curricula focus on the development of concepts, skills, and applications related to numbers. Math has been characterized as a spiraling curriculum because some skills are repeated over time as review or as part of more advanced operations. For example, addition facts taught in earlier grades will emerge later when students are required to compute multiple-digit multiplication problems. Because of the interconnection of basic skills, math is largely cumulative in nature; certain skills must be taught and mastered before introduction of others.

The domain of mathematics includes a wide variety of general goals or skills. In 1977, the National Council of Supervisors of Mathematics developed a list of goals for developmental mathematics instruction. These goals were intended to delineate the overall domain of mathematics; 10 general goals were included.

1. *Problem solving.* Students should be able to apply acquired skills to unfamiliar situations that require analysis, logic, and translating solutions into numerical expressions.

2. *Applying mathematics to everyday situations.* Given everyday situations, students should be able to select and use appropriate computational skills.

3. *Alertness to the reasonableness of results.* Students should be able to inspect computational results to see if their answers make sense in light of the original problem.

4. *Estimation and approximation.* Using "rounding off" procedures, students should quickly estimate calculations. Also, simple techniques for estimating quantity, weight, distance, and so forth should be acquired, as well as the ability to decide how precise a result should be in a particular situation.

5. *Appropriate computational skills.* While many long or complicated calculations are done with computers or pocket calculators, students should be able to compute mentally single-digit number facts, simple fractions, and percentages—especially as they apply to consumer situations.

6. *Geometry.* Geometric concepts and properties as they relate to communicating about environment and solving problems involving measurement are important in everyday living. These concepts and properties include point, line, parallel, and perpendicular lines, as well as simple geometric figures (e.g., circle, triangle).

7. *Measurement.* Measurement of time, distance, volume, and temperature are important, and students should be able to measure them using both metric and imperial systems.

8. *Reading, interpreting, and constructing tables, charts, and graphs.* Summarizing and considering numerical data make the data more meaningful and manageable. Students also should be able to read and to draw conclusions when given data visually.

9. *Using mathematics to predict.* Basic knowledge of probability is useful in predicting future events. Students should know how mathematics is used to make a variety of predictions.

10. *Computer literacy.* Because of the computer's increasing role in society, it is important for people to understand what computers can and cannot (as yet) do.

While these broad curricular goals have been established for typical students, some students have difficulty learning all of the skills. Many educationally handicapped students require repeated exposure to skills and concepts before achieving mastery. Thus, the amount of material covered during their educational careers necessarily will be limited. For these students a less inclusive curriculum, with the overall goal of helping them to function independently in society, is needed.

A functional mathematics curriculum is intended to teach application of numerical skills and concepts in the context of everyday situations. While many of the basic skills usually found in a functional mathematics curriculum are also included in a typical developmental curriculum, the goal is to help students cope in the contexts of work, leisure, consumer, residential, and transportation situations.

The goals discussed above provide a global description of instructional intent and content within the domain of mathematics. However, most curricula are more precise as to the behaviors or skills taught and the order in which they are presented.

Scope and Sequence of Mathematics Curricula

"Scope" and "sequence" refer to skills and concepts included (scope) and when they occur (sequence) within the math curriculum. Many published math curricula include a scope and sequence chart within the instructor's manual.[1] However, before developing CBA materials, it is best to ensure that skills included in the chart coincide with the skills actually taught. It is also important to ascertain whether the order of presentation matches the sequence presented in the chart. Since students' texts do not always correspond to the scope and sequence chart, teachers should verify the actual scope and sequence by scanning each page of text or material and noting the skill(s) included, as well as the number of each type of problem. If done systematically (i.e., as a written outline), this procedure provides the teacher with the specific skills covered, how often they are presented, and on what page they are presented.

Scope and sequence vary between curricula. There is no universal agreement as to content or order of skills. In one curriculum, third-graders may be introduced to problems that require regrouping in the division of two-digit numbers by one-digit numbers. In another curriculum, this type of problem may not be introduced until the fourth grade. Some curricula stress the development of vocabulary as a readiness skill while others cover vocabulary in a cursory fashion. Finally, the level of mastery set for certain skills may also vary. Schmidt (1978) and Freeman et al. (1983) have analyzed mathematics curricula and have found wide variation in their contents. Similarly, Shriner and Salvia (in press) compared the content of *Scott Foresman Mathematics* (Bolster et al., 1983) and *Distar Arithmetic* (Engelman & Carnine, 1976) in the first three grades. They found that the two curricula differed significantly on their coverage and emphasis on:

- *Operations* (i.e., identification of equivalents, ordering, addition without regrouping, addition with regrouping, column addition, subtraction without regrouping, subtraction with regrouping, multiplication, division without remainder, division with remainder, combinations of operations, concepts and terms, properties, place value, and estimation)
- *Materials* on which the operations were performed (i.e., single digits, single and multiple digits, multiple digits, number sentences, algebraic sentences, single like fractions, unlike fractions, mixed numbers, decimals, percent, measurements, geometry, and other)
- *Types of cognitive demands* (knowledge, computation, comprehension, and application).

Although the emphases placed on content and the way in which content spirals across curricula *vary*, it is, nonetheless, possible to discuss in the most general terms strands of mathematics content and typical sequences *within* strands that

---

[1]When student texts are not appropriate, teachers may wish to consult general professional texts that usually contain suggested scopes and sequences for mathematics. Also, many local and state education agencies have developed their own.

FIGURE 7.1. Curricular strands and components.	*Readiness Skills:* Classification, one-to-one correspondence, ordering and seriation, conservation of quantity, conservation of number, and rote counting.
	Vocabulary and Concepts: Quantity concepts (e.g., same, equal, larger, greater, bigger, more than, smaller, less than, taller, fewer, longer, and so on) and positional/spatial concepts (e.g., left, right, above, below, top, bottom, front, under, over, behind, next to, between, and so forth).
	Numeration: Writing numbers, recognizing/identifying numbers, comparing and ordering whole numbers, and counting by 2s, 3s, 5s, and 10s.
	Whole Number Operations: Addition, subtraction, multiplication, and division.
	Fractions: Writing and identifying fractions, conversion to lowest terms, addition, subtraction, multiplication, and division.
	Decimals: Writing and identifying, rounding off to designated place, addition, subtraction, multiplication, and division.
	Ratio and Percent: Converting (fractions to percents, decimals to percents, ratios to fractions).
	Measurement: Linear, time, money, weight, temperature, and capacity.
	Geometry: Identifying shapes, identifying lines, identifying angles, identifying congruency of lines and shapes, and measurement of geometric figures.

are more or less representative. Figure 7.1 contains common strands and their components.

It is generally assumed that certain number-readiness skills and concepts must be mastered prior to instruction in math operations. Once students have demonstrated mastery of concepts related to quantity, order, and number, they are usually instructed in *numeration*. This curricular strand emphasizes identifying numerals, writing and ordering them, and rote counting. Later numeration skills include identifying place value and rounding off whole numbers to the nearest 10s, 100s, and so forth places.

Whole numbers are the core of the elementary math curriculum. They require students to solve whole-number problems using the operations of addition, subtraction, multiplication, and division. While the order of instruction of these operations is usually the same as indicated here,[2] presentation of subcomponents of the operation is more varied. For example, while addition problems are introduced first in a curricular sequence, subtraction is often introduced after students master single-digit problems with sums between 0 and 9. Then, after single-digit subtraction facts with differences between 0 and 9 are memorized, the curriculum may return to addition facts with sums between 10 and 18.

The *fraction* strand commonly begins with readiness activities such as dividing

[2]The order is not invariant. For example, addition may be followed by multiplication with instruction in subtraction and division following.

figures into regions, introducing vocabulary (e.g., numerator, denominator, lowest common denominator). Once readiness skills are introduced and mastered, computation begins using the basic operations. Again, the sequence is variable. For example, fifth-graders may be asked to solve fraction problems using addition and subtraction but will not be asked to multipy or divide fractions until the sixth grade.

Finally, *decimals*, *ratios*, and *percents* are usually introduced after fractions. *Measurement* and *geometry* are included in curricula at several levels.

An additional strand not included in Figure 7.1 (but sometimes identified as a separate strand) is *problem solving*. Problem solving also may be viewed as a component of most strands in which students may be asked to answer word problems that require comprehension of what is read and varying sentence structures, logic (especially set inclusion and exclusion), and a variety of operations (Bachor, Steacy, & Freeze, 1986). Therefore, students are required to go beyond using correct algorithms and computation. They must be able to:

- Understand what is called for in the problem
- Identify relevant and irrelvant information
- Estimate and organize multiple steps into a correct sequence
- Select the correct operations
- Compute the answer
- Check the answer

Since a variety of skills and competencies are required for solving problems, teachers should examine where problems occur. Was the reading level too high? Is the student actually capable of the computation required? Does the student have problems when two or more steps are required? Is the amount of information a factor? More information can help or hinder completion of word problems. Increasing the amount of relevant information reduces the difficulty of the problem (Bachor, Steacy, & Freeze, 1986). For example, a student might be given the following problem. Fay and Jim went to the seashore. Fay saw 3 starfish, 5 crabs, and a porpoise. Jim saw 13 clams and 2 whales. Fay and Jim are children. Starfish, crabs, and clams are shellfish. How many shellfish did the children see? Telling a student that Fay and Jim are children and that starfish, crabs, and clams are shellfish lengthens the problem but adds information about set inclusion. Thus, this problem would be easier than the same problem without that information. Too, when teachers give word problems with additional, but irrelevant, information, they complicate the problems. For example, a student might be given the following problem. Fay and Jim went to the seashore. Fay saw 3 starfish, 5 crabs, and a porpoise. Fay's dog, Mike, barked at 3 more starfish. Jim saw 13 clams and 2 whales. They enjoyed the visit to the shore. How many shellfish did the children see? Mike is not a child, and its actions are irrelevant to the solution of the problem. Moreover, when some students read the word "more" they use it as a cue to add. Thus, the information about Mike is not only irrelevant, it may actually mislead some students. Englert, Cullata, and Horn

(1987) found that the addition of irrelevant linguistic and numerical information to addition word problems significantly increased their difficulty for students with learning disabilities. Additionally, it was found that word problems containing irrelevant numerical information were more difficult for the subjects used in the study than problems including irrelevant linguistic information. According to these and the findings of others (e.g., Goodstein, Cawley, Gordon, & Helfgott, 1971; Thibodeau, 1974), teachers can gain important information about a student's problem-solving skills by systematically varying the amount of irrelevant information contained in a word problem. Assessments of this type can allow teachers to discern whether errors are due to computation errors or difficulties in comprehending the problem to be solved.

Assessment of Mathematics Skills

In the assessment of a student's skills in mathematics, teachers have several options related to performance measures and proficiency levels. They also need to decide if they will conduct a careful analysis of student errors. All of these options depend, at least in part, on their reasons for assessment and on the curriculum, especially the forms that instruction and practice take.

Performance Measures

A variety of presentation and response modes exist for math assessment. One method for stating the different ways problems are presented and students are asked to respond is through learning channels, as used in precision teaching. Examples are provided in Figure 7.2. The stimulus is stated in terms of the sensory or internal process used by a student and the response is stated in terms of how a student will answer. Which one to choose depends largely on how the skill

FIGURE 7.2. Methods of presentation and response.

Presentation	Problem	Response	Explanation
See	subtraction of 2-digit numbers with regrouping	**Write**	Student is given a worksheet with written problems and writes answers
Hear	addition problems with sums to 18	**Write**	Teacher dictates problems and student writes answers on answer sheet
See	multiplication problems with answers from 0 to 9	**Say**	Teacher presents problems visually (e.g., on flashcards) and student answers orally
Hear	subtraction facts with minuends from 0 to 9	**Say**	Teacher dictates problems and student answers orally
See	reducing fractions to lowest common denominator	**Select**	Student is given a worksheet and selects correct answers from multiple-choice arrays

is taught and practiced during instruction, and the functional importance of a student responding in one or more ways to a variety of stimuli.

Moreover, skill components may be measured in more than one way. For example, knowledge of geometric shapes may be measured by requesting a student to draw a trapezoid or to select one when presented with several shapes (including a trapezoid). Some students might be required to solve computational problems mentally, while others may be given a calculator to use. Some students might be required to perform simulations (e.g., complete a worksheet in which a student compares similar grocery items and chooses the best buy), while others may be required to perform the task physically (e.g., to go to the store and select the best buy). Finally, the criterion (e.g., percent correct, rate, quality) included in a behavioral objective and the performance measure used should be parallel, as illustrated by the following peformance measures.

Performance measure 1: Percentage correct. Regardless of the target behavior, percentage correct can be an appropriate performance measure for almost any component or subcomponent (e.g., operations, measurement, vocabulary, concepts) in a math curriculum. The use of percentage correct is appropriate in four circumstances. First, it should be used when accuracy and acquisition are of primary interest. Second, it should be used if the purpose of assessment is to survey student ability to perform a variety of skills in order to identify possible problem areas, although attention should be paid to which types of problems give trouble to a student. Third, when it is not practical to have a free operant, percentages are appropriate. Fourth, percentages should be used when establishing rate criteria may be too cumbersome. For example, it is difficult to establish rate criteria for word problems since there are so many variables that may influence the rate at which they are solved—linguistic and numerical distractors, number and type of operations needed to solve the problem, number of words, reading level, using pronouns versus nouns, and so forth. It is simpler, then, to score student performance as percentage correct.

To use percentage correct, a teacher first establishes criteria for what constitutes a correct response. For example, a teacher may want students to show all their work, count the number of correct digits in a problem (as opposed to counting completely correct answers), or circle their answers. Next, a teacher must set criteria for acceptable performance. Since percentage correct is so often used at the acquisition stage of learning, 90% is often selected for stand-alone skills.

Performance measure 2: Rate of correct responses. Rate is the measure of choice when assessing performance on a single, discrete skill and if fluency (accurate and fast performance) is of primary concern. Like percentage correct, rate can be used with most skills taught in typical math curricula.

When measuring rate of performance, a teacher administers timed probes and calculates rate per minute. The development of probes is discussed in Chapter 4, and two examples of written probes are included in the first extended example in this chapter (see Figures 7.7 and 7.8). A teacher first establishes criteria for what constitutes a correct response. The same criteria used for establishing correct responses for percentage correct may be used. Finally, teachers must set criteria for acceptable performance. Suggested performance rates for whole number op-

FIGURE 7.3.		Digits Correct/Minute
Suggested performance rates for visually presented mathematics exercises.	*Numeration*	
	Write random numbers	80
	Say random numbers	100
	Addition	
	Write addition facts (0–9)	50
	Write addition facts (10–18)	60
	Write sums of 1- and 2-digit addends, no regrouping	80
	Write sums of 1- and 2-digit addends, regrouping	70
	Write sums of 2- and 2-digit addends, no regrouping	70
	Write sums of 2- and 2-digit addends, regrouping	60
	Subtraction	
	Write subtraction facts (minuends 2–9)	50
	Write differences, 2-digit less 1-digit problems, no regrouping	80
	Write differences, 2-digit less 1-digit problems, regrouping	70
	Write differences, 2-digit less 2-digit problems, no regrouping	70
	Write differences, 2-digit less 2-digit problems, regrouping	60
	Multiplication	
	Write multiplication facts, 0–9	50
	Write products of 1-digit and 2-digit multiplicands, no regroup-ing	40
	Write products of 1-digit and 2-digit multiplicands, regrouping	30
	Division	
	Write quotients for single-digit divisors, no remainders	50
	Write quotients for two-digit divisors, no remainders	40
	Write quotients for two-digit divisors, remainders	40

[a]Adapted from Florida Department of Education, 1983); Howell and Kaplan (1980); Great Falls (1981); Mercer and Mercer (1985); and Mercer, Mercer, and Evans (1982).

erations are presented in Figure 7.3. If the skill in question is not included in Figure 7.3, teachers can use other methods for establishing rate criteria described in Chapter 3.

Level of Assessment

In most classrooms assessment of math computation takes place on the abstract level. At this level a student is required to solve problems using numerals that are abstractions or symbols of actual things (i.e., 3 balls plus 4 balls is written as the math sentence, $3 + 4 = ?$). Some writers in the area of mathematics (Mercer & Mercer, 1985; Reisman, 1984; Underhill, Uprichard, & Heddens, 1980) maintain that assessment and instruction should also take place at other more concrete levels in order for a student's skill to be measured adequately and instruction to be planned. Underhill, Uprichard, and Heddens (1980) stated that later problems in math may, in part, result from earlier failure to understand fully these underlying (and basic) concepts. It therefore behooves teachers to assess for the level of understanding when measuring a student's performance on a particular skill. These levels include the concrete, semiconcrete, and abstract.

A student is presented with the problem, "9–6," and given the following directions: "Here are nine marks. Draw a circle around three marks. How many marks are left?"

/   /   /   /   /   /   /   /   /

FIGURE 7.4.
A math problem at the
semiconcrete level.

The *concrete* level requires a student to manipulate objects to solve problems. It involves attending to both the objects and procedures used to solve the problems. For example, a student may be presented with the problem, "9 − 6," and then be required to count out 9 blocks, to remove 6 of them, and to count the remaining blocks in order to find the difference. Students with documented learning difficulties often use concrete methods (e.g., counting on fingers) more often than their normally achieving peers (Connors, 1983).

The *semiconcrete* level involves assessing whether a student requires other aids such as illustrations, tally lines, or fingers to solve a problem. For example, a student is presented with the problem, "9 − 6." If the student cannot recall the fact immediately, a teacher could present the problem, as shown in Figure 7.4, to see if the student solves the problem at the semiconcrete level.

The *abstract level* requires a student to solve problems using numerals only. Thus, if a teacher asked, "What is 9 − 6?" the student would be expected to write or to say "3."

Error Analysis

A typical method used to score student performance on math computation is to mark answers correct or incorrect, compute the percentage or rate correct, and place the score on the top of the paper—perhaps along with a letter grade or "smiley face." If assessment is carried out in this way, the teacher may be missing important information. For example, two students may miss the same problems but for different reasons. Therefore, it is not only important to discover that students cannot compute a particular type of problem, but also "why" they cannot; in many instances the student is applying a rule to solve the problem but it happens to be the wrong one. This information is critical since the type of error pattern may directly influence instructional objectives and, perhaps, instructional methods used to remediate the performance.

If a teacher notices frequent errors in certain types of problems, for either individual or groups of students, a closer examination may be warranted using the following guidelines (Ashlock, 1986; Howell & Kaplan, 1980):

1. Make sure enough problems of the type being assessed are included so an adequate sample of a student's work is obtained.
2. Make notes on patterns of performance while the student is solving the problems to guide later questioning. Do not provide instruction during the assessment since its purpose is data collection and not remediation. If errors are

continually pointed out to students, they may be less likely to perform in their usual fashion.

3. Ask students to tell how the problems were worked after they have finished answering or while they are solving them, and record their responses. Here, too, it is better to accept responses without comment and any time pressures and to leave the teaching for later.

Various schemes for classifying student errors in arithmetic exist (cf. Ashlock, 1986; Enright, 1983; Roberts, 1968). Five distinct types of computational errors emerge.

1. *Lack of prerequisite skills.* More advanced operations such as multiplication and division require that a pupil has mastered more basic operations (e.g., addition). Miller and Milam (1987) examined the types of errors made by students with learning disabilities when solving mulitplication and division problems. They found that most errors were due to lack of prerequisite skills. For example, poor memory for basic multiplication facts and addition facts accounted for most of the errors in multiplication. For division problems there was evidence of subtraction errors; however, the most common problem was omitting the remainder from the answer (quotient).

2. *Wrong operation.* The student performs an operation other than the operation required to solve the problem. For example, a student adds when he should

---

FIGURE 7.5.
Examples of defective algorithms (adapted from Ashlock, 1982).

1. Adds from left to right

$$
\begin{array}{r}
6\,{}^{\text{\scriptsize1}}2 \\
+5\ 4 \\
\hline
1\ 7
\end{array}
$$

2. Adds all three digits together

$$
\begin{array}{r}
2\ 2 \\
+3 \\
\hline
7
\end{array}
$$

3. Subtracts the smaller number from the larger when the larger number is the subtrahend

$$
\begin{array}{r}
4\ 1\ 6 \\
-3\ 2\ 5 \\
\hline
1\ 1\ 1
\end{array}
$$

4. Regroups when not required

$$
\begin{array}{r}
{}^{1}\ {}^{17}{}^{1} \\
\cancel{2}\,\cancel{8}\,6 \\
-5\ 7 \\
\hline
1\ 1\ 2\ 9
\end{array}
$$

5. Adds the regrouped number to the multiplicand in the tens column *before* multiplying

$$
\begin{array}{r}
{}^{2}\ \\
5\ 7 \\
\times 4 \\
\hline
2\ 8\ 8
\end{array}
$$

have subtracted. This error may be due to a number of factors (e.g., not knowing the meaning of the sign, carelessness).

3. *Obvious computational error.* With this type of error, a student uses the correct operation but incorrectly recalls basic fact.

4. *Defective algorithm.* A student tries to apply the correct operation and knows the basic facts but makes errors in using the steps necessary to solve the problem. For example, a student might add three-digit problems from left to right. Figure 7.5 (adapted from Ashlock, 1986) contains examples of this type of error.[3] In a study of students labeled mildly handicapped, Lepore (1979) noted frequent problems in regrouping and place value.

5. *Random responses.* This category describes answers that have no readily apparent relationship to the problem given. Usually, the answer is "way off" and may be due to guessing and/or lack of motivation. Roberts (1968) found this type of error to be common among low-functioning students.

Summary

Many people read for pleasure and some write for enjoyment, but few calculate for fun. Accordingly, the major outcome of mathematics instruction is to provide individuals functional skills that can be applied to everyday life in personal finance, employment, homemaking activities, and so forth. Most elementary mathematics curricula stress whole-number operations that require memorization of basic facts; however, other strands such as readiness skills, concepts, vocabulary, and problem solving are also typically included.

Several options are available for developing performance measures of math skills. Presentation and response modes—visual, oral, motoric—can be varied depending on the purpose of instruction. Moreover, the level of assessment can be varied to assess whether the student can compute a problem on the abstract level or is operating on a concrete or semiabstract level of understanding. When developing word problems the teacher can alter several variables in order to assess student ability. These variables include irrelevant information, number of operations needed to solve the problem, and so forth.

Error analysis is a critical part of the assessment process in mathematics. Identifying what type of error the student makes when solving a problem gives the teacher crucial instructional information. Types of errors discussed were lack of prerequisite skills, wrong operations, obvious computational errors, defective use of algorithms, and random responses or guessing. Procedures for performing an error analysis include examining written responses to certain types of problems, observing the student solving a problem, and interviewing students about how they solved the problem.

---

[3]Ashlock presents a detailed description of a variety of errors and includes suggested remediation procedures for each type of error.

Extended Example 1

Scenario

Mr. Good teaches in a resource room in an urban elementary school. He has 8 to 10 students per period. It is the beginning of the second semester, and 2 new students are being placed in his third-period class for instruction in math.

Step 1: Specify Reason for Assessment

The 2 students, Tom (a second-grader) and Lois (a fourth-grader), both have individualized education plans (IEPs) and, therefore, have different math objectives. Mr. Good decides to monitor each student's progress through their instructional objectives.

Step 2: Analyze Curriculum

Since curriculum has been broadly defined as instructional intent, goals for students in special education are defined for the most part by the goals and objectives in the IEPs that were formulated by the MDTs. Therefore, analysis of curriculum is essentially the same as an analysis of the goals and objectives contained in the IEP. These goals and objectives are usually written as a result of systematic testing with both formal devices (i.e., standardized, norm-referenced tests) and informal ones (e.g., criterion-referenced tests). However, since there may be considerable delay between the time that the testing occurred and the physical change in placement, it is usually a good idea for a teacher to verify that the objectives on the IEP are still appropriate—that is, that the student has not mastered an objective during the period of time between assessment and placement. Typically, several objectives are written for each academic and/or social goal.

2a. Tom

Content analysis and sequence. The math goal for Tom is to "improve numeration." The behaviors included in those objectives for Tom's goal are identifying numbers, counting by rote, writing numbers, and ordering numbers. Mr. Good selects *identifying numbers* as the first behavior to be taught[4] since this behavior is an enabler for the remaining ones on Tom's IEP and, therefore, logically would precede the rest. For instructional purposes, however, Mr. Good breaks these behaviors into smaller units. For example, he would not attempt to teach the identification of the numerals 0 through 100 simultaneously. Rather, he groups the numbers in an instructionally logical fashion—0–9, 10–19, and so forth. These groupings represent subcomponents or subobjectives.

Levels of proficiency. It is also clear that all of these goals lie in the beginning of the area of *operations* and are at the *knowledge* level.

[4]Teachers often teach two or more goals within the same strand simultaneously when they are not hierarchially related although IEP objectives are usually written in a sequence from easy to hard.

Quantification of the curriculum. Since all of the objectives lie at the knowledge level, Mr. Good did not need to develop a formal table of specifications to quantify the curriculum. He only needed to decide relative instructional emphases for the subobjectives. He believed that identifying the numerals 0 through 19 was the most important. The remaining numerals could be learned by learning 17 rules. For example, the numerals 20 through 29 could be learned by two rules:

- 20 is called "twenty"
- The remaining 9 numbers are named by calling the digit in the tens place "20" and recalling the already-learned numeral in the units place

Therefore, he decided to devote about 60% of his instructional effort to the mastery of 0 through 19 with the rest of his effort expended for teaching 20 through 100.

2b. Lois

Content analysis and sequence. For Lois, the IEP lists "improving subtraction" as the goal for mathematics. The behaviors included in those objectives for Lois's goal are subtracting two-digit minuends without zeros but with regrouping, and subtracting large numbers that require regrouping (problems with up to 8 digits in the minuend). Mr. Good decides to start with the subtraction of two-digit minuends without zeros but with regrouping. This objective seemed to logically precede the second and third objectives.

For his purposes, Mr. Good would teach all of Lois's objectives at knowledge (computation) level using the standard "borrowing" algorithm and to emphasize subtraction with regrouping using two-digit minuends and subtrahends. His rationale was that problems of this type provide the basis for all of the remaining higher level subtraction that Lois would be required to do. He also decided to stress subtraction using three-digit subtrahends and three-digit minuends containing one zero since problems of this type form the basis of subtraction with any number of zeros in the minuend. Quantification of Lois's curriculum appears in Figure 7.6

Step 3: Formulate Behavioral Objectives

Often, specific student objectives, written as behavioral objectives, may have been formulated already by the MDT and included in the IEP at the time eligibility was determined. Thus, MDTs can facilitate a teacher's CBAs.

	Knowledge	Comprehension	FIGURE 7.6.
2 digits − 2 digits, regroup once	35	0	Percent of instructional
3 digits − 3 digits, regroup once	10	0	effort for Lois's
3 digits − 3 digits, regroup twice	10	0	subtraction
3 digits − 3 digits, 1 zero in minuend	30	0	curriculum.
3 digits − 3 digits, 2 zeros in minuend	15	0	

Behavioral objectives contain three components (i.e., the behavior, the conditions under which the behavior is to be demonstrated, and the criterion of successful performance). The *behavior* components come directly from Mr. Good's analyses of the curricula. The *conditions* that he selected were based upon the actual conditions he used in instruction—how the students' text series and his supplementary materials actually presented the material. The *criteria* for successful performance were based upon Mr. Good's decision to use rate as a performance criterion: He expected both Tom and Lois to be both accurate and fluent in their instructional objectives. To select appropriate rates for the particular objectives, Mr. Good consulted a table that he had prepared and that was based on several sources (e.g., Florida Department of Education, 1983; Mercer, Mercer, & Evans, 1982) (see Figure 7.3). In Tom's case, Mr. Good noted that, according to experts,[5] 100 digits per minute was about the averge proficiency rate for responding orally to visually presented random numbers (i.e., "see–say"). Lois's criterion rate (60 correct digits per minute) was also selected using the data in Figure 7.3.

Mr. Good wrote the following objectives for the 2 students:

- Tom's specific objective: When given worksheets with the numbers 0 through 100 printed in random order, Tom will say the numbers correctly at a rate of 100 digits per minute with 2 or fewer errors per minute.

- Lois's specific objective: When given worksheets containing two-digit subtraction problems that require regrouping, Lois will write the correct answers at a rate of 60 digits per minute with 2 or fewer errors per minute.

Step 4. Develop Appropriate Assessment Procedures

Since Mr. Good decided to assess rate of correct and incorrect responses, he selected probe sheets as a measure of the students' progress on their objectives. He allotted 1 minute for daily assessments that would follow instruction or practice. Given this amount of time and the criteria set for the objectives, the minimum number of digits on Tom's probe sheets would be 100 and on Lois's, 60. However, the minimums would not allow Mr. Good to measure student progress beyond the criteria that he had set. Therefore, he made sure that there were many more problems than the students could complete in the allotted time.

Mr. Good constructed[6] the probe sheets for Tom and Lois displayed in Figures 7.7 and 7.8. Tom's probe sheets assess all of the numerals in the objective and do not directly reflect the daily instruction. They contained an equal number of numerals for 0 to 9, 10 to 19, and 20 to 100. The rationale for doing this was that the probe sheets would allow Mr. Good to assess progress toward the complete goal (see Deno and Mirkin, 1977). Should Tom's progress be inadequate, Mr. Good would develop probe sheets to monitor each instructional subobjective

---

[5]If the particular skill had not been included in Table 7.6, the methods for establishing rate criteria that are described in Chapter 3 could have been used.

[6]Although Mr. Good constructed the probes himself, he could have purchased similar probes from the sources mentioned in Chapter 4.

5	3	12	62	75	0	19	10	20	2	11	44
13	22	4	100	8	17	99	16	5	23	13	1
18	4	6	31	14	36	73	9	46	15	10	0
35	96	14	7	9	47	1	18	48	19	8	15
1	11	87	5	23	10	9	68	17	80	2	18
71	16	65	17	12	3	19	2	8	36	5	60

FIGURE 7.7. See-say random numerals (0–100).

73	45	40	54	94	70	82	71	99	22	62	71
−54	−38	−17	−17	−85	−38	−67	−22	−19	−14	−23	−46

59	32	84	51	97	71	45	96	60	99	60	83
−39	−16	−48	−45	−39	−14	−16	−79	−15	−58	−46	−17

50	87	74	96	34	73	93	46	90	43	55	95
−33	−76	−69	−17	−26	−15	−29	−38	−12	−28	−43	−29

98	70	66	61	82	31	85	87	43	20	53	99
−19	−24	−45	−58	−49	−17	−17	−28	−27	−19	−28	−48

non-instance

61	86	64	89	95	62	85	80	53	73	71	67
−53	−57	−17	−38	−67	−35	−16	−56	−14	−16	−54	−19

FIGURE 7.8 Probe sheet for Lois.

Skill: 2-digit subtraction with regrouping

Student: Lois. Date: _____   Class period _____

Correct _____   Incorrect _____

Adapted from Orange County Public Schools, Precision Teaching Project, Orlando, Florida

precisely (i.e., 0 to 9, 10 to 19, and 20 to 99). The problems included on Lois's probe sheets mirror the behaviors included in her behavioral objectives with the exception of two diagonal rows on her probe sheets. Mr. Good has included some nonexamples of the skill (i.e., two-digit subtraction *without* regrouping) to see if she can discriminate between problems that require regrouping and those that do not. (The reader should note that the diagonal lines would not actually appear on Lois's probe sheet.) In addition to the problems themselves, Mr. Good has included space for student name, date, class period, objective assessed, number correct and incorrect, and scoring aids in digits to the right of each row.

5. Collect Data

Mr. Good administers the 1-minute probes following daily instruction or practice. Since Lois's timings result in permanent, written products, her probe sheets can be scored later, at Mr. Good's convenience. However, since Tom's probes require an oral response, he can choose among several administration and scoring procedures. First, Mr. Good could administer the probe individually—sitting with Tom and marking correct and incorrect responses on a duplicate probe as Tom says the numbers. Second, if he does not always have time, he could have Tom say his responses into a tape recorder and score them later. Third, he could use others (e.g., a competent peer, student aide, teacher's aide) to administer and score the probe. In the beginning, it may be a good idea to administer a probe in an untimed fashion prior to the timed assessment so that the students are familiar with the format. This also may make the probes less stressful. Finally, he developed several forms of the probe sheets to control for practice effects over multiple timings. The total number of correct and incorrect responses are recorded in the appropriate space on the probe sheet.

Steps 6 and 7: Summarize and Display Data

Since the purpose of Mr. Good's assessments of Tom and Lois was to monitor their progress on behavioral objectives, he decided to display the data on a graph. Since a rate criterion was selected, he charts the data using semilogarithmic graph paper (see Figures 7.9 and 7.10). First, he adds pertinent information to the chart—student name, behavior, goal, and so on. Next, he estimates a reasonable date on which Tom and Lois should reach the criteria and places a star where the rate and date intersect.[7] For example, in Tom's case Mr. Good decided that Tom should reach his goal of 100 digits per minute in five weeks. Then, after the number correct on several more probes are plotted and Tom's average rate of correct responses on these probes is calculated, Mr. Good draws an aimline from the mean rate of correct responses to the star. This aimline will be used later when making decisions about adequate or inadequate progress. Thereafter, Mr. Good plots the rate of correct responses as he scores each timed probe; additionally, he writes the raw data in the appropriate box on the right side of the graph paper. Mr. Good also has the option of allowing students to chart their own performance.

Step 8: Interpret Data and Make Decisions

After a week or so of data collection, Mr. Good begins to analyze the data and make judgments about Tom's and Lois's progress. In Tom's case, visual inspection shows an improving picture—rate of correct response is increasing at or above the aimline and rate of incorrect response is decreasing. Based on this

---

[7]Remember that the dates when the goals should be attained—and hence the rate of student progress—may be revised as a function of student performance. Right now, these decisions are "good guesses."

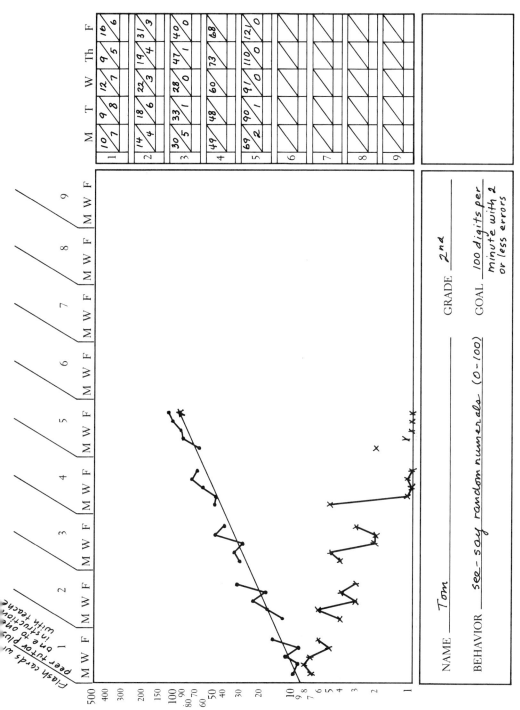

FIGURE 7.9. Tom's progress chart. (Copyright by Eugene M. Berquam, Performance Data Co., P.O. Box 13289, Gainesville, FL 32604. Used by permission.)

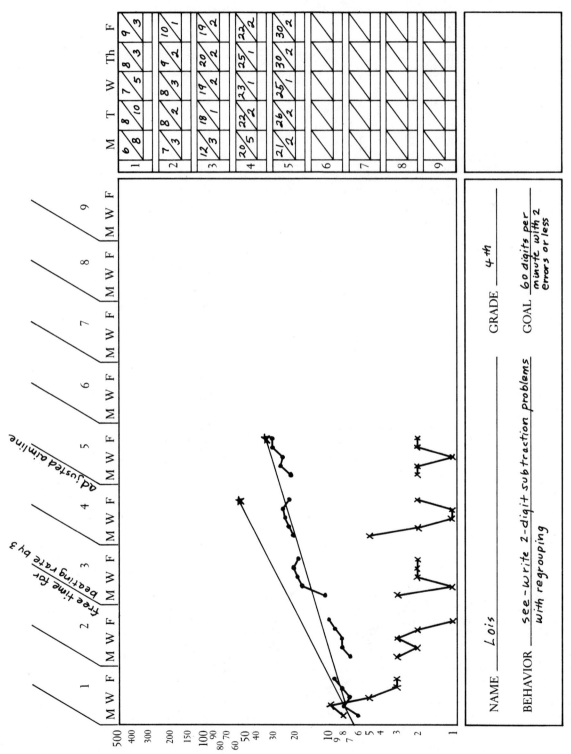

FIGURE 7.10. Louis's progress chart. (Copyright by Eugene M. Berquam, Performance Data Co., P.O. Box 13289, Gainesville, FL 32604. Used by permission.)

information, Mr. Good decides to maintain the current instructional program. Analysis of Tom's performance over the following weeks shows continuing adequate progress, and in five weeks Tom reached his goal. Mr. Good decides to begin instruction on a new math objective but makes a note to administer periodic probes to see if Tom is maintaining the skill at an acceptable criterion.

While Tom's performance is ideal (he responds well to the intervention and progresses steadily to the criterion), Lois's performance is not that good. After her aimline was drawn and two weeks of instruction had elapsed, Lois had decreased her error rate, but her rate of correct responses was not improving as hoped. In order to quantify the little improvement that she made, Mr. Good calculated a celeration value by finding the median rate for both weeks—7.5 and 8.5. He then divided the larger number by the smaller and found the celeration rate to be ×1.13. This value is below the suggested minimum rate of ×1.25. Since Lois was performing accurately but slowly, Mr. Good hypothesized that her problem may be one of motivation to work faster. Accordingly, he provided an incentive (i.e., free time) if she increased her previous rate by more than three digits. During the next two weeks, she improved but her rate of correct response began to flatten out. At that point, Mr. Good decided to investigate the possibility that motor speed may be interfering with Lois's ability to write her answers quickly. If this was the case, the rate criterion might have to be adjusted downward. To assess the tool skill of writing digits, he administered three probes in which Lois was instructed to write, in sequence, the digits from 0 to 9 as many times as she could for a minute. Since this skill should be performed at an automatic level, it should indicate how fast she can write numbers. Her totals (number correct/number of errors) for the three timings were 58/0, 63/0, and 61/0; the means were 61 and 0. Mr. Good then multiplied the mean rate of correct responses (61) by one-half (0.5) and adjusted his instructional criterion to 31 digits per minute. He then adjusted the aim on the graph by drawing a new aimline (see Figure 7.9). Lois reached her new aim several days later. Since her motor speed was a problem that affected performance on other objectives in math as well as in other academic areas, Mr. Good decided to begin working to increase her speed in digit and letter writing concurrently with instruction on the next math objective.

Summary

Mr. Good has monitored Tom's and Lois's progress in their individualized math curricula. For each student, he analyzed the content and levels of proficiency for curricula and quantified his analyses. He formulated specific behavioral objectives and probes to assess student progress toward their goals. As he taught the students, he administered and scored the probes. He transferred student scores to graphs. He analyzed these performances, adjusted educational programs as necessary, and continued teaching. This process continued until the students met their instructional objectives.

Extended Example 2

Scenario

Ms. Hudson is a fifth-grade teacher is a suburban school and has 20 students enrolled in her class. It is the beginning of the year. She has decided to use small-group instruction.

Step 1: Specify Reason for Assessment

Ms. Hudson wants assessment information in order to form three instructional groups and to decide where to begin instruction for each. Her groupings will be based on the current levels of skills that her students have. The first group will consist of students who have not acquired a majority of basic computational skills included in the first several chapters of the math text and are, therefore, in need of more intensive remediation in skills taught prior to fifth grade (e.g., material covered in the fourth grade). Group two will include students who have acquired some of the initial components in the computational strand (e.g., can multiply one-digit numbers but not two-digit numbers). Thus, students in group two are ready to begin instruction in Chapter 1 and are believed to have the skills needed to move through the curriculum at a normal pace. The third group will consist of more advanced students who have mastered most or all computational skills introduced in the first part of the text. This advanced group could move quickly through the first portion of the curriculum emphasizing problem solving and additional enrichment activities.

Step 2: Analyze the Curriculum

The school system in which Ms. Hudson works has adopted the McGraw-Hill Mathematics Program (Bitter et al., 1987). She has noted that the *table of contents* of the student text is organized by *strands* (i.e., addition, subtraction, and so forth) and includes *components* for each (e.g., adding two-digit numbers, adding three-digit numbers). Since she intends to follow the text, she does not need to develop her own scope and sequence chart. From scanning the student text, Ms. Hudson learns that the actual content does, indeed, follow the scope and sequence presented in the *table of contents*.

Content Analysis. Ms. Hudson decided to focus her assessment on student ability to complete the whole-number operations included in the first five chapters. Since this curriculum emphasizes (devotes more pages, more problems to) computation, she believed that only including this aspect would provide enough survey information for her decisions about grouping.[8]

Levels of proficiency. Next Ms. Hudson decided upon the levels of proficiency at which she would assess the content. Inspection of the curriculum indicated that all objectives were at the computation, comprehension, or application levels.

---

[8]Several strands and components were not assessed. These included problem solving, using graphs, and estimation. A simple rationale for not assessing these strands and components is that failure to master them will not impede learning new whole-number operations.

However, as discussed earlier, the purpose of this screening test was to assess computation only. Computation of math facts is at the knowledge level, and for her purposes the only behavioral level assessed is acquisition.

Quantification of the curriculum. Ms. Hudson looked at the curriculum to see how much *student time* (i.e., number of pages) was spent on each component and saw that approximately the same number of problems (and pages) were included for each component. Since the general form and content of the test is implicit, in this instance it is unnecessary to construct a precise table of specifications. Such a table would be more precise than the test itself. What was needed was a clear understanding of the content to be assessed.

Step 3: Formulate Objectives

For this purpose of assessment (to survey student skills in computing whole-number operations and to use that information to form three instructional groups), a formal behavioral objective is not as critical as it would be for identifying an instructional intent for an individual student.

Nonetheless, behavioral objectives are implicit in Ms. Hudson's assessment. As noted throughout this text, behavioral objectives include three components: behavior, conditions, and criteria. Specific behaviors are already included in the left-hand column on the student record sheets (see Figure 7.11). The conditions are also apparent: The students will be given a written test on these behaviors.[9]

However, Ms. Hudson must be specific in establishing the relevant criteria for performance. How will she decide, based on student performance, which student will be placed in what group? There are two considerations to which she must attend. *First*, criteria for an adequate performance are unclear and variable. As yet there are no research data upon which she can rely in order to guide her decision. Because the bases for selecting criteria are so uncertain, she must realize that all such placement decisions are tentative. Consequently, she must be ready to move students between groups based on their actual learning performances. *Second*, she must understand the risks associated with poor decisions. Setting criteria too low risks placing students who meet a weak criterion into groups where they lack sufficient skill to progress with the rest of the group. Setting criteria too high risks placing students who fail to meet a rigorous criterion into groups where the pace of instruction and the material covered are not sufficiently challenging. Ms. Hudson decided that about 70% would be a sufficiently rigorous criterion.

Step 4: Develop Appropriate Assessment Procedures

Next, she needed to decide upon an efficient procedure to assess mastery on curricular strands. Since she wanted to begin instruction as quickly as possible, she decided not to use preexisting probes to assess the students.[10] Since students in

---

[9]See the sections of developing assessment tools in Chapter 4 for a description of the test.

[10]Because 16 probes would be needed to assess the components of addition and subtraction and because Ms. Hudson thought that each probe should be administered three times, she would need 48 minutes over at least three days to complete the assessment. In addition she would need to allocate sufficient time to score the 48 probes.

FIGURE 7.11. Student record sheets for Ms. Hudson's class.

Components	Item Numbers	James	Shirley	Sam	Chris	Joey	Leslie	Jenny	Soud	Ben	Ceila	Ronnie	Bill	. . . .
Add. Facts 0–9	1–3													
Add. Facts 10–18	4–6													
Missing Addend 0–9	7–9													
Missing Addend 10–18	10–12													
2-digit Add. no regroup	13–15													
2-digit Add. regroup	16–18													
3-digit Add. 1 regroup	19–21													
3-digit Add. 2 regroup	22–24													
more than 2 addends	25–27													
Subtract facts 2 dig − 1 dig.	28–30													
Subtract 2 dig. − 2 dig. no regroup	31–33													
Subtract 2 dig. − 2 dig. regroup	34–36													
Subtract 3 dig − 3 dig. 1 regroup	37–39													
Subtract 3 dig. − 3 dig. 2 regroup	40–42													
Subtract 3 dig − 3 dig. 1 zero	43–48													

Subtract 3 dig − 3 dig. 2 zeroes	46–48	
Subtract 3 dig − 3 dig. 3 zeroes	49–51	
greater numbers	52–54	
TOTAL	___/54	
PERCENT CORRECT		

the lowest instruction group would be those who could not meet criterion on previously taught material, she decided to develop two tests. She developed a three-step procedure.

Step 1. All students will be administered a survey test over the types of addition and subtraction problems included in Chapter 2 (see Figure 7.12).

Step 2. Students scoring less than 70% correct on the survey test will be placed in instruction group one (IG-1). Ms. Hudson will examine the record sheets and identify all types of problems where an individual student scored less than two of three correct and analyze the type of error made.

Step 3. Students scoring more than 70% correct on the addition and subtraction survey test will be administered a second survey test on the following day. This test will cover the types of multiplication and division problems included in Chapters 3–5 of the mathematics text. Students scoring less than 70% correct on this test will be placed in instructional group two (IG-2); students scoring more than 70% correct will be placed in instructional group three (IG-3). Ms. Hudson will again examine the record sheets to identify problems of students who scored less than two of three correct and perform an error analysis on these items.

To develop the *first* screening test, Ms. Hudson carefully examined the problems contained in Chapter 2 of the *McGraw-Hill Mathematics Program.* This chapter reviews basic whole-number addition and subtraction facts.

If there had been an unlimited amount of time available for assessment, Ms. Hudson would only have to decide which subcomponents to assess and how many problems to include for each subcomponent. However, and in most cases, unlimited testing time is not available since it must come from teaching time. Thus, Ms. Hudson first had to fix the maximum amount of time she could spend on this assessment, and this decision then would affect which types of problems are assessed and how many problems are assessed per problem type. Ms. Hudson decided to allow a maximum of 60 minutes for testing.

Next she had to decide upon the format of problems she would use on the test. Since "supply" was the most frequently used format, she decided to use that type of problem.

FIGURE 7.12.
Ms. Husdon's first
math placement test:
addition and
subtraction.

1

Ms. Hudson

5th Grade, Math

Name: _____

Directions: Please show your work, and write your answer right on the test. If a problem is too hard, try your best but don't spend more than a minute or two on it.

1)	5 +3	2)	2 +7	3)	5 +4	4)	5 +7	5)	6 +9	6)	5 +6

7) 5 + _____ = 7   8) 3 + _____ = 9   9) 2 + _____ = 8

10) 6 + _____ = 14   11) 7 + _____ = 15   12) 8 + _____ = 17

13)	67 +32	14)	62 +25	15)	35 +54	16)	56 +38	17)	39 +46	18)	47 +36

19)	462 +357	20)	874 +55	21)	786 +193	22)	555 +376	23)	354 +267	24)	487 +419

25)	292 315 +249	26)	612 42 348	27)	356 82 11 +183	28)	16 −7	29)	14 −6	30)	15 −8

31)	79 −29	32)	68 −63	33)	75 −45	34)	64 −25	35)	87 −38	36)	93 −25

2

37)	756 −327	38)	841 −512	39)	648 −353	40)	817 −332	41)	574 −467	42)	347 −265

43)	346 −237	44)	513 −425	45)	621 −134	46)	402 −258	47)	106 −48	48)	901 −256

49)	500 −67	50)	800 −186	51)	200 −154	52)	4203 −1637	53)	81036 −2667	54)	145214 −124225

Next, she estimated the number of problems that she could expect her students to complete within the allotted time. Her experience with students in this grade led her to conclude that, on the average, such problems could be completed in about 30 seconds. By dividing 30 seconds into 60 minutes allowed for assessment, she could ask no more than 120 problems. This number of problems would not allow her to assess the target domain exhaustively. Thus, she had to balance the number of problems per subcomponent with the number of subcomponents.

Next, she had to decide how many problems to include for each type of problem since she could, of course, choose to use less than the maximum number. Thus, for example, she had to decide how many two-digit problems without regrouping would give her a sufficiently precise estimate of her students' abilities. Ms. Hudson decided against using only one problem per subcomponent since a student might miss it due to carelessness. On the other hand, she believed that inclusion of several items for each skill (subcomponent) would decrease the likelihood that she might mistake a student's carelessness for inability to perform the operation. In the end, she felt three problems per type would be adequate.

Finally, she had to construct her test within these parameters. As a sample of addition and subtraction facts, Ms. Hudson decided to assess the more difficult ones. For single-digit addition problems with sums less than 10, she used addends 2, 3, and 4 with addends 5, 6, and 7; the six combinations with sums less than 10 were divided between column problems and missing addend problems. The same addends were used for two- and three-digit addition problems that did not require regrouping. For single-digit addition problems with sums less than 18, she used addends of 5, 6, and 7 with addends of 6, 9, and 8; the six combinations were also divided between column problems and missing addend problems. As far as possible, the same addends were used for two-digit addition problems that required regrouping. For subtraction, she followed the same general procedure of selecting and balancing the more difficult facts. For example, in problems where a one-digit number was subtracted from a two-digit number, she used minuends of 18 through 14 and subtrahends of 9 through 5. Figure 7.12 contains the first test she constructed and used with her class. The second column of the record sheet (Figure 7.11) shows the problem numbers that correspond to the subcomponents that were assessed.

Also note that Ms. Hudson was careful to allow sufficient space around each problem, and she made a two-page probe. This helps students by providing adequate room to write their answers and calculations (e.g., regrouped numbers). It also makes scoring easier since the students' answers are less likely to run together. In addition, Ms. Hudson allowed the students to write their answers directly on the test. This reduced the likelihood of clerical errors by the students when transferring their answers to a separate answer sheet and teacher errors resulting from misalignment of test and answer form.

Procedures for developing and scoring the *second* survey test (covering multiplication and division facts), as well as recording and analyzing student performance, are essentially the same as those used for the first test. First, Ms. Hudson examines Chapters 3–5 to identify the types of basic facts that are covered and the way they are presented. She includes three of each type on the second test.

5. Collect Data

Ms. Hudson had to decide on the directions that she would give the students. On both screening tests, she told them why she was testing, how she would use the test results, and what they should do when taking the test.

When Ms. Hudson administered the first test, she told the students:

> This test is not part of your grade but a way for me to find out what types of addition and subtraction problems you know how to do. How you do on the test will help me teach you better. You can write your answer right on the test. Also, please show your work. If you come to a problem that's difficult, try your best but don't spend more than a minute or two on it. Just go to the next problem. Remember, even though this is not for a grade, I want you to do your best.

When she administered the second test, she simply substituted multiplication and division for addition and subtraction.

Steps 6, 7, and 8: Summarize and Display the Data; Interpret Data and Make Decisions[11]

When the students are finished with the first test, Ms. Hudson scores the tests and records performance of each type of problem (subcomponent) on the record sheet (see Figure 7.12). After she writes the number correct on each type of problem for each student, she records the total and calculates the percent correct. In order to make it easier to identify problems (types of problems where a student missed more than one out of three), she circles the score. This will help her later to identify types of problems on which to perform error analysis prior to planning instruction. When the record sheet is completed, the data analysis and resulting decision only require the identification of students who scored lower than 70% and placing them into instructional group one.

When the students are finished with the second screening test, Ms. Hudson follows the same general procedures she used with the first screening test: She writes the number correct on each type of problem for each student; she records the total and calculates the percent correct; and she circles the score to indicate problems that may require error analysis. When the record sheet is completed, she identifies those students who scored more than 70% and places them into IG-3.

Summary

Ms. Hudson wished to form three instructional groups for her students. She analyzed and quantified the curriculum. She did not need to formulate specific behavioral objectives for this purpose of testing. She developed two screening tests that were sufficient for her purpose of assessment. After administering the tests, she scored them and displayed and analyzed the students' performances.

[11]Because the decision-making process for the two tests are so interrelated, the final three steps in the model are considered together.

With approximately 5 hours of teacher effort,[12] Ms. Hudson was able to identify instructional groups and tentative starting points for her instruction. She had identified specific types of problems each student was experiencing and could use this information to start error analyses for individual students.

After completing the testing, Ms. Hudson should have three relatively distinct groups. IG-1 will consist of students who are having some difficulty computing some types of addition and subtraction problems. Students in IG-2 will have acquired most addition and subtraction facts but have some difficulty with multiplication and division facts. Students in IG-3 will have few problems in any of the whole-number operations and should soon be able to move into measurement and fractions.

As with any type of instructional grouping, Ms. Hudson will be flexible and allow movement between groups based on student growth. For example, if some students in IG-2 master multiplication and division facts at a higher rate than other members of their group, they could be placed in IG-3. It is important to remember that Ms. Hudson should make this decision using frequent, formative, curriculum-based assessment.

Ms. Hudson will also be able to use the tests at different times and for different reasons. For example, either test could be used as a mastery test at the end of a unit or could be given for periodic maintenance checks.

---

[12]Some of this time could be spent while the students are taking the tests. For example, she could develop the record form and score tests.

Chapter 8

Curriculum-Based Assessment in Written Language

Key Terms

Atomistic scoring	Penmanship
Diction	Punctuation
Grammar	Spelling
Holistic scoring	Style
Mechanics	T-unit
Organization	Writing fluency

There are several reasons to teach written language systematically (cf. Evans et al., 1986). Writing is necessary for success in school; students must be capable of writing answers to essay questions, preparing essays and term papers, and taking notes. Writing is usually necessary for successful adaptation by adults after formal schooling; individuals must be capable of completing a variety of application forms (e.g., employment, insurance, credit), of writing letters, of preparing short communications (e.g., writing notes, taking telephone messages, making shopping lists), and sometimes of preparing business and professional reports. Writing may be a leisure or creative activity; many people enjoy (and some earn a living) writing poetry, short stories, and so forth.

Instruction in written language varies considerably depending on a student's repertoire of skills vis-à-vis the content being taught, as well as a teacher's orientation toward the teaching of writing. The emphasis in this chapter is on the evaluation of grammatical, mechanical, lexical, organizational, and production skills that are systematically taught. We consider *systematic* instruction essential if handicapped and low-functioning students are to learn how to write. However, we recognize that this approach may be unsatisfactory to some. Finally, a few teachers stress the process of writing (i.e., production of ideas) and give little attention to technical skills, and some teachers stress the interpretative, evaluative, creative, and artistic uses of language in prose and poetry. As is the case with reading comprehension, we consider such uses of written language to be more indicative of language arts or general reasoning and therefore have not considered them in this chapter.

Systematic instruction in written language is a multifaceted area of the school curriculum, and several different taxonomies for written language could be prepared (cf. Issacson, 1988). In practice teachers provide instruction on several components at more or less the same time. For example, after students have learned to form the letters of the alphabet and spell a few words, they may be taught to capitalize the first words of a sentence, to end declarative sentences with periods, and to write simple sentences. Next, in one curriculum a student might be taught to end interrogative sentences with a question mark, while in another curriculum a student might be taught the use of commas within dates or the capitalization of proper names. Moreover, instruction in written language generally follows a spiraling curriculum—each rule or principle of written language is repeated and practiced over time as review or as part of more advanced instruction.

For the purposes of this chapter, we have classified written language into four major instructional strands: penmanship, spelling, content, and style. (Although spelling might well be considered a subcomponent within mechanics, we have treated it separately since it is taught so often as a separate part of the curriculum.) In the following sections, scope and sequence, assessment, and error analyses are discussed for each of the four strands.

Penmanship

Students are expected to produce permanent records of their words that can be read by others. These records can be prepared on a typewriter or computer with a word-processing program, in Braille, or with pencil (or pen) and paper. The latter mode of recording is the focus of this section. *Penmanship* is the general term used to describe the production of written symbols that can be read by others and, in this case, the production of upper- and lower-case letters of the English language.

Scope and Sequence

Penmanship contains three major strands: prewriting skills, printing, and cursive writing. Prewriting skills include pencil grip, pencil control, pencil pressure, posture, and paper angle. Within the printing and cursive writing strands, the same two components are usually included: letter recognition and letter formation. Letter formation includes six subcomponents: shape, slant, and size of individual letters; line quality; spacing between individual letters and words; and general legibility of individual letters and words. There is some controversy about the sequence in which penmanship is taught. Advocates of teaching printing before or in place of cursive writing note that printing bears a closer relationship to the printed word and is easier to learn since it consists of straight lines and circles. Moreover, it can be used in legal signatures, is legible, and can be written as rapidly as cursive. Those who advocate teaching cursive without first teaching printing can point to several benefits as well: Many students have difficulty in making the transition from printing to cursive; cursive minimizes spatial judgments and, therefore, problems with letter spacing; and letter reversals are much less common in cursive than in printing. In practice teachers usually have little say in whether to teach printing; that decision is usually made administratively.

Older students and adults are expected to individualize the style in which they produce written symbols. Indeed, graphologists believe that idosyncratic letter formation can provide valuable insights into personality—a claim about which we are skeptical. Nonetheless, beginning students are expected to learn a particular shape for each letter as well as appropriate slant and size.

Assessment

Penmanship is often evaluated through systematic observations of pupil performance during teaching and evaluation of a pupil's written products. Three performance measures are used.

Performance measure 1: Quality of letters produced in isolation. The most fundamental measure of acquisition is a student's skill in forming letters in isolation, and many beginners have difficulty forming letters correctly. The letters formed by a student are compared to standard letters that the student is expected to copy. Letters are scored in terms of their deviations from the standard in terms of letter shape, size, and line quality (e.g., even pressure). Because this performance measure is used only during acquisition, criteria for mastery should be stated in terms of percentage of letters correctly formed. Moreover, since letter production is a skill that will be practiced throughout the school career of most students, a criterion level of 80% should be adequate. Teachers vary considerably in the degree of deviation that they will accept and are likely to be influenced by factors such as a student's age, experience, motoric capacities, and peer performances.

Performance measure 2: Quality of letter sequences. After students have mastered the production of individual letters in isolation, they are usually expected to produce them in sequences (i.e., writing the alphabet, their own names, or words). The assessment of writing letters in sequence includes the evaluation of individual letters, as well as spacing between and size consistency of letters and words.[1] As a basic acquisition skill, criteria for mastery should be at 90% or higher.

Performance measure 3: Fluency in letter production. Students are expected to produce letters automatically—without thinking about how to form each letter. However, many beginning students, and especially handicapped beginners, are painfully slow writers. It is not uncommon to find 12- or 13-year-olds with tool-skill rates of less than 30 letters per minute. For such students, increased speed and accuracy of the tool skill is critical for future academic success. Timed probes

[1]Occasionally, an additional criterion of general legibility is used. (For example, if a teacher must deduce the letter from the surrounding letters, that teacher might evaluate the letter as illegible.

Process Problems
- _____ pencil grip (i.e., finger positions or pressure)
- _____ posture (e.g., sitting erect, angle of paper to body, nonwriting hand holding paper)
- _____ incomplete erasures

Writing Problems
- _____ appropriate use of space (e.g., spacing between lines, margins)
- _____ consistency of letter size
- _____ line quality (e.g., lines too heavy or light)
- _____ slant of letters
- _____ slow writing speed
- _____ spacing between letters and words
- _____ writing on line

Letter Formation[a]
- _____ failure to close letters (e.g., *o* written like a *u*)
- _____ closing open letters (e.g., *h* written like a *b*)
- _____ top loops closed (e.g., *e* written like an *i*)
- _____ substitution of straight-up strokes for rounded strokes (e.g., *i* written like an *e*)
- _____ end stroke difficulty (e.g., not ending a *w* with a horizontal stroke)
- _____ top of letter too short (e.g., *d* written like an *a*)
- _____ crossing letters (e.g., *t* written like an *l*)
- _____ letter reversal (e.g., *b* written like a *d*)

[a]Source: Newland, T. (1932). An analytic study of the development of illegibilities in handwriting from the lower grades to adulthood. *Journal of Educational Research*, 26(4), 249–258.

FIGURE 8.1. Checklist of common errors in penmanship.

are ideally suited for the assessment of the rate at which students produce letters correctly. For example, a teacher might ask students to write the alphabet or their names as many times as possible in 2 minutes. Fluent students should be able to write the alphabet at a rate of 80 to 100 letters per minute (Florida Department of Education, 1983). However, for students with motor deficiencies (e.g., students with cerebral palsy), 80 letters per minute may not be realistic. For such students, a teacher should consider using experience with the student to set aims. For example, a teacher could use a changing criterion design[2] (with increments of about 10%) until the student's progress begins to level off.

[2]A changing criterion design is used in single-subject research to increase performance (e.g., go from writing 40 letters per minute to writing 100 letters per minute). In this design, individuals are told that they will receive a reinforcer for attaining a specified level of performance (e.g., writing letters at a rate of 50 per minute). After that level of performance has been reached for a few successive trials, they are told that the criterion has been raised (e.g., to 60 letters per minute), and they will again receive reinforcement when their performance reaches the new criterion. The process of raising the criterion continues until the individual reaches the target level of performance (e.g., 100 letters per minute). A changing-criterion design is used in an extended example at the end of this chapter.

Error Analysis

Teachers may use a simple checklist to guide observation and error analysis (see Figure 8.1). One particular error not included in this checklist waves a red flag for teachers—reversals. Perhaps because many individuals with identifiable handicaps reverse letters and numbers, students who reverse symbols come under close scrutiny. However, teachers should bear in mind that reversals are commonly made by pupils in the primary grades and that reversals are not synonymous with problems in visual–motor integration—some children simply may not remember which way a letter or number faces. The latter point is important because interventions for students with visual–motor problems are different from those for children with memory problems.

Spelling

Reading and spelling make similar demands on a student. While reading is the recognition that a sequence of characters represents sounds and words, spelling requires the production of the correct sequence of letters to represent a word. However, recognition is usually an easier process for students than production since context cues will not help a student to spell a word.

Scope and Sequence

The scope and sequence of spelling instruction varies as a function of the curriculum and the student's skill level. Like reading curricula, some spelling curricula follow a specific strategy for teaching spelling words (i.e., structural analysis and/ or phonics). Since written standard American English (SAE) is fairly regular phonetically—80% of consonants have a single spelling in SAE words (Hanna, Hanna, Hodges, & Rudorf, 1966), students should be able to spell most words accurately by learning to apply a few rules of phonics. However, students learn the individual spelling of some words—homonyms whose spellings vary with the meaning, and phonetically irregular words (Wallace & Larsen, 1978).

Spelling curricula are intended to teach students the spelling of important words.[3] What makes a word important depends on the criteria the curriculum developer applies. For example, some teachers select spelling of words that appear frequently in written English (e.g., the Thorndike list, the American Heritage Word List, the Dolch list), lists of words frequently found in children's literature, or lists of specialized words (e.g., scientific words).

Assessment

To assess spelling teachers can choose between testing and analysis of a student's writing. Testing can take two forms: (a) dictation tests in which students write or say the letters of a word said by the teacher and (b) recognition tests in which

---

[3]Systematic instruction in spelling may also include instruction in dictionary use.

students identify either correctly spelled or misspelled words. Written dictation tests have intuitive appeal since writing fluency is the reason that spelling is taught. However, recognition of misspelled words is also a relevant skill for more advanced students who are expected to edit and revise their own writing. Dictation tests are much easier to prepare than recognition tests but they have two potential disadvantages: (a) student writing may be so poor that scoring can be difficult and (b) teachers occasionally cue the correct spelling of a word by distorting its pronunciation somewhat. The primary advantage of recognition tests is the speed with which they can be given—several times faster than dictation tests; however, students may learn incorrect spelling from recognition tests. While these dictation and recognition tests may appear quite different, student performances on the two measures are highly correlated (Freyberg, 1970). Analysis of spontaneous writing is an appealing procedure because it is the most direct measure of a teacher's ultimate objective—the correct spelling of words in written discourse. However, this approach to the assessment of spelling has two major disadvantages. First, record keeping is burdensome for a teacher who must compile lists of misspelled words for each student. Second, students can easily avoid using words when they are unsure of their spelling. For all of these reasons we much prefer written dictation tests.

Performance measure 4: Rate of words correctly written from dictation. Teachers should present the words[4] to be spelled in isolation (i.e., not use them in a sentence or paragraph) since this format is generally easier for students (Horn, 1954, 1967). Teachers can expect students to write words at a rate of about 15 to 25 words per minute, depending on the length of the word (Florida Department of Education, 1983). Thus, if teachers dictate spelling words at a rate of one word every 7 seconds, a student should have ample time to write the word in the 7-second interval (cf. Greene & Petty, 1975; Shinn, Tindal, & Stein, 1988). If the number of words is constant from assessment to assessment, student performance can be recorded as the number of correctly spelled words. When the number of words that are assessed varies from assessment to assessment, student performance should be recorded as the percent correct. For most assessments a 2-minute probe can be used. Moreover, it is generally a good idea to include review words on the probe to check retention of previously learned words as well as words missed on previous probes.

Error Analysis

When instruction is directed toward teaching spelling strategies, error analysis focuses on the correct application of the strategy. For example, if a teacher taught a student to apply phonic rules to spelling, that teacher would examine a student's spelling test to evaluate the extent to which that student applied each rule correctly to phonetic words. Teachers also often look for rule overgeneralization (e.g., forming all plurals by adding an s, such as writing *foots* instead of *feet*) and teach exceptions to the rule when overgeneralizations are noted. In addition

---

[4]Bryant, Drabin, and Gettinger (1981) noted that learning-disabled students performed better on spelling tests when the number of words they had to study was limited to seven or eight words per week and were introduced three at a time.

teachers also note spelling errors in aphonetic words. Finally, teachers often look for commonly made errors: omission of silent letters, omission of sounded letters, addition or omission in doubled letters, letter reversals, plurals, and words with apostrophes (e.g., posessives and contractions). Burns (1980) noted that most errors occur in vowels in mid-syllables; about two-thirds of those errors were substitutions and omissions.

Content of Written Expression

Content refers to *what* a writer communicates to the intended audience. Often, writing instruction is divided into three processes: prewriting, draft writing, and draft revision. Prewriting consists of finding and narrowing a topic, explicating the purpose (including the main idea), defining the intended audience, and preparing an outline. Draft writing consists of the first exposition of written product. Revising and editing consist of checking for violations of writing conventions (Thoburn, (1987).

Scope and Sequence

Four components can be included in content preparation (Isaacson, 1988). First is *idea generation*, which refers to brainstorming the possible ideas that could be included in the text. Second is *coherence*, which refers to the relationship among ideas. Writers should convey a sense of the whole text and how the parts fit together. Third is *organization*, which refers to sequencing ideas into cohesive prose. Within paragraphs, organization includes the use of explicit (or implicit) topic sentences, subordination, pronoun referents, and parallelism. Across paragraphs, organization refers to the sequencing of ideas and paragraphs. Fourth are *audience considerations* which refer to a writer's awareness of a probable reader's sophistication, both in terms of background information and linguistic competence.

In the earliest stages of instruction and assessment in writing, greater emphasis is placed on fluency (i.e., writing more words) in addition to the correct use of simple grammatic conventions (i.e., construction of declarative sentences and subject–verb agreement) and mechanics (i.e., spelling, punctuation, and capitalization). To improve a student's skills in written language, teachers must have written products with which to work. As a rule, students who are experiencing difficulties in written language tend to produce written responses of a few sentences or words. Thus, the first consideration in teaching written language is to get students to write more words and sentences. A teacher often provides a story starter (e.g., a topic sentence or a stimulus picture) to prompt writing.[5] Next, a teacher sets the amount of time that students will be allowed to write (3 minutes is usually sufficient).

---

[5]The format of the story starter appears to make no difference in terms of student performance (Deno, Mirkin, & Marston, 1980).

The simplest general measures of content production that yield valid estimates of student achievement are based on the number of words or the number of correctly spelled words that a student writes (Shinn, Tindal, & Stein, 1988).

Performance measure 5: Number or rate of words written. To use the frequency of words written, a teacher must decide what constitutes a word [e.g., should only correctly spelled words count or should single-letter words (i.e., *a* or *I*) count?] and the amount of time to allot. This performance measure is simply the number of words written in the time period that meet the criteria for being a word. Rate of writing words is an appropriate measure, especially for students in the beginning stages of instruction when the primary instructional goal is to get more words written quickly.

Although criteria that can be used for setting aims are not readily available from the research literature, teachers can set reasonable initial aims based on normative comparisons or tool rates. Aims can be based on the average performance of peers who are producing acceptable written products (i.e., social comparison). Using a student's tool rate to set initial aims is best saved for instruction in the earliest stages of writing or when a student's production is so atypical that aims based on normative data are unrealistic. A teacher might use one half a beginning student's tool rate of writing letters in isolation to estimate the number of letters an essay should contain. (Dividing the number of letters written per minute by five will provide a rough estimate of the number of words that can be written per minute.)

Teachers may find the use of simple word counts unappealing: A student's writing might contain many words but make no linguistic sense or contain numerous errors in grammar, punctuation, and capitalization. In such cases, a teacher might also use a performance measure based on correctness of the words in the student's writing.

Performance measure 6: Percentage of correct words. To use this performance measure, a teacher first prepares criteria for what constitutes a correct word. The criteria will in part depend upon the grade level of the students as well as their linguistic backgrounds. For example, students whose first language is not English may write word sequences that are acceptable translations of their native languages but are incorrect in English—that is, incomplete verb forms or incorrect preposition usage. Criteria for correct words usually include spelling, grammar, capitalization, and punctuation (cf. Isaacson, 1988). As shown in Figure 8.2, a teacher indicates incorrect words. (We have underlined them in the figure.) If a punctuation error occurs, the word preceding the incorrect or omitted punctuation is scored as incorrect. The percentage of words correct can be found by dividing the number of correct words by the total number of words and multiplying the quotient by 100.[6]

---

[6]Videen, Deno, and Marston (1982) recommend using the number of correct word sequences (i.e., two or more adjacent words that use correct style; e.g., spelling, capitalization, punctuation). Isaacson (1988) recommends using the proportion of correct sequences. While there is some evidence (Videen, Deno, & Marston, 1982) that correct word sequences are related to other measures of written language, we believe

FIGURE 8.2. Assessing words in correct sequence.	Ths sumar[1] I <u>visit</u>[2] my grammy.[3] She___[4] in <u>Tuscon</u>.[1] It is very hot <u>their</u>[1] and I <u>swim</u>[2] <u>alot</u>.[1] We went on <u>picknicks</u>[1] and saw <u>alot</u>[1] of <u>cactises</u>.[1] <u>Their</u>[1] are tall <u>montens</u> <u>evarywhere</u>.[1] I ha<u>d fun. I wan</u>t to go back next <u>sumar</u>.[1] Number of incorrect words = 16 Number of words = 43 Percent words correct = 63%

[1] = spelling
[2] = verb tense
[3] = punctuation
[4] = word omitted

With more advanced students, teachers may teach particular strategies intended to facilitate the production of written content. These strategies teach students to follow a sequence of steps when writing, and the steps are designed to ensure organization, subordination, and so forth. For example, Ms. Li might teach her students how to write topic and other declarative sentences and begin instruction on writing simple paragraphs that consist of a topic sentence, two or more descriptive sentences, and a concluding sentence. Some strategies are embodied in commercial materials that a teacher can use to teach written language. For example, Macmillan's *Thinking and Writing Processes* is intended to facilitate idea generation, coherence, organization, and audience considerations. Other strategies may be used independently of or in addition to commercial materials. For example, the TOWER strategy, described in an extended example in Chapter 10, can be used to teach organization of expository prose. Whenever a writing strategy is taught, the first assessment should get at how well a student knows the steps in the strategy. This assessment can be accomplished by constructing a test that specifically assesses a student's knowledge and comprehension, but frequently strategy use is inferred from a student's prewriting products (e.g., notes, outline) or final written product. When inferring strategy usage, a teacher looks for evidence that students have actually used the strategy to produce a written passage that contains the outcomes of strategy use. For example, Ms. Li might evaluate each outline or essay to ascertain the presence of a topic, descriptive, and concluding sentence.

Performance measure 7: Following the strategy during production. To use this performance measure, a teacher first prepares criteria for what constitutes strategy usage. For example, Ms. Li would set criteria for what constitutes topic, descriptive, and concluding sentences. Next, each essay is scored for the use of each step in the strategy. The percentage of strategy use is found by dividing the number of steps used by the total number of steps and multiplying the quotient by 100. Generally, the criterion for appropriate strategy use should reflect a high rate

that this index may be misleading if the number of words in correct and incorrect sequences are not equal. For example, suppose a college student wrote a 20-page term paper that contained six nonsequential spelling errors in the body of the paper. That term paper would contain 13 sequences, and 6 sequences would be incorrect. About 54% of the word sequences would be correct, although more than 99% of the words in the paper would be in correct sequence.

of accuracy—90% or higher—and students should receive systematic feedback on their accuracy of strategy utilization.

Although a student might have followed the strategy and written many correct words, the written product may or may not have many ideas. Thus, teachers may view appraisal of ideas as an independent and critical component of the assessment of written language. *Holistic scoring*—summary ratings of the quality of the entire piece of writing—are a popular method of assessing this aspect of a student's writing. The meaning of *quality* can vary (Mishler & Hogan, 1982). A teacher might take into consideration the clarity and development of the main ideas, logical and empirical support for the main idea, match between what has been written and a reader's level of sophistication, grammatical and lexical cohesion and coherence, transitions used to link paragraphs, and the sensibility of the writing as a whole (Perkins, 1983).

Holistic scoring has three advantages and two disadvantages. The advantages are its perceived sensitivity to differences in content (Cooper, 1977) and the speed with which an essay can be scored—1 or 2 minutes per essay. The third advantage is that holistic scoring can allow a teacher to reinforce a student's ideas without regard for the technical aspects of presentation. Thus, even students who lack skill in punctuation and spelling can find writing to be a rewarding experience. There are two major disadvantages of holistic writing. First, the single, impressionistic score provides teachers insufficient information with which to remediate student errors or to plan or monitor instruction. Second, unless there is a substantial time commitment prior to scoring, holistic ratings may vary considerably from scorer to scorer (i.e, they may be unreliable).

Because of these disadvantages in holistic scoring, there have been several attempts to objectify and quantify the scoring of content. Several indices related to the quality of content have been investigated, but their use does not seem to have found their way into the classroom—probably because of their complex scoring. Five other common indices are the percentage of particular grammatical structures (e.g., adjectives, the number of nouns), number of T-units,[7] number of cohesive ties,[8] number of mature words,[9] and type–token ratio.[10] These indices of content fluency are related to each other and to more general judgments about the quality of written content (Golub & Kidder, 1974; Page, 1968) as well as the impressions of the writer's maturity (Loban, 1976; Steward & Leaman, 1983).

Error Analysis

One of the more common errors that teachers detect in a student's writing is incomplete sentences or sentence fragments. For beginning students, production of sentence fragments may indicate incomplete learning of what constitutes a

---

[7]A T-unit is "a single main clause (or independent clause) plus whatever subordinate clauses or nonclauses are attached to, or embedded within that one main clause" (Hunt, 1965, p. 93).

[8]Cohesive ties include conjunctions, pronouns that allude to preceding antecedents, and so forth and "presuppose the existence of another element elsewhere in the text" (Isaacson, 1988, p. 539).

[9]Mature words are words that do not apprear frequently in SAE (Carroll, Davies, & Richman, 1971).

[10]A type–token ratio is an index of vocabulary diversity. This index is calculated by dividing the number of unrepeated words by the square root of two times the total number of words that the student has written (Carroll, 1964).

sentence. With more advanced students, sentence fragments probably indicate poorly developed proofreading skills.

Style

Style refers to how the ideas that the writer wants to convey are presented. Thus, style does not refer to content but to form. It should be noted that there is some controversy over the relative importance of style conventions vis-à-vis content. Some teachers believe that the style is relatively unimportant, while others may place greater emphasis on style than on the content—although they might not admit it. We believe that students should have sufficient mastery of style to communicate their ideas appropriately to the intended audiences. In school, the expectations for using the correct style are much higher than in nonacademic settings. However, even in nonacademic settings, individuals are expected to write in a literate fashion.

Scope and Sequence

Style consists of four components: grammar, mechanics, diction, and diversity. Each component has several subcomponents.

Grammar

Grammar refers to the sequencing and interrelationships among words that give meaning to written expression. Six subcomponents of grammar are generally taught.

Parts of speech refer to the use to which words are put. Traditionally, parts of speech include verbs, nouns, pronouns, adjectives, adverbs, conjunctions, prepositions, and interjections. However, these classifications are somewhat misleading since a word's classification actually depends on its particular use within a sentence. For example, in the sentence, "Special-education students often have difficulties learning school material," both *education* and *school* are nouns, but they are used as adjectives.

Sentence construction refers to expression of a complete thought unit with a minimum of a subject (sometimes subjects are understood as, for example, in the case of imperatives) and verb. Sentence construction also includes proper word order to convey meaning and knowledge of simple, compound, and complex sentences.

Pronoun case refers to different forms of the same word. In English (and unlike other languages), the use of case is restricted to changes in pronouns. Pronouns change to show different uses in sentences (i.e., subjects, objects, and possessives). For example, *she* might refer to Mary Kay. However, *she* is used to refer to Mary Kay only when Mary Kay is the subject or predicate nominative in a sentence. *Her* is used when Mary Kay is used as an object of a verbal or preposition. *Hers* will be used to show possession by Mary Kay. Similar changes are made with *I* (me, my), *he* (him, his), *they* (them, their), and other pronouns.

Agreement refers to consistency in number and gender between pronouns and

	TABLE 8.1
He says he wants to go.	Some Examples of
He says he will want to go.	Sequences of Verb
He says he wanted to go.	Tenses in English
He says he had wanted to go.	

He says he wants to go.
    He says he will want to go.
    He says he wanted to go.
    He says he had wanted to go.

He will say he wants to go.
    He will say he will want to go.
    He will say he wanted to go.
    He will say he had wanted to go.

He said he wants to go.
    He said he would want to go.
    He said he wanted to go.
    He said he had wanted to go.

antecedents and consistency in number between subjects and verbs. *Verb tense* refers to the time at which the action (or state of being) expressed by the verb occurs. In English, several tenses are used: future, present, present perfect, past perfect, and future perfect. Sequence of verb tenses shows the relative timing of two or more verbs. For example, the meanings of the sentences given in Table 8.1 change as a function of the verb tenses.

Verb voice refers to whether the subject of a clause acts or is acted upon. English sentences are classified as active (e.g., "The dog *bit* the boy") and passive ("The boy *was bitten* by the dog").

Verb mood refers to the way verb action takes place. In English, three moods are used: indicative, imperative, and subjunctive. Indicative verbs are the most common and are used to state facts (e.g., "She *is reading* a book"). Imperative verbs command or request (e.g., "While you're up, *get* me a cup of coffee"). Subjunctive verbs are used to show doubt, a situation that is contrary to fact, a wish, or a regret (e.g., "If I *were* the teacher, . . .").

Mechanics

Mechanics refer to the conventions used to write English. These conventions, sometimes called rules, are arbitrary and variable. Seven subcomponents usually are taught.

Punctuation refers to the various rules for adding symbols (other than letters and numbers) to one's writing in order to add clarity and meaning to written communications. These symbols include periods, commas, question marks, exclamation marks, apostrophes, quotation marks, colons, semicolons, dashes, parentheses, and hyphens.

Capitalization refers to the various conventions for using uppercase and lowercase letters. For example, capitalization is required for the first word in a sentence, proper names, and months of the year.

Font styles refer to changes in the style in which letters are formed within a communication. In printed materials, font style refers to boldface, roman, and italic print. In handwritten materials, font style refers to underlining and interchanges of printed and cursive styles. Changes in font style may indicate emphasis, foreign words, and titles (e.g., ships, works of art).

Abbreviations refer to commonly accepted shortenings of spelling in which the abbreviated word typically ends with a period such as *Mr.* (mister), *Dr.* (doctor), *etc.* (et cetera), *i.e.* (id est), *amt.* (amount), *lbs.* (pounds), and so forth. Abbreviations can also refer to the substitution of a single symbol for an entire word such as $ (dollar), & (and), and so forth.

Number usage refers to the conventions for using Arabic numerals versus writing a number in words. For example, street addresses and dates are usually written in Arabic numerals, while single-digit numbers (e.g., *three* men and a dog) are usually written as words.

Referencing refers to the acknowledgment of the source of information or quotation. Depending on the particular style, references may appear in the body of the text (e.g., in this text) or they may appear in footnotes.

General format refers to the visual–spatial presentation of the written communication. Included under the rubric of general format are margin widths, use of headers and footers, pagination, tabs, spacing between lines, and inside addresses and salutations for letters.

Diction

Diction refers to word usage, and three aspects are generally considered. First, diction refers to using the word that means precisely what the writer intends. For example, a writer might intend to convey that a child is unattractive but friendly by describing that child as homely but personable. Such a description would be an oxymoron[11] since personable means attractive. Correct word usage also refers to the tone that particular words carry. For example, a writer could describe an individual of a different nationality as a *foreigner*, an *alien*, or a *visitor from another country*. The particular word chosen will set a tone for the description. Second, *diction* refers to wordiness. Probably as the result of E. B. White's influence, modern writers are thought to be good writers if they convey their meaning in few words (cf. Strunck & White, 1959). For example, the phrase, *the residents of England*, could be written more parsimoniously as *the English*. Third, *diction* also refers to the omission of words; necessary words should not be left out.

Diversity

Diversity refers to the use of different vocabulary, sentence structures, and grammatical transformations. Good writers use diverse forms more often than poor writers (Hunt, 1970).

Assessment

Assessment of a student's knowledge and comprehension of the conventions of style is straightforward and similar to the assessment of content in most of the other academic content areas. Teachers can use probes or tests. Criteria for

---

[11]An oxymoron combines incongruous or contradictory terms such as beautifully ugly or mournful joy.

acceptable performance for objectives prepared at knowledge and comprehension levels should be set between 90% and 100% (cf. Stephens, Hartman, & Lucas, 1978).

Performance measure 8: Percentage correct on comprehension of style conventions. Teachers can prepare objective tests or probes to ascertain students' understanding of any convention. Part 1 of Figure 8.3 contains examples of how test questions might be worded to assess understanding of various conventions. Part 2 contains two probes—one to assess capitalization and one to assess punctuation— of commas and periods.

Performance measure 9: Percentage correct on prompted application. Teachers can also prepare tests or probes that prompt the application of various written-language conventions. Figure 8.4 contains examples of prompted convention usage.

Error Analysis

After style conventions have been mastered in isolation, students are expected to apply them spontaneously in their writing. Typically, teachers point out consistent errors to students and offer explanations about why the students' product was incorrect and what the students should have written. If explanation of an error is not sufficient for a student to correct the mistake, additional drill can be provided. With more advanced students, teachers often note errors by writing an abbreviation or number that refers to a scoring guide (see Figure 8.5). Advanced students are expected to seek further explanation when the scoring guide is not self-explanatory.

Summary

In the assessment of written language, teachers can choose among several performance measures within each spiraling instructional strand. The choice of a particular performance measure will depend upon the purpose of instruction and the level of the students.

The assessment of penmanship and spelling is less complex than that of content and style. In the assessment of penmanship, the quality of individual letters produced in isolation and in sequence is usually stressed during acquisition, while fluency in letter production is usually assessed at more advanced stages of instruction. While teachers can choose among a variety of procedures with which to assess spelling, generally dictation tests are more useful than recognition tests or an analysis of spelling in spontaneous writing. The content of written exposition is the most difficult strand to assess. Criteria such as coherence and audience are difficult to define and will probably always retain some degree of subjectivity, although organization can be defined precisely. For beginners, the number of words written and the percentage of correct words are probably the most useful measures of content production, although they are not without limitations. For more advanced students, the generation of ideas and the elimination of systematic

FIGURE 8.3.
Examples of test
questions and probes
to assess
understanding of
writing style.

Part 1: Test Questions

1. What punctuation mark is used after the day when writing the date? For example, June 1___ 1994.

   a) period

   b) comma

   c) dash

   d) colon

2. The picture was _____ over the fireplace.

   a) hanged

   b) hung

   c) hunged

   d) hang

3. The first word of a sentence is always capitalized.

   a) true

   b) false

4. What is the antecedent of *who* in the following sentence? While the dogs and cats gamboled in the back yard, the boys who were working on the car watched them.

   a) dogs and cats

   b) boys

   c) them

   d) automobile

Part 2: Probes

Directions: Circle the words that should **not** be capitalized, and draw a line under the words that should be capitalized.

It was john's birthday—december 7, 1981. it was saturday, and there was no School. john and mary went to mr. Rodger's store to buy Candy. because They liked gummy bears, licorice sticks, and chocolate turtles, They wanted to buy a pound of each to eat while they watched the Grinch on tv. On the way back home, They took the shortcut, across the san diego freeway, but they were careful to dodge all the cars and trucks. mary dropped her candy, and all the cars stopped while she picked it up. When They got home, the kids washed mary's candy, and They watched the Grinch with mom and dad.

Directions: Put in all of the commas and periods that should be in the story.

It was John's birthday—December 7 1981 It was Saturday and there was no school John and Mary went to Mr Rodger's store to buy candy Because they liked gummy bears licorice sticks and chocolate turtles they wanted to buy a pound of each to eat while they watched the Grinch on TV On the way back home they took the shortcut across the freeway but they were careful to dodge all the cars and trucks Mary dropped her candy and all the cars stopped while she picked it up When they got home the kids washed Mary's candy and they watched the Grinch with Mom and Dad

---

Directions: Write the correct punctuation mark in space provided.

It was John___s birthday___December 7___1981___ It was Saturday___and there was no school___John and Mary went to Mr.___Rodger's store to buy candy___ Because they liked gummy bears___licorice sticks___and chocolate turtles___they wanted to buy a pound of each to eat while they watched the Grinch on TV___ On the way back home___they took the shortcut across the freeway___but they were careful to dodge all the cars and trucks___ Mary dropped her candy___and all the cars stopped while she picked it up___When they got home___the kids washed Mary's candy___and they watched the Grinch with Mom and Dad___

FIGURE 8.4
Examples of test questions that prompt punctuation.

AGR = subject-verb or pronoun-antecedent agreement

CE = comma error

D = word choice

DM = dangling modifier (i.e., a word or phrase lacks an antecedent)

FRAG = sentence fragment

lc = make lowercase

SP = spelling error

SS = sentence sense

SUB = subordination

W = wordiness

== capitalization (e.g., new york city)

___/ = punctuation mark (e.g., ?// means use a quotation mark)

^ = omitted word

// = parallel construction

ɣ = delete

FIGURE 8.5.
Commonly used abbreviations for scoring guides that can be attached to student essays (adapted from Hodges, 1956).

errors in organization appear more important. In the style strand, during acquisition, grammar, mechanics, and diction are readily assessed with tests or worksheets intended to assess students' understanding of particular conventions in written English. For more advanced students and during maintenance and generalization, systematic analysis of errors is a common practice.

Extended Example 1[12]

Scenario

It is the beginning of the year, and Mr. Rogers teaches a secondary English class for educable mentally retarded students. Most of his students' IEPs list improvement in written language, particularly in spelling, as instructional goals. Since these students are new to Mr. Rogers's high school class, he decides to pretest his students to learn their relative spelling mastery of basic words. As an initial screening, he assesses their ability to spell the 500 most common words in written English that are contained in the American Heritage Word List. He developed a screening test to assess his students' ability to write from dictation 50 words selected at random from the list. The results of this screening test indicated that 12 of his students could spell approximately 25% of the words, while 6 students could spell at least 90% of these words. Consequently, he decided to form two instructional groups and to teach the lower group to spell all of the words on the list. He has reasoned that if these students could spell the words, they would substantially increase their ability to communicate their ideas in writing. Further assessment of the students in this group indicated that they had limited phonetic skills (e.g., knowledge of initial sounds of consonants and consonant blends).

Step 1: Specify Reason for Assessment

The reason for assessment is to monitor ongoing pupil performance in spelling the words on the 500 words from the word list and simple variants of these words. Specifically, he wanted to monitor (1) the number of new words that are learned, (2) the number of simple variants of the basic spelling list that are generalized, (3) the number of previously learned words that are retained, (4) the number of errors that are made in initial sounds, and (5) the number of errors that are made in the spelling of the word-family stem.

Step 2: Analyze the Curriculum

Mr. Rogers's curriculum contained four basic components: word families, other words, previously learned words, and simple spelling rules. The objectives were formulated at three levels: acquisition, maintenance, and generalization.

---

[12]Please note that the extended example in Chapter 10 deals with using a strategy for written language.

face, place	find, kind, mind, wind	**TABLE 8.2**
act, fact	fine, line	Word Families Based
all, call, fall, shall, small, wall	being, bring, king, thing	on the American
came, became, name, same	is, his	Heritage Word List
an, can, man, human, plan, than, began, woman	it, its	
and, demand, hand, land, stand, thousand	five, live	
any, many	go, no, so	
car, far, war	often, men, ten, then, when, women	
part, start	old, hold, told	
as, has	alone, done	
at, sat, that, what	not, got	
cause, because	other, another, mother	
day, pay, may, play, say, way, away, today, always	could, should, would	
be, me, she, the, we	found, round, around, sound	
dear, fear, hear, near, year	our, hour, your	
tell, well	out, about	
best, rest	cover, over	
get, let, set, yet	how, low, now, show	
fight, light, might, night, right	down, town, own	
bill, fill, still, will	much, such	
in, begin	by, cry, my, try, why	

1. Components

Mr. Rogers's analysis of the curriculum was based on the words to be learned and on the method he chose to use in teaching spelling. Because the students in the lower spelling group lacked sophisticated phonic skills, he decided to teach the spelling of word families.[13] He reasoned that his students could use their skills in producing consonants and consonant blends in conjunction with memorization of family stems. Therefore, he clustered words that had common ending sounds but that differed in their initial sounds. Words that could not be clustered according to families were placed in a separate category, "other words." His clustering of the word list into word families appears in Table 8.2. In the absence of data about the optimal sequencing of word families, he chose to sequence the families according to his perception of the sequence of easy to hard word families. He believed that shorter and phonetically simple word families would be easier to learn than longer and phonetically complex families. In addition, he decided to teach several words per week from the "other word" category.

Since students with learning problems often have trouble generalizing rules, Mr. Rogers's curriculum included several rules for spelling words with changed final morphemes. The particular rules are shown in Table 8.3. Also, since students with learning problems often have trouble retaining what they have

[13]Word families are words that have common endings but differ in initial sounds. For example, the *-ug* family consists of bug, hug, mug, pug, rug, and tug.

TABLE 8.3	*Ending*	*Rules*
Rules for Changing Final Morphemes Selected by Mr. Rogers	Plural:-s[a]	add -s unless the word ends in a consonant and *y* words ending in consonant + *y*, add -*ies*
	Past tense: -*ed*	words ending in -*e*, add -*d* words ending in consonant + *y*, add -*ied* words ending in a vowel + consonant, double the *consonant* and add -*ed*
	-*ing* words	words ending in -*e*, drop -*e* and add -*ing* words ending in a vowel + consonant, double the *consonant* and add -*ed*

[a]Latin words such as gymnasium, curriculum, and so on were not taught as exceptions.

learned, Mr. Rogers had to be concerned about maintenance of the newly learned words and rules. Thus, his sequence of instruction would include periodic review of words that had already been mastered as well as the application of very basic spelling rules to unfamiliar words (e.g., words that have not been assigned).

2. Levels

Three levels of objectives are implicit in the foregoing analysis. At the acquisition and maintenance levels are the individual new words, word families, and the simple spelling rules. At the generalization level is the application of the simple spelling rules to previously untaught instances.

3. Quantification of the Curriculum Analysis

Table 8.4 shows the initial quantification that Mr. Rogers used for his spelling curriculum. Most of his effort was directed at the acquisition and maintenance of the spelling words.

Step 3: Formulate Behavioral Objectives

No specific behavioral objectives were formulated by the MDTs and included in the IEPs. Therefore, Mr. Rogers had to formulate his own objectives.

Mr. Rogers had several choices for the *behavior* in the behavioral objective: to produce the correct spelling of words orally or in writing, to recognize correctly spelled words, or to recognize incorrectly spelled words. He chose writing words.

Mr. Rogers had two options for the *conditions:* a test format where the student would spell words from dictation or an analysis of spontaneous spelling. Since his students were not fluent writers and since students often avoid using words when they are unsure of their spelling, he chose to use a test format. However, he also wanted his students to incorporate the spelling words in their written language. Therefore, he required the students to use the week's spelling words in their weekly writing assignments.

Mr. Rogers decided that he would be satisfied if his students learned to spell about 300 words during the year, which would break down to about 8 words per

	Individual Words	Word-Family Rules	Simple, Final Morpheme Rules	TABLE 8.4 Mr. Rogers's Curriculum Quantification
Acquisition	25%	25%	25%	
Maintenance	10%	10%	5%	
Generalization	—	—	—	

week. His *criterion* for successful performance was percentage correct on newly assigned words and review words. Ideally, he would have preferred 100% accuracy, but he also had to allow for the possibility that his students would make careless errors. Therefore, he selected 90% accuracy for new words and simple variants; he selected 95% accuracy for review words, initial sounds, and word family stems.

Mr. Rogers wrote the following objectives for his students.

Objective 1. When given spelling words from dictation, the student will write the words with 90% accuracy.

Objective 2. When given simple (rule-governed) variants of spelling words from dictation, the student will write the words with 90% accuracy.

Objective 3. When given previously assigned and mastered spelling words from dictation, the student will write the words with 95% accuracy.

Objective 4. When given a week's eight new words, the student will use six of the eight words in a weekly essay. Criteria for correct use included both correct spelling and grammatical sense.

Step 4: Develop Good Assessment Procedures

First, Mr. Rogers estimated the time that would be required if he assessed 8 new spelling words per week, reviewed an additional 18 words per week, and assessed rule generalization with 4 unfamiliar words. Dictating 1 word every 7 seconds, he figured his students could write the 30 words in about 3.5 minutes. In addition, he would need 2 or 3 minutes to hand out and collect the tests. In all, he would need about 7 minutes to give each test. Mr. Rogers thought that this amount of time would be acceptable. Therefore, he allotted 7 minutes for the biweekly assessments.

He then constructed two forms of each test and answer sheet to allow for easy scoring of the tests. The format of these answer sheets is shown in Figure 8.6. In addition to placing new and review words in different columns, he put the rule-application words in a box in the middle of the page. In addition, Mr. Rogers included spaces for student name, date, number of review words correctly spelled, number of new words correctly spelled, and the number of correct rule generalizations.

Steps 5 and 6: Collect and Summarize Data

Mr. Rogers announces to his class each Monday that there will be spelling tests on Wednesday and Friday. If a student got all of the words right on Wednesday's quiz, they were excused from Friday's quiz. When students failed to meet the

FIGURE 8.6.
General format of Mr.
Rogers's spelling tests.

Name ———————————   Today's Date ——————————

1.	new	2.	old	3.	old	4.	old
5.	old	6.	old	7.	new	8.	old
9.	new	10.	old	11.	old	12.	old
13.	old	14.	generalization	15.	generalization	16.	new
17.	new	18.	generalization	19.	generalization	20.	old
21.	new	22.	old	23.	old	24.	old
25.	old	26.	old	27.	new	28.	old
29.	new	30.	old				

——————— * Rev. Wds.   ——————— * New Wds.   ——————— * Gen.

——————— * errors Initial Consonants

criterion by Friday's quiz, they were quizzed on succeeding days until they mastered the words missed. At the appropriate times on Wednesdays and Fridays, he hands out the response forms while the students clear their desks and take out pencils. He begins each test with the following directions: "I will say each word that you are to spell. Write the word in the correct space on your answer sheet. Ready. Word one is ———." Since the spelling tests result in permanent, written products, the tests can be scored later. The total number of correctly spelled new words, the total number of correctly spelled review words, and total number of correctly spelled generalization words are recorded in the appropriate space on the answer sheet.

Each Thursday, each student also writes a 10-minute essay in which six of the eight new spelling words must be used. In addition to scoring the essays for mechanics and the number of words used, he scores them for the presence of the weekly words.

Step 7: Display Data

Since the purpose of Mr. Rogers's assessments was to monitor his students' progress, he used two graphs for each student: one for weekly mastery of words (Figure 8.7) and one for cumulative mastery of words (Figure 8.8). After he has scored each quiz and tabulated the percentage correct for new words and review words, Mr. Rogers enters the data points on each student's chart. He also used a table so that he could monitor each student's mastery of the rules he was teaching (Figure 8.9). In addition he recorded in his grade book the number of words correctly used in each week's essay.

Step 8: Interpret Data and Make Decisions

Mr. Rogers reviews each student's charts and his gradebook and decides to make modifications to the programs of individual students when they fail to meet criterion for two or more consecutive weeks. Jim's (JS) graphs are shown in Figures 8.6 and 8.7. Although Jim's use of spelling words in the weekly essays was always perfect during the first three weeks, his performance on new and review

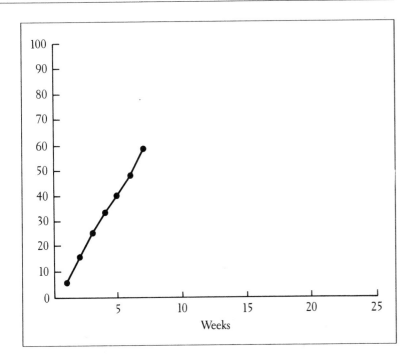

FIGURE 8.7.
JS's weekly spelling
quiz results.

FIGURE 8.8
Cumulative spelling
words mastered.

| | Students | | | | | | | | | | | |
	BA	WC	JF	JG	CH	TJ	LM	RP	JS	CT	HT	DW
Rules												
Plurals[a]												
add *-s* unless the word ends in a consonant and *y*	x	x	x	x	x	x	x	x	x	x	x	x
add *-ies* to words ending in consonant + *y*	x	x	x	x	x	x	x	x	x	x	x	x
Past Tense *-ed*												
add *-d* to words ending in *-e*	x	x	x	x	x	x	x	x	x	x	x	x
drop *-y* and add *-ied* to words ending in consonant and *y*	x	x		x	x			x		x	x	x
double the consonant and add *-ed* to words that end in a vowel and consonant	x				x					x	x	
Present Progressive *-ing*												
drop *-e* and add *-ing* to words ending in *-e*												
double the consonant and add *-ing* to words ending in a vowel and cosonant												
	BA	WC	JF	JG	CH	TJ	LM	RP	JS	CT	HT	DW

FIGURE 8.9   Mastery of simple rules by Mr. Rogers's students.

words were below the targeted criteria. Even though Jim appeared to be highly motivated and paying attention, his performance was not satisfactory. After the third week, Mr. Rogers decided to increase the amount of purposeful rehearsal. Mr. Rogers indicated the change in instructional procedures on Jim's chart by inserting a vertical line and not connecting points that the line separated. After the change in instruction, Jim's performance increased. Some of this information can be gleaned from his cumulative progress chart (Figure 8.8), but it is not nearly as useful as adjusting instruction.

Mr. Rogers also monitored his students' acquisition of simple spelling rules (Figure 8.9). The first three rules were known by several of his students prior to his instruction. The remaining students mastered the rules easily. The next two rules proved more difficult. While Mr. Rogers could come to this conclusion by reviewing individual charts, it is abundantly clear from his table (Figure 8.9) that his instructional procedures were not effective. Mr. Rogers will have to redesign his instructional program for teaching simple rules.

Summary

Mr. Rogers screened his students and formed an instructional group that needed systematic instruction in the spelling of commonly used English words. He set up several instructional programs and developed appropriate assessment procedures

for each program. He used biweekly quizzes to monitor acquisition and maintenance of spelling words and spelling-rule usage and particular types of errors
made by each student. After using his programs and evaluating student performance, Mr. Rogers discovered that his initial programs were not always working
as he had hoped. Therefore, he modified instruction.

Extended Example 2

Scenario

Marc is a second-grader receiving special-education services in Ms. Li's resource
room for his problems in written language and mathematics. Although he has no
sensory or motor impairments, he prints manuscript letters (and writes numbers)
so slowly—at a rate of 27 letters per minute—that his assignments are seldom
completed. Moreover, his performance on any type of timed test is unsatisfactory
because so little is written although what he does write is generally correct.

Ms. Li decided upon a two-pronged strategy to improve Marc's poor tool-skill
rate. First, she decided to intervene directly to try to increase his rate of writing
letters and words. She communicated her belief to Marc that he could write faster
with practice and that they would be working on that skill for a few minutes each
day. Each day she would have him copy a passage; he would be allowed 3 minutes
to copy as much as he could. Additionally, to see if his printing speed generalized to
spontaneous production, Ms. Li tallied the number of correctly formed letters in
each Friday's story-writing session in which students were given a story starter and
allowed 5 minutes to write. Second, she allowed Marc to use a microcassette tape
recorder to complete homework assignments orally. (She also urged Ms. Clayburg,
Marc's teacher in the regular classroom, to allow Marc to complete his assignments
orally whenever possible so that he would not be penalized for his slow writing.)

Step 1: Specify Reason for Assessment

Ms. Li performed daily assessment of Marc's copying and weekly assessments of
the number of letters written in each story to monitor his progress.

Step 2: Analyze the Curriculum

Since Marc demonstrates no problems in the formation of letters in isolation or
sequence or problems with particular letters, whether capitals or lowercase, Ms.
Li did not believe curriculum analysis was required. However, Ms. Li did make
sure that Marc copied material that contained numerous capital letters and
formed both capital and lowercase letters correctly.

Step 3: Formulate Behavioral Objectives

Ms. Li decided to use a changing-criterion design to accelerate Marc's rate. Her
aim was 100 letters per minute, and her initial criterion was 36 letters per minute.
Since Marc appeared to enjoy using the Apple IIG computer located in the

learning center to practice his math, he would be allowed an extra 5 minutes each day that his writing rate exceeded 36 letters per minute for the 3-minute session. In addition, if his rate exceeded 30 letters per minute in his written story, he would be given 5 minutes to play a computer game. The initial objectives for Marc are:

Objective 1. Given a pencil and lined paper, Marc will copy words from his basal reader at a rate of 36 letters per minute.

Objective 2. Given pencil, lined paper, and a story starter, Marc will write a 5-minute essay at a rate of 30 letters per minute.

When the first objective is met or exceeded on three consecutive sessions, Marc will be told that the criterion level has been increased. Ms. Li did not specify the criterion for the second objective since that decision will rest in part on how long it takes Marc to reach 36 letters per minute. (The longer it takes him, the smaller will be the increase.) This procedure will be followed until Marc reaches the aim of 100 letters per minute or his progress levels off at a lower, but minimally acceptable, rate (e.g., 80 letters per minute).

Step 4: Develop Good Assessment Procedures

Ms. Li photocopied passages from stories that Marc had already read in his basal reading series. The passages for the first objective contained between 250 and 275 letters to guarantee that Marc could exceed the initial objective.

Steps 5 and 6: Collect and Summarize Data

Each day at about 11:00 A.M., Ms. Li would take Marc to the learning center for him to practice. He was to bring his pencil and paper, and she would give him a page with the passage to be copied. Ms. Li used a kitchen timer that would ring after a predetermined interval to time the session. She explained that he was to begin copying on her signal and to stop when the timer rang. Then he was to bring his paper and the other materials to her desk. Since the other students in her class were usually engaged in seatwork at that time, Ms. Li would count the number of correct letters and calculate Marc's rate. A letter was counted if it was legible, and no deductions were made for omissions.

Each Friday all students wrote short stories for 5 minutes from a variety of story starters. In addition to the things she checked in all students' stories, Ms. Li counted the number of letters correctly formed in Marc's story to see if increases in his tool-skill rate were generalizing to other written work.

Steps 7 and 8: Display Data; Interpret Data and Make Decisions

Ms. Li entered Marc's daily rate of writing letters on an equal-interval graph. As shown in Figure 8.10, it took Marc three days to reach the first criterion (35 letters per minute), and Ms. Li kept the criterion at that level for four more days; that week his essay was written at a rate of 31 letters per minute. Then Ms. Li raised the criterion to 45 letters per minute. Within four days, Marc was copying letters at a rate of 45 or more letters per minute, and his weekly essay also

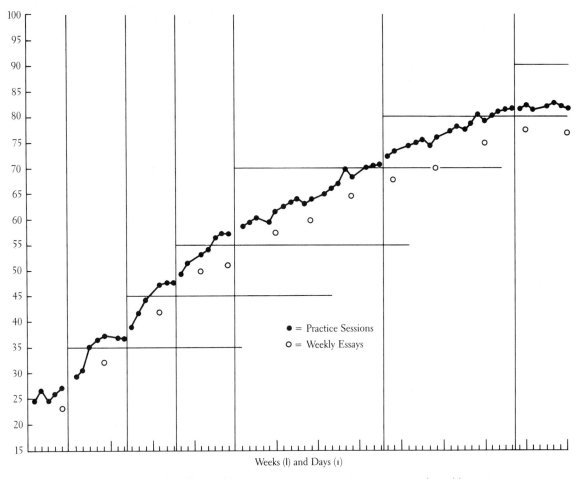

FIGURE 8.10.   Marc's rate of producing letters per minute in practice sessions and weekly stories.

contained more letters. Ms. Li continued to raise the criterion and provide practice. After 11 weeks, Marc's progress slowed considerably. He was consistently performing at a rate of between 80 and 85 letters per minute but was unable to attain 85 letters per minute. Ms. Li decided to consolidate gains at that level. Marc was put on a maintenance program in which he was reinforced for producing letters at a rate greater than 80 letters per minute, and practice sessions were reduced to Mondays, Wednesdays, and Fridays. Ms. Li was satisfied with Marc's progress, and he continued on maintenance until the end of the semester.

Summary

In the beginning of the year, Ms. Li noted that Marc was producing letters and numbers in spontaneous work at a very low rate. She decided to intervene using a changing-criterion design in which Marc practiced printing faster and faster and was reinforced for increases in his production. As Marc's rate of producing letters per minute increased, his fluency in weekly essays also increased, although these rates of increase generally lagged behind increases in his tool skill. As Marc was reaching a minimally acceptable rate, his progress flattened out, and Ms. Li put him on a maintenance program. Nonetheless, he continued to show modest improvement in his rate of letters per minute, and Ms. Li again raised the criterion.

Chapter 9

Curriculum-Based Assessment in Adaptive and Social Behavior

Key Terms

Adaptive behavior
Critical incident log
Daily living skill
Nomination

Rating scale
Social behavior
Sociogram

Social and adaptive behavior are general concepts that have nebulous meanings. Despite their fuzziness, these concepts play important roles in education. Philosophers, social scientists, and professional organizations whose ideas have been important in American education have promulgated a variety of goals for social and adaptive behavior—for example, civic responsibility, worthwhile use of leisure time, self-actualization (cf. Gross, 1978; Maslow, 1954; National Education Association, 1918). In the schools, the social behavior of a student plays an important role in decisions made about what, where, and how to teach that student. Poor social or adaptive behavior (coupled with other student characteristics) can result in a student being classified as exceptional—mentally retarded, emotionally disturbed, behaviorally disordered, and so forth. Relative levels of social behavior and relative absence of maladaptive or disruptive behavior are important determiners for the type of educational setting into which students are placed. Usually, the more disruptive or the lower the adaptivity of behavior, the more restrictive is the educational placement.

Much of what is called social behavior is culturally determined. Communication is a ready example. Not only is the language that one learns culturally determined, but the pragmatics of that language (e.g., speaking distance, eye contact, accompanying gestures) are also cultural. Perhaps in the strictest sense these concepts describe behavior that is valued by society. Certainly the converse is true: Maladaptive and antisocial behavior is not valued. Almost all behavior is neutral;[1] its value depends primarily on three factors.

- *The context in which the behavior occurs.* The context or circumstances in which an act occurs have a major influence on how that act will be evaluated. For example, aiming and firing a pistol at another person is a neutral act even when that other person is shot and killed. Most people cannot tell if it is a good act or a bad act without knowing the context. Did the shooting occur in a war? Did the shooting occur in self-defense? Was the shooting an accident? Did he or she know the gun was loaded? Since American society condones shooting people under certain circumstances, shooting cannot be viewed as inherently bad.
- *The status of the person exhibiting the behavior.* Some behaviors are generally devalued by American society, but they are valued even less when individuals of lower social status perform them. Airline pilots who report UFOs are given the benefit of the doubt, while eccentric individuals may be thought to be hallucinating or seeking attention.
- *The presence of an observer.* If the behavior is never observed (or reported), it will never be evaluated negatively by another person.

Scope of Adaptive and Social Behavior

The scope of adaptive and social behavior depends on the definitions that one uses to limit these domains. It quickly becomes apparent that these two categories are not mutually exclusive. *Social behavior* is an inclusive term for any action that affects another individual. Most behavior can be classified as social. For example, smoking tobacco may be seen as a highly personal action. Yet it has social consequences beyond the smoker: passive smoking by nonsmokers, increased mortality and morbidity rates of smokers that affect health insurance rates of nonsmokers, and so forth. Thus, much of what is taught in the schools could be considered part of a social behavior curriculum. For example, whenever communication is involved, the academic area has social implications: Verbal communication obviously plays a major role in the reading and writing of English and foreign languages; nonverbal communication plays a major role in mathematics, music, and visual arts. Social curricula are distingushed by the relative emphasis on the application of information and skills and not their content.

Adaptive behavior is an inclusive term for any action that increases people's likelihood of physical survival and ability to cope with social and physical de-

---

[1]Some behavior approaches universal devaluation—for example, smearing oneself with excrement (Murphy, 1976). However, these behaviors are most extreme, as evidenced by our example.

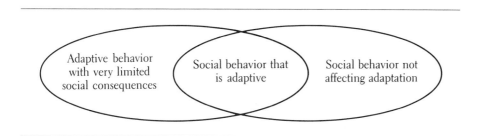

Figure 9.1.
Relationship between
adaptive and social
behavior.

mands of their environments. Coping takes two forms—adjusting one's behavior to conform with these environmental demands and modifying environmental demands to conform with one's personal abilities and preferences. Two additional restrictions are generally imposed before a behavior can be considered adaptive. First, ability to perform the behavior is insufficient; the behavior must be performed consistently. Second, the behavior must be performed by the individual, not for the individual; adaptive behavior is performed independently.

In the sections that follow, these two domains are discussed separately, although they have much in common. The Venn diagram in Figure 9.1 illustrates how these two concepts overlap and where their primary differences lie.

Adaptive Behavior

Over the years, various classifications and components have been offered (Doll, 1935; Nihira, 1969), and six major strands of adaptive behavior have been consistently identified.

1. Daily living skills. This term has been applied to the collection of skills necessary for managing one's life. Subsumed in this category are four subcomponents.

- Self-help skills are those skills and subskills involved in eating, food preparation, dressing, and personal health and hygiene. Any of these subcomponents can be subdivided further. For example, eating can be subdivided into ordering foods outside of the home and proper use of eating utensils.

- Domestic skills are those skills involved in maintaining one's immediate environment in a neat and clean manner. Within this subcomponent, several subsets can be identified: laundry skills, dishwashing, doing routine household chores (e.g., setting the table for a meal), and taking care of one's belongings.

- Play or leisure-time skills are those necessary for participation in recreational activities (e.g., knowing the rules of games and sports, locating and getting to recreational sites).

- Resource management skills are those skills necessary for budgeting one's time and money.

2. Communication skills. This term that has been applied to a set of skills necessary for expressing one's own thoughts and feelings and understanding those of others. Subsumed in this category are three subcomponents.

- Expressive skills in communication refer to the production of communication: speaking, writing, drawing, gesturing, and using more artificial means of communication (e.g., language boards).
- Receptive skills in communication refer to the understanding of speech, written language (both literal and figural), and gestures.
- Pragmatic aspects of communication include such language-related factors as speaking distance, eye contact, volume, inflection, affect, formality (e.g., friendly letters versus business letters), and accompanying gestures.

3. Locomotion and transportation skills. These skills are necessary for mobility in one's environment. Subsumed under the subcategory of transportation are three subcomponents.

- Use of person-powered vehicles refers to the safe and appropriate use of vehicles and toys (e.g., bikes and rowboats).
- Use of motorized personal vehicles refers to the safe and appropriate use of conveyances for transportation and recreation.
- Use of public transportation includes locating, getting on, getting off, paying fares, planning arrivals and departures in accordance with published schedules, and using appropriate language when using public transportation.

4. Prevocational and vocational skills. These skills are associated with the acquisition and performance of job-related skills necessary for economic independence as an adult. Vocational skills usually consist of four subcategories.

- Prevocational preparation refers to the acquisition of the general skills necessary for gainful employment. Included in this category are social skills (e.g., social interaction on the job, punctuality, dependability, following instructions), as well as basic literacy and computational skills.
- Job preparation includes learning the general skills required for an occupation and obtaining the necessary working papers (e.g., a social security or a green card).
- Job application refers to the collection of skills needed to secure employment (e.g., using classified advertisements, completing application forms, dressing and speaking appropriately when applying for work, completing tax withholding forms).
- Job performance skills are the particular skills that one is paid to perform (e.g., a carpenter is paid for sawing, measuring, trueing, fastening, planing).

5. Self-Control skills. These skills are associated with inhibiting undesirable behaviors and selectively exhibiting behavior that can be inappropriate under certain circumstances.

- Selective exhibition implies knowing the social expectations associated with public display of certain behavior and conforming to these expectations. Many behaviors that are quite appropriately performed privately are considered inappropriate when performed publicly. While some violations of social expectations merely label the person as uncouth (e.g., picking teeth or clipping fingernails publicly), others mark the individual as immature (e.g., having one's food at a restaurant cut by someone else) or deviant (e.g., public masturbation).

- Inhibiting undesirable behavior refers to knowing that certain acts, whether performed publicly or privately, are not acceptable and conforming to these social taboos. Behavior included in this category is likely to cause harm to the person exhibiting the behavior (e.g., head banging) or to the target of the behavior (e.g., spouse abuse).

6. *Social graces.* Social graces are those actions and words that the use of which label one as polite, mannerly, cool, or suave.

- Verbal indices of a socially graceful person include using polite words and phrases (e.g., "thank you," "please," "may I," "excuse me"), giving appropriate compliments (e.g., "My, you look nice tonight, Bill"), and avoiding critical comments (e.g., "Boy, have you gotten fat").

- Actions that indicate social graces include consideration (e.g., holding a door for a person whose arms are occupied), deference (e.g., rising when a person of special status enters a room), and cooperation (e.g., turn taking).

7. *Civic responsibility.* Civic responsibility refers to fulfilling one's obligations to one's community, state (provincial), and national government. With young children, it refers to meeting obligations to family. With school-age children, civic responsibility is expanded to include responsibility to the school and community—following school rules, participating in civic-minded organizations such as the scouts. For individuals who have reached legal majority, civic responsibility includes obeying the law, voting, being informed on political issues, and so forth.

8. *Absence of maladaptive behavior.* In recent years adaptive behavior has come to include the absence of maladaptive behavior—behavior that is incompatible with adaptive behavior or that increases one's chances of being socially ostracized.

- Behavior incompatible with adaptive behavior might be stereotypic (e.g., arm flapping, rocking, refusing to touch objects), noncompliant, either hyperactive or hypoactive, or self-injurious (e.g., head banging, suicide).

- Behavior that leads to social isolation can be disturbing (e.g., public sexuality), annoying (e.g., constant humming), odd (e.g., dressing inappropriately), rude (e.g., cursing or using offensive words), or otherwise offensive (e.g., having body odor).

Social Behavior

When social skills are viewed as any behavior critical to successful interaction with another person, almost all behavior can be classified as social in nature. Thus, any compilation of behaviors or competencies would be staggering. In the schools, the nature and extent of social curricula depend to a large extent on where a child is educated. Typically, in mainstream classes the socialization process is somewhat informal; parents are expected to have taught their children how to act in socially appropriate ways. Minor exceptions are handled without resorting to a formal curriculum. If a student has major deficits or excesses in social behavior, they will more likely receive more intensive and systematic instruction in how to behave in socially acceptable ways. Such instruction may be delivered in a special classroom with students labeled "emotionally disturbed" or "behaviorally disordered." In this setting, teaching prosocial behaviors becomes a priority and more attention is given to the scope and sequence on an individual level. However, even teachers of students with severe behavior problems may lack access to special curricula for two possible reasons. First, school systems for the most part have not adopted existing social curricula to the same extent as academic curricula. Second, publishers may not perceive a large enough market to develop and market this type of product. However, some curricula do exist and a partial list, compiled by Carter and Sugai (1988), are included in Table 9.1

Cartledge and Milburn (1986) have reviewed several commerical curricula. Although different categorization plans are used by the various authors, the skills to be acquired from these curricula can be grouped into six strands.

- *Self-related skills* include accepting the consequences of one's own behavior, expressing one's feelings, being organized, and possessing various self-help skills of the type commonly termed "adaptive" (cf. Bursuck & Lessen, 1987; Stephens, 1978 [in Table 9.1]; Walker et al., 1983 [in Table 9.1]).

TABLE 9.1
Sources of Social Skills Curricula

Goldstein, A. P., Sprafkin, R. P., Gershaw, M. J., & Klein, P. (1980). *Skillstreaming the adolescent: A structured learning approach to teaching prosocial skills.* Champaign, IL: Research Press.

Jackson, J. F., Jackson, D. A., & Monroe, C. (1983). *Getting along with others: Teaching social effectiveness to children.* Champaign, IL: Research Press.

McGinnis, E., & Goldstein, A. P. (1984). *Skillstreaming the elementary school child: A guide for teaching prosocial skills.* Champaign, IL: Research Press.

Spence, S. (1981). *Social skills training with children and adolescents: A counselor's manual.* Windsor, Berks, London: NFER-Nelson.

Stephens, T. M. (1978). *Social skills in the classroom.* Columbus, OH: Cedar Press.

Waksman, S. A., & Messmer, C. L. (1985). *Assertive behavior: A program for teaching social skills to children and adolescents.* Portland, OR: Enrichment Press.

Walker, H. M., McConnell, S., Holmes, D., Todis, B., Walker, J., & Golden, N. (1983). *The Walker social skills curriculum: The ACCEPTS program.* Austin, TX: PRO-ED.

Wilkinson, J., & Canter, S. (1982). *Social skills training manual: Assessment, program design, and management of training.* New York: Wiley.

- *Interpersonal skills* include accepting authority, greeting and bidding farewell to others, having conversations, having acceptable physical contact with a person or a person's property, basic interaction skills (e.g., eye contact, taking turns, talking, sharing, using polite words), and making and keeping friends (cf. Germann & Tindal, 1985; Stephens, 1978 [in Table 9.1]; Walker et al., 1983 [in Table 9.1]).

- *Environmental skills* include caring for the environment and dealing with emergencies (cf. Stephens, 1978 [in Table 9.1]).

- *Task-related skills* include completing tasks, listening to the teacher and other students, beginning work, staying with and completing a task, and paying attention (cf. Bursuck & Lessen, 1987; Stephens, 1978 [in Table 9.1]; Walker et al., 1983 [in Table 9.1]).

- *Classroom skills* include following classroom rules and teacher directions, asking and answering questions, and seeking assistance as needed (cf. Bursuck & Lessen, 1987; Walker et al., 1983 [in Table 9.1]).

- *Absence of undesirable behavior* includes not making noises that distract peers and/or teacher from the current activity (e.g., talking out, tapping), *not* being out of place (e.g., being out of seat, being in the wrong place), not being off the task (i.e., any movement off assigned task/activity that does not fall into the above categories such as staring or doodling), and lacking social behavior (i.e., being withdrawn or socially isolated) (cf. Germann & Tindal, 1985).

Concluding Comments

Many adaptive and social skills may manifest themselves in a variety of ways that depend on a student's cultural milieu. For example, children might show deference to high-status adults by not questioning the adults with whom they deal or by speaking politely (e.g., with eyes lowered, using polite words, and the correct *tone* and volume). Students who experience difficulty with this type of social skill may be taught both the cultural manifestation preferred by the teacher and the majority in the child's cultural community.

Teachers often target for intervention adaptive and social behaviors that are disruptive to the educational process—to the students themselves, to their peers, or to their teachers. Such intervention targets are quite reasonable when a student's behavior violates established school rules, society's laws, or will significantly interfere with a student's social or personal development. Thus, interventions have the potential to benefit either the students who are candidates for social skill training or their peers (or both). However, in many instances, the targeted behavior may lack social validity. For example, while truly disruptive classroom behavior should be modified, some behavior that is personally disturbing to teachers may not bother, offend, or disturb the students in the classroom or even other teachers. Furthermore, noncompliance with classroom or teacher rules may have no impact on either learning or peer acceptance—a variable that can affect a student long past his school career. The ultimate criterion for selecting target behavior is to teach skills that will help students in as many situations as possible.

Sequence of Adaptive and Social Behavior

The actual sequence followed in instruction varies as a function of several parameters. Some social behavior follows a developmental sequence. For example, play usually occurs first as a solitary activity, then as a parallel activity, and finally as a cooperative activity; the skills involved in locomotion are primarily developmental in nature—creeping, crawling, walking, running. Students who are delayed in the acquisition of developmental social skills are placed in curricula that follow the typical developmental sequence.

Other social skills do not follow a typical developmental sequence. In such cases, the target behavior is taught directly. When a social skill is complex, it may be broken down in smaller slices, and the components taught individually. For example, using a public bus requires knowing where to be to get it, paying, appropriate behavior while on the bus, and when and how to signal the driver to get off. These subskills can be taught in almost any sequence, although local conditions may necessitate some ordering of the skills (e.g., if exact change is required, that skill should be taught before getting on is taught).

Assessment of Adaptive and Social Behavior

Four types of problems can make the assessment of adaptive and social behavior particularly difficult. *First*, some behavior of interest is difficult for teachers to observe. Many deviant social behaviors (e.g., extortion of lunch money) occur at relatively low frequencies (e.g., once a day) and students deliberately avoid observation by adults (e.g., the money is extorted when no teachers are present to protect the victim). Other socially and instructionally important behaviors occur off the school campus (e.g., using public transportation) or at night (e.g., dating). *Second*, we are interested in the impact of some adaptive and social behavior on other people. The impact of these behaviors often cannot be observed directly because it is internal; the behaviors can only be inferred from the verbalizations and actions of classmates. Moreover, teachers may be upset by behavior that is well tolerated by a student's peers. This point is especially important when teachers try to establish interventions to increase peer acceptance. There is the danger that teachers will target the wrong behavior for intervention. *Third*, many adaptive and social behaviors are emotionally laden. Teachers and parents may feel uncomfortable discussing and developing interventions for some behavior because of the cultural values associated with them—sexuality, bodily functions (e.g., elimination or menstruation), recreational drug use, and so on. *Fourth*, many adaptive and social behaviors are targeted for intervention because they are exhibited with excessive amplitude (e.g., overreactions, talking too loudly). Such behavior is difficult to assess directly (outside of laboratories) and can be a function of a teacher's personal tolerance. Because of these problems, indirect assessment strategies may be the only realistic assessment option available. Teachers and psychologists sometimes must rely on less precise ratings or impressions of behavior for screening, placement, program planning, and program evaluation.

Indirect Measures of Social Behavior

Because of the problems associated with low-frequency and out-of-school behavior, teachers and psychologists often must rely upon the *reports* of behavior. While such reports themselves may not be completely accurate, they offer an efficient but less accurate alternative to the observation of difficult-to-observe behavior.

Measure 1: Adult ratings of social behavior. Some information about a student can be obtained from adults who have had sufficient opportunity to observe the student outside of the school situation and who are willing to report what they have seen. However, the relationship between ratings and direct observations is weak.

Teachers can do five things to objectify adult ratings. *First*, they can state the behavior as objectively as possible. For example, ask the respondent, "Does the child do [behavior of interest]?" *Second*, when asking about the behavior, also ask about the circumstances or conditions under which the child performs the behavior: "Does the child do [behavior of interest] when [circumstances]?" *Third*, teachers can ask the respondent to estimate the frequency, duration, or intensity of the behavior. For example, how often does the child make a fuss at bedtime? How long does the fussing usually last? *Fourth*, teachers and psychologists can maintain a nonevaluative and accepting demeanor because a parent's or teacher's own self-esteem may come into play (cf. Mealor & Richmond, 1980; Soyster & Ehly, 1986; Wall & Paradise, 1981). For example, parents might overstate the accomplishments or minimize the deviance of their child for fear that they might appear to be inadequate parents. In addition, teachers and psychologists should be sensitive to the possibility of an "acquiescent response set" in which parents may respond as they think the interviewer expects them to respond (cf. Reschly, 1982). *Fifth*, when possible a teacher or psychologist should try to get the same information from more than one person (e.g., from both mom and dad).

Measure 2: Self-ratings of social behavior. With older students and adults, self-ratings can often result in more accurate appraisals than those obtained from parents. While self-ratings can be used to pinpoint and monitor behavior, the same precautions used with adult ratings should be used with self-ratings.

Measure 3: Peer ratings of social behavior and acceptance. Sociometrics, a commonly used form of peer ratings (Moreno, 1953), is used to establish relative status and/or acceptance of students within a classroom. They can be used to screen students for social-skill problems, predict later social adjustment difficulties (e.g., delinquency), and measure the general impact of an intervention on a student's status with peers (Cartledge & Milburn, 1986). There are two basic types of sociometric procedures—nomination and rating.

With *nomination* measures, students are requested to name several (usually three) classmates on the basis of some social criterion. For example, students could be asked to name three students in the class with whom they would most like to play or to name three classmates with whom they would most like to work on a social studies project. These positive nominations can identify popular students but cannot tell a teacher if unnominated students are actively rejected or

Figure 9.2.
A Sociogram for the
question, "With whom
would you most like to
study?"

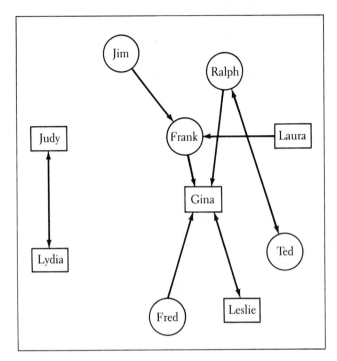

their peers just don't feel strongly about them one way or the other. If the intent is to identify students who are unpopular,[2] then nominations can be worded negatively (e.g., "Name three students with whom you would *not* like to work"). Also, a combination of both positive and negative nominations can be used in the same process. Some concern exists that asking children to identify classmates with whom they do not want to play is insensitive to the feelings of those students who know (or suspect) that they are unpopular. Another concern is that negative nomination will foster an undesirable attitude toward nominated students and perhaps create a self-fulfilling prophesy of rejection (e.g., Deno, Mirkin, Robinson, & Evans, 1980). Others, such as Hayvren and Hymel (1984), state that this phenomenon does not occur. Since there does not appear to be consensus about the effects of negative nomination, teachers must rely on their own judgment and be sensitive to any problems that might arise through use of this technique.

When scoring and reporting nomination data, teachers have two options. Scores can be reported as the total number of nominations received for each student. The results can be displayed in a *sociogram* such as the one depicted in Figure 9.2.

When *rating procedures* are used, students are asked to evaluate each classmate on some social criterion. Unlike nomination procedures in which students are asked to select a few favorites or nonfavorites, all students are judged. Ratings can

[2]Other variables besides social behavior can effect popularity or acceptance within the classroom setting—for example, physical characteristics such as facial attractiveness or obesity (Salvia, Sheare, & Algozzine, 1975).

Directions: Circle the number that best describes how you feel about each of your classmates. Please do not allow others to see your form or discuss it with other students.

	like a lot	like	don't know very well	don't like	don't like at all
Richie C.	5	4	3	2	1
▪					
▪					
▪					
Ginger R.	5	4	3	2	1

Figure 9.3.
A sociometric rating procedure using a Likert-type scale.

be made either by ranking classmates or by using a Likert-type scale. Figure 9.3 contains an example of the latter procedure adapted from Cartledge and Milburn (1986).

Five guidelines for administering sociometric measures have been identified by Hughes and Ruhl (1984): (1) Increase the validity of the measurement by administering in classes where students have opportunities for a variety of interactions (e.g., academic and social). (2) Repeat sociometrics over the school year in order to assess the stability of student attitudes. This is especially critical for younger students since the nature of their relationships tend to vary more than for older students. (3) Ensure privacy and confidentiality of results (e.g., do not ask students to pass their forms forward). (4) For young students or poor readers, use photographs of students with their names printed on the picture. The students may then copy the name when completing the sociometric rating or put pictures in an envelope coded with the sociometric criterion. (5) Administer individually with younger or mentally handicapped students to ensure they understand what is being required of them.

Finally, there are four important considerations in using sociometric techniques. First, Gronlund (1985) warns against generalizing results from one sociometric criterion to another: A student may not receive a high number of nominations for working on an academic project but may for participating in a social activity. Second, relationships are not always stable—even best friends may hate each other for a short period. Third, being popular does not always mean a student is well behaved; "tough guys" and "class clowns" can be respected or liked by their peers. Therefore, sociometrics may not be sensitive to compliance problems that may be interfering with successful functioning in the classroom. Fourth, knowledge of a student's popularity or lack thereof does not help identify specific behavioral excesses or deficits that may contribute to social acceptance (Cartledge & Milburn, 1986; Deno et al., 1980).[3]

[3]One method for dealing with this problem is to follow up the sociometric rating with an interview in which students are asked questions such as, "Could you tell me what Janie does that makes you not like her?"

Figure 9.4.
Examples of items
rating the quality of
performance.

Directions: Check the highest level of performance attained by the student.

Drinks from a cup
_____ cup must be held for the student
_____ cup must be steadied for the student
_____ student drinks from small cup using two hands and with some spilling
_____ student drinks from large glass using one hand without spilling
_____ student holds wine glass by stem

Directions: Check all that apply to the student's written assignments.
_____ papers not handed in
_____ papers handed in late
_____ papers are rumpled
_____ papers contain food stains
_____ papers contain messy cross-outs
_____ papers contain too many misspelled words

Figure 9.5.
Example of a scale to
rate independent
performance.

Directions: Check the level of assistance required by student to complete task.
_____ Physical guidance required
_____ Physical prompting required
_____ Verbal prompting required at each step
_____ Verbal prompting required at some steps
_____ Performs task on request

Measure 4: Adult ratings of the quality of performance. Adult ratings are also used to pinpoint areas of adaptive behavior in need of instruction as well as to assess acquisition and maintenance. While such scales are conceptually similar to the Likert-type scales used with social behavior, they assess how the behavior is performed rather than the impact of the behavior on others.

Two types of ratings are typically used. One type (Figure 9.4) examines the quality of performance. Quality is assessed in terms of approximation of error-free performance or approximation of performance by a person judged competent. The second type (Figure 9.5) examines the degree of independence with which the performance is accomplished. Independence is assessed by the amount of help a student requires to produce the behavior.

Direct Measures of Social Behavior

Assessment of classroom behavior typically begins with a screening process designed to pinpoint behavior for intervention. Often, teachers form an impression that a student is having a problem. At this stage terms such as "troublemaker," "hyperactive," "disorganized," or "poor work habits" are used to describe the student in question. Once teachers are aware of a problem, they must move beyond general, imprecise descriptions and develop hypotheses about the specific behavior that interferes with academic and social success in their classrooms.

1. Keep a *critical incidents log* in which are noted descriptions of antecedents, behavior, and consequences, as well as dates and times of incidents of important behavior.
2. Develop a rating form if the data in the log indicate that a problem of sufficient seriousness exists. The behavior can be rated on a four-point scale (e.g., frequently a problem, occasionally a problem, seldom a problem, or never a problem). Ratings are obtained for at least three days, from several settings (e.g., large group, independent work, transitions, recess), and in several academic subjects (e.g., reading, math, social studies). Before proceeding with more intensive assessment and intervention, a teacher must decide if decreasing or increasing the behavior is likely to help a student enough to justify the amount of time and effort needed. Also, a teacher must ask if the behavior is being selected because it is personally disturbing rather than so maladaptive that it affects the student's ability to function in a variety of settings.
3. Make direct observations if the ratings indicate a problem of sufficient magnitude. The antecedents and consequences of the target behavior also should be noted. In addition, data should be taken at the same time on up to five peers to ascertain if the target student's behavior is atypical of the rest of the class.

When the specific behavior is selected, the three-step procedure shown in Table 9.2 can facilitate decision making about the accuracy of the teacher's initial perceptions and the extent to which and under what circumstances the behavior is occurring.

These three steps allow a teacher to decide if the behavior in question should be targeted for intervention, as well as provide a teacher with three bits of information useful for formulating interventions: (1) likely stimuli that cause a student to behave inappropriately, (2) possible discriminative stimuli for the undesirable behavior,[4] and (3) events that are likely to reinforce (and therefore maintain) the undesirable behavior. For example, it is not enough to know that Jimmy sometimes rips up his papers in Ms. Clayburg's class. Ms. Clayburg could better plan an intervention if she knew that Jimmy rips up only worksheets containing long division problems or that he rips up worksheets only when his best friend, Waldo, is present or that Ms. Clayburg gives him easier problems after he rips up the worksheet. Finally, the data gathered on peers also can be used to set criteria for objectives in interventions on the target behavior. For example if the mean rate of talk-outs for nonproblem students were two per day, the aim for the target student should be the same.

As discussed in Chapter 4, teachers can assess behavior conveniently and directly through systematic observation. As is the case for any systematic observation, the target behavior must be carefully defined, and criteria for successful performance must be set. Most often criteria are determined through social comparison. Teachers must also decide which characteristic of behavior they wish to use in their performance measures: frequency (or rate), duration, or latency.

[4]Discriminative stimuli are events, conditions, or people that provide a signal that a particular behavior will occur. They set the stage for a stimulus to elicit a response.

Performance Measures Using Frequency and Rate

Frequency or rate data can be obtained through event recording and momentary time-sampling procedures. To use event recording, behavior should be discrete (i.e., have a clear ending and beginning), of brief duration, easily counted, and not occur at a high frequency. Data derived from event recording can be reported as the number of occurrences during the observational period if the times for each observation remain constant and the opportunities to respond are equivalent between sessions. However, because it is unlikely, except under very controlled situations, that a student will have exactly the same number of opportunities to exhibit the target behavior, data from event recording are better reported as the percentage of correct responses (i.e., correct responses divided by the opportunities to respond).

Momentary time sampling is best used with behavior that occurs at a high rate (e.g., stereotypic behaviors such as hand flapping), is nondiscrete (e.g., on or off task), or is of long duration (e.g., out of seat). Data are summarized as the number of intervals provided that the number of intervals between observations is constant; when they are not constant, the data should be converted to percentage of intervals at the end of which the student exhibited the target behavior.

An advantage of time sampling over event recording is that the teacher does not have to observe continuously and can be involved in other instructional activites. Also, it is easier to record the behavior of several students since recording is noncontinuous. Since it can be very difficult for a teacher to keep track of observation times, a cueing device (e.g., a kitchen timer or a series of taped tones) should be used.[5]

Performance Measures Using Duration

When the length of time a behavior occurs is of major concern (e.g., length of a tantrum, length of an appropriate social interaction), duration recording is appropriate. Duration can be assessed in two ways—direct timing of the target behavior and duration estimated from the proportion or percentage of an observation period that the behavior lasts. In direct measurement, a teacher times and notes the duration of each occurrence of the behavior. (Behaviors observed in this manner must be discrete—have an obvious beginning and ending.) In momentary time-sampling procedures, the only stipulation is that the observation intervals remain constant. When they are constant, percentage duration is accurately estimated by the percentage of intervals during which the behavior was noted. Momentary time sampling is usually a more accurate method of estimating duration than other interval sampling procedures and more convenient than duration recording.

---

[5]If a timer of some sort is used, it should be kept out of sight of the students so they cannot behave well only at the recording time.

Performance Measures Using Latency

Performance measures using latency are used when the teacher is concerned about how long it takes the student to respond after an antecedent stimulus is presented. For example, when a teacher or student asks Zena a question, she seems to take a long time to respond, and her teacher wishes to decrease this period of time. In this instance, the length of time between a question or other form of initiation and Zena's response is what is observed and recorded.

While systematic and direct observations are sensitive to changes in behavior, changing problem behavior may not be associated with changing peer acceptance (Deno, Mirkin, Robinson, & Evans, 1980; Gottlieb, 1978; Kuehnle, Deno, & Mirkin, 1982). Indeed, preliminary results indicate that reduction in problem behavior is not as important as increasing the frequency of initiations/interactions of peers and the target child. Therefore, in addition to observing frequency of target behavior teachers should assess if the intervention impacts how well the student is liked or accepted by peers.

Levels of Assessment

When assessing adaptive and social behavior, two types of learning are evaluated. First, understanding of social conventions (e.g., classroom rules) are assessed at the comprehension level. While such assessments are typically conducted orally with younger children and for simple conventions ("Do you know how to line up for lunch?"), older students and more complicated conventions may be assessed with paper-and-pencil tests. Selecting criteria for acceptable performance follows the usual procedures for cognitive tasks.

Performance of the behavior itself is assessed for mastery at the levels of acquisition, maintenance, and generalization. Criteria for mastery at these levels depend upon the nature of the target behavior. For some behavior, the quality of performance or the frequency of the behavior used in mastery criteria are derived from a knowledge of normal human development. For example, is a particular eating skill typically within the repertoire of an 8-year-old? For other behavior, mastery criteria are developed through peer comparison. For example, are the other children in the class completing their homework assignments 90% of the time?

Error Analysis

Error analysis can be applied routinely to ascertain why social behavior is not performed. Three reasons are common. First, students may not perform a particular action because they do not know how. In this case, interventions are developed to teach the student the particular skill. Second, students may know how to perform but do not know when to perform. In this case, students are taught strategies to help them know when performance is desired. Third, students may know how and when to perform but choose not to perform. In this case, a teacher usually tries to increase compliance by modifying the contingencies that control the behavior or by reinforcing incompatible behavior.

Summary

Much of what is considered appropriate adaptive and social behavior is culturally determined and many of the behaviors included in these two areas typically are not taught in mainstream classes; students are *expected* to exhibit them. However, some students, especially those labeled exceptional, do not perform these critical behaviors at an acceptable level or rate, and a variety of curricula have been developed to directly teach these students appropriate social and adaptive behaviors.

Adaptive behavior is an inclusive term for any action that increases a person's likelihood of physical survival and ability to cope with social and physical demands of the environment. *Social behavior* refers to actions that affect interpersonal relationships with others in the environment and can include in- and out-of-school behavior, although teachers usually focus on day-to-day compliance with rules, task-related behavior, and student interpersonal relationships with their peers in the classroom setting. Often, it is difficult to make a clear distinction between adaptive and social behavior.

Adaptive and social behavior can be measured indirectly or directly. Indirect measures are frequently used in educational settings and typically take the form of ratings or estimations by self, adults, or peers. When it is possible to obtain them, direct measures of adaptive and social behaviors are preferred. Direct measures include observing and recording the frequency, rate, duration, or latency of the behavior(s) in question. When direct observation is used, it is critical to pinpoint the behavior of concern by defining it in precise, observable terms and then selecting an appropriate observation and recording system (e.g., event or time sampling).

Extended Example 1

Scenario

Ms. Cline is a second-grade teacher with 19 students in her class. She is in the process of assigning grades for the first nine-week period of the year. While filling out the deportment section on the back of Patsy's report card, she is reminded of a growing concern she has about this student. In many ways Patsy is a model student. She follows directions, gets her work done punctually, and bothers no one during instructional time (behavior Ms. Cline wishes a couple of her other students would imitate). When Ms. Cline is asked to describe Patsy, the terms quiet, shy, or withdrawn are used. As Ms. Cline fills out the comments section of the report card, she realizes that Patsy rarely plays or talks with classmates when it is appropriate to do so—during free time. Ms. Cline is concerned with more than academics and decides she must do something to help Patsy.

Step 1: Specify Reasons for Assessment

Ms. Cline's school system recently adopted a prereferral system, the major purpose of which is to try to help students in their mainstream classes prior to referring them for eligibility testing. Ms. Cline met and discussed her concern about Patty with some of the members of the child-study team. Based on this meeting, it was decided that three aspects of Patsy's behavior should be investigated: her relative status among her classmates, the number of her interactions vis-à-vis the number of interaction of her peers, and, if Patsy is found to have a deficit in this area and intervention is indicated, a formative assessment of the intervention's effectiveness.

Step 2: Analyze Curriculum

The curriculum consists of two components—playing board games or talking with peers.

Step 3: Formulate Behavioral Objectives

When writing an objective for Patsy, Ms. Cline first defines the behavior she wants Patsy to exhibit in as precise and measurable terms as possible. She knows that she wants to increase the amount of time Patsy spends interacting with other students and that she must define interacting in the context of Patsy's free-time period. She informally observes what other students do during this time and sees that students either play board games or just talk with each other while engaging in activities such as coloring. She decides that interacting will be defined as engagement in any of these activities. Additionally, she decides to measure the duration of interaction because frequency would not be appropriate due to the characteristics of the target behavior. Ms. Cline decided to set the criterion for desired performance after the initial observation of Patsy and several peers. She will use the median duration of peer engagement as measured over three days. The condition under which the behavior will be performed is during the three daily 15-minute free-play periods. Patsy's objective is that, during three daily free-time periods, she will interact with another student 65% of the time.

Step 4: Develop Appropriate Assessment Procedures

Since there are several reasons for assessment, several procedures are used. First, to get a general idea of Patsy's status within the classroom, Ms. Cline and members of the child-study team decided to use sociometric nominations. Since Patsy's objective dealt with interaction during free time, students were asked to name three students with whom they would *most* and *least* like to play during free time. The sociometric assessment also would be administered later to see if there were any changes in Patsy's status after intervention.

A second measure, direct observation, was used to establish a baseline for the duration of Patsy's interactions and peer norms. While the amount of time interacting is the dimension to be measured, duration recording would be too time consuming. Since momentary time sampling would allow an accurate estimation of duration and be more efficient, it was used. A time-sampling observation form was developed to record interaction for Patsy and five peers during free-time periods over three school days (see Figure 9.6). Observations were made at 60-second intervals for each child. Since six students (Patsy and five peers) are being observed, Ms. Cline observes one student at the end of 10 seconds, the next student 10 seconds later and so on. Since there is a total of 45 minutes of observation time per day (three 15-minute periods), each student will have 45 observations per day. Estimated duration will be calculated by multiplying the number of times a student

TOTAL "HITS"

Free Time #1

	1	2	3	4	5	6	7	8	9	10	11	12	13	14	15
Patsy															
Fred															
Gina															
Leslie															
Rhonda															
Jack															

Free Time #2

	1	2	3	4	5	6	7	8	9	10	11	12	13	14	15
Patsy															
Fred															
Gina															
Leslie															
Rhonda															
Jack															

Free Time #3

	1	2	3	4	5	6	7	8	9	10	11	12	13	14	15
Patsy															
Fred															
Gina															
Leslie															
Rhonda															
Jack															

Figure 9.6.   Momentary time-sampling form for Patsy and five peers.

was observed interacting (sometimes referred to as a "hit"), multiplied by the number of observation intervals. For example, if Patsy were observed interacting five times, Ms. Cline would multiply five times 60 seconds, which equals 300 seconds (5 minutes), which is 11% of the 45 minutes of free time.

Finally, a 60-second time-sampling observation form was developed to record Patsy's interaction time for the purpose of formative assessment. Procedures for calculating estimated duration for this procedure are the same.

Steps 5, 6 and 7: Collect, Summarize, and Display Data

Ms. Cline decided to administer the sociometric device to groups of six so she could monitor students closely and answer any questions that they might have. At the beginning of the school year, a poster was made for each primary class; the poster displayed Polaroid pictures and names of all the students and was labeled "Our Class." Ms. Cline used this poster to help the students remember who is who. She tells them:

> Listen carefully so you will know what to do. First I want you to write down the names of the three classmates you would *most* like to play with during free time. If you can't remember somebody's name or don't know how to spell it, look at the chart. Don't look at anybody else's paper, and don't let anybody look at yours. Any questions?
> Okay. Go ahead.
> Has everybody finished?
> Now I want you to do something a little different. On the next three lines I want you to write down the names of three classmates you would *least* like to play with during free time.
> Finished?
> Thank you for following directions so well.

After the sociometric is administered, Ms. Cline totals the number of positive and negative nominations for Patsy. Her total for each is zero; this shows Patsy to be isolated rather than rejected. This finding confirms Ms. Cline's initial perceptions about Patsy and indicates the need for further assessment. Because it will be helpful when she plans an intervention, Ms. Cline also notes Patsy's nominations for children with whom she would most like to play during free time. Ms. Cline decides not to plot a total sociogram at this time since she is only concerned about Patsy for the moment.

Ms. Cline enlists the help of the school psychologist and her part-time aide to conduct systematic observations of Patsy's (and the five target peers') interactions. After ensuring that all persons understand exactly what is being measured and how data are to be collected, observations are made for three days. Observers are careful to be discreet about what they are doing in order to avoid possible student reactivity. On the first of the three days, the two people will observe simultaneously and their interobserver agreement will be calculated.[6]

Data are converted to percentage of time interacting daily for Patsy and the target peers. Patsy's average interaction lasted about 10% of the time, while her peers' inter-

---

[6]See Chapter 4 for a discussion of calculating observer agreement.

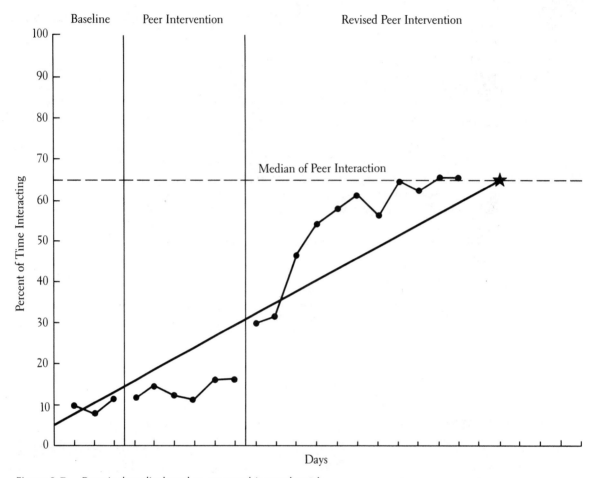

Figure 9.7. Patsy's data displayed on an equal-interval graph.

actions averaged about 65% of the time. These data further confirmed Ms. Cline's impression that Patsy was not interacting with her peers and that an intervention to increase both Patsy's interactions and her peer acceptance would be desirable.

Ms. Cline enlists the aid of the three girls Patsy nominated. She instructs them on some simple peer initiation procedures centered on inviting Patsy to play (i.e., "Do you want to play?). At the same time, she prepares an equal-interval graph to monitor Patsy's progress during intervention. The first three data points on this graph are baseline data (data collected prior to intervention). Ms. Cline first estimates about how long the intervention should last and checks her calendar to learn the date of the last day of intervention. She puts an aim on the graph at the intersection of the last day and her criterion for satisfactory interactions—65%, the median duration of the interactions of Patsy's five peers. Then she draws an aimline between Patsy's baseline rate today (10%) and the aim (65%)[7] (see Figure 9.7).

---

[7]See Chapter 5 for the discussion on setting aims and drawing aimlines.

Step 8: Interpret Data and Make Decisions

Based on sociometric results and peer rates of interaction, Ms. Cline decided that intervention is necessary. However, as the data in Figure 9.7 indicate, the initial intervention did not appear to be working as well as hoped; the data are well below the aimline with no noticeable increase. Ms. Cline decides to modify her intervention and provide more structure for the initiations to interact. For example, Patsy's peers are instructed to be more specific (i.e., "Do you want to play Old Maid?" vs. "Do you want to play?") and to ask questions during play (i.e., "Do you have any Barbie dolls?" or "Do you like to swim?"). After providing more structure, Patsy's data showed an increase in interaction and ultimately she reached criterion. Ms. Cline, smart teacher that she was, took pride in helping Patsy, but knew she should not stop there. She realized that responding to initiations to play was only a part of this area of social skills. Patsy had to learn how to initiate interaction as well as respond to it. Accordingly, Ms. Cline decided to write a new objective.

Summary

Ms. Cline was concerned about the nature and extent of Patsy's interactions with her classmates. She decided to approach the problem by attempting to increase the amount of time Patsy spends interacting with some of her peers during free-play periods. She used both sociometric and direct observations to establish the extent of Patsy's interactions and how she was perceived by her peers before and after intervention. When initial data indicated an unacceptable rate of improvement, Ms. Cline decided to alter her intervention. The revised intervention was successful.

Extended Example 2

Scenario

It is late in October, and Mr. Chesterfield notices some of the trainable mentally retarded students in his primary classroom arriving at school with their coats properly buttoned but that Ellen has trouble buttoning hers for recess and when it is time to go home. Moreover, he noticed that she always wore slacks with elasticized waistbands and pullovers that required little or no buttoning. That evening he telephoned Ellen's parents, who confirmed that Ellen had not learned to button and that they would like her to learn that skill. Therefore, Mr. Chesterfield decided that he would teach it to her.

Step 1: Specify Reasons for Assessment

There were two reasons to conduct assessments. First, Mr. Chesterfield wanted to ascertain which, if any, components of the skill Ellen currently could perform. Second, he wanted to monitor Ellen's progress on those skills that required instruction.

Figure 9.8.	1. Aligns front botton of coat.
Steps for putting on and buttoning a coat.	2. Locates bottom buttonhole.
	3. Locates bottom button.
	4. Buttons bottom button.
	a) Orients bottom button to bottom buttonhole.
	b) Inserts bottom button in bottom buttonhole.
	c) Pulls bottom button through buttonhole.
	5. Buttons next-to-bottom button, etc.

Step 2: Analyze Curriculum

In developing this small instructional unit, Mr. Chesterfield first performed a task analysis (see Figure 9.8). Each of the steps in the sequence were to be learned to fluency. To facilitate Ellen's acquisition of the various subskills involved, Mr. Chesterfield decided to begin instruction with oversized materials—a coat that was one size too large with large buttons and even larger buttonholes. When Ellen could succeed with the larger materials, Mr. Chesterfield would switch to a coat that was Ellen's correct size with medium-size buttons. When Ellen could succeed with those materials, Mr. Chesterfield would switch to a shirt with medium buttons and then to a shirt with small buttons. Backward chaining was selected as the method to integrate the steps in the sequence.[8]

Step 3: Formulate Behavioral Objectives

A behavioral objective was formulated for each step in the task analysis. Because backward chaining was used, each step would be practiced as part of the instruction in the subsequent step. Therefore, Mr. Chesterfield set his criterion at a fairly low level of mastery—3 consecutive correct trials. He defined a correct trial as one in which Ellen performed the skill without verbal cues, manual prompts, or manual guidance. Thus, each objective took the following format: Given coat or shirt, Ellen will _____ correctly for three consecutive trials.

Step 4: Develop Appropriate Assessment Procedures

Mr. Chesterfield developed a single checklist to record his evaluation of Ellen's performance on each subskill involved in putting on and buttoning a coat (see Figure 9.9). When he used the checklist as a pretest, he instructed Ellen to put on and button her coat; he watched her but offered no help. He indicated if she performed the skill correctly by making a check mark in the last column; if her performance was incorrect, he made no mark. When he used the checklist to monitor instruction, he modified his recording procedure so that he could keep

[8]In backward chaining, the last step is taught to mastery first, then the penultimate step is taught and the last step is practice. Thus, after every trial, a student has met the terminal objective.

Skill	Independence of Performance				Figure 9.9. Checklist for putting on and buttoning a coat.
	physical guidance	physical prompting	verbal prompting	independent performance	
Locates coat	————	————	————	————	
Orients coat	————	————	————	————	
Inserts left arm	————	————	————	————	
Inserts right arm	————	————	————	————	
Adjusts fit at shoulder	————	————	————	————	
Checks collar	————	————	————	————	
Aligns front bottom of coat	————	————	————	————	
Locates bottom buttonhole	————	————	————	————	
Locates bottom button	————	————	————	————	
Buttons bottom button	————	————	————	————	
a) Orients button to hole	————	————	————	————	
b) Inserts button in hole	————	————	————	————	
c) Pulls button through hole	————	————	————	————	
Buttons next button	————	————	————	————	
Buttons next button	————	————	————	————	
Buttons next button	————	————	————	————	
Buttons next button	————	————	————	————	
Buttons next button	————	————	————	————	
Buttons next button	————	————	————	————	

track of the number of trials at each level of assistance. He wrote a slash (/) in the column that best exemplified Ellen's performance. In the column indicating independent performance, he would cancel all previous slashes if they were followed by a trial in which assistance had to be provided or an error was made.

Step 5: Collect Data

On the pretest, Ellen could select her own coat from the cloakroom and put it on. She could not button. Therefore, Mr. Chesterfield began instruction on the last step with an oversized coat. First, he buttoned all of the buttons but the last one. Then he oriented the button, inserted it into the buttonhole, and modeled how to pull the button through the hole. Then he unbuttoned the button, oriented it, pushed it into the buttonhole, and gave Ellen a prompt to try it herself: "Now you button it, Ellen." He watched Ellen perform, provided help (e.g., guidance or prompts) as needed, and recorded his evaluation of her performance. When Ellen had mastered buttoning the bottom button, Mr. Chesterfield then unbuttoned the last two buttons, pointed to the next-to-last button, and told Ellen to button her coat. Instruction progressed in this way through two coats and a shirt.

Steps 6 and 7: Summarize and Display Data

Ellen made two errors in orienting the button on the first trial with the first button. When she progressed from buttoning one button to buttoning two, she required a verbal prompt to button the last button. Thereafter, she made no errors until she had to button the collar button on her shirt. It took Ellen three trials to pull the button through the buttonhole correctly, two trials to insert the button into the hole, and three trials to orient the button.

Since Ellen's progress was so rapid and the learning task was so concrete, Mr. Chesterfield did not graph her progress. His rating form provided the data he needed to make instructional decisions.

Step 8: Interpret Data and Make Decisions

Mr. Chesterfield made three instructional decisions. First, Ellen's progress was so fast that Mr. Chesterfield decided to lower the criterion to two consecutive correct trials. When the instructional chain had progressed to four buttons, Ellen said the task was too easy. Because she had made no errors since she needed one prompt to continue buttoning, Mr. Chesterfield lowered the criterion to one trial. The third instructional decision occurred as a result of her performance on the shirt with small buttons. Since she failed to button the top button correctly twice, he raised the criterion for this button to five consecutive correct trials.

Summary

Ellen was unable to button her clothing. Lack of skill in buttoning could seriously impede her adaptation in many social situations (e.g., using school showers, going out in cold weather) and jeopardize her health (e.g., not buttoning up in cold weather). Mr. Chesterfield developed an instructional sequence to teach the skill to Ellen. Because Ellen's progress was so rapid and unremarkable, he adjusted his criterion for mastery. In approximately 18 minutes of instruction, over four days, Ellen learned to button.

Chapter 10

CBA in Learning Strategies

Key Terms

Active learner
Cognition
Learning strategy
Metacognition

Mnemonic device
Paraphrasing
Study skill

Learning strategies are a particular type of study skill. Ellis and Lenz (1987) defined study skills as a wide variety of skills necessary for success in the classroom (e.g., bringing paper and pencil to class, using a dictionary, and writing down homework assignments). Learning strategies are more cognitive and require the student to engage in problem solving. Learning strategies have been conceptualized in a variety of ways. Thus, some confusion exists about what a learning strategy is and what is included in strategy instruction. When examining three approaches described as strategy instruction, deBettencourt (1987) noted that major differences centered on the specificity of the strategy. For example, one approach might teach students a step-by-step strategy to solve a particular type of problem (e.g., the steps needed to solve multiplication problems with regrouping). A more general approach might involve teaching students step-by-step procedures that can be used with several similar tasks (e.g., a reading comprehension strategy that could be used across different textbooks and different content areas). Other approaches to strategy instruction might be even more general and stress skills such as self-questioning (e.g., "Why am I reading this—to discuss the material in class, to study for a test, to help me write an assigned paper?") and self-monitoring (e.g., "Is my approach to this problem effective? Am I using the strategy effectively?").

A learning-strategies curriculum teaches *how* to learn rather than *what* to learn—that is, *what* is to be learned is *how* to learn. Therefore, the major purpose of learning-strategies instruction is to influence how a learner "interacts with learning situations" (Palincsar, 1986). Numerous definitions of learning strategies have been offered. Alley and Deshler (1979) defined learning strategies as "techniques, principles, or rules that will facilitate the acquisition, manipulation, integration, storage, and retrieval of information across situations and settings" (p. 13). Similarly, Dansereau (1978) defined a learning strategy as a "set of processes or steps that can be used by an individual to facilitate the acquisition, storage, and/or utilization of information" (p. 4). Stevens (1987) characterized a strategy as a "plan, consisting of a set of steps, which is used flexibly and adaptively, depending upon the situation, to perform a particular task" (p. 1). Finally, Ellis and Lenz (1987) succinctly defined learning strategies as "a set of steps the student uses to talk his or her way through a problem" (p. 96). The common elements of these definitions are that learning strategies are made up of steps a student performs when acquiring and expressing information and can be used and adapted to a variety of tasks and situations.

Successful students generally use some form of strategic behavior to help themselves to master information to which they are exposed and expected to learn as they progress through school. Indeed, when they reach high school, most successful students have developed a repertoire of strategies (Meyers & Lytle, 1986). Consider the following scenario.

Eddie and Vince are enrolled in Ms. Parker's tenth-grade social studies class. The boys' records contain data that are remarkably similar; their IQs fall within normal range, and their reading scores on published norm-referenced tests are comparable.

Ms. Parker has returned a recently completed test that covered three chapters in the text and information from class lectures. Eddie received a B and Vince a D. Earlier Ms. Parker had advised the class to prepare for the test by reading the chapters, answering study questions at the end of each chapter, and studying class notes. Neither Eddie nor Vince had missed any class meetings. Both took lecture notes. They also spent approximately the same amount of time studying for the test. Why the difference in their test scores? If Ms. Parker had been able to closely observe Vince and Eddie in and out of class she may be able to answer this question to some extent.

Ms. Parker would have observed that Eddie's class notes were more organized (i.e., in outline form) and included more important information (i.e., what was on the test) than Vince's. She would have noticed that when Eddie read his text he wrote, then studied, paraphrased summaries of chapter sections. Vince, however, read each chapter twice—word for word. When Eddie answered the chapter study questions, he scanned the chapter to find the section where the answer might be found. Vince started at the beginning of the chapter and read (word for word) until he found the answer. Ms. Parker would then have observed that Eddie organized lists of related facts and fashioned them into first-letter mnemonic devices and rehearsed them several times. Vince read and reread.

When Vince and Eddie were taking their tests, Ms. Parker would have seen Eddie quickly write his mnemonic devices on the test margin—he knew Ms. Parker, unlike some of his teachers, didn't mind. Eddie was careful to read each question/stem carefully before responding and when he came upon an item he was unsure of, he skipped it. After he answered the "easy ones," he returned to the skipped items. When answering the essay question he wrote a short outline to help him organize his response.

Upon receiving his test, Vince immediately chose the first option or answer he thought was correct. When he came to a tough question, he would spend 5 minutes thinking about it before going to the next question. When Ms. Parker collected the test, several of his items were yet to be answered. Ms. Parker marked unanswered items as incorrect.

Based on these observations, Ms. Parker could have concluded that Eddie knew how to approach the task (i.e., organize information from lecture and text in a meaningful way, manipulate pertinent information in a manner that promoted recall, and express the information in a testing situation) in an efficient manner; Vince did not.

Interest in learning strategies as a curricular emphasis is evident both in the professional literature (e.g., special issues of *Exceptional Children* and *Educational Psychologist* have been devoted to learning strategies) and in practice (e.g., both California and Florida have adopted learning-strategies curricula as approved electives in secondary resource classes). Deshler and Schumaker (in press) reported that 15,000 teachers have been trained in the learning-strategies curriculum (LSC) developed through the Kansas University Institute for Research in Learning Disabilities (KU-IRLD).

Two major reasons for this interest are the learning characteristics of students with learning problems and the perceived shortcomings of typical intervention approaches used in special classes. These two concerns are basic to the rationale for teaching learning strategies (Deshler et al., 1984).

Students with learning disabilities have been characterized as inactive or passive learners (Torgeson, 1979) who do not spontaneously use effective strategies in problem resolution and/or task completion. For example, the response of an active learner to presentation of a list of words to memorize that includes animals, cars, and colors, would include use of one or more strategies to assist later recall (e.g., categorization, visual imagery, verbal rehearsal). An inactive or passive learner might use serial rehearsal only and not recognize that the task could be made more manageable by categorical memorization. Some writers have suggested this lack of strategic learning is due to metacognitive deficiencies—that is, a lack of knowledge of one's cognitive processes or abilities that negatively affects one's learning (e.g. Armbruster, Echols, & Brown, 1983).[1] While students with learning difficulties, especially those classified as learning disabled, do not use appropriate learning strategies effectively and independently, it is becoming increasingly clear that they can and should be taught to do so (Schumaker et al., 1983).

The second rationale for a curriculum emphasizing learning strategies relates

---

[1] Definitions of metacognition usually include four executive functions: (1) knowledge of one's own learning behavior (e.g., strategies in repertoire), (2) knowledge of most effective strategy choice, (3) implementation of the strategy, and (4) monitoring the effectiveness of a strategy. Implicit in these components is a student's ability to consider task attributes when selecting a strategy and regulating its use. For example, metacognition can be inferred when a student, confronted with a lengthy chapter including many new and/or difficult concepts, outlines instead of rereading. Palincsar (1986) presents a similar example by describing a student who "notes that it is necessary to prepare differently for essay and true/false tests" (p. 118).

to the shortcomings of intervention approaches commonly used in resource classes at the secondary level. Deshler et al. (1984) have identified three common approaches to interventions used in resource rooms at the secondary level: tutorial, compensatory, and basic skills remediation.

In a tutorial approach the resource teacher typically tutors students on content currently presented in mainstream classes. This approach may include helping students answer chapter questions, explaining difficult concepts, or assisting them in studying for an upcoming test. Tutoring, therefore, focuses on immediate difficulties that a student faces. While the tutorial approach offers solutions to immediate problems students experience when coping with mainstream curriculum, potential shortcomings exist. For example, Laurie et al. (1978) noted that tutoring is effective on a short-term basis but does not address the need for students to learn curriculum content independently; the student is dependent on the teacher's presence. The immediate gains of this approach may not in many cases justify the long-term patterns that are established (i.e., single project learning and dependency).

A compensatory approach involves adapting curriculum materials and/or the method of presenting curriculum to compensate for students' learning problems. These curriculum modifications may include rewriting textual materials at a lower reading level, modifying testing procedures, using detailed advance organizers before lectures, use of peer tutors, and taping textbooks. As with the tutorial, the compensatory approach minimizes student involvement and does not directly address the need for students to be independent learners.

An approach to remediate basic skills has as its goal the raising of academic performance to a level where a student can cope with curricular materials or meet minimal competency standards. Deshler et al. (1984) noted three potential drawbacks with this approach. First, many of the materials available to teach students basic skills are written for elementary students, thus some motivational problems may arise when adolescents are presented with "baby books." Second, remedial instruction does not prepare students to cope with material used in mainstream classes (e.g., texts written at the twelfth-grade level). Third, skills emphasized in this approach typically do not include critical study skills such as skimming reading material or organizing large amounts of information.

Scope and Sequence of Learning-Strategies Curricula

Since learning strategies have not been viewed as a separate curriculum[2] until recently, specific scopes and sequences of instruction have not been validated empirically or been given much attention. Virtually nonexistent, too, are

---

[2]Some writers in the area of cognitive-learning strategies (e.g., Dansereau [1985] and Sheperd [1987]) caution that LSC should not be taught as a separate curriculum—that is, taught in isolation—but rather should be taught and practiced within the context of mainstream course content. We concur and believe that the cornerstone of effective instruction in learning strategies is the use of these strategies with tasks required of students in mainstream settings.

published learning-strategies curricula except in supplementary, "how-to" formats.[3] One exception is the learning-strategies curriculum developed by the KU-IRLD for use with adolescents with learning disabilities. The Institute has been in existence since 1978 and is primarily concerned with development and validation of learning strategies. As a result of this work, a learning-strategies curriculum has been developed and is available commercially.[4]

One method of determining the scope of a learning-strategies curriculum is to ascertain the skills necessary for successful functioning in a specific setting (e.g., school, job) and to identify skill deficiencies relevant to the population of students in question. (The KU-IRLD followed these procedures when developing a curriculum for learning-disabled secondary students resulting in the LSC.[5])

Necessary Skills

Frequently occurring academic demands in secondary mainstream classrooms were identified by Schumaker and Deshler (1984). They categorized demands into three areas: work habits, knowledge acquisition, and knowledge expression.

- *Work habit demands.* Work habits include assignment completion, class participation, time management, and following classroom/school rules. For example, middle and high school students are expected to work independently; teachers at these levels do not provide as much individualized attention and feedback as those at the elementary level. Teachers in middle and high schools may be assuming that students understand task requirements or ask questions of the teacher or other students if they need assistance.

- *Knowledge-acquisition demands.* Knowledge acquisition includes various skills related to listening, reading, and locating information as well as those related to note taking, skimming, scanning, and summarization. For example, students must be able to locate appropriate resources (e.g., find a library book) as well as relevant material within the resource.

- *Knowledge-expression demands.* Knowledge expression includes both written and oral expression as well as test taking.[6]

Skill Deficiencies

After identifying the necessary skills in secondary settings, researchers at the KU-IRLD examined abilities of learning-disabled adolescents to meet those demands. Not surprisingly, many students labeled learning disabled have diffi-

---

[3]The reader is directed to an article by Cronin and Currie (1984) for a comprehensive list of materials published regarding study skills and strategies.

[4]These materials are available only by receiving training provided by KU-IRLD–associated trainers. Information about training can be obtained by contacting Dr. Frances Clark, Coordinator of Training, Kansas University Institute for Research in Learning Disabilities, 223 Carruth-O'Leary Hall, Lawrence, KS 66045.

[5]Other areas have been studied by the KU-IRLD (e.g., social skills, motivation); however, the prior discussion focuses on findings related to accademic learning strategies.

[6]Other modes of expression also could be included for students who are unable to communicate either orally or in written form. Other modes include manual expression, language boards, Braille, and so forth.

TABLE 10.1 Learning-Strategies Curriculum	Acquisition	Storage	Expression and Demonstration of Competence
	Word identification	First-letter mnemonic	Sentences
	Paraphrasing	Paired Associates	Paragraphs
	Self-questioning	Listening and note taking	Error monitoring
	Visual imagery	Themes	Interpreting visual aids
	Assignment completion	Multipass	Test taking

culty in coping with the variety of expectations for successful performance in mainstream settings. For example, as indicated by achievement test scores, most of the students studied read at a level significantly below the grade level at which their texts are written. Also, many of the learning-disabled adolescents studied were deficient in text usage strategies such as skimming and scanning. Also, analysis of notes taken during class lectures indicated learning-disabled students' notes contained only half as much key information as the notes of nonhandicapped peers. Finally, other observations showed these students to have difficulty expressing their knowledge on objective, short answer, and essay tests. For example, when taking objective tests, learning-disabled students did not use time-management strategies, make use of cues, or read items/choices carefully.

In summary, the KU-IRLD compared necessary skills and skill deficiencies to develop the scope of the learning-strategies curriculum. This curriculum is organized into three strands: acquisition, storage, and expression and demonstration of competence (see Table 10.1).

The acquisition strand includes strategies to assist students in gaining information from written materials.

- The word-identification strategy (Lenz et al., 1984) provides students with a strategy to decode polysyllabic words.
- The paraphrasing strategy (Schumaker, Denton, & Deshler, 1984), designed to improve reading comprehension, requires a student to paraphrase the main idea and related details of each paragraph in a reading passage.
- The self-questioning strategy (Clark et al., 1984), designed to improve reading comprehension, is used to formulate questions on information not included by an author and to locate answers to those questions later in a passage.
- The visual-imagery strategy (Clark et al., 1984), also designed to improve reading comprehension, requires a student to form mental pictures of events included in passages that lend themselves to visual imagery.
- The interpreting visual aids strategy (Lenz, Schumaker, & Deshler, in press) is designed to help students to acquire information from pictures, diagrams, charts, tables, and maps.

- The multipass strategy (Schumaker et al., 1982) requires a student to make three passes over a textbook chapter (1) to survey it, (2) to obtain key information from it, and (3) to study important information.

The storage strand includes two strategies to promote identification and storage of important information.

- The first-letter mnemonic strategy (Nagel, Schumaker, & Deshler, 1986) requires a student to identify textual material that can be organized into lists, to develop lists, and to arrange (or rearrange) the list to form a mnemonic. For example, most students are familiar with ROY G BIV—a mnemonic used to remember the colors of the spectrum: red, orange, yellow, green, blue, indigo, and violet.
- Paired-associates strategy (Bulgren & Schumaker, in preparation) helps a student to associate two things (e.g., states with their capitals or individuals and their accomplishments) in various ways—for example, visual imagery.

The third strand, expression and demonstration of competence, contains six strategies for facilitating written expression, assignment completion, and test taking.

- The sentence-writing strategy (Schumaker & Sheldon, 1985) provides students with steps and formulas for writing sentences.
- The paragraph-writing strategy (Schumaker, in press) aids organization and writing of paragraphs.
- The theme-writing strategy (Schumaker, in press) facilitates writing organized and integrated themes.
- The error-monitoring strategy (Schumaker, Nolan, & Deshler, 1985) is used to detect and correct errors in student-generated written products.
- The assignment-completion strategy (Whitaker, 1982) is used by students to increase assignment completion by teaching scheduling and organization behaviors.
- The test-taking strategy (Hughes et al., in press) helps students avoid careless errors, use time-management procedures, and attend to cues when taking classroom tests.

Educators interested in providing systematic instruction in learning strategies could either use the strategies included by the KU-IRLD to form the scope of the curriculum or develop their own by interviewing mainstream teachers and/or observing their classrooms in order to determine crucial setting demands and assess student need for strategies to meet those demands. Table 10.2 displays examples of the type of information needed to identify frequent demands or requirements in mainstream classes.

TABLE 10.2 Academic Demand Inventory	*Reading Demands*	
	Reading level of text(s):	_____
	Typical reading requirement (number of pages or chapters):	_____
	Typically must answer chapter questions?	_____
	Lecture Demands	
	Approximate time spent lecturing (%)	_____
	Lecture outlines provided?	_____
	Advance organizers provided?	_____
	Approximate test content from lectures (%)	_____
	Written Expression Demands	
	Are short papers/essays (2–5 pages) assigned?	_____
	How often?	_____
	Are term papers assigned?	_____
	How often?	_____
	When papers are graded, approximately what percentage of the grade is given for:	
	Mechanics (grammar, spelling, punctuation, etc.):	_____
	Organization:	_____
	Content:	_____
	Testing Demands	
	How often are tests administered?	_____
	Typically, what percentage of the test scores are based on:	
	Multiple-choice/true-false	_____
	Matching	_____
	Fill in Blank	_____
	Short Answer	_____
	Essay	_____

Assessment of Strategic Learning

When a student's achievement is a source of concern, as is often the case with those who are in remedial and special-education settings, assessment personnel should consider the possibility that the student does not have or cannot use learning strategies appropriately. Assessment of learning strategies can occur in three ways.

Tests of Metacognition

Some underachieving students, especially those who are mentally retarded or learning disabled, may be metacognitively deficient; they may lack awareness of strategies and/or the ability to devise, employ, or modify efficient strategies for a particular task (Cavanaugh & Borkowski, 1979; Lloyd & Loper, 1986). Assessment of metacognitive abilities is in the first stages of development, and currently no technically adequate devices exist to assess metacognitive ability. There are several specific problems associated with the use of metacognitive assessment devices that do exist. First, one might question whether self-reports truly reflect metacognitive activities, especially the self-reports of handicapped students who may have difficulty understanding the questions or expressing their responses (Merriwether & Hughes, 1987). Second, correlations between metacognitive tasks and actual academic tasks are relatively low (Cavanaugh & Borkowski, 1979); this finding suggests that a student may be *aware* of strategies but does not *use* them appropriately and independently in academic settings.

In assessing awareness of cognitive processes, one attempts to get at what students *think* they are doing—or should be doing—as opposed to what they are actually doing. Thus, assessment provides general indications of students' knowledge of when and what type of planned activities are necessary to assist in later recall.

Assessment typically involves multiple-choice questionnaires or interviews. Questionnaires—for example, the informed strategies for learning (ISL) (Paris, Cross, & Lipson, 1984)—have been developed to measure awareness of appropriate strategies. Lloyd and Loper (1986, p. 1244) gave the following example of an item from the ISL: "The best way to focus on the important points of a story that you read is to: a) Underline the main ideas. b) Read the story 3 or 4 times. c) Ask someone to explain it." While all three choices in this item describe behaviors that may assist a student in understanding the story, *a* would be the most appropriate choice since active identification of main ideas is typically more efficient than nondirected rereading and requires more student independence than relying on another person for the answer.

Interviews are similar to questionnaires but are given orally and ask open-ended questions. The following interview is adapted from a metamemory test by Kreutzer, Leonard, and Flavell (1975).

The other day I played a record of a story for a little girl. I asked her to listen carefully to the record as many times as she wanted so she could tell me the story later. Before she began to listen to the record she asked me one question, "Am I supposed to remember the story word for word or can I tell it in my own words?"

1. Why do you think she asked this question?
2. Would knowing the answer to the question help her know how to study the story?
3. If I told her to learn it word for word what do you suppose she did?
4. If I told her to learn it in her own words what do you suppose she did?
5. Would it be easier to learn it word for word, or in her own words?

Informal Assessment of Strategic Behavior

Since tests of metacognition cannot, as yet, provide educators with useful information about student use of strategic behavior, a more valid approach is to observe and to question students while they complete academic tasks. With this type of assessment, a teacher can determine if students are having difficulty meeting a particular academic demand (e.g., reading comprehension, note taking, test taking), if they are using appropriate strategic behavior, and at what stage they are experiencing difficulty (e.g., selecting an effective strategy, implementing it, error monitoring, or error correction). One method of direct assessment, similar to a procedure described by Meyers and Lytle (1986), requires the teacher to select a task with which a particular student is having difficulty, present the task, observe student performance, probe for student strategic behavior, and analyze performance on a student product. For example, Mr. Franklin has noticed that Joe has difficulty understanding what he reads and has limited recall of important facts from reading passages. First, Mr. Franklin selects a reading passage from Joe's social studies text. He asks Joe to read aloud from the passage to see if Joe is capable of recognizing a majority of the words. If he cannot, his problem may be due to limited sight vocabulary rather than poor comprehension. To discover whether Joe applies strategies to facilitate comprehension, Mr. Franklin stops Joe at the end of each paragraph and asks him to verbalize any thoughts he has had while reading the paragraph to learn whether Joe spontaneously paraphrases, summarizes, or uses other comprehension strategies such as visual imagery or self-questioning. If Joe's responses indicate that he is using any strategic behavior, Mr. Franklin asks him to paraphrase the paragraph (i.e., identify the main ideas and two or three pertinent details) to see if Joe is capable of using the strategy effectively. After Joe reads an entire selection, Mr. Franklin administers a short test to check for comprehension. Based on this initial procedure, Mr. Franklin can obtain a general idea of Joe's spontaneous use of comprehension strategies, if prompts are required for Joe to use a strategy, or if Joe will need instruction in strategy use.

Direct Assessment of Learning-Strategies Instruction

While the previous procedures can be considered general screening processes for identifying areas of deficiency, assessment for instruction provides more detailed and varied information about student strategic behavior and the effectiveness of strategy instruction. The instructional procedures used to teach learning strategies to students with learning problems are crucial to successful acquisition, maintenance, and generalization (Gelzheiser, Sheperd, & Wozniak, 1986; Palincsar, 1986). A detailed description of a set of instructional steps used for strategies instruction is provided by Deshler, Alley, Warner, & Schumaker (1981) and is found in Table 10.3. First, a pretest to determine the student's current approach to an academic task is administered and scored using specific criteria; second, instruction is provided if indicated; third, a formative evaluation of acquisition is completed; and fourth, generalization and maintenance of strategy usage is checked periodically.

Pretesting

Pretesting typically requires examination in two areas of student ability: how well a student performs an academic task (e.g., remembers facts, answers comprehension questions on content read) and how well a student uses a particular strategy when completing an academic task (e.g., uses mnemonic strategy, paraphrases). The former measure, *task performance*, is taken by presenting the student with a

Acquisition Steps	TABLE 10.3 Steps in Acquisition, Maintenance, and Generalization of Strategies

Step 1: **Prestest and Obtain Commitment to Learn**
Obtain measure(s) of current functioning
Make the student aware of inefficient/ineffective habits
Obtain student's commitment to learn

Step 2: **Describe**
Give rationales for using the strategy
Give general characteristics of situations
Solicit example situations
Describe results that can be expected
Supervise goal setting
Describe the steps of the strategy

Step 3: **Model**
Demonstrate the entire strategy "thinking aloud"
Involve the students in a demonstration

Step 4: **Verbal Rehearsal of the Steps**
Lead rapid-fire verbal rehearsal
Require mastery

Step 5: **Controlled Practice and Feedback**
Supervise practice in "easy" materials
Provide positive and corrective feedback to individuals
Require mastery

Step 6: **Grade-Appropriate Practice and Feedback**
Supervise practice in materials/stimuli from regular coursework
Provide positive and corrective feedback to individuals
Require mastery

Step 7: **Posttest and Obtain Commitment to Generalize**
Obtain measure(s) of progress
Make the student aware of progress
Obtain the student's commitment to generalize

Step 8: **Phase 1 of Generalization—Orientation**
Make the students aware of situations in which the strategy should
  be used
Discuss adaptations of the strategy
Make the students aware of cues for using strategy

Step 9: **Phase 2 of Generalization—Activation**
Program the students' use of the strategy in a variety of situations
Provide feedback

Step 10: **Phase 3 of Generalization—Maintenance**
Conduct periodic reviews
Test maintenance of strategy usage
Provide feedback

Source: Training materials produced by the University of Kansas Institute for Research in Learning Disabilities. Reprinted by permission.

task similar to one required in several subject areas and is critical to success in those areas. For example, if a student is frequently required to read textual materials, understand the material, and answer multiple-choice questions designed to assess comprehension, a teacher would present the student with a selection from a textbook—one not previously read, requesting that the passage be read, and administer a test the following day.

To measure *strategy performance*, a teacher would select an appropriate strategy (e.g., summarization, paraphrasing, visual imagery) and give the student general instructions to use the strategy when reading the selected passage. For example, Schumaker, Denton, and Deshler (1984), in their paraphrasing strategy manual, direct a teacher to tell the student to read the passage silently and stop at the end of each paragraph to describe what has been read. Scoring the task performance is straightforward—the percentage of comprehension questions answered correctly is computed. At this point, the teacher selects a criterion for acceptable performance, usually between 70 and 90% correct. Next, a teacher must decide if the student performed the steps of the strategy in a required manner. For example, Schumaker, Denton, and Deshler (1984) provided the following evaluation guidelines for scoring student paraphrases.

Points are given for general statements about the main idea of a paragraph (one per paragraph) and for statements about specific details (two per paragraph) included in the paragraph. Additionally, specific requirements must be met in order to award points for student responses. These requirements are that student responses must (1) be a complete thought, (2) contain accurate information, (3) contain new information from prior responses, (4) make sense, (5) contain relevant information, (6) not be a further general statement about the content, and (7) be in the students' own words. A percentage score is calculated by dividing the points earned by the total number of points availabe (three per paragraph). Again, an acceptable performance criterion is set—usually about 80%.

Strategy Instruction

At this point, based on the scores of both task performance and strategy performance, the teacher decides whether the strategy needs to be taught. If one or both scores are at or above the set criteria, then instruction in the strategy is not appropriate.

Formative Evaluation of Acquisition

If strategy instruction is indicated, the next step in the assessment process is to provide formative evaluation of strategy acquisition. After a strategy has been presented to students, a series of practice sessions are provided in which a student applies the strategy with appropriate materials. After each attempt, assessment of student performance takes place. Assessment procedures are the same as those used in the pretest. Student performance for each session is graphed to provide a visual display of progress. After criteria for acceptable performance for both task and strategy have been reached, a more formal (e.g., no assistance or feedback during assessment) posttest is administered.

Generalization and Maintenance Checks

Upon demonstration of strategy acquisition, maintenance and generalization usage—both generalization to other settings and to other materials and teachers—are assessed. (These generalizations are explained in the context of Schumaker, Denton, and Desher's [1984] assessment of generalization of a paraphrasing strategy.) To assess generalization to other settings (as well as maintenance over a two-week period), students were given daily reading assignments and instructed to read and paraphrase them in a setting other than the class in which they were taught the strategy. The following day the teacher asked the students three questions about the main ideas and details included in the assigned reading. To assess generalization to other materials and teachers, students used the strategy for assignments made in their mainstream classes. Their resource-room teachers evaluated the effectiveness of strategy usage with a three-step procedure.

1. Students noted each assignment with which they used the strategy.
2. Teachers read the reading passages assigned in the mainstream themselves.
3. Teachers asked four questions on main ideas and details within the passage.

Maintenance assessment is an ongoing process to ensure appropriate use of strategy over time. Periodic probes are administered during the school year (and subsequent years if possible) using the same procedures employed during pre- and posttesting. To continue with the paraphrasing example, maintenance assessment is executed by providing reading selections to students and measuring strategy performance with the same scoring guidelines and criteria used previously. If a student falls below mastery requirements, then remedial instruction in strategy use is required.

Summary

Many students with academic problems do not generate and use strategies when acquiring, storing, or expressing information. Moreover, they may not monitor the effectiveness of a strategy and adapt it when necessary. If students do not exhibit efficient strategic behavior when presented with academic tasks, then it becomes necessary to teach them appropriate learning strategies. A learning-strategies curriculum teaches students *how* to learn rather than *what* to learn. Typically, a strategy is a set of problem-solving and self-questioning steps a student follows in order to complete a task.

Assessment of learning strategies can take different forms. Since deficient strategy use may be viewed as a metacognitive deficit, it has been proposed that assessment take place at the metacognitive level. However, metacognition is a construct, and it is not possible to measure it directly. Moreover, current attempts at measuring metacognition lack reliability and validity. A more useful method of assesment, at least for a classroom teacher, is to present a pertinent academic task and then directly assess both task and strategy performance. If strategy instruction is indicated, formative assesment is conducted until the strategy is mastered and the student performs the task at an acceptable level. A critical part of instruction and assessment is to ensure generalization of strategy use (e.g., the student uses the strategy effectively with mainstream materials).

Extended Example

Scenario

Ms. Hirai teaches in a resource room for learning-disabled students in a suburban high school. Most of her students are mainstreamed in several content classes (e.g., science, social studies).

Step 1: Specify Reasons for Assessment

Several of her students are not doing well in the content classes. She is interested in beginning instruction in strategies to help them meet the demands of those classes. Therefore, she wants to identify a frequent requirement with which the majority of students are having difficulty, to teach a strategy to assist them in meeting the requirement, and to monitor both strategy usage and task performance.

Step 2: Analyze the Curriculum

Since a strategies curriculum is designed to teach students how to learn and/or perform curricular requirements, Ms. Hirai first analyzes frequent curricular requirements or demands. Over several days she asks mainstream teachers about the nature and extent of class requirements and the ones with which her students are having difficulty. Through this informal analysis, she discovers that her students are frequently expected to write essays and themes and that the students are not performing well on these tasks—especially in organization, rather than mechanics. Ms. Hirai then went to several sources (e.g., texts, journals, other teachers) to see what strategies exist to help students organize and express ideas in writing. She decided to use the TOWER strategy (author unknown), designed to assist students organize themes and refine their ability to formulate paragraphs into main ideas and supporting details. The acronym TOWER stands for

T— Think of a topic and write an introduction to the topic.

O— Order ideas (subtopics) related to the topic and list supporting details about each subtopic.

W—Write paragraphs on the topic and subtopics.

E— Edit the paper for errors.

R— Rewrite a final draft.

Step 3: Formulate Objectives

Ms. Hirai writes two sets of objectives; one for student strategy performance and one for task performance. The task-performance objectives require evidence of student ability to complete a TOWER form before writing a theme, writing on every other line, monitoring capitalization and punctuation errors, and rewriting the essay. The TOWER form is displayed in Figure 10.1. When filling out this form, the student is required to write the topic/title, write an introductory paragraph, identify subtopics, and list supporting details for each subtopic. Figure 10.2 illustrates a completed TOWER form.

Ms. Hirai wrote four objectives for strategy performance:

- When given an essay topic, the student will correctly fill out the TOWER form.
- When writing a theme, the student will write a first draft using every other line.
- The student will correct 80% of capitalization and punctuation errors made on the first draft
- The student will rewrite the first draft.

Figure 10.1.
A TOWER form.

TOPIC:

INTRODUCTION

Subtopic   Subtopic   Subtopic

Details   Details   Details

Figure 10.2.
A completed TOWER
form.

TOPIC

Drug abuse

INTRODUCTION

Drug abuse is a serious problem in today's society. People who are addicted to drugs cause problems for themselves, other people, and all of society.

Subtopic	Subtopic	Subtopic
Personal Problems	*Problems for Others*	*Problems for Society*
Details	**Details**	**Details**
health	*divorce*	*crime*
money	*violence*	*productivity*
legal	*family relations*	

The following task performance objectives for the final written products were prepared.

- Assigned themes will include an introductory paragraph followed by a minimum of three subtopic paragraphs.
- Student subtopic paragraphs will begin with a topic sentence followed by sentences about supporting details.
- Eighty percent of student sentences will be complete (i.e., subject and verb).

Step 4: Develop Appropriate Assessment Procedures

Ms. Hirai needed to develop several assessment procedures. First, she developed pretests to measure the students' current performance on both strategy and task-related objectives in order to establish the need for strategy instruction. For this purpose, she decided to instruct the students to write a theme on a familiar topic (they selected the topic from a list) so they would not have to read materials to complete the assignment. She also instructed the students to outline their response before writing the essay and told them that they would have to edit their first draft and execute a final draft. Assessment procedures and scoring criteria for the pretest are as follows.

Strategy Performance

1. Examine student outlines for evidence of an introduction, subtopics, and details for each subtopic. Students must obtain at least 90% of available points for mastery; points are awarded in the following manner:

Introduction: 2 points. Introduction must include the major topic.

Subtopic: 1 point for each subtopic. Subtopic must relate to the topic and at least three subtopics must be included for credit.

Details: 1 point for each detail. Detail must relate to the subtopic. Additionally, student must include at least two details for each subtopic for credit (**11+ points**).

2. Examine first drafts to establish if students wrote on every other line. Students will be awarded 1 point for writing on every other line. (1 point).

3. Examine first and second drafts for corrected capitalization and punctuation errors. To receive credit, students must correct at least 80% of capitalization and punctuation errors they made on the first draft.[7] (5 points).

Task Performance

1. Examine the final draft to establish whether the student included an introductory paragraph followed by at least three subtopic paragraphs. One point for each paragraph will be awarded. The introductory paragraph must relate to the topic and the subtopic paragraphs must relate to the topic (4+ points). Students must obtain 100% of available points for mastery.

2. Examine each paragraph to establish whether it began with a topic sentence followed by at least two sentences about details supporting the subtopic. Each topic sentence and detail sentence will be awarded 1 point (9+ points). Students must obtain at least 90% of available points for mastery.

3. Examine the final draft for complete sentences and calculate the percentage of complete sentences (number of incomplete sentences/number of sentences in theme). Students must score at least 80% for mastery.

If a student met the three criteria for task performance, then strategy instruction is not indicated. However, if students wrote less than 80% of their sentences in a complete manner, Ms. Hirai would decide that instruction in sentence writing was indicated and was prerequisite to instruction in theme writing. Additionally, if students had extreme difficulty in detecting and/or correcting basic capitalization and punctuation errors, Ms. Hirai would decide that instruction in this area was needed before instruction in theme organization. If a student did not have

---

[7] If no capitalization or punctuation errors were made on the first draft, students would earn all of the points available for correction.

major difficulty in these two areas but was not able to perform the other task *and* strategy objectives, Ms. Hirai would begin instruction in the TOWER strategy.

Once Ms. Hirai begins to teach acquisition of TOWER, she wishes to perform formative assessment to provide information on how well the students are learning and using the strategy. However, before students begin practicing the strategy, she wants to assess student ability to memorize and state fluently what each letter of the mnemonic TOWER stands for at a criterion of 100% correct. (See step 4 in Table 10.3). After allowing students to rehearse strategy steps orally, she requires them to verbalize strategy steps to her until 100% accuracy is attained. Ms. Hirai then instructs her students how to complete the TOWER form. After instruction, students must complete the form with 100% accuracy on two separate occasions when presented with a topic. Then Ms. Hirai instructs and provides practice on use of the TOWER form and writing a theme based on information from the form. Practice test scores are recorded. When a student masters all task and strategy performance objectives, a posttest identical (except for the topic) to the pretest is administered.

After a student has demonstrated mastery, Ms. Hirai begins assessment for generalization. She instructs the students to apply the strategy when writing themes somewhere other than her class and to bring back both the completed TOWER forms and their themes for grading. She requires four of these out-of-class assignments. Concurrently, she tells students to use the strategy when assigned a theme to write in a mainstream class and to bring both the form and theme to her for scoring. Finally, Ms. Hirai schedules maintenance tests (again identical in format to pre- and posttests) over the next few months to ensure student strategy maintenance.

Steps 5 and 6: Collect and Summarize the Data

When administering the pretest, Ms. Hirai told her students:

- Why she was testing them
- Directions for taking the test
- How long they would have

In addition, she told them:

> I need to know how you organize your thoughts before you write a theme or short essay and how well you put these thoughts down when you actually write the paper. This is an important skill since you are required to use it in social studies, science, and so forth, and I want to see if you need help. I am going to show you a list of topics from which you can choose one to write about. Pick one that you like and know a lot about. Before you write the theme, I want you to organize your thoughts for your theme on a separate paper. Once you have done that, I want you to write about the topic. You will have the whole class period to do this. Tomorrow, you will edit your theme and rewrite it to make it better.
>
> Any questions?
>
> The theme will not be given a letter grade and will not be counted as part of your grade

in this class. I just want to get a better idea of how you organize and write short themes and essays.

Similar directions are given for the posttest. When assigning students themes to write outside of class (generalization to other settings), Ms. Hirai tells the students:

> Over the next few weeks I will give you some topics to write a paper on. On the day I assign the topic, I will ask you to write the paper at home or in study hall. I want you to use the TOWER form and to write a first draft, edit it, and then write a final draft. The following day I will score it and discuss the results with you.

When instructing students to use the strategy in mainstream settings (generalization to other materials and teachers), Ms. Hirai tells her students:

> For the next few weeks when you are assigned to write an essay or theme by one of your other teachers, I want you to use the TOWER strategy. Bring the graded paper to me so I can look at it and discuss whether the strategy worked for you in that class.

Steps 7 and 8: Display Data; Interpret Data and Make Decisions

In order to have a record of student performance, Ms. Hirai uses a graph to display student data (see Figure 10.3). On the graph she records scores from the pre- and posttests, TOWER form completion, practice strategy, task perfor-

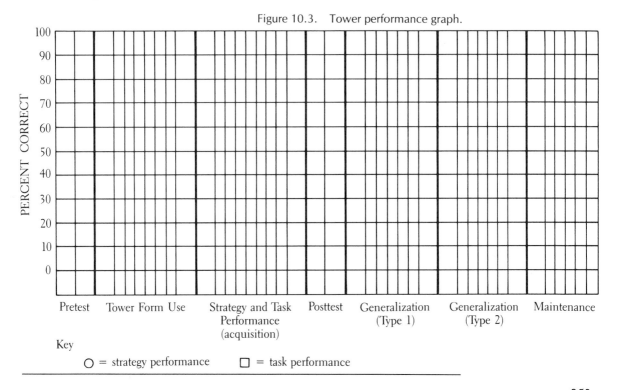

Figure 10.3. Tower performance graph.

Key

○ = strategy performance   □ = task performance

mance, generalization (both generalization to other settings and to other materials and teachers), and maintenance. Additionally, Ms. Hirai records grades on themes written for mainstream teachers prior to and after strategy instruction and displays them in order to interpret student performance.

Ms Hirai was especially concerned with analyzing TOWER form completion and strategy/task performance to see if steady progress was being made toward mastery in these areas. She decided that if a student made little progress three sessions in a row, she would sit with the student, occasionally asking questions, while he or she was filling out the form and/or writing the theme in order to get a better idea of where the student was experiencing difficulty.

Summary

Concerned about several students' essay- and theme-writing abilities—a frequent requirement in mainstream classes—Ms. Hirai decided to discover if they approached the task in a systematic or strategic manner. After identifying a group of students who did not outline before writing, edit first drafts, or execute drafts organized into complete paragraphs, Ms. Hirai taught them a strategy incorporating these skills. She used pre- and posttests to demonstrate student strategy acquisition and conducted formative assessment over multiple practice sessions to measure student progress toward acquisition. Finally, knowing that students often do not generalize and maintain newly acquired skills, she provided opportunities to do so and conducted performance assessments in these areas.

Chapter 11

CBA in Early Childhood Education

John T. Neisworth and Stephen Bagnato

Key Terms

Curriculum-embedded assessment
Curriculum-referenced assessment
Developmental curricula
Developmental domain

Developmental norms
Functional range
Transitional skill

The mission of contemporary early childhood education is far different from that of a traditional nursery school or daycare center. In the past, services for youngsters focused on safe, custodial care and opportunities for socialization. As our knowledge and recognition of the importance of early childhood expanded, the demand for more *educational*, rather than *custodial* services intensified. Early education programs for youngsters now often include comprehensive developmental curricula that are composed of developmental goals. In addition to child care and socialization, other aspects of development are encouraged, including physical health and growth, language stimulation, and cognitive development. Enrichment programs aim to promote the child's general welfare and developmental progress, to reduce the usual problems associated with early childhood, and to heighten the child's readiness for school. These general goals are appropriate and feasible for children who are not burdened with a developmental handicap or who are not at risk for serious problems.

Youngsters who are at risk or who display delays or deviations in development require even closer consideration, special and specific treatment, and a great deal of instructional precision. If special-needs preschoolers are not to be excluded, the mission of contemporary early-childhood education must include preventive and therapeutic instruction, as well as care and socialization.

Scope and Sequence of Developmental Curricula

Developmental domains may include hundreds of tasks or goals arranged in a hierarchical sequence. The hierarchies are lists of activites that correspond to sequences of skills displayed by normal children during their development. Drawing on a large body of observational research, experts have compiled lists of tasks that are ordered from easy to hard or early to later in development (e.g., Havighurst, 1956).

The progression of these developmental tasks is usually orderly, and they create a kind of ordinal scale in which a later skill is rarely evidenced before an earlier one. However, there are two major criticisms of the use of lists of developmental tasks for curricular goals. *First,* although the task sequences are quite consistent from culture to culture and generation to generation, they are not consistently demonstrated in the same order by children with certain handicaps. Children with congenital and severe sensory deficits may exhibit a less predictable sequence of concept development, and motoric disabilities are related to a different sequence of motor skills. Always requiring a handicapped child to learn in the normal (nonhandicapped) sequence may not be beneficial. *Second,* developmental tasks are not necessarily worthwhile instructional or curricular tasks. Many of the developmental tasks included on developmental assessment instruments are skills that are psychometrically useful, but they may not necessarily be important to teach in their own right. For example, stacking three blocks to form a tower may accurately discriminate among youngsters, but the skill itself has little social value, either when it is acquired or in later life.

Regardless of the criticisms, an empirically derived developmental test provides the basis for most early childhood curricula. Development is indeed quite predictable, and helping a child to progress evenly across the several domains of development is a sound goal. Certainly this approach is consistent with normalization, both in approach and content. Thus, in early childhood education, lists of sequenced, developmental landmarks become curricular goals. The developmental tasks or landmarks are accompanied by lists of precursive skills, and these skills are frequently task analyzed to provide even more goals. Table 11.1 displays some of the developmental landmark skills in the gross-motor and hand–eye domains as an example. As stated, these milestones usually do not include precise statements of criteria. Teachers in early education settings often must prepare these for themselves.

Because of the paramount position of the curriculum in instruction and therapy, a federally sponsored program was begun more than a decade ago to develop curricula suited to special-needs youngsters. This effort, the Handicapped Children's Early Education Program, funded hundreds of projects designed to pro-

Stage 1 (1–3 mos.)	Lifts head in prone position; moves arms and legs in forceful manner from flexion toward extension; begins to roll onto side.	Eyes begin to fix on objects; fists hands; grasps by reflex; brings objects to mouth.	TABLE 11.1 Normal Sequence of Motor Development in the First 36 Months
Stage 2 (4–6 mos.)	Lifts head and looks around; rolls supine to prone; holds head erect while sitting with support; pushes self up on hands in prone position and pulls toys toward self.	Turns head to look, looks at objects coming into visual field and reaches for them with arms; releases objects voluntarily; fingers toys being held.	
Stage 3 (7–9 mos.)	Moves from prone to crawling and standing positions; uses hands to pull self to standing.	Handles and bangs large objects on supporting surfaces; fixates on stationary objects; slaps, rakes, and scratches with hands.	
Stage 4 (10–12 mos.)	Spends most of time vertical, not horizontal; walks with widely spread feet.	Picks up beads with thumb and index finger; explores objects with fingertips.	
Stage 5 (13–24 mos.)	Develops better balance; begins climbing stairs with one foot leading; sits self in chair.	Plays with blocks; removes socks and shoes; feeds self with spoon; holds cup; imitates a vertical stroke.	
Stage 6 (25–36 mos.)	Runs, jumps.	Turns pages of books carefully.	

Source: Bigge, J. (1982). Teaching individuals with physical and multiple disabilities, second edition. Columbus, OH: Charles Merrill Publishing Co. Reprinted with permission.

duce experimental curricula. As a result, numerous curricula are now commercially available (see Bagnato, Neisworth, & Capone, 1986). Depending on the purpose of instruction, several approaches to curricular content are available.

Five Approaches to Preschool Curricula

The needs and characteristics of the child are the basic considerations in selecting a curriculum. Of course, the selection is also influenced by the teacher's intent, theory choice, and prior training. The five approaches differ in their scope or coverage of developmental goals, but all are sequenced according to demonstrable milestones or inferred processes typically acquired at predictable ages (given a typical environment).

Basic skills approach. Key or fundamental skills and knowledge form the basis of content for this approach. The goals and objectives included are usually said to be the basis for later development. For example, expressive and receptive language skills are essential for school success. Therefore, such skills would be stressed on the presumption that instruction in such key skills is the best use of a child's time and program resources.

Psychological constructs approach. A construct, of course, cannot be observed and measured. However, a construct or psychological process can be defined or operationalized by expected behaviors. Thus, constructs such as creativity, motivation, self-esteem, and cognition are postulated and then described in terms of skills or behaviors that would be subsumed by the construct. This approach emphasizes the attainment of inferred processes, and instruction is aimed at enhancing the child's mastery of increasing levels of the process or trait. As examples, special curricula are available for attempting to promote creativity, ego strength, achievement motivation, and locus of control.

Preacademic approach. Kindergarten and certain preschool *acceleration* programs often employ curricula that concentrate on getting children ready for the academic content of the primary grades. Training in initial reading, numbers, arts, science, and language is seen as a downward extension of elementary school curricula. This sort of curriculum appeals to some parents who are dedicated to an early academic start for their children. Many parents, however, do not favor pushing academic content in the preschool and argue that school will come soon enough and that early childhood programs should be more comprehensive in scope.

Remedial approach. Children's deficits or weaknesses are the basis for remedial curricula. Once identified, a child's developmental problems become a source of instructional goals and objectives (i.e., the curriculum). This approach is often the choice when working with handicapped youngsters, although preoccupation with deficits may mean neglecting progress in nondeficit areas. Indeed, these areas may become deficits themselves through neglect and later may become remedial targets. A remedial approach can be an efficient way to provide an immediate boost in development, helping a child to catch up with peers. As suggested, however, many educators would prefer a comprehensive, balanced, and steadily paced curricular approach.

Developmental tasks approach. Traditionally, nursery school authorities have advocated a *whole-child* approach (e.g., Hymes, 1968). Their position is that preschool experiences should foster progress within and across all important areas of development. With a whole-child philosophy, the curriculum must include goals and objectives coming from all basic developmental domains: communication (speech and language), socialization, self-care, both fine- and gross-motor behavior, affective or emotional, and intellectual or cognitive development.

Curricula for Handicapped Youngsters

Some curricula are designed to be comprehensive and to accommodate children with delays or special problems in any developmental domain, while other curricula address the specific needs created by particular handicapping conditions (i.e., physical handicap, visual limitations, severe retardation). Table 11.2 contains a list of several curricula designed for handicapped or potentially handicapped infants, toddlers, and preschoolers. In such curricula, objectives are usually provided in the four basic areas of social, cognitive, language, and motor development. Other areas (e.g., self-help, creativity, school readiness) can be subsumed within one or more of these four major areas. Such curricula may be employed

TABLE 11.2
Some Curricula
Designed for
Handicapped or
Delayed Youngsters

- Carolina Curriculum for Handicapped Infants (Johnson-Martin, Jens, & Attermeier, 1985)
- Clark Early Language Program (Clark & Moores, 1979).[a]
- Individualized Assessment and Treatment for Autistic and Developmentally Delayed Children (Schopler, Lansing, Reichler, and Waters, 1979)
- Oregon Project for Visually Impaired and Blind (Brown, Simmons, & Methvin, 1979)
- Portage Curriculum (Bluma, Shearer, Frohman, & Hillard, 1976)

[a]This curriculum is designed for the hearing impaired.

by Head Start or other programs devoted to helping children catch up. Clearly, then, early childhood special educators are not without sequences of specific developmental, instructional objectives for use with youngsters who cannot profit from the more general goals of early education. To facilitate curriculum-based assessment, the curriculum chosen should include many goals in all major areas of development. In addition to comprehensiveness of goals, the steps between goals must not be too great—a graduated continuum of skills is much more useful. The more graduated, the more easily children of varying levels and rates of progress may be accommodated.

Targeting Objectives for Intervention

When compared to students in elementary and secondary programs, mastery of developmental objectives is considered in somewhat different terms: full acquisition $(+)$, absence $(-)$, or emergence $(\pm)$. Emerging skills are usually targeted for systematic instruction since children have usually acquired the components of the final skill but are unable, or inconsistently able, to complete the tasks as expected. Intervention is directed toward full skill acquisition on these tasks in the developmental sequence. Skills in transition are ideal sources for instructional objectives since such skills are usually at the optimal level of challenge for the youngsters—not too hard, not too easy. Once a child's transitional skills are identified, individualized goal planning is accomplished by designing lessons that involve these transitional skills in various purposeful activities (e.g., drawing and writing, matching shapes in group circle-time activites, labeling pictures during storytelling). Instruction is most effective when clusters of related skills are taught together across people and settings as well as across curricular areas for two reasons. First, the chances of uneven development are reduced. Second, instruction is integrated so that the chances of teaching isolated tasks that result in a child's learning nonpurposeful splinter skills are also reduced. Most commercially available developmental curricula include field-tested strategies for grouping transitional skills for individual and group instruction and for matching appropriate instructional techniques (e.g., shaping and prompting) for teaching certain tasks.

Criteria for mastery of specific objectives are established by the program and each teacher. However, criteria typically involve 80 to 90% completion of a task without prompting over a number of trials or when the skill occurs under several conditions. Most intervention specialists believe that mastery and generalization of trained skills has occcurred when that skill is repeatedly displayed with different people, in different settings, with different materials, and under circumstances distinct from the training conditions.

After emerging skills have been mastered, the process is repeated by determining the next range of fully acquired, emerging, and absent skills so that a child's individualized goal plan can be revised. Newly emerging skills are targeted for intervention. If no new skills within a curriculum are emerging, the next objectives in the overall developmental sequence are selected.

Assessment in Preschool Curricula

CBA at the preschool level differs markedly from CBA in elementary and secondary schools for four reasons.

1. *The content that is taught is different.* Normal developmental curricula are based on developmmental landmarks (i.e., skills manifested by most children at specific ages without formal and systematic instruction). Many sensory, motor, and language skills come close to being universal; they have been observed in comparisons of widely differing cultures and divergent social strata within individual cultures. While other skills are more closely tied to a particular culture or social stratum, their development is quite consistent with a specific cultural milieu. Because curricula are based on developmental milestones, there is little divergence among curricula in terms of important curricular goals.

2. *CBAs within early childhood curricula rely more heavily on norm-referenced assessments.* Because developmental milestones form the basis of both curricula- and norm-referenced assessment for infants, toddlers, and preschoolers, all CBAs are, in a very real sense, norm referenced. Using two-word sentences, for example, is characteristic of 2-year-olds. This capability is both a developmental landmark and a curricular objective. When curricular goals are based on child development norms, attainment can be judged relative to other same-age children. A 3-year-old who just learns to walk shows mastery of the curricular objective but also a serious delay relative to the 1-year norm for walking. Good developmental CBA, then, also yields at least a rough measure of the child's status with respect to developmental norms. Thus, early childhood educators typically use existing norm-referenced tests rather than reinventing them. See Table 11.3 for a partial list of such devices.

3. *The growth, cognitive, and affective characteristics of preschoolers are quite different.* Infants, toddlers, and preschoolers change rapidly; they may not sustain attention to a task for as long a period; they are often noncompliant (e.g., "But I don't want to"); and they are quite heterogeneous in terms of background experiences and enabling skills. Thus, the assessment of preschoolers often requires adaptations in assessment that may violate the standardization procedures.

4. *The purposes of assessment are usually restricted to placement within a curriculum and monitoring progress on selected instructional objectives.* Diagnostic assessment (i.e., finding the category of handicap) with preschoolers usually does not fulfill the mission of early intervention. Educators are much more concerned about what children can do or cannot do—not whether they are retarded, disturbed, or learning disabled. Determining what categorical label fits a child does not provide a prescription for what objectives and methods should be used.

Two Types of Developmental CBAs

There are two major approaches to curriculum-based measurement within early childhood programming: curriculum-embedded and curriculum-referenced assessment.

Curriculum-Embedded Assessment

In its purest form, curriculum-embedded assessment refers to the use of the curriculum itself as the source for both testing and teaching; the instructional and assessment items are identical. In this case, the curriculum is the CBA. Thus, an obvious advantage of curriculum-embedded assessment is its unquestionable content validity. However, assuming the curriculum is comprehensive and thorough, the assessment process can be quite time and effort consuming. When a new child is referred to a preschool program, it may be necessary to spend up to two weeks in observation and testing to find the entry points within each developmental domain. (Once this is done, however, progress monitoring is relatively easy.) Another major disadvantage of this approach is that preschool programs use a variety of curricula. Children's status in their former curricula may, at best, only roughly correspond to their position in a new program's curriculum.

The most prominent and frequently used system for preschool children is the *Learning Accomplishment Profile—Revised Prescriptive Edition* (LAP) (Sanford &

Zelman, 1981). There are two curriculum-embedded scales within the total system: (1) *Early Learning Accomplishment Profile* (ELAP) (Glover, Preminger, & Sanford, 1978) that covers the birth to 36-month age range and (2) the *LAP Prescriptive Component* that surveys the 36- to 72-month range. Both scales provide a developmentally task-analyzed sequence of prerequisite skills appropriate for both at-risk and handicapped infants and preschool children. ELAP/LAP serve as individualized guides for the teacher to identify the child's mastery level, appraise the behavioral components of the subsequent level, and plan activities that facilitate skill acquisition and movement along a continuum of increasing developmental competence. The LAP system enables the analysis of 400 developmental capabilities within seven domains: cognitive, language, fine motor, gross motor, prewriting, personal/social, and self-help.

The assessment–prescriptive approach used with the LAP rests upon the fact that the content of assessment and teaching tasks is identical; thus, these developmental tasks provide a framework through which assessment, individualized programming and teaching, and progress evaluation are integrated. A child's initial baseline level of skill development is determined, teaching is directed toward mastery of prerequisites for later skills in the sequence, and individual progress is analyzed using these curriculum objectives as benchmarks and the child's baseline level as a reference point. Indices such as the number or percentage of curriculum objectives achieved within a period of treatment and gains in developmental skills comparatively across several domains of functioning are the typical performance measures employed by programs.

Another curriculum-embedded assessment system with unique features is *Developmental Programming for Infants and Young Children* (DPIYC) (Schafer & Moersch, 1981). DPIYC encompasses two developmental assessment scales that function as the treatment or instructional sequence. The *Early Intervention Developmental Profile* (EIDP) (Rogers, D'Eugenio, Brown, Donovan, & Lynch, 1981) surveys the birth to 36-month range, while the *Preschool Developmental Profile* (PDP) (Rogers, D'Eugenio, Drews, Haskin, Lynch, & Moersch, 1981) covers functioning across the 36- to 72-month levels. The programming system arranges functional skills by age and difficulty level into six developmental domains: cognitive, language, perceptual/fine motor, social-emotional, gross motor, and self-care. Embedded within the curriculum are task analyses of skills in various subdomains such as object constancy, cause–effect, and means–end problem solving in the cognitive domain. There are several unique aspects of DPIYC. Each of the six domains was designed by a developmental specialist with expertise in the area and is intended to be used by an interdisciplinary child development team. For example, the language domain was designed by a speech/language specialist and the gross-motor domain was constructed by a physical therapist. Next, DPIYC incorporates recent research in child development into its structure and content. Piagetian tasks are included in the cognitive area; attachment and separation skills are included in the social–emotional domain; a sequence of primitive reflexes integrated with functional movement skills comprise the gross-motor areas. Finally, a set of stimulation activites completes the DPIYC system. In addition to standard teaching strategies, field-tested adaptations to accommodate the sensory and response deficits of children with visual, auditory, and neuromotor impairments are provided for each skill cluster. Use of the EIDP and PDP allows the team to identify a child's range of fully acquired (+) absent (−) and emerging (±) capabilities and thus a child's transitional level to most effectively guide individualized teaching.

Curriculum-Referenced Assessment

The diversity of available curricula and the mobility of today's families make it unlikely that the same curriculum will be used by the several programs in which a young child may participate. Further, children may require specific instruction in areas of difficulty that involve specialized curricula (e.g., speech/language objectives). Teachers, specialists, and parents need a common curricular yardstick or measure that can be used across programs and times. Curriculum-referenced instruments, devices that assess the attainment of developmental milestones but are not specific to any one curriculum, fill this need. Professionals who plan children's programs are able to use curriculum-referenced measures to make suggestions applicable to a variety of curricula. A curriculum-referenced instrument is compatible with most good developmental curricula but is specific to none. Most developmental assessment batteries contain at least one good curriculum-referenced instrument.

The *Battelle Developmental Inventory* (BDI) (Newborg et al., 1984) is a standardized developmental scale that is the only current example of a norm-referenced diagnostic measure that also integrates criterion- or curriculum-referenced features into its structure (although it is not a curriculum). The BDI analyzes the acquisition of 341 critical developmental skills across birth to 8 years and within 5 functional domains and 22 subdomains. Functional capabilities are assessed in the following major domains: personal–social, adaptive, motor, communication, and cognitive. Unique clusters of subdomain skills are sampled in such areas as adult interaction, expression of feelings and affect, coping, attention, and reasoning. The battery's multidimensional structure allows a comprehensive analysis of fucntional capabilities that incorporates diagnostic data from many people and multiple sources (teachers, therapists, parents, observation, interviews, and child performance). In addition, the developmental and behavioral content of the BDI is congruent with the goals and tasks of frequently used infant and preschool curricula. Finally, the organization of the BDI enables interdisciplinary team members to assess children independently so that formative and summative evaluations of progress and program efficacy can be accomplished.

The *Diagnostic Inventory of Early Development* (IED) (Brigance, 1978) surveys the birth to 7-year age range while analyzing child performance across 96 skill sequences within 11 major developmental domains, including prespeech behaviors, general knowledge and comprehension, fine-motor skills, and preambulatory motor skills. Item placement and skill sequencing were accomplished by reviewing the organization of items in traditional developmental scales; moreover, the IED uniquely references the source of these placements for each item. Multisource procedures for scoring child performance are provided (interview, observation, diagnostic teaching, and pragmatic task modifications). The scale links assessment with intervention by arranging tasks in a hierarchical manner and by matching appropriate objectives to these tasks in each subdomain. Computer-based programs are available to translate child assessment data directly into IEP plans. *Prescriptive Readiness: Strategies and Practice* (Brigance, 1985) is a curriculum-based package of instructional activities appropriate for preschool, kindergarten, and early first-grade levels that match with assessment tasks on the IED. These activities detail objectives, rationale, instructional sequences, teaching recommendations, and indicators of learning difficulties for 400 developmental and behavioral skills.

Conducting CBAs in Early Childhood Education

Mastery of developmental objectives is usually judged from a child's performance on standardized norm-referenced tests, systematic observations during structured and unstructured situations, or parents' reports of mastery.

Norm-Referenced Tests

Certain norm-based scales such as the *Bayley Scales of Infant Development* (Bayley, 1969) and the *Battelle Developmental Inventory* (Newborg et al., 1984) can be used as objective-referenced tests. Compared to the curriculum-based scales, they contain similar but more global developmental sequences. However, unlike school-age curricula and intelligence tests, the parallel content of norm-based developmental skill measures and preschool curriculum-based measures generates some valid assessment–curriculum linkages (Bagnato & Neisworth, 1981; Bagnato, Neisworth, & Munson, in press).

The skills and the developmental domains surveyed in both types of instruments are similar. Thus, a diagnostic specialist such as the developmental school psychologist or the early childhood special educator can use norm-based scales to appraise landmark developmental skills.

Curriculum-embedded scales may be used to appraise general developmental levels also. Both curriculum-referenced and curriculum-embedded scales can be used to establish developmental levels and thus enter a child into an appropriate level within the curriculum, such as skill sequences appropriate for the 24- to 36-month level.

Systematic Observations

For many developmental objectives, systematic observation is the most efficient and effective method of assessment. Generally, the procedures and performance measures discussed in Chapter 9 may be applied appropriately to attainment of various objectives in early childhood education.

Performance measure: Percentage of occasions an emerging skill is used in place of the established, but lower-level, skill During the course of the day, a teacher (or parent) has many opportunities to observe a child's spontaneous use of various emerging skills. For example, a teacher can observe a child's unprompted mode of locomotion—crawling versus walking. In this example, when the percentage of walking exceeds 90% or 95%, the skill has emerged. The criteria for mastery of other developmental skills (e.g., associative play) should be set at a lower level and should be based on the opportunities to demonstrate the behavior rather than the total number of activities in which a child plays. (Some contexts or activites may not allow a child to engage in associative play).

Parent Ratings

For some developmental objectives, systematic observations conducted by teachers may not be possible. In such cases, the estimates of parents or caregivers may be the most efficient method of assessment. Once again, the procedures, performance measures, and cautions discussed in Chapter 9 may be applied appropriately to parent ratings of the attainment of various objectives.

Summary

Curriculum-based developmental assessment is the primary technique used to plan instructional and therapeutic programs for even the most severely handicapped preschool child. Among all other forms of CBA, is it unique. First, it is distinguished by the fact that it projects a practical blend between developmental assessment and developmental treatment with child developmental theory providing the unifying thread; no other form of CBA reflects this tight merger of theory and practice. Second, it places the greatest reliance on standardized testing since those tests so accurately reflect curricula. Third, educational interventions in early childhood education are aimed not only at the children's skills but also at various dimensions of the physical and social environment that influences them. Thus, future curricula and assessment strategies will need to be devised to identify and to modify relevant characteristics of a child's environment, including family circumstances, stress, classroom arrangements, and adult–peer interactions.

Extended Example

Scenario

At the age of 4, Kevin entered a Head Start program. Initially, his mother was concerned about the slow development of his speech and language skills. Everyone regarded Kevin as smart, but he never seemed to be able to keep pace with his peers in the preschool. After six months in the program, Kevin's articulation improved considerably, but he was still unable to complete work individually or in small groups. The teachers and aides described Kevin as restless, inattentive, and impulsive; he rarely waited, shared, or took turns like the other children. In addition, Kevin seemed to have problems listening and remembering during small-group activities. Also, he had problems in drawing and coloring tasks.

The Head Start teacher, Ms. Martin, arranged a conference with Kevin's mother to discuss Kevin's difficulties. His mother reported that Kevin had been active and "unsatisfied" ever since he was a toddler. It was very difficult for her to manage his behavior at home, but since enrollment in the preschool, Kevin's behavior problems decreased considerably. Ms. Martin believed that Kevin's chances for success in kindergarten next year would be limited unless his school readiness could be improved in the areas of behavioral control and preacademic skills. Ms. Martin thought that enrolling Kevin in the school district's transitional kindergarten program would be helpful because that setting was more structured and was specifically designed for children who were at risk of a learning handicap. Ms. Martin helped Kevin's mother contact the public school kindergarten transitional program (KTP).

The KTP referred Kevin to determine his eligibility for placement in the program. Data were collected from the *Perceptions of Developmental Status* (PODS) (Bagnato & Neisworth, in press). Figure 11.1 uses the PODS profile to synthesize the judgment-based ratings by Ms. Martin and Kevin's mother. A review of this graph shows that all seem to agree about Kevin's near-average intellectual skills and have similar concerns about his ability to get along with peers, his motivation, his attention and self-control, his mastery of basic concepts, and his fine-motor abilities. A school psychologist then administered the *Woodcock–Johnson Psychoeducational Battery—Preschool Cluster* (WJPEB) (Woodcock, 1978), and the *Bracken Basic Concept Scale* (BBCS) (Bracken, 1984). Kevin's performances were similar to those judged and reported by Ms. Martin and his mother. The personnel from the KTP viewed Kevin as a likely candidate for placement in the program and found him eligible for their services.

Step 1: Specify Reasons for Assessment

In order to plan an individual program of instruction in the transitonal kindergarten, it was first necessary to ascertain Kevin's current mastery in various preacademic and behavioral readiness areas. Attainment of unmastered skills would increase his chances for success in a regular kindergarten or first-grade setting as he approached 6 years of age.

Step 2: Analyze the Curriculum

The KTP team wanted to select a curriculum that would meet Kevin's instructional needs by translating clear goals into developmentally task-analyzed and behaviorally specific objectives and that placed a high premium on skills that were deficient or absent in Kevin's repertoire. They chose the *Help for Special Preschoolers Activities Binder* (Santa Cruz County Office of Education, 1987). This widely field-tested curriculum was chosen because its content and objectives focus on such developmental curricular subdomains as reasoning skills, basic reading and math skills, auditory perception and listening comprehension, attention and task completion, and interpersonal relations.

Step 3: Formulate Behavioral Objectives

Specific behavioral objectives would be formulated after a pretest of skills from the *Help* curriculum had been completed.

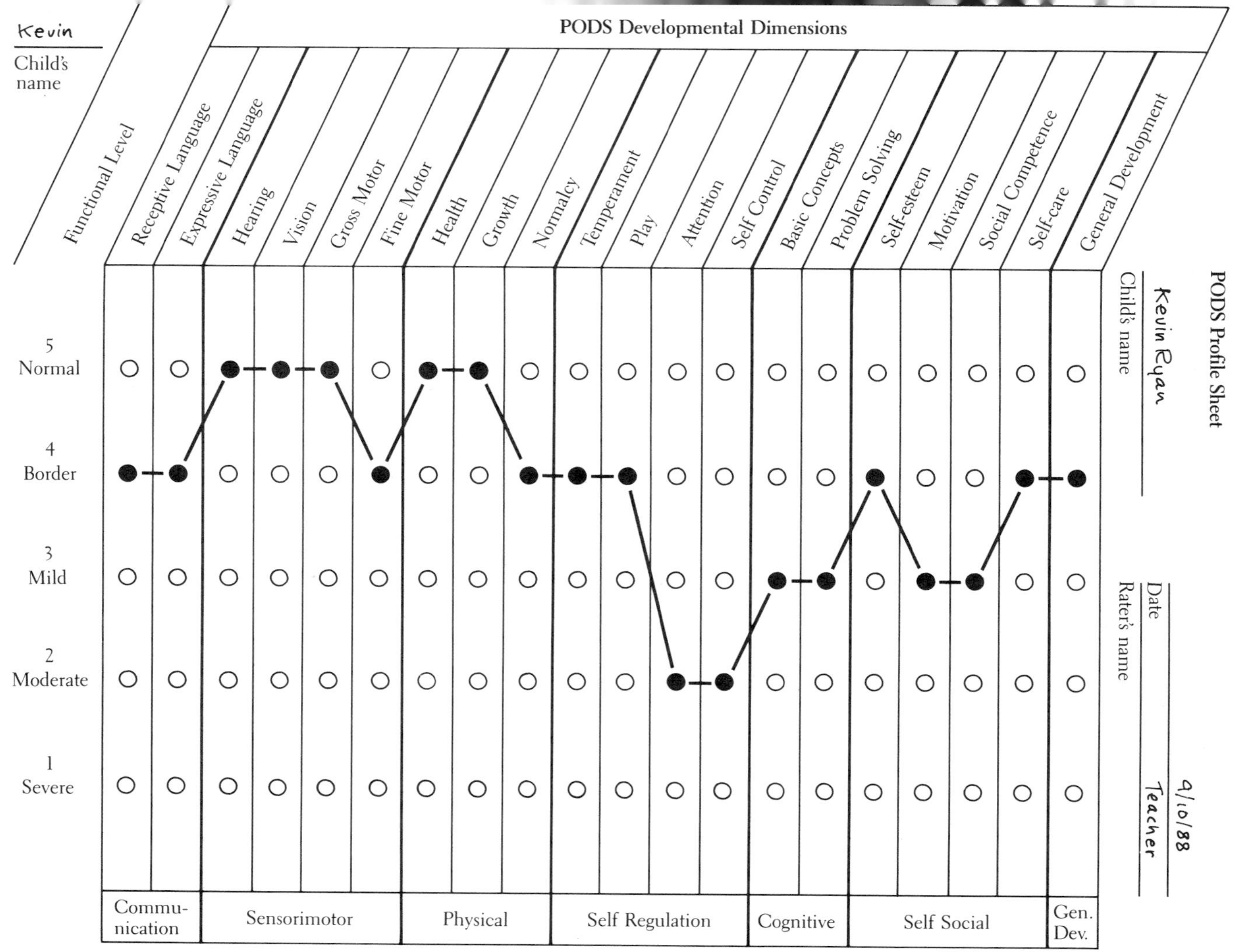

Figure 11.1. Kevin's PODS profile. (Source: Bagnato, S. & Neisworth, J. [1990]. *System to Plan Early Childhood Services* [SPECS]. Circle Pines, MN.: American Guidance Service. Reprinted with permission.)

Step 4: Develop Appropriate Assessment Procedures

As part of the system, a *Help* checklist is included. This checklist is completed on the basis of direct observations, play interactions, and parent interview. Since mastery of individual skills would be systematically observed and graphed as part of ongoing instruction, the current impressions of teachers, aides, and parent were considered sufficiently precise to use as an initial screening. The KTP provided individualized instruction, and Kevin's program and objectives would be modified on the basis of his ongoing performance.

Step 5: Collect Data

The team conducted a two-day appraisal of Kevin within the kindergarten classroom of 10 children. Available adults included two teachers and an aide. The morning of the third day, Kevin's mother was interviewed by one of the teachers to estimate Kevin's mastery of those behaviors and skills that could not be observed in the two-day period.

Steps 6 and 7: Summarize and Display Data

Kevin's emerging or transitional skills, indicated by ± on the record form, were targeted for intervention. These skills are shown in Table 11.4.

Step 8: Interpret Data and Make Decisions

Based on the results displayed in Table 11.4, an IEP was prepared for Kevin. The long-term and short-term objects are displayed in Table 11.5.

TABLE 11.4	*Communication*
Kevin's Transitional Skills in Communication, Basic Reading, Math, and Attention Span/Task Completion, Based on *HELP for Special Preschoolers Activities Binder*	tapping rhythms
	repeating melodies
	rephrasing comments
	carrying out implied tasks
	Attention Span/Task Completion
	attending to task without supervision
	completing task independently
	Basic Reading
	matching words
	naming consonants
	Math
	locating objects of relative size
	locating objects by position
	reading and writing numbers to ten

Short-Term Objectives to Be Accomplished Within Four Weeks:

When presented with a rhythm or melody consisting of five notes, Kevin will reproduce it on request.

When requested to complete a series of three tasks, Kevin will perform the tasks independently and in the order requested.

After participating in a discussion and upon his teacher's request, Kevin will restate portions of the discussion in his own words.

Given a stimulus word of five letters, Kevin will select a matching word from a four-stimulus array in which the response options differ in only one letter. (The differing letter will appear in initial, medial, and end positions.)

When shown any upper- or lowercase letter, Kevin will say the letter's name.

When given a series of objects in random order, Kevin will point to the one that best represents bigger, smaller, biggest, smallest, and so forth.

When given a sequence of five objects, Kevin will point to the object that is first, middle, and last in the sequence.

Given the numerals from 1 to 3 written in various sizes, Kevin will say the number upon request.

Without a model, Kevin will write the numerals 1, 2, and 3.

Given activities that are generally appealing to him, Kevin will continue to participate for durations of at least 5 minutes without redirection.

Given appropriate classroom activities, Kevin will complete 90% accurately and without prompting.

Long-Term Objectives to Be Accomplished by Year-End:

When requested to complete a series of four tasks, Kevin will perform the tasks independently and in the order requested.

After listening to a story and upon his teacher's request, Kevin will restate portions of the story in his own words.

Given oral communications said with different intonations, Kevin will distinguish between questions, commands, anger, humor, and *regular* talk.

When shown any upper- or lowercase consonant, Kevin will say the letter's hard and soft sounds.

When shown any upper- or lowercase vowel, Kevin will say the letter's long and short sounds.

Given concrete objects, Kevin will count the elements up to sets of 20.

Given the command, "Show me," Kevin will demonstrate 20 relational concepts (e.g., front, back, left, right, inside, outside).

Upon his teacher's request, Kevin will begin and complete tasks working in small groups without prompting or assistance for 5 to 10 minutes.

TABLE 11.5
Kevin's Long-Term and
Short-Term Objectives

Chapter 12

Managing CBA in the Classroom
Deborah A. Bott

Curriculum-based assessment is related to positive results in student learning (Fuchs & Fuchs, 1986a), and many teachers are familiar with CBA. Nevertheless, of the teachers surveyed by Wesson, King, and Deno (1984) who reported that they had some knowledge of frequent and direct measurement, nearly half did not use CBA in their classrooms. The primary barrier reported by the teachers was that CBA is time consuming. There is no denying that quality CBA procedures do take time, but the benefits to efficacy of instruction and student learning cannot be ignored. The issue becomes one of efficiency.

Management of CBA in the classroom is efficient when teachers invest some time in planning and preparation, use assessment routines that are quick and accurate, involve other persons as assistants, and make optimal use of available time, technology, and resources. Since many CBA activites are ongoing or repetitive, they may be organized in ways that will save time. Other tasks within CBA can probably be done just once if they are well designed and well constructed. The purpose of this chapter is to consider each step of the CBA model presented in this text and provide practical suggestions for effective and efficient curriculum-based assessment. Ideas for efficient management are described within categories of resources typically available to classroom teachers—the teacher's own time and energy, other adults, students, and microcomputers.

Step 1: Specify Reasons for Assessment

The first step in the CBA model requires decisions about what to teach, how to teach, and where to teach that will set the direction taken during all subsequent assessment steps. Groups of adults or individual classroom teachers make these decisions, although students may be consulted. Technology is rarely involved at this stage, as the process requires clarification of goals and values.

If a large group (e.g., a department, a team of teachers, a school, or a district) is responsible for specifying reasons for assessment, then the group must come to a consensus, clearly communicate the policies to stakeholders, and offer meaningful leadership in implementation. The membership of a group making this decision should be representative of the people affected by the decision, and the decision should reflect best practice based on research evidence and previous school-based applications.

Even if the classroom teacher has participated in shaping a policy or has received a policy statement from the school or district administration, the process of specifying a reason for assessment also involves developing a personal rationale for assessment that is relevant to the teacher and his or her instructional goals. Regardless of the number of persons involved in this step, the outcome should be a clear rationale for the assessment process. A written statement will facilitate communication (and memory) and can provide a starting point for any revisions made in response to new information or situations.

Steps 2 and 3: Analyze Curriculum and Formulate Behavioral Objectives

The next two steps of the CBA model, analyzing curriculum and formulating behavioral objectives, share many efficiency considerations. Obtaining appropriate curriculum and behavioral objectives involves three possibilities used separately or in combination—use existing materials, adapt existing materials, and write original materials. These activities primarily involve the classroom teacher and other professionals. Students may be consulted at this stage for suggestions about curriculum and objectives, and microcomputer applications can help people write, revise, and distribute the curriculum and accompanying behavioral objectives. Details about strategies for professionals, student involvement, and microcomputer applications are described within this section.

Strategies for Teachers and Other Professionals

Several considerations for teachers and other professionals are appropriate across all of the activities mentioned above—selecting, adapting, or writing curricula. Involving persons who have a vested interest in obtaining a quality curriculum and also have experience in and knowledge about the curricular area is critical. If curriculum development activities are not part of these individuals' job descriptions, motivation will certainly improve if compensation is provided for time spent on the task. Compensation may include any combination of salary supplement, released time, or in-service credit. Direct support from the school district reflects a commitment by administrators to the curriculum development project that may improve chances for implementation and dissemination of the final product. Other sources of support include grants from state and federal governmental agencies or private foundations. Announcements of federal grant programs are published in the *Federal Register,* and references such as Eckstein's (1988) funding directory describe sources of grants for special projects in education.

Additional considerations for teams working on curriculum development include attention to work conditions and processes. Scheduling work sessions on a consistent basis throughout a reasonable period of time (e.g., one session every other week for three months) can avoid pressuring team members and promote progress. If possible, sessions scheduled early in the day may be more productive than those scheduled after members have worked a full day in the classroom or office. Some curriculum development teams have used district-wide in-service days, released time, Saturdays, and the summer months to avoid after-school meetings. Providing adequate and comfortable work space and necessary supplies (including reference materials) will help team members work efficiently. Periodic reviews of the product by independent readers can help identify areas that need clarification, redundancies that need to be omitted, or additional goals and objectives that need to be included.

A final consideration is planning for a functional product, one that will be convenient for consumers—classroom teachers and their students. The curriculum should be organized into logical chunks that correspond to normal subject area boundaries and typical teaching sequences. Often a coding system cross-referenced to probes, tests, and observation systems is appropriate.

Selecting existing curricula and objectives. When identifying curricula and accompanying objectives, it is most efficient to avoid writing original materials if useful curricula and objectives already exist. Whether the purpose is updating, replacing, or implementing new curricula, the first step should be to look for existing curricula and objectives that match the needs of the students, are logically conceptualized and well written, and are organized in a functional way. Persons to contact for existing curricular materials include other teachers, local district consultants or supervisors, and curriculum specialists at state departments of education, colleges, or universities. Some curricula developed by funded projects or public agencies appear in the ERIC Document Reproduction Service that may be found in many university libraries. One example found in ERIC is *Math Objectives Guide: Project CAST,* a comprehensive listing of functional life-skills objectives in arithmetic for persons with mild and moderate handicaps published by the Charles County (Maryland) Board of Education (1981). Other sources of published curricula are professional organizations, commerical instructional materials, and reference books. If the curricular material is not public domain material, that is, the materials are copyrighted and some form of payment is required before they may be used, teachers should write to the author or publisher and request a review copy that may be used for decision making only. If the material is to be adopted in part or whole, a fee should be negotiated for use of the copyrighted material.

Adapting existing curricula and objectives. Available published curricula and objectives may not be an exact match for the needs of a specific group of students, and they may require some adaptation before serving as a basis for CBA. Modifying a relatively large curriculum may be most efficient if it is accomplished by a team of educators who are experienced in the content domain, but it is possible for an individual to accomplish this task. Analysis of curriculum may be easiest if portions of the domain are considered separately and the task is divided into manageable chunks. Individuals or teams who work on curricular adaptation should always cite the original source(s) of the curriculum and objectives on all printed material but should feel free to add necessary content or skills, subtract inappropriate portions, and improve the clarity of curricular descriptions or objectives. In subject areas that change quickly, especially the sciences, curricula and objectives will require constant updating; an established schedule for periodic reviews will help ensure that updates actually are accomplished. Teachers working with special student populations will need to be alert to the match between curriculum and unique needs of students.

Writing original curricula and objectives. If published curricula and objectives are not satisfactory or are unavailable, a third option is to write all or part of the material needed to begin CBA. Even in this case, curriculum development need not start from scratch; high-quality existing curricula may serve as models for organization and format even if the content does not match what is needed. If a comprehensive curriculum is required, this may be a staggering task for an individual to face, but it is reasonable to expect that a team of educators can write a curriculum that will meet the needs of students. If the authoring task is quite large, the team may function most efficiently as several smaller working groups, each of which work toward a specific and publicly stated outcome. Indeed, the first task of the curriculum-writing team may be to write a series of objectives for their own work and establish a timeline for completion of the task.

Student Participation

Students may serve as advisers during the adoption, revision, or authoring of curricula and objectives. In some situations adults may wish to consult with students regarding curricular emphasis and goals. The advisory role given to students will vary with the purpose of the curricula and the students' ages, maturity levels, and backgrounds. Students may suggest how existing curricula and objectives should be modified or they may review proposed curricula and objectives after adults have completed a draft copy.

Student involvement may also occur at a very personal level when designing a student's individual program, as occurs during individual educational program planning for students placed in special education. The *Educational Planning Strategy* (VanRusen et al., 1987) provides a structured process in which students analyze their own strengths and weaknesses, develop personal instructional objectives, practice communicating their goal statements using role playing, and present their suggestions to the adults present at the IEP meeting. The *Educational Planning Strategy* or similar techniques may be used with any student who is involved in making decisions about the content and direction of the school experience. Outcomes of such an approach can increase student awareness of short- and long-term goals, motivation for goal attainment, and practice in self-assessment and planning for the future.

Microcomputer Applications

If classroom teachers who will be using the curriculum and the development team members have access to compatible microcomputers, curriculum and objectives that are written using a word processor or database will be easy to access and revise. Objectives entered into a database using a code followed by the objectives will allow teachers to locate them quickly and create individualized lists of objectives for students' program plans including the IEP required for students in special education. The Fayette County (Kentucky) Special Education Curriculum Project produced an example of a teacher-authored curriculum that includes coded and cross-referenced short-term objectives, accompanying assessment tasks, and suggested teaching strategies. The objectives exist on a large mainframe computer at the central office, and the multidisciplinary team that develops the IEP selects objectives from a *Thesaurus of Instructional Objectives for Special Education Programs* (1987). IEP teams in this district also have the option of writing original objectives for students with unique needs or for content areas not included in the thesaurus. After objectives are selected, the codes are noted on a form, and the form is sent to the central office where someone who works at a computer accesses objectives by their codes and creates the IEP document. (See Figure 12.1 for sample codes and objectives from this curriculum, and see Table 12.1 for additional information.)

The first two steps of the CBA model are best managed when persons involved

Figure 12.1.
Selected codes and objectives from the Fayette County (Kentucky) thesaurus of instructional objectives for special-education programs (1987).

Sample Language Arts Codes and Objectives

Oral Language (OL)
LA-OL-023 Given the question "What is your address?" the pupil will state mailing address (street number, street, apartment, city, and state) on five different days with 100% accuracy.
Oral Reading (OR)
LA-OR-017 Given the months of the year and abbreviations for each, the pupil will read the words and abbreviations with 100% accuracy.
Spelling (SP)
LA-SP-031 Given ordinal numbers (first to tenth) orally, the pupil will write the words with 90% accuracy.

Sample Mathematics Codes and Objectives

Calendar (CA)
MA-CA-015 Given 20 dates and a calendar, the pupil will locate the day on which the specific date occurs with 100% accuracy.
Measurement-Linear (ML)
MA-ML-005 Given a 12-inch ruler and 10 lines of varying inch lengths, the pupil will measure each line to the inch and write its length with 100% accuracy.
Numeration (NU)
MA-NU-004 Given isolated printed numerals (1 to 10) in random order, the pupil will orally identify the numeral with 100% accuracy.

Title	Description	Address	
AIMSTAR	Computer (Apple II) software for generating line graphs depicting student performance and decision rules	ASIEP Education Co. 3216 NE 27th Portland, OR 97212	TABLE 12.1 Descriptions of Selected CBA Material
Classroom Learning Screening Manual	System of printed probes for times assessments of basic skills	Psychological Corp. 555 Academic Court San Antonio, TX 78204	
Computer-Based Measurement Software Applications	Computer (Apple II series) software with four major components: generate printed probes, collect performance data on computerized probes, data management system, and data-based decision rules	Dr. Lynn Fuchs Peabody College Vanderbilt University Nashville, TN 37203	
Fayette County Special Education Curriculum	Thesaurus of objectives, assessment tasks, and teaching activities; all teaching activities are cross-referenced using a coding system	Dr. Eve Proffitt Special Pupil Services & Alternative Programs Fayette County Public Schools 301 East Main Street Lexington, KY 40502	
Fact Sheets	Computer software (Apple) package, produces printed math fact probes and answer keys for all four operations	Hartley Courseware Box 419 Dimondale, MI 48821	
MECC Mastering Math Worksheet Generator	Creates and prints arithmetic worksheets (Apple II series)	MECC 3490 Lexington Ave., N St. Paul, MN 55126	
Pine County Special Education Cooperative Total Special Education System	Behavioral classification system, methods for establishing local district norms using curriculum-based assessments, formal problem-solving system, computerized data management	Gary Germann Box 228 Court at Fifth Sandstone, MN 55072	
Precision Teaching Probes	Printed sets of probes for timed assessments	Precision Teaching Project Skyline Center 3300 Third Street, NE Great Falls, MT 59404	
Sheri	Microcomputer (Apple II) software package creates line or bar graphs, applies data decision rules, generates reports	Performances Monitoring Systems PO Box 148 Cambridge, MN55008	

work within clearly identified goals, have the necessary skills and knowledge of the curricular domain, are appropriately compensated for their work, and have access to adequate resources for curriculum development. After the curriculum and objectives are adopted, adapted, or developed, they may be used as the basis for assessment procedures that will provide the classroom teacher with information necessary for effective instruction.

Step 4: Develop Appropriate Assessment Procedures

Decisions made during the development of classroom assessment procedures greatly influence the efficiency and efficacy of assessment. Initial development of practical and appropriate procedures is important, but ongoing refinement and adjustment are of equal value. This section provides descriptions of development strategies for teachers and suggestions for how other adults, students, and technology may assist teachers at this step in the CBA process.

Strategies for Teachers

At the third step within the CBA model, an effective teacher establishes assessment routines, prepares tests and probes, creates standard forms, and organizes assessment materials. For teachers new to CBA, it may be wise to select one small area of the curriculum (e.g., oral reading or arithmetic facts), develop procedures and materials, and work with the procedures for several weeks. After some experience, the teacher will find parts of the procedures that work well and parts that need modification. This experience can then be applied to the development of procedures and materials for other parts of the curriculum.

Establishing assessment routines. When the same systematic assessment procedures are used across skills or domains, CBA becomes less time consuming than when the teacher has to deliver detailed instructions to students each time an assessment is conducted. Routines should be identified as such for the students (e.g., "We will do this *every* time you take an arithmetic probe"), and initially the teacher will need to give detailed, direct instructions and encourage the students to ask questions about the procedure. Routines include how students take a test or probe and, if they are to be allowed to administer probes, how they give a probe to another student.

When students are learning CBA routines, it is best to model or demonstrate the routine. Then students can be given practice using easy content on which they will not be graded and can recieve feedback regarding their mastery of the routine. Practice should continue until students are proficient and independent in using the routines. Time spent in familiarizing students with CBA routines will pay off when a teacher merely has to provide a simple prompt such as, "It's time for oral reading probes for Group X," and students immediately get their materials, locate the correct page, label their performance charts, and go to the reading station when it is their turn. When the teacher identifies a portion of the routine that needs modification, the instruction again should be direct, and students should be allowed to practice the new routine before they must use it during an actual assessment.

Some standard measurement procedures for oral reading, written spelling, written expression, and arithmetic were developed at the Institute for Reasearch on Learning Disabilities at the University of Minnesota (Deno & Fuchs, 1987; Germann & Tindal, 1985). These procedures are included in Figure 12.2 and

Figure 12.2.   Assessment routines developed at the University of Minnesota, Institute for Research on Learning Disabilities (Deno & Fuchs, 1987, pp. 8–9).

Measuring and Scoring Oral Reading Performance

1. Select a reading passage that corresponds to the appropriate level for the student's long-range goal.

2. For each passage there are two forms—an unnumbered copy for the student and a numbered copy for the teacher. Put the student copy in front of and facing the student.

3. Put the teacher copy in front of and facing yourself.

4. Say to the student: "When I say 'start,' begin reading aloud at the top of this page. Try to read each word. If you wait for a word too long, I'll tell you the word. You can skip words you don't know. At the end of one minute, I'll say 'stop.' " (Give students 3 seconds before supplying words.)

5. Turn on the stopwatch as you say "start."

6. Follow along on your copy, circling with a pencil incorrectly read words (omissions, substitutions, mispronunciations, insertions).

7. At one minute, say "stop" and turn off the stopwatch.

8. Place a slash after the last word read.

9. Count the number of words correct and the number of errors. (The teacher copy lists the number of words per line.)

10. Record both correct and incorrect scores on an equal-interval graph labeled "Number of Words Read Aloud from Text Passages."

11. Repeat steps 1–10 at least twice weekly.

Measuring and Scoring Written Expression Performance

1. Give the child a pencil and a response form. (Story starters may be individually or group administered.)

2. Give the student the following instructions. "Today I want you to write a story. I am going to read a sentence to you first, and then I want you to write a short story about what happens. You will have 1 minute to think about the story you want to write and then have 3 minutes to write it. When I say 'begin,' start writing."

3. Time the student as he or she writes for 3 minutes.

4. When 3 minutes have elapsed, tell the student to stop writing.

5. Count the total number of words or letters written in the composition, including words spelled incorrectly. Count all personal nouns and names. Do not count numbers.

6. Record the total number of words or letters written by the student on an equal-interval chart labeled "Number of Words (or Letters) Written."

7. Repeat steps 1–6 at least twice weekly.

---

are examples of CBA routines that may be used in any classroom in which reading, spelling, written expression, or arithmetic are part of the curriculum. Teachers may adapt these procedures to fit other curricular areas.

Preparation of assessment materials for CBA. The collection, development, production, and organization of materials for CBA is an ongoing process. The classroom teacher probably never has a finished and complete set of probes and tests because curricula and student needs are constantly changing. Recognizing this somewhat discouraging fact, there is still much that the classroom teacher can do to prepare materials before assessment takes place in the classroom. As with most organizational tasks, the more care and thought put into the process ahead of time, the better the outcome.

As is the case with curriculum development, if appropriate probes or tests already exist, then the most efficient practice is to adopt or adapt them. (See Table 12.1 for sources of probe and test materials.) If a teacher is unable to locate existing probe materials that match the curriculum, then teacher-made probes are an option.

Developing a standard format for a probe or test will make administration and future development of probes easier. As one example, the staff of the Precision Teaching Project listed in Table 12.1 has developed a common format for written probes, and teachers may use this same structure when creating original probes. This probe format is designed to be consistent and easy to use; it includes the following four features.

1. The 8½ × 11–inch page is turned 90 degrees so that rows are longer and contain more items. Longer rows require students to make fewer moves to new lines and can save a few seconds during a timed assignment.

2. At the top of the page, identifying information is written, including student's name, date, instructional objective (complete statement, brief paraphrase, or code), and criterion for mastery. Any special directions also appear at the top of the page.

3. There is a place to record the results of the assessment task in terms of number of correct responses and number of errors. If the assessment is timed, the time limit appears in this section also.

4. A cumulative total number of movements required for correct responses is noted at the end of each line. This allows for quick scoring of the completed probe. (For an example of an arithmetic probe using this format, see Figure 4.7 in Chapter 4.)

Sometimes probes consist of a group of randomly selected items from a larger pool such as spelling words, story starters, or one-page reading samples. Wesson (1987) suggests some techniques for streamlining random selection of material for probes. For spelling words, she suggests printing words on 3 × 5–inch cards, shuffling the cards, and randomly selecting the ones to present during probe. Wesson estimates that 30 different story starters should be sufficient for an entire academic year of twice-weekly written-expression probes, and that these should also be written on notecards. As a card is randomly selected for a writing probe, the student's initials are printed on the back; after students have used the same story starter three times, they may not use the card again. Reading passages for oral reading probes may be selected by identifying 30 pages—10 from the beginning, middle, and end of a book. A container is labeled with the book's title, previously identified page numbers are printed on separate pieces of paper, and the slips of paper are placed in the container. When students prepare to read, they draw a slip of paper and write their initials on the back of the slip. After students have read a passage three times, they may not use the same page again.

Use of standard forms. In addition to the development of probes and tests, CBA will be more efficient if standard forms are developed for collecting, summarizing, and displaying the data. Standardized procedures are especially helpful if persons other than the teacher are involved in CBA because they only need to be taught to use one kind of graph or one kind of performance chart. A sample performance chart designed for recording data on a series of objectives is presented in Figure 12.3. When standard forms are used, a large supply of the forms may be duplicated at the beginning of the school year. Some school districts and commerical printers offer reduced printing costs for large jobs, and it may be

---

Student __*Kenny*__   DOB __*6-6-82*__

Teacher __*Jackson*__   School Year __*89-90*__

Figure 12.3. Sample performance chart to display progress on multiple objectives (Fayette County, 1984).

IEP Monitoring Sheet

Objectives for Spelling
SP-002 Initial or final
diagraphs (CRITERION: 85%)   40%   65%   70%   85%   M/90%
                      Date   9-5   9-7   9-11 9-13 9-20

SP-003 l,r,s blends
        (CRITERION: 85%)   80%   85%   M/85%
                      Date   9-13 9-15 9-22

SP-004 two-letter clusters
        (CRITERION: 85%)   85%   M/85%
                      Date   9-15 9-27

SP-005 long "a" words
        (CRITERION: 85%)   55%   60%   75%
                      Date   9-18 9-19 9-20

SP-006 long "i" words
        (CRITERION: 85%)
                      Date

Key: M/%   =   Maintenance check
        %   =   Assessment
        obj*   =   Added objective (circled in red marker)
        0%   =   Criterion met (block is colored with yellow marker)

realistic for several teachers to develop standard forms and have them mass produced at a relatively low cost.

Organizing materials. After probes and forms are produced, it is essential that they be organized in ways that make them convenient and accessible. If instructional objectives are coded, then this same code should be used to organize a filing system with large sections for each content or skill area and subsections for each objective. If objectives are not yet coded, it may be helpful to develop a coding system that is simple yet allows for future additions to the curriculum. (Numbering by tens or twenties will allow for additions that are made at a later date to be inserted into the sequence.) Wesson (1987) suggests color coding probes, graphs, and plan sheets for each instructional area so that materials can be easily identified and returned to their designated storage areas. Assessment materials should be stored in an area close to where they will be used, especially if students will be accessing the files. Thus, filing cabinets or storage boxes should be placed in several different locations around the classroom. File folders should be clearly labeled and kept in a rack or box for easy access. (Note: Originals used for duplicating should be clearly labeled as such and should never be placed in a file to which students have access.) Some teachers prefer to organize students' individual graphs and charts in a tabbed, loose-leaf notebook with one section for each student.

Involving Other Adults and Students

One strategy for reducing the amount of teacher time devoted to assessment and thus freeing the teacher for other instructional activities is to involve other persons in CBA tasks. Delegating assessment tasks to others requires an initial investment in organization and training, but delegation results in increased efficiency. If a classroom teacher has access to a teacher's assistant or paraprofessional, the assistant may help at nearly every stage of the CBA model. Volunteers such as parents or senior citizens may also assist in CBA, but if their schedule is variable, these persons may be of most help by doing "behind the scenes," preparatory tasks such as duplicating materials and organizing files. If there is a teacher-education program in the area, a classroom teacher also may be assisted by practicum students. Tasks assigned to college students should match their skill level and the amount of time they are assigned to the classroom.

The largest group of people available to assist teachers is their students. Local conditions may prevent teachers from having a paid assistant, volunteers, or college students in the classroom; however, every teacher has students, and they are a valuable source of assistance for a teacher committed to CBA. Involving students in some managerial task is not ruthless; it is good classroom management. In addition to making CBA easier to manage, students may learn other important skills. Lovitt (1973) describes student participation in classroom management as valuable for students who learn independence, gain satisfaction by helping the teacher, practice many functional skills, and frequently are motivated by participating in classroom management. Teaching students to participate in the management of their classroom can reinforce the values of self-sufficiency and helping others.

Teaching students to assist with CBA. There are many tasks within CBA that students, even very young ones, can perform. If a teacher is to be successful in involving students, time must be devoted to teaching them what is expected, selected materials must be organized and accessible to students, and assisting the teacher must be established as a desirable activity within the classroom. Helping a teacher should never be used as a punishment; it always should be presented as a positive activity or privilege for students. Some tasks may be expected of all students—for example, placing a finished probe in the "in box" and freeing a teacher from collecting papers. Other jobs, such as administering a probe, may be earned after a student has demonstrated competency in required skills. Some teachers require students to pass a competency test before they are *certified* to administer probes to peers. Competencies may include such skills as operating a stopwatch, using an answer key, calculating correct/error totals or percentages, delivering corrective and positive feedback, and entering data on a performance chart or graph. Teaching students the competencies required to assist in CBA procedures should be direct, and mastery should be required before students are allowed to work independently. A sample script for a lesson designed to teach students to enter data on a line graph (Florida Department of Education, 1983) appears in Figure 12.4.

Assisting the teacher in assessment also may be used as a reinforcer within a classroom's behavior-management system. One teacher administered a survey to her class to determine what they would like to have included on a menu of reinforcers for reaching academic and behavioral goals. To her surprise, many of the items listed by students involved assisting in classroom management tasks. The students wanted to help the teacher grade papers, file papers, and run the photocopy machine. A classroom teacher may promote appropriate behavior and delegate time-consuming tasks if some aspects of CBA are identified as privileges contingent on following classroom rules and meeting individual goals.

Delegation of tasks to assistants. Delegating tasks to others is sometimes viewed as more time consuming than doing the task oneself. A small investment in training and preparation may avoid this trap and allow teachers to delegate appropriate tasks to others more freely. One strategy to avoid writing long notes or descriptions of tasks for assistants is to develop a checklist of common management tasks and take the time to familiarize the assistant with each task on the list initially. Later, the teacher duplicates the list, checks the necessary tasks on one copy of the list, and gets it to the assistant. If several adults and students are involved as assistants, a comprehensive list may be publicly posted. As time allows, they can go to the list, select a task, put their name by the item, and check it off the list when it has been finished. Sample task sheets for adults and students appear in Figure 12.5. All delegation requires some level of monitoring and supervision, and adult and student assistants need feedback about the job they did. Teachers using assistants should check to see how well assigned tasks are completed. They should praise assistants for what was completed satisfactorily, as well as clearly and tactfully describe any aspects of a job that need to be improved.

Figure 12.4
Teaching script for a
lesson on basic skills
involved in plotting
data on a line graph.

Point to each box and the day of the week that goes with it. Practice entering several more raw scores.

Now we are ready to plot our score on the line graph. Find the week with the "1" above it. This is week one, and we always start our graph with week one.

Look at the correct score we wrote in the box. It is 5, so we go up the number line to 5 and then across to the Monday day line. We put a small dot on the day line for correct. Now look at the incorrect score. It is 4, so we go up the number line to 4 and then across to the Monday day line. We put an X on the day line for incorrect. Don't make the dot and the X too big or too small. Remember to put the dot and the X on the day line. (Demonstrate plotting data.)

What do we use to mark corrects? (Students respond.)

What do we use to mark errors? (Students respond.)

Where do we put the dots and Xs? (Students respond.)

On a day when you do not take a timing or a probe, skip that day on the graph. What do you do with the graph on days you do not take a probe? (Students respond.)

Make up correct/error scores for two weeks and practice plotting these scores. **After you have more than one day on the graph, you connect the dots to the dots and the Xs to the Xs for one week at a time. Do not draw lines through Sunday lines. What do you connect on the graph?** (Students respond.)

Do you draw lines through the Sunday line? (Students respond.)

We have just practiced putting scores on a line graph. You can do the same thing with graphs that show your spelling score or your oral reading score or your arithmetic score. We will practice this again, and then you will be responsible for keeping your own graphs.

Microcomputer Applications for Developing CBA Materials

Even if the teacher must make original tests or probes, there are microcomputer software packages that make this process easier and faster. (See Table 12.1 for descriptions of selected software.) Several microcomputer programs are available to assist teachers in test and probe construction. Pieces of software called "authoring systems" or "teacher utilities" can help teachers produce tests or probes that students complete at a microcomputer keyboard. Software packages that create computerized assessment tasks typically include a record-keeping feature that allows the teacher to view or print results of the students' work at a later time. Record-keeping features vary from providing only a percentage correct to an item-by-item error analysis and a record of time spent on the task. Other software packages allow teachers to use the microcomputer to develop probes or tests and answer keys that can be sent to a printer and duplicated for distribution to students. Sometimes a

Sample Task Sheet for Adult Assistants

Figure 12.5.
Sample task sheets for
adult and student
assistants.

Please complete all of the items I have checked by _____ (date). Thanks so much for your help.

_____ Xerox (_____) of probes #_____

_____ Laminate all probes in the "To Be Laminated" folder

_____ Make audio tape(s) for spelling test—list(s) of words are attached

_____ Enter data from probes in AIMSTAR files and file probes to students' records folders.

_____ Print updated progress graphs from AIMSTAR files for (names of students, instructional groups, or class period).

_____ Listen to and score oral reading tapes from the "In Box for Tapes," return tapes to students' envelopes, put score sheets in my "Oral Reading Probes" notebook.

Sample Task Sheet for Students

(To be posted on a bulletin board)

JOBS FOR THE DAY

Please put your last name beside the job you want to do. When it is finished, put an X in the box.

_____ ☐ Sharpen red pencils in Checking Station

_____ ☐ Count words per line and write running total in right margin for these pages: (book title) (page numbers).

_____ ☐ Get answer keys and correct probes in the "Needs Grading" folder

_____ ☐ Count probes in folders at the (name) station and write down the codes for any folders with less than 10 probes

---

teacher provides the content; for example, a test generator allows the teacher to develop a bank of test questions on any topic and then to go back and to select those items desired for a specific test. Other pieces of software already contain the content, as is the case of some arithmetic utilities that can generate worksheets or probes containing math facts in any combination that a teacher specifies. These convenient microcomputer programs allow teachers to create several versions of a probe for the same objective and thus prevent students from inflating their rate correct on a probe simply because they have memorized the first few items.

Step 5: Collect Data

Data collection is the step during which students perform an academic behavior, and their responses are recorded in such a way that they may be summarized, displayed, and used for instructional decisions. There are many ways in which teachers may be assisted in data collection by other adults, students, and technology. It is especially important that teachers look for time-saving techniques at the data collection step because it happens so frequently. If a teacher adopts a procedure that will save a minute every time a probe is administered, then the minute will be multiplied across two or three measures each week for each child for each week of the school year. It is evident that a large chunk of time could be involved, and the time saved in assessment may be spent teaching new concepts, helping a child who is having difficulty, or any other valuable instructional task.

Data Collection Strategies for Teachers

When scheduling data collection, a teacher should consider available classroom resources, the anticipated rate of behavior change, and the complexity of the assessment task. Some educators advocate daily measurement, but there is evidence that a twice-weekly measurement schedule is just as functional in terms of student achievement as is daily measurement (Fuchs, 1986). It is suggested that teachers establish a schedule for data collection to ensure that targeted skills are not overlooked for long periods of time. The data collection schedule should provide the information necessary to make timely instructional decisions. Staggering data collection by content area and instructional groups may make data collection more manageable. For example, oral reading samples may be collected twice each week, but different reading groups can be scheduled for probes on alternate days of the week—for example, Group X on Monday and Thursday, Group Y on Tuesday and Friday, and Group Z on Wednesday and Friday. Additional specific suggestions for managing data collection are discussed in terms of the two most common forms in which students demonstrate learning—written responses and oral responses.

Teacher-directed assessment procedures for written responses. Because written responses provide a permanent product that may be scored at a later time, there are many possible versions of efficient routines for collecting written responses. The degree of control or supervision a teacher must use to ensure an accurate sample is one factor to be considered when collecting written responses. For example, in some situations homework or seatwork assignments may serve as a CBA sample; however, if a teacher is concerned that such work is not completed independently by a student, then the assignment is not an accurate reflection of student learning and a more controlled routine is required.

Teacher-directed assessment routines for written responses may involve several students at one time, and all students need not be working on the same skill or objective. For example, a class of 25 second-graders may simultaneously complete a daily probe on math facts; the probes may be identical or they may be different for each student. A teacher may distribute the probes at the end of arithmetic period, announce a 1- or 2-minute timing, and have all students complete the probe at once. If the time period during which students are working on the probe is long enough, the teacher may periodically scan the classroom, work at grading papers, enter data on graphs, or pull the next set of probes from a file.

In some situations, excessive paper use is a problem when students are completing frequent probes on a large number of skills. It is not suggested that data be taken less frequently to avoid paper use, but there are several strategies that may help avoid using reams and reams of paper to collect the data necessary for quality instruction. First, frequently used probes may be laminated, and students may write on the probes with washable acetate markers. After the probes are scored and the measures are recorded elsewhere, students clean the probes with paper towels and glass cleaner leaving them ready for the next assessments. A second idea is to tape an $8\frac{1}{2} \times 11$–inch sheet of clear acetate to the outside of a manila folder, attaching only two or three sides. The printed probe is inserted between the folder and the acetate, and again students write on the plastic with a washable acetate marker. With the folder arrangment, one folder per student may be prepared and labeled with the students' names. The appropriate probe(s) may be inserted inside the folder before class, thus preventing students from having to visit files before completing their probes. The drawback to any of these paper-saving arrangements is that the probe must be scored and summarized before the material may be used again since a student's work will be washed away.

Teacher-directed assessment procedures for oral responses. Academic learning demonstrated by oral responses includes such skills as reading aloud, saying math facts from a flashcard, and stating personal information (home address and tele-phone). Assessment routines for oral responses are typically not as time efficient as those for written responses because a teacher or an assistant must listen to an individual's performance (live or recorded). For this reason, if there is a logical and functional written substitute for an oral response, it may be best to avoid oral responses. For example, see–say math facts from flashcards are a typical class-room activity, but a see–write probe is more efficient because several students may complete it at once and scoring may be done at a later time. In this case, written responses to math facts also may be more functional since learners will typically demonstrate and use math facts in written rather than oral form. In addition, scoring an oral performance will always take at least as long as the time it took to perform the skill, but a written probe may be scanned much faster, especially if the skill is quite simple or answer keys are used. In other situations, oral responses are essential; for example, the most direct measure of a student's decoding skills is oral reading.

A few simple tactics will make data collection for oral responses easier and faster. For example, in oral reading a teacher should write the number of words per line in a passage before duplicating a probe to make scoring easier because a teacher will not have to count words after a probe is completed. Some reading materials such as the *Time Reading Series* (Spargo & Williston, 1980) include word totals printed in the margins. Working with two copies of the text—one for the reader and one for the scorer—allows the scorer to sit opposite the reader and easily monitor the reading. If the scorer's copy is laminated, he or she may use a washable acetate marker and circle errors or keep a running tally of the number of errors.

Data Collection by Other Adults and Students

Teachers who are assisted in data collection by other adults and students have additional scheduling considerations. The more people involved in the assess-ment process, the more important a system for organizing data collection becomes. Providing an assessment schedule that is publicly posted and clearly understood by everyone involved can add to the smooth operation of CBA. Involving students in data collection as peer assistants should never interfere or compete with attendance at group lessons, completion of assignments, or practice activities. Many teachers who allow peers to assist with probe administration insist that a student assistant complete all assignments before helping with assessment. Some scheduling difficulties may be avoided if probes are given at standard times with students working in pairs and taking turns administering probes to each other.

If an assistant is administering a timed probe, the timing device may be a stopwatch, egg timer, digital watch with seconds feature, or standard clock with a second hand. Self-administration of timed probes can be facilitated by using a timing tape that provides an audible tone. Thus, a student can avoid visual monitoring of a timer. Timing cassette tapes may be made by recording a series of tones (a soft bell, a click, or a buzz) at specific intervals, usually one, two, or three times. It is not necessary to say, "Please begin," and "Please stop," because students quickly understand to start when they hear a tone and stop when the next one occurs. A timing tape may be played on a standard tape player with or without earphones. If electric outlets are a problem or the tape player is already in use elsewhere, then a small, battery-operated tape player may be a solution.

After receiving appropriate direction and practice, peers may administer probes for both oral and written responses. Unlike written probes for which only test administration competencies are required, assistants administering and scoring oral probes must have previously mastered the content of the probe. If assistants have not mastered all of the content, they will be unable to distinguish correct and incorrect oral responses accurately. In some situations, students from higher grades may assist with oral reading probes, but these students should be required to read the passages aloud at a proficient rate without error before working with another student.. Placement in a higher grade does not ensure that students can read the passages assigned to another student.

Assessment stations. One way in which assessment may be made time efficient for a teacher is to have it occur when a teacher is doing other things. Assessment stations can be designed to provide students with appropriate directions and materials to collect data themselves without a teacher's direct supervision. Students may administer probes to other students, or the station may be designed for self-administration of probes.

Printed probes requiring written responses are relatively easy to include in an assessment station. Coble (1982) describes an arithmetic station set up to assess rate and accuracy on basic facts using printed probes organized in a simple and accessible filing system. For example, the procedure for a student to complete a probe on long division can be quite simple.

·1. Look at your task sheet and find the code for the probe you must do today.

2. Use the code to find this probe in the file box.

3.   If this is a timed probe, start the timing tape. Start and stop when you hear the tones. If it is untimed, work on the probe until you finish all the items you know how to do.

4.   Put the finished probe in the "in box" on the table, and put away all other materials.

If an audible stimulus is involved for an untimed written probe, this procedure can be modified in several ways: An adult or a student can read from a probe; the student taking the probe may put a prerecorded stimulus tape in a cassette player or run a set of prepared language-master cards through the language-master machine. As one example, a spelling test may be recorded by the teacher (or an assistant) in the same format as the teacher would deliver a spelling test in person: "The word is *jellybean*. I ate a watermelon-flavored jellybean. Spell *jellybean*." After hearing the task command, the student presses the pause button on the tape player, writes the word, and presses the pause button again to hear the next word. A version of the same technique may be used with a language master; each audio card contains a recording of one spelling word and its accompanying sentence. For timed tests with audible stimuli, a student may use a small battery-operated tape player with headphones and a timing tape. Since a timing tape only emits tones to signify when to start and stop, a student is still able to hear the stimuli tape while wearing the lightweight headphones.

Self-administration of probes for oral responses is also a useful procedure. Oral responses may be collected using a tape recorder; for example, students may read aloud for 1 minute into a tape recorder; and a teacher or an assistant may listen to all recorded samples at another time during the same day. Students may use a tape recorder and follow these steps to collect data on oral reading:

1.   Put the timing tape in the Walkman and put the earphones on.

2.   Find the assigned passage in your reading book and mark it with a bookmark.

3.   Find the cassette tape labeled with your name, rewind it to the beginning, and press the *record* and *play* buttons down at the same time.

4.   Allow the tape to run for 10 seconds, and then say your name, the date, the title of the book, and the page number.

5.   Open your book, start the timing tape on the Walkman, and when you hear a tone, begin reading out loud. Read as fast and as accurately as you can. Skip any words you cannot figure out.

6.   Stop reading when you hear a second tone.

7.   Rewind the tape in the recorder and rewind the tape in the Walkman.

8.   Put the tape with your name on it in the "in box for tapes." Put away all other materials.

Assessment stations may be organized in a variety of ways. To avoid traffic jams, a teacher may find it best to set up separate stations for different skill areas in different parts of the classroom. Rules should be established for use of a station, including how many students may be at a station at any one time. Materials for an assessment station include any or all of the following: desks and chairs, probe materials (e.g., worksheets, cards, reading books), charts or graphs, storage containers, colored pencils and pens for self-correction, answer keys, tape player or language master, area for displaying charts such as a bulletin board, and a timing device.

Microcomputer Applications for Data Collection

Microcomputers are not only helpful to teachers during preparation of assessment materials, but they may also deliver assessment tasks to students and collect performance data. Teachers using microcomputers to collect data on students' skill development are assured that an assessment task is presented in a consistent format and that a probe is scored accurately. Some pieces of instructional software (especially drill and practice packages) include record-keeping capabilities that save to the disk a summary of student performance after a student has completed the lesson. Teachers using such performance summaries should be cautious and analyze the scope of the lesson's content and what students must do to make a response within the microcomputer lesson or probe. Some tasks performed within a microcomputer lesson may not relate directly to how a teacher wants students to be able to respond away from the microcomputer. For example, suppose a computerized arithmetic lesson requires students to select correct answers in a multiple-choice format. A teacher may not be satisfied that, even after scoring 100% correct, a student can supply answers to the same problems with 100% accuracy. In this instance, a teacher should provide a follow-up computerized or pencil-and-paper probe that requires a student to supply answers rather than select them.

A computer-based measurement software application currently being developed by researchers at Peabody College of Vanderbilt University (Fuchs, Hamlett, & Fuchs, 1988) allows teachers to use microcomputers to collect student performance data in reading, spelling, and arithmetic. The "Checkup" disks within the package contain graded reading passages, spelling lists, and arithmetic probes. When students are ready to take a probe, they sit down at a microcomputer, insert the "Checkup" disk, and follow a series of prompts to record name and date and then select the area to be assessed (i.e., reading, spelling, or arithmetic). A student enters responses from the keyboard, and performance data are saved on the student's disk. These data may be summarized, graphed, and analyzed using other features of the software package. The software package will also generate printed probes for use with pencil-and-paper assessments. (See Table 12.1 for additional information about this software package.)

Step 6: Summarize Data

Summarizing assessment data involves scoring a test or condensing observational data and then calculating a measure such as rate correct or percentage correct. The time-honored process of grading students' work has typically been managed by teachers and often requires many hours of work. The more tests or probes administered in a classroom, the more grading there is to be done. However, because few performance measures involve high-level calculations, usually summarization can be accomplished by assistants or students appropriately trained to help.

This section describes individual and group self-correction as management strategies that involve students in summarizing data. The section also addresses how to prevent and respond to cheating that can occur when students are allowed to score their own work. Finally, computer software packages, designed to assist teachers with the summarization step, are also described.

Student Involvement in Summarizing Data

When tests and probes are scored using an answer key or a correct model of the desired response, individual and group self-correction may be appropriate. Self-correction is usually inappropriate for correcting written expression and scoring essay exams in which student responses will vary a great deal, but they are very efficient techniques for assessments such as spelling tests and arithmetic probes in which there is only one correct response to each item.

When students score and summarize some of their own assessments, several important instructional outcomes can occur. First, students who participate in scoring and summarizing their own performance are likely to be more aware of the goals held for them. Second, students can gain valuable practice in such arithmetic skills as addition, division, subtraction, comparison, and calculation of percentages (Lovitt, 1973). Third, feedback is immediate, and this may prevent students from practicing an error response until it is learned (Mercer, Mercer, & Bott, 1984). Fourth, self-correction also may promote the development of independence and responsibility (Paine et al., 1983). However, individual self-correction by students is productive only if the procedures are carefully designed to prevent abuse and cheating.

Individual self-correction. Self-correction by students working alone is best managed and controlled when it takes place in a checking station, such as the one described by Paine et al. (1983). A checking station is used after students finish a probe, and only one student may be at a station at any time (to avoid talking and cheating). Materials for a station include answer keys, colored pens or pencils, and a box or folder for completed work. Student performance charts or graphs also may be located at a station. The checking station should be located in an area of a classroom that is easy for a teacher to scan and supervise. When students go to a station, they leave all writing tools at their desk and work only with the colored pens available at the station. If permitted, students may take a paper back to their desk after all errors are circled and make corrections before putting the probe in the box or folder at the station.

Group self-correction. It is common to see students trading papers and correcting them, but some students are reluctant to let peers see their work, and often students are more concerned about looking to see what is happening to their papers than they are about scoring their classmate's work properly. When several students or even the entire class complete the same probe at the same time, group self-correction is appropriate. The following procedure allows for group self-correction, provides immediate feedback to students, and prevents a stack of ungraded papers from appearing on the teacher's desk after school (Paine et al., 1983).

1. Students make all corrections with a colored pen or pencil that is to be used only for correction; all other writing tools must be put away.

2. The teacher prepares an answer key for the probe and is ready to display the answers using an overhead projector or the chalkboard. (Answers may be written on the chalkboard beforehand and concealed by a pull-down map or screen.)

3. After all students have completed the probe or the timing has concluded, the teacher reveals the answers and students mark their own papers using the colored pencils. Students are allowed to ask questions about the test items, and the teacher may use this opportunity for clarification or reteaching.

4. After all items have been scored, students count correct and incorrect items and calculate the appropriate measure (e.g., rate, percentage).

Preventing cheating. Some teachers react negatively to the concept of self-correction because of their concern about cheating, but there are steps that can be taken to prevent cheating and to provide consequences for cheating if it does happen. First, the procedures described above discourage cheating because students only have access to answer keys and colored marking pens under controlled circumstances. In addition, teachers using self-correction should reinforce accurate scoring with recognition, bonus points in a token economy, or access to privileges.

Initially, a teacher should double check students' scoring of their own work and let students know that they are doing a good job or that they need to be more careful and honest. After students are familiar with the routine of self-correction, a teacher will still find spot checks to be valuable. Teachers should tell their classes that self-scored tests will be checked at random, and that positive and negative consequences will occur for accurate and inaccurate scoring. It is important for students to understand that there is always a possibility that their scoring may be double checked by the teacher. If a teacher does detect cheating, negative consequences may include loss of the self-correction privilege for a specified time period or points deducted from a classroom token economy system. Random checking of student-scored probes does take teacher time, but it is only a small fraction of what would be required to grade all the papers for all students.

Another alternative for checking students' self-scoring is to have peers or assistants verify the scoring. Students who have completed their assignments may take completed papers from a checking station and check the work against the answer key. After students have scored their own work in a group, they may also trade papers and check for scoring accuracy on each other's papers. Even though self-correction is desirable, it needs to be controlled by the teacher if it is to be accurate and worthwhile.

Step 7: Display Data

Displaying assessment data on performance charts or graphs gives an ongoing picture of learning that serves as the basis for instructional decisions. This section describes data display strategies for the teacher that are quick and accurate. The section also addresses how classroom assistants and students can graph data and leave the teacher free for more complex instructional tasks. Microcomputer software packages available to assist with data display are also described.

Data Display Strategies for Teachers and Other Adults

Often data may be displayed on a graph or chart immediately after it is collected. This strategy can avoid making the data display task one that requires a large block of time because graphs are updated throughout the school day. If the teacher is using a data display procedure that involves calculation of trend lines, split middles, or celeration values, then it may be most convenient to plot data on performance graphs immediately after the probe is summarized but do all the calculations together at a later time. The risk in this approach is that graphs needing additional attention may pile up and not be used for timely instructional decisions. If graphs are saved for additional steps required to display the data, a routine should be established for taking care of this task at a specific time each day.

Student Participation in Data Display

The teaching script presented in Figure 12.4 is designed to teach students to enter data on a line graph. Teachers who involve students in graphing their own data find that students are motivated by seeing direct evidence of their progress. Moreover, the need for backup reinforcers for meeting instructional goals is replaced by a students' personal satisfaction of seeing hard work pay off in progress. If students are involved in graphing their own data, then graphs need to be kept in accessible locations such as open file boxes placed on a counter, a lower drawer in a file cabinet, or posted at students' eye-level on a bulletin board.

Microcomputer Applications for Data Display

Some teachers who have access to microcomputers find it convenient to use utility software to generate displays of student performance data. There are several microcomputer software packages available for this application, and a sample of these are listed in Table 12.1. The computer-based measurement software described in a previous section (Fuchs, Hamlett, & Fuchs, 1988) will display the data collected using the "Checkup" disks. Another software package developed by researchers at Vanderbilt University, AIMSTAR (Hasselbring & Hamlett, 1983), is currently available for the Apple II series of computers. AIMSTAR accepts data in a variety of formats (i.e., rates, percentages, and ratios) and keeps an ongoing record of progress for an unlimited number of students and objectives. A teacher (or an assistant) enters the raw data, and the computer will plot data points on a logarithmic graph. If an aim date and criterion level are entered, the aimline is drawn on the graph. The program will also calculate trend lines. Teachers may view updated performance graphs on the computer's monitor or may send the graph to a printer and obtain a hard copy for student files or progress reports. The program is easy to use and includes a tutorial diskette that provides instruction on how to use the AIMSTAR features. It is not necessary for the teacher to have a microcomputer in the classroom in order to make use of software that creates data displays, as data may be entered on the computer in a nearby classroom, the school computer lab, or at home.

Step 8: Interpret Data and Make Decisions

The final step in the CBA model is interpreting data and making instructional decisions. Developing curriculum and objectives, designing assessment procedures, collecting data, summarizing data, and plotting the data on charts or graphs are pointless activities unless the data are used to guide instruction. Decision making is a high-level instructional task to which teachers must bring their knowledge of curricula, individual student characteristics, instructional strategies, and data-based decision rules. Instructional decision making is one CBA task for which teachers are uniquely qualified, although microcomputer technology may assist them, other persons may be consulted when particularly difficult instructional problems arise, and students should suggest what they think needs to happen with their own programs.

Decision-Making Strategies for Teachers

Guidelines for decision making are discussed at length in Chapter 5. The most frequently made decisions are those that involve monitoring pupil progress and modifying instruction. For such decisions, it is a good idea for teachers to establish a consistent time during which to review all performance graphs and charts. This practice can ensure that each student's progress on each objective is periodically evaluated and probably will make instructional decisions more consistent across students. Although a daily review of progress may be important for selected skills, reviewing graphs and charts once or twice each week is sufficient for making timely changes in students' programs. If charts and graphs are reviewed less frequently, the teacher runs a risk of allowing students to continue in an ineffective instructional program for several weeks before an appropriate change is made. However, a teacher may want to review progress more frequently for programs that have been changed recently in order to ascertain the effects of the program modification.

Teachers who have used CBA for one or more years often begin to see common problems with instructional objectives that students find particularly difficult or similarities in students' performances. When the same objectives are difficult for many students, a teacher should review instructional procedures. Future instructional decisions will be easier if some record is kept of successful instructional strategies for certain objectives, skill areas, or students. A loose-leaf binder or card file containing strategies or tactics that (a) worked for an individual student, (b) were generally effective for several students, (c) worked for another teacher, or (d) were described in research articles can be a valuable resource when a problem recurs. Some ideas will be specific to a particular skill (e.g., long vowel sounds or multiplying by zero), but others will be applicable across domains and will relate to motivation or a stage of learning (e.g., fluency building or maintenance). If a solution relates to a specific student, the intervention may be cross-indexed; the complete description of the solution is noted in a teacher's comprehensive idea file and a description is entered in the student's cumulative folder or IEP so that other teachers may benefit from the finding.

Microcomputer Applications That Assist in Decision Making

Many of the same software packages that generate data displays will also assist the teacher in making instructional decisions. (See Table 12.1 for descriptions of software packages.) These computer programs are designed to follow specific decision rules, and they work quickly and systematically. The data decision rules discussed in Chapter 5 are examples of rules applied by several of the available software packages including the computer-based measurement programs described in the previous section. Teachers should read manuals and documentation accompanying the software to determine if the rules used in the computer program fit their preferences for decision making. It is important that teachers who use a software package understand and agree with the decision-making model executed by the program.

The fastest decision making is accomplished by integrated software (e.g., Fuchs, Hamlett, & Fuchs, 1988) that collects and displays data, as well as recommends decisions because such programs eliminate the need to reenter data. Data collected by hand may be entered into a computerized decision-making program, as is the case with AIMSTAR. After entering data into the computer and requesting a graph, a teacher then requests an instructional decision. The computer program compares the student's performance to decision rules and arrives at an instructional decision. Computer analysis may indicate that the student is having an acquisition problem. This problem suggests several possible solutions: provide additional models, give more extensive corrective feedback, or implement an errorless learning procedure—all of which are appropriate at the acquisition stage of learning. Given another data set to analyze, computer analysis may indicate that the student's progress is satisfactory and that the instructional program should not change. A teacher may request that the data decision rules be applied only to specified students and objectives or to all objectives for all students.

The use of decision-making software not only saves teachers' time, but also ensures that data decision rules are applied consistently and accurately. It is important, however, for teachers to realize that a computer-generated instructional decision reflects only the performance data entered into the program. The output of these helpful computer programs contributes to a teacher's knowledge about students' learning, but it is up to the teacher to decide how to interpret the

References

ALBERTO, P., & TROUTMAN, A. (1986). *Applied behavior analysis for teachers* (2nd ed.) Columbus, OH: Merrill.

ALGOZZINE, B., SIDERS, J., SIDERS, J., & BEATTIE, J. (1980). *Using assessment information to plan reading instructional programs: Error analysis and word attack skills.* (Monograph No. 14). Minneapolis: University of Minnesota, Institute for Research on Learning Disabilities.

ALLEY, G., & DESHLER, D. (1979). *Teaching the learning disabled adolescent: Strategies and methods.* Denver: Love.

ANDERSON, R. & FAUST, G. (1973). *Educational psychology.* New York: Dodd, Mead.

ARRINGTON, R. (1943). Time sampling in studies of social behavior. A critical review of techniques and results with research and suggestions. *Psychological Bulletin, 40* 81–124.

ARMBRUSTER, B. B., ECHOLS, C. H., & BROWN, A. L. (1983). The role of metacognition in reading to learn: A developmental perspective. *Volta Review, 84*(5), 45–56.

ARY, D. & SUEN, H. (1983). The use of momentary time sampling to assess both frequency and duration of behavior. *Journal of Behavioral Assessment, 5*(2), 143–150.

ASHLOCK, R. B. (1986). *Error patterns in computation: A semi-programmed approach* (4th ed.). Columbus, OH: Merrill.

BACHOR, D., & CREALOCK, C. (1986). *Instructional strategies for students with special needs.* Scarborough, Ontario: Prentice-Hall Canada.

BACHOR, D., STEACY, N., & FREEZE, D. (1986). *A conceptual framework for word problems: Some preliminary results.* A paper presented at the conference of the Canadian Society for Studies in Education. Winnipeg, Manitoba.

BAILEY, D. B. (1984). Effects of lines of progress and semilogarithmic charts on ratings of charted data. *Journal of Applied Behavior Analysis, 17,* 359–365.

BAGNATO, S. & NEISWORTH, J. (in press). *Perceptions of developmental status.* Circle Pines, MN: American Guidance Services.

BAGNATO, S., & NEISWORTH, J. (1981). *Linking developmental assessment and curricula: Prescriptions for early intervention.* Rockville, MD: Aspen.

BAGNATO, S., NEISWORTH, J., & CAPONE, A. (1986). Curriculum-based assessment for the young exceptional child: Rationale and review. *Topics in Early Childhood Special Education, 6*(2), 97–109.

BAGNATO, S., NEISWORTH, J., & MUNSON, S. (in press). *Linking developmental assessment and early intervention: Curriculum-based prescriptions.* Rockville, MD: Aspen.

BARTEL, N. (1986). Teaching students who have reading problems. In D. Hammill & N. Bartel (Eds.), *Teaching students with learning and behavior problems,* (4th ed.) (pp. 23–89). Austin, TX: PRO-ED.

BARTON, L. (1981). *An analysis of error due to interval recording method and interval length in observational recording strategies.* Unpublished doctoral dissertation, Northern Illinois University, DeKalb, IL.

BAYLEY, N. (1969). *Bayley scales of infant development.* New York: Psychological Corp.

BERQUAM, S. (1979). AC-4. Gainesville, FL: Performance Data.

BITTER, G., GREENE, C., HILL, S., MALETSKY, E., SCHULMAN, L., SHUFELT, G., SOBEL, M. & THOMPSON, L. (1987). *McGraw-Hill mathematics (level 5).* New York: McGraw-Hill.

BLANKENSHIP, C. (1985). Using curriculum-based assessment data to make instructional decisions. *Exceptional Children, 52,* 233–238.

BLANKENSHIP, C., & LILLY, M. S. (1981). *Mainstreaming students with learning and behavior problems: techniques for the classroom teacher.* New York: Holt, Rinehart, & Winston.

BLOOM, B., HASTINGS, T., & MADAUS, G. (1971). *Handbook of formative and summative evaluation of student learning.* New York: McGraw-Hill.

BLUMA, S., SHEARER, A., FROHMAN, A., & HILLAR, J. (1976). *Portage guide to early education.* Portage, WI: CESA Publishers.

BOLSTER, L., GIBB, E., HANSEN, T., KIRKPATRICK, J., McNERNEY, C., ROBITAILLE, D., TRIMBLE, H., VANCE, I., WALSH, R., & WISNER, R. (1983). *Scott, Foresman mathematics. Teachers edition (Books 1, 2, 3).* Glenview, IL: Scott, Foresman.

BORKOWSKI, J., & CAVANAUGH, J. (1979). Maintenance and generalization of skills and strategies by the retarded. In N. Ellis (Ed.), *Handbook of mental deficiency* (2nd ed.) (pp. 569–617). New York: McGraw-Hill.

BRACKEN, B. (1984). *Bracken basic concept scale.* New York: Psychological Corp.

BRADLEY, M., & AMES, W. (1978). Readability parameters of basal readers. *Journal of Reading Behavior, 11*(2), 175–183.

BRANDSTETTER, G., & MERZ, C. (1978). Charting scores in precision teachinng for skill acquisition. *Exceptional Children, 45*(1), 42–48.

BRIGANCE, A. (1985). *Prescriptive readiness: Strategies and practice.* North Billerica, MA: Curriculum Associates.

BRIGANCE, A. (1978). *Diagnostic inventory of early development.* North Billerica, MA: Curriculum Associates.

BROWN, A. L. (1978). Knowing when, where, and how to remember: A problem of metacognition. In R. Glasser (Ed.), *Advances in instructional psychology* (pp. 77–165). Hillsdale, NJ: Erlbaum.

BROWN, D., SIMMONS, V., & MEHTVIN, J. (1979). *Oregon project curriculum for visually impaired and blind preschoolers.* Medford, OR: Jackson County Education Service District.

BRULLE, A. (1981). *The accuracy of momentary time sampling procedures when used in applied settings.* Unpublished doctoral dissertation, Northern Illinois University, DeKalb, IL.

BRULLE, A. & REPP, A. (1984). An investigation of the accuracy of momentary time sampling procedures with time series data. *British Journal of Psychology, 75,* 481–488.

BRYANT, N., DRABIN, I., & GETTINGER, M. (1981). Effects of varying unit size on spelling achievement in learning disabled children. *Journal of Learning Disabilities, 14,* 200–203.

BUGELSKI, B. (1964). *The psychology of learning applied to teaching.* Indianapolis: Bobbs-Merrill.

BULGREN, J. A., & SCHUMAKER, J. B. (in preparation). *Learning strategies curriculum: The paired-associates strategy.* Lawrence: University of Kansas, Institute for Research in Learning Disabilities.

BURNS, P. (1980). *Assessment and correction of language arts difficulties.* Columbus, OH: Merrill.

BURSUCK, W. D., & LESSEN, E. (1987). *A classroom-based model for assessing learning-disabled students.* Unpublished manuscript.

CARNINE, D., & SILBERT, J. (1979). *Direct instruction reading.* Columbus, OH: Merrill.

CARROLL, J. (1964). *Language and thought.* Englewood Cliffs, NJ: Prentice-Hall.

CARROLL, J., DAVIES, P., & RICHMAN, B. (1971). *Word frequency book.* Boston: Houghton Mifflin.

CARTER, J., & SUGAI, G. (1988). Teaching social skills. *Teaching Exceptional Children, 20*(3), 68–71.

CARTLEDGE, G., & MILBURN, J. (1986). *Teaching social skills to children: Innovative approaches* (2d ed.). New York: Pergamon.

CAVANAUGH, J. C., & BORKOWSKI, J. G. (1979). The metamemory-memory "connection": Effects of strategy training and maintenance. *The Journal of General Psychology, 101,* 161–174.

CHARLES COUNTY BOARD OF EDUCATION (1981). *Math objectives guide: Project CAST.* LaPlata, MD: Office of Special Education. (ERIC Document Reproduction Service No. 242 146)

CLARK, C., & MOORES, D. (1981). *Clark early language program.* Allen, TX: DLM/Teaching Resources.

CLARK, F. L., DESHLER, D. D., SCHUMAKER, J. B., ALLEY, G. R., & WARNER, M. M. (1984). Visual imagery and self-questioning: Strategies to improve comprehension of written materials. *Journal of Learning Disabilities, 17*(3), 145–149.

COBLE, A. (1982). Improving math fact recall: Beating your own score. *Academic Therapy, 17*(5), 547–553.

CONNORS, F. P. (1983). Improving school instruction for learning disabled children: The Teachers College Institute. *Exceptional Education Quarterly, 4*(1), 23–44.

COOPER, C. (1977). Holistic evaluation of writing. In C. Cooper & L. Odell (Eds.), *Evaluating writing: Describing, measuring, judging* (pp. 3–31). Buffalo, NY: National Council of Teachers of English.

CRONIN, M. E., & CURRIE, P. S. (1984). Study skills: A resource guide for practitioners. *Remedial and Special Education, 5*(2) 61–69.

CROWL, T., & MACGINITIE, W. (1974). The influence of students' speech characteristics on teachers' evaluations of oral answers. *Journal of Educational Psychology, 66*(3), 304–308.

DANSEREAU, D. F. (1985). Learning strategy research. In J. Segal, S. Chipman, and R. Glaser (Eds.). *Thinking and learning skills, vol. 1: Relating instruction to research* (pp. 209–239). Hillsdale, NJ: Erlbaum.

DEBETTENCOURT, L. U. (1987). Strategy training: A need for clarification. *Exceptional Children, 54*(1), 24–30.

DENO, S. (1985). Curriculum-based measurement: The emerging alternative. *Exceptional Children, 52, 219–232.*

DENO, S. L., & FUCHS, L. S. (1987). Developing curriculum-based measurement systems for data-based special education problem solving. *Focus on Exceptional Children, 19(8), 1–16.*

DENO, S., MARSTON, D., MIRKIN, P., LOWRY, L., SINDELAR, P., & JENKINS, J. (1982). *The use of standard tasks to measure achievement in reading, spelling, and written expression: A normative developmental study.* (Research Report No. 87). Minneapolis: Institute for Research on Learning Disabilities, University of Minnesota.

DENO, S., & MIRKIN, P. (1977). *Data-based program modification: A manual.* Reston, VA: Council for Exceptional Children.

DENO, S., MIRKIN, P. K., & CHIANG, B. (1982). Identifying valid measures of reading. *Exceptional Children, 49(1), 36–45.*

DENO, S., MIRKIN, P., LOWRY, L., & KUEHNLE, K. (1980). *Relationships among simple measures of spelling and performance on standardized achievement tests* (Research Report No. 21). Minneapolis: University of Minnesota, Institute for Research on Learning Disabilities.

DENO, S., MIRKIN, P., & MARSTON, D. (1980). *Relationships among simple measures of written expression and performance on standardized achievement tests* (Research Report No. 22). Minneapolis: University of Minnesota, Institute for Research on Learning Disabilities.

DENO, S., MIRKIN, P., ROBINSON, S., & EVANS, P. (1980). *Relationships among classroom observations of social adjustment and sociometric ratings* (Research Report No. 24). Minneapolis: University of Minnesota, Institute for Research on Learning Disabilities.

DESHLER, D., ALLEY, G., WARNER, M., & SCHUMAKER, J. (1981). Instructional practices for promoting skill acquisition and generalization in severely learning disabled adolescents. *Learning Disabilities Quarterly, 4(4), 415–421.*

DESHLER, D. D., & SCHUMAKER, J. B. (1988). An instructional model for teaching students how to learn. In J. L. Graden, J. E. Zins, & M. J. Curtis (Eds.), *Alternative educational delivery stystems: Enhancing instructional options for all students,* (pp. 391–411). Washington, D.C.: National Association of School Psychologists.

DESHLER, D.D., SCHUMAKER, J.B., LENZ, B. K., & ELLIS, E. (1984). Academic and cognitive interventions for LD adolescents: Part II. *Journal of Learning Disabilities, 17(3), 170–179.*

DOLCH, E. (1950). *Dolch word list.* Morristown, NJ: General Learning.

DOLL, E. (1935). The Vineland social maturity scale. *Training School Bulletin, 32, 1–74.*

DUNBAR, R. (1976) Some aspects of research design and their implications in the observational study of behaviour. *Behavior, 58, 78–98.*

DUNN, L., & MARKWARDT, F. (1970). *Peabody individual achievement test-revised.* Circle Pines, MN: American Guidance Service.

EATON, M. D. (1978). Data decisions and evaluation. In N. G. Haring, T. C. Lovitt, M. D. Eaton, & C. L. Hansen, (Eds.), *The fourth R: Research in the classroom* (pp. 167–190). Columbus, OH: Merrill.

ECKSTEIN, R. M. (1988). *Handicapped funding directory.* Margate, FL: Research Grant Guides.

THE EDUCATON OF ALL HANDICAPPED ACT. PUBLIC LAW 94-142, 1975.

EEDS, M. (1985). Bookwords: Using a beginning word list of high frequency words from children's literature, K–3. *The Reading Teacher, 38, 418–423.*

EKWALL, E. (1981). *Locating and correcting reading difficulties* (3d ed.). Columbus, OH: Merrill.

EKWALL, E. & SHANKER, J. (1983). *Diagnosis and rememdiation of the disabled reader* (2d ed.). Boston: Allyn and Bacon.

ELLIS, E. S., & LENZ, B. K. (1987). A component analysis of effective learning strategies for LD students. *Learning Disabilities Focus, 2*(2), 94–107.

ENGLEMANN, S. & CARNINE, D. (1976). *Distar arithmetic I, II, & III.* Circle Pines, MN: American Guidance Service.

ENGLERT, C., CULLATA, B., & HORN, D. (1987). Influence of irrelevant information in addition word problems on problem solving. *Learning Disabilities Quarterly, 10*(1), 29–36.

ENRIGHT, B. E. (1983). *Enright diagnostic inventory of basic arithmetic skills.* North Billerica, MA: Curriculum Associates.

EVANS, S. S., EVANS, W. H., & MERCER, C. D. (1986). *Assessment for instruction.* Boston: Allyn & Bacon.

FAYETTE COUNTY PUBLIC SCHOOLS (1987). *Thesaurus of instructional objectives for special education programs.* Lexington, KY: Department of Special Pupil Services.

FAYETTE COUNTY PUBLIC SCHOOLS (1984). *Policy and procedures manual for handicapped pupils.* Lexington, KY: Department of Special Pupil Services.

FEUERSTEIN, R., & RAND, Y. (1979). *The dynamic assessment of retarded performance.* Baltimore: University Park.

FEWELL, R., & LANGLEY, B. (1984). *Developmental activities screening inventory.* Austin, TX: PRO-ED.

FITZGERALD, G. (1980). Reliability of the Fry sampling procedure. *Reading Research Quarterly, 15*(4), 489–503.

FLORIDA DEPARTMENT OF EDUCATION. (JUNE 1983). *Techniques of precision teaching, Part I: Training manual.* Tallahassee, FL: Florida Department of Education.

FLORIDA DEPARTMENT OF EDUCATION (1983). *A resource manual for the development and evaluation of special programs for exceptional students* (Volume V-D, Part 1). Tallahassee, FL: Bureau of Education for Exceptional Students.

FOLIO, R., & FEWELL, R. (1983). *Peabody developmental motor scales.* Austin, TX: PRO-ED.

FOSTER, G., & SALVIA, J. (1977). Teacher response to the label of learning disabled as a function of demand characteristics. *Exceptional Children, 43*(8), 533–534.

FOSTER, G., YSSELDYKE, J., & REESE, J. (1978). I wouldn't have seen it if I hadn't believed it. *Exceptional Children, 41,* 469–473.

FREEMAN, D., KUHS, T., PORTER, A., FLODEN, R., SCHMIDT, W., & SCHWILLE, J. (1983). Do textbooks and tests define a national curriculum in elementary school mathematics? *The Elementary School Journal, 83,* 501–513.

FREYBERG, P. (1970). The concurrent validity of two types of spelling test. *British Journal of Educational Psychology, 40,* 68–71.

FRISINA, R. Report of the committee to redefine deaf and hard of hearing for educational purposes. Cited by Kirk, S., & Gallagher, J. (1983). *Educating exceptional children* (4th ed.). Boston: Houghton Mifflin.

FUCHS, L. S. (1986). Monitoring progress among mildly handicapped pupils: Review of current practice and research. *Remedial and Special Education, 7*(5), 5–12.

FUCHS, L., & DENO, S. (1981). *A comparison of reading placements based on teacher judgment, standardized testing, and curriculum-based assessment* (Research Report No. 56). Minneapolis: University of Minnesota, Institute for Research on Learning Disabilities.

FUCHS, L., DENO, S., & MIRKIN, P. (1983). Data-based program modification: A continuous evaluation system with computer technology to facilitate implementation. *Journal of Special Education Technology, 6*(2), 50–57.

FUCHS, L., & FUCHS, D. (1986a). Effects of systematic formative evaluation: A meta-analysis. *Exceptional Children, 53,* 199–208.

FUCHS, L., & FUCHS, D. (1986b). Linking assessment to instructional intervention: An overview. *School Psychology Review, 15,* 318–323.

FUCHS, L., FUCHS, D., & DENO, S. (1983). *The nature of inaccuracy among readability formulas* (Research Report No. 129). Minneapolis: University of Minnesota, Institute for Research on Learning Disabilities.

FUCHS, L., FUCHS, D., & HAMLETT, C. (in press). Effects of alternative goal structures within curriculum-based measurement. *Exceptional Children.*

FUCHS, L., FUCHS, D., & MAXWELL, L. (1988). The validity of informal reading comprehension measures. *Remedial and Special Education, 9*(2), 20–28.

FUCHS, L., FUCHS, D., & WARREN, L. (1982). *Special education practice in evaluating student pupil progress toward goals* (Research Report No. 21). Minneapolis: University of Minnesota, Institute for Research on Learning Disabilities.

FUCHS, L., HAMLETT, C., & FUCHS, D. (1988). *Improving data-based instruction through computer technology: Description of software: Year 3.* Unpublished manuscript, Vanderbilt University, Peabody College, Nashville.

FURUNO, S., INATSUKA, T., O'REILLY, K., HOSAKA, C., ZEISLOFT, B., & ALLMAN, T. (1987). *Hawaii early learning profile: Help for special preschoolers: Assessment checklist and activities binder.* Palo Alto, CA: VORT Corporation.

FURUNO, S., INATSUKA, T., O'REILLY, K., HOSAKA, C., ZEISLOFT, B., & ALLMAN, T. (1984). *HELP checklist (Hawaii early learning profile).* Palo Alto, CA: VORT Corporation.

GELZHEISER, L., SHEPERD, M., & WOZNIAK, R. (1986). The development of instruction to induce skill transfer. *Exceptional Children, 53*(2), 125–129.

GERBER, M., & SEMMEL, M. (1984). Teachers as imperfect test: Reconceptualizing the referral process. *Educational Psychologist, 19,* 137–148.

GERMANN, G., & TINDAL, G. (1985). An application of curriculum-based assessment: The use of direct and repeated measurement. *Exceptional Children, 52,* 244–265.

GICKLING, E., & THOMPSON, V. (1985). A personal view of curriculum based assessment. *Exceptional Children, 52,* 205–218.

GLOVER, M., PREMINGER, J., & SANFORD, A. (1978). *Early learning accomplishment profile.* Winston-Salem, NC: Kaplan.

GOLUB, L., & KIDDER, C. (1974). Syntactic density and the computer. *Elementary Journal, 11,* 175–231.

GOOD, R. (1981). *An examination of curriculum bias in reading achievement measures.* Unpublished master's thesis. University Park, PA: Pennsylvania State University.

GOOD, R., & SALVIA, J. (in press). Curriculum bias in reading achievement tests: Utility of content-validity grade equivalents. *School Psychology Digest.*

GOODMAN, K. (1969). Analysis of oral reading miscues: Applied psycholinguistics. *Reading Research Quarterly, 5,* 9–30.

GOODMAN, Y., & BURKE, C. (1972). *Reading miscue inventory: Manual of procedure for diagnosis and evaluation.* New York: Macmillan.

GOODSTEIN, H., CAWLEY, J., GORDON, S., & HELFGOTT, S. (1971). Verbal problem solving among educable mentally retarded children. *American Journal of Mental Deficiency, 77,* 238–241.

GOTTLIEB, J. (1978). Observing social adaptation in schools. In G. P. Sackett (Ed.), *Observing behavior (Vol. 1): Theory and applications in mental retardation,* Baltimore: University Park.

GRADEN, J., CASEY, A., & BONSTROM, D. (1985). Implementing a prereferral intervention system: Part II, the data. *Exceptional Children, 51,* 487–496.

GREAT FALLS PUBLIC SCHOOLS. (1981). *Precision teaching project training manual.* Great Falls, MO: Great Falls Public Schools.

GREEN, S., MCCOY, J., BURNS, K., & SMITH, A. (1982). Accuracy of observational data with whole interval, partial interval, and momentary time sampling recording techniques. *Journal of Behavioral Assessment, 4*(2), 103–118..

GREENE, H., & PETTY, W. (1975). *Developing language skills in the elementary schools* (5th ed.). Boston: Allyn and Bacon.

GRONLUN, N. (1985). *Measurement and evaluation in teaching* (5th ed.). New York: Macmillan.

GRONLUND, N. (1982). *Constructing achievement tests* (3d ed.). Englewood Cliffs, NJ: Prentice-Hall.

GROSS, R. (1978). Seven new cardinal principles. *Phi Delta Kappan, 60,* 291–293.

GROSSMAN, H. (1983). *Manual of terminology and classification in mental retardation.* Washington, DC: American Association on Mental Deficiency.

GUTKIN, T., HENNING-STOUT, M., & PIERSAL, W. (1988). Impact of a district-wide behavioral consultation prereferral intervention service on patterns of school psychological service delivery. *Professional School Psychology, 3,* 301–308.

HAEUSSERMAN, E., JEDRYSK, E., KLAPPERT, Z., POPE, L., & WORTIS, J. (1958; 1972). *Psychoeducational evaluation of the preschool child.* New York: Grune & Stratton.

HAMMILL, D. (1986). Improving spelling skills. In D. Hammill & N. Bartel (Eds.), *Teaching students with learning and behavior problems* (4th ed.) (pp. 123–152). Boston: Allyn & Bacon.

HAMMILL, D., & LARSEN, S. (1983). *Test of written language, 2.* Austin, TX: PRO-ED.

HANNA, P., HANNA, J., HODGES, R., & RUDORF, E. (1966). *Phoneme grapheme correspondence as cues to spelling improvement.* Washington, DC: U.S. Department of Health, Education, and Welfare.

HARARI, H., & MCDAVID, J. (1973). Name stereotypes and teachers' expectations. *Journal of Educational Psychology, 65*(2), 222–225.

HARING, N. G., LIBERTY, K. A., & WHITE, O. R. (1980). Rules for data-based strategy decisions in instructional programs. In W. Sailaor, B. Wilcox, & L. Brown (Eds.), *Methods of instruction for severely handicapped students* (pp. 159–192). Baltimore: Brooks.

HARING, N., WHITE, O., EDGAR, E., AFFLECK, G., & HAYDEN, A. (1981). *Uniform performance assessment system.* San Antonio, TX: Psychological Corp.

HARRIS, A., & SIPAY, E. (1980). *How to increase reading ability: A guide to developmental and remedial methods* (7th ed.). New York: Longmann.

HASSELBRING, T. S., & HAMLETT, C. L. (1983). *AIMSTAR.* Portland, OR: ASIEP Education Company.

HAVINGHURST, R. (1956). Research on the developmental task concept. *School Review* (May), 215–123.

HAYVREN, N., & HYMEL, S. (1984). Ethical issues in sociometric measures on interaction behavior. *Developmental Psychology, 20,* 844–849.

HENDRICK, D., PRATHER, E., & TOBIN, A. (1975). *Sequential inventory of communication development.* Seattle, WA: University of Washington Press.

HODGES, J. (1956). *Harbrace college handbook* (4th ed.). New York: Harcourt Brace.

HORN, E. (1967). *What research says to the teacher: Teaching spelling.* Washington, DC: National Education Association.

HORN, E. (1954). Phonics and spelling. *Journal of Education, 136,* 233–235, 246.

HOWELL, K. W., & KAPLAN, J. S. (1980). *Diagnosing basic skills: A handbook for deciding what to teach.* Columbus, OH: Merrill.

HOWELL, K. W., & McCOLLUM-GAHLEY, J. (1986). Monitoring instruction. *Teaching Exceptional Children, 19,* 47–49.

HOWELL, K., & MOREHEAD, M. (1987). *Curriculum-based evaluation for special and remedial education.* Columbus, OH: Merrill.

HUGHES, C., & RUHL, K. (1984). Social skills training. In B. Algozzine (Ed.), *Educators' resource manual for management of problem behaviors in students.* Rockville, MD: Aspen.

HUGHES, C., SCHUMAKER, J. B., DESHLER, D. D., & MERCER, C. (in press). *The learning strategies curriculum: The test-taking strategy.* Lawrence, KS: Excel Enterprises.

HUNT, K. (1965). *Grammatical structures written at three grade levels.* Urbana, IL: National Council of Teachers of English.

HUNT, K. (1970). Syntactic maturity in school children and adults. *Monographs of the Society for Research in Child Development, 134*(35), 1–44.

HYMES, J. (1968). *Early childhood education: An Introduction to the Profession.* Washington, DC: National Association for Education of Young Children.

IDOL-MAESTAS, L. (1983). *Special educator's consultation handbook.* Rockville, MD: Aspen.

ISSACSON, S. (1988). Assessing the writing product: Qualitative and quantitative measures. *Exceptional Children, 54*(6), 528–534.

IVARIE, J. J. (1986). Effects of proficiency rates on later performance of a recall and writing behavior. *Rememdial and Special Education, 7*(5), 25–30.

JENKINS, J., & PANY, D. (1978). Standardized achievement tests: How useful for special education? *Exceptional children, 44,* 488–453.

JOHNSON-MARTIN, N., JENS, K., & ATTERMEIR, S. (1986). *The Carolina curriculum for handicapped infants at risk.* Baltimore: Brooks.

KEMPER, S. (1983). Measuring the inference load of a text. *Journal of Educational Psychology, 75*(3), 391–401.

KERR, M. M., & NELSON, C. M. (1983). *Strategies for managing behavior problems in the classroom.* Columbus, OH: Merrill.

KREUTZER, M. A., LEONARD, S. C., & FLAVELL, J. H. (1975). Interview study about children's knowledge about memory. *Monographs of the Society for Research in Child Development, 40,* 1–57.

KUBISZYN, T., & BORICH, G. (1984). *Educational testing and measurement: Classroom application and practice.* Glenview, IL: Scott, Foresman.

KUEHNLE, K., DENO, S., & MIRKIN, P. (1982). *Behavioral measurement of social adjustment: What behaviors? What settings?* (Research Report No. 82). Minneapolis: University of Minnesota, Institute for Research on Learning Disabilities.

LARSEN, S., & HAMMILL, D. (1986). *Test of written spelling.* Austin, TX: PRO-ED.

LAURIE, T. E., BUCHWACH, L., SILVERMAN, R., & ZIGMOND, N. (1978). Teaching secondary learning disabled students in the mainstream. *Learning Disability Quarterly, 1,* 62–72.

LEINHARDT, G., & SEWARD, A. (1981). Overlap: What's tested, what's taught? *Journal of Educational Measurement, 18,* 85–95.

LEINHARDT, G., ZIGMOND, N., & COOLEY, W. (1981). Reading instruction and its effects. *American Educational Research Journal, 18*(3), 343–361.

LERNER, J. (1985). *Learning disabilities: Theories, diagnosis, and teaching strategies* (4th ed.). Boston: Houghton Mifflin.

LENKOWSKI, R., & BLACKMAN, I. (1969). The effect of teachers' knowledge of race and social class on their judgments of children's academic competence and social acceptability. *Mental Retardation, 6*(6), 15–17.

LENZ, B. K., SCHUMAKER, J. B., & DESHLER, D. D. (in press). *The interpreting of visual aids strategy.* Lawrence, KS: Excel Enterprises.

LENZ, B. K., SCHUMAKER, J. B., DESHLER, D. D., & BEALS, V. L. (1984). *The learning strategies curriculum: The word identification strategy.* Lawrence: University of Kansas, Institute for Research in Learning Disabilities.

LEPORE, A. (1979). A comparison of computational errors between educable mentally handicapped and learning disability children. *Focus on Learning Problems in Mathematics, 1,* 12–33.

LLOYD, J. W., & LOPER, A. B. (1986). Measurement and evaluation of task-related learning behaviors: Attention to task and metacognition. *School Psychology Review, 15*(3), 336–345.

LOBAN, W. (1976). *Language development: Kindergarten through grade twelve* (Report No. 18). Urbana, IL: National Council of Teachers of English.

LOVITT, T. (1973). Self-management projects with children with behavioral disabilities. *Journal of Learning Disabilities, 6*(3), 15–28.

LOVITT, T., & HANSEN, C. (1976). The use of contingent skipping and drilling to improve oral reading and comprehension. *Journal of Learning Disabilities, 9,* 481–487.

MAGER, R. P. (1961). *Preparing objectives for program instruction.* San Francisco: Fearon.

MARSTON, D. (1988). Measuring progress on IEP's: A comparison of graphing approaches. *Exceptional Children, 55*(1) 39–44.

MARSTON, D., & MAGNUSSON, D. (1985). Implementing curriculum-based measurement in special and regular education settings. *Exceptional Children, 52,* 266–276.

MARSTON, D., TINDAL, G., & DENO, S. L. (1984). Eligibility for learning disabilities services: A direct and repeated measurement approach. *Exceptional children, 50*(6), 534–556.

MASLOW, A. (1954). *Motivation and personality.* New York: Harper and Row.

MEALOR, D., & RICHMOND, B. (1980). Adaptive behavior: Teachers and parents disagree. *Exceptional children, 46,* 386–389.

MERCER, C., & MERCER, A. (1985). *Teaching students with learning problems* (2d ed.). Columbus, OH: Merrill.

MERCER, C., MERCER, A., & BOTT, D. (1984). *Self-correcting learning materials for the classroom.* Columbus, OH: Merrill.

MERCER, C., MERCER, A., & EVANS, S. (1982). The use of frequency in establishing instructional aims. *Journal of Precision Teaching, 3*(3), 57–63.

MERRIWETHER, A., & HUGHES, C. (1987). *Learning disabled children: Memory remediation through strategy instruction.* Unpublished manuscript.

MEYERS, J., & LYTLE, S. (1986). Assessment of the learning process. *Exceptional Children*, 53(2), 138–144.

MILLER, C., McLAUGHLIN, J., HADDON, J., & CHANSKY, N. (1968). Socioeconomic class and teacher bias. *Psychological Reports, 23*, 806.

MILLER, J., & MILAM, C. (1987). Multiplication and division errors committed by learning disabled students. *Learning Disabilities Research, 2*(2), 119–122.

MISHLER, C., & HOGAN, T. (1982). Holistic scoring of essays: Remedy for evaluating the third R. *Diagnostique, 8,* 4–16.

MORENO, J. (1953). *Who shall survive? Foundations of sociometry, psychotherapy, and sociodrama* (2d ed.). New York: Beacon House.

MURPHY, J. (1976). Psychiatric labeling cross-cultural perspective. *Science, 191,* 1019–1028.

NAGEL, D., SCHUMAKER, J. B., & DESHLER, D. D. (1986). *The learning strategies curriculum: The first-letter mnemonic strategy.* Lawrence, KS: Excel Enterprises.

NATIONAL EDUCATION ASSOCIATION. (1918). *Seven cardinal principles of secondary education: A report of the commission on the reorganization of secondary education* (Bulletin 1918, No. 35). Washington, DC: U.S. Government Printing Office.

NEWBORG, J., STOCK, J., WNEK, L., GUIDUBALDI, J., & SVINICKI, J. (1984). *Battelle developmental inventory.* Allen, TX: DLM/Teaching Resources.

NEWLAND, T. (1932). An analytic study of the development of illegibilities in handwriting from the lower grades to adulthood. *Journal of Educational Research, 26,* 249–258.

NIHIRA, K. (1969). Factorial dimensions of adaptive behavior in mentally retarded children and adolescents. *American Journal of Mental Deficiency, 74,* 130–141.

PAGE, E. (1968). The use of the computer in analyzing student essays. *International Review of Education, 14,* 210–225.

PAINE, S., RADICCHI, J., ROSELLINI, L., DEUTCHMAN, L., & DARCH, C. (1983). *Structuring your classroom for academic success.* Champaign, IL: Research.

PALINCSAR, A. S. (1986). Metacognitive strategy instruction. *Exceptional Children, 53*(2), 118–124.

PARIS, S. G., CROSS, D. R., & LIPSON, M. Y. (1984). Informed strategies for learning: A program to improve children's reading awareness and comprehension. *Journal of Educational Psychology, 76,* 1239–1252.

PEARSON, P., & JOHNSON, D. (1979). *Teaching reading comprehension.* New York: Holt, Rinehart, & Winston.

PENNYPACKER, H. S., KEONIG, C. H., & LINDSLEY, O. R. (1972). *Handbook of the standard behavior chart.* Kansas City, MO: Precision Media.

PERKINS, K. (1983). On the use of composition scoring techniques, objective measures, and objective tests to evaluate ESL writing ability. *TESOL Quarterly, 17*(4), 651–664.

PONTI, C., ZINS, J., & GRADEN, J. (1988). Implementing a consultation-based service delivery system to decrease referrals for special education: A case study of organizational considerations. *School Psychology Review, 17,* 89–100.

POPHAM, W. (1978). *Criterion-referenced measurement.* Englewood Cliffs, NJ: Prentice-Hall.

POWELL, J., MARTINDALE, A., & KULP, S. (1975). An evaluation of time sample measures of behavior. *Journal of Applied Behavior Analysis, 8*(4), 463–469.

POWELL, J., MARTINDALE, B., KULP, S., MARTINDALE, A., & BAUMAN, R. (1977). Taking a closer look: Time sampling and measurement error. *Journal of Applied Behavior Analysis, 10*(2), 325–332.

Powell, J., & Rockinson, R. (1978). On the inability of time sampling to reflect frequency of occurrence data. *Journal of Applied Behavior Analysis, 11*(4), 531–532.

Power, D., & Quigley, S. (1973). Deaf chidren's acquisition of the passive voice. *Journal of Speech and Hearing Research, 16*(1), 5–11.

Quay, H., & Peterson, D. (1983). *Revised behavior problem checklist.* Coral Gables, FL: University of Miami.

Rasool, J., & Royer, J. (1986). Assessment of reading comprehension using the sentence verification technique: Evidence from narrative and descriptive texts. *Journal of Educational Research, 79*(3), 180–184.

Reisman, F. K. (1984). *Sequential assessment of mathematics inventory.* Columbus, OH: Merrill.

Repp, A., Roberts, B., Slack, D., Repp, C., & Berkler, M. (1976). A comparison of frequency interval and time sampling methods of data collection. *Journal of Applied Behavior Analysis, 9*(4), 501–508.

Reschly, D. (1982). Assessing mild mental retardation: The influence of adaptive behavior, sociocultural status, and prospects for nonbiased assessment. In C. Reynolds & T. Gutkin (Eds.), *The handbook of school psychology* (pp. 209–242). New York: Wiley.

Ritter, D. (1978). Effects of a school consultation program upon referral patterns of teachers. *Psychology in the Schools, 15*, 239–243.

Robert, G. H. (1968). The failure strategies of third grade arithmetic pupils. *The Arithmetic Teacher, 15*, 442–446.

Rogers, S., D'Eugenio, D., Drews, J., Haskin, R., Lynch, E., & Moersch, M. (1981). *Preschool developmental profile.* Ann Arbor: University of Michigan.

Rogers, S., Donovan, C., D'Eugenio, D., Brown, S., Lynch, E., Moersch, L., & Schafer, D. (1981). *Early intervention developmental profile.* Ann Arbor: University of Michigan.

Rojahn, J., & Kanoy, R. (1985). Toward an empirically based parameter selection for time sampling observation systems. *Journal of Psychopathology and Behavioral Assessment, 7*(2), 99–120.

Rosenshine, B. (1980). Skill hierarchies in reading comprehension. In R. Spiro, D. Bruce, & W. Brewer (Eds.), *Theoretical issues in reading comprehension* (pp. 535–554). Hillsdale, NJ: Erlbaum.

Ross, M., & Salvia, J. (1975). Attractiveness as a biasing factor in teacher judgments. *American Journal of Mental Deficiency, 80* (1), 96–98.

Royer, J., & Cunningham, J. (1981). On the theory and measurement of reading comprehension. *Contemporary Educational Psychology, 6*, 187–216.

Royer, J., Hastings, C., & Hook, C. (1979). A sentence verification technique for measuring reading comprehension. *Journal of Reading Behavior, 11*(4), 355–363.

Salmon-Cox, L. (1981). Teachers and standardized achievement tests: What's really happening? *Phi Delta Kappan, 62*(9), 631–634.

Salvia, J., Algozzine, B., & Sheare, J. (1977). Attractiveness and school achievement. *Journal of School Psychology, 15*(1), 60–67.

Salvia, J., Sheare, J., & Algozzine, R. (1975) Facial attractiveness and personal-social development. *Journal of Abnormal Child Psychology, 3*(7), 171–178.

Salvia, J., & Ysseldyke, J. (1988). *Assessment in special and remedial education* (3d ed.). Boston: Houghton Mifflin.

SANFORD, A., & ZELMAN, J. (1981). *Learning accomplishment profile-revised prescriptive edition*. Winston-Salem, NC: Kaplan.

SANSON-FISHER, R., POOLE, A., & DUNN, J. (1980). An empirical method for determining an appropriate interval length for recording behavior. *Journal of Applied Behavior Analysis*, 13(3), 493–500.

SCHAFER, D., & MOERSCH, M. (1981). *Developmental programming for infants and young children*. Ann Arbor: University of Michigan.

SCHLOSS, P. J., HALLE, J. W., & SINDELAR, P. T. (1984). Guidelines for teachers' interpretation of student performance data. *Remedial and special education*, 5(4), 38–43.

SCHMIDT, W. (1978). *Measuring the content of instruction*. East Lansing: Michigan State University, Institute for Research on Teaching.

SCHOPLER, E., LANSING, M., REICHLER, R., & WATERS, L. (1979). *Individualized assessment and treatment for autistic and developmentally delayed children*. Austin, TX: PRO-ED.

SCHUMAKER, J. B. (in preparation). *The learning strategies curriculum: The theme writing strategy*. Lawrence: University of Kansas, Institute for Research in Learning Disabilities.

SCHUMAKER, J. B., DENTON, P. H., & DESHLER, D. D. (1984). *The learning strategies curriculum: The paraphrasing strategy*. Lawrence: University of Kansas, Institute for Research in Learning Disabilities.

SCHUMAKER, J. B., & DESHLER, D. D. (1984). Setting demand variables: A major factor in program planning for the learning disabled adolescent. *Topics in Language Disorders Journal*, 4(2), 22–40.

SCHUMAKER, J. B., DESHLER, D. D., ALLEY, G. R., & DENTON, P. H. (1982). Multipass: A learning strategy for improving reading comprehension. *Learning disability quarterly*, 5(3), 295–300.

SCHUMAKER, J. B., DESHLER, D. D., ALLEY, G. R., & WARNER, M. M. (1983). Toward the development of an intervention model for learning disabled adolescents: The University of Kansas Institute. *Exceptional Education Quarterly*, 4(1), 45–74.

SCHUMAKER, J. B., NOLAN, S., & DESHLER, D. D. (1985). *The learning strategies curriculum: The error monitoring strategy*. Lawrence: University of Kansas, Institute for Research in Learning Disabilities.

SCHUMAKER, J. B., & SHELDON, J. (1985). *The learning strategies curriculum: The sentence writing strategy*. Lawrence: University of Kansas, Institute for Research in Learning Disabilities.

SEAVER, W. (1977). Effects of naturally induced teacher expectancies. *Journal of Personality and Social Psychology*, 28, 333–342.

SHEPERD, M. J. (1987). *Learning strategies*. Paper presented at Conference on Cognition and Metacognition. Pittsburgh: Pennsylvania Resources and Information Center for Special Education.

SHINN, M. (1988). Development of curriculum-based local norms for use in special education decision-making. *School Psychology Review*, 17(1), 61–80.

SHINN, M., TINDAL, G., & STEIN, S. (1988). Curriculum-based measurement and the identification of mildly handicapped students: A review of research. *Professional School Psychology*, 3(1), 69–85.

SHRINER, J., & SALVIA, J. (1988). Content validity of two tests with two math curricula over three years: Another instance of chronic noncorrespondence. *Exceptional Children*, 55(3), 240–248.

SKIBA, R., MARSTON, D., WESSON, C., SEVCIK, B., & DENO, S. (1983). *Characteristics of the time-series data collected through curriculum-based reading measurement* (Research Report No. 125). Minneapolis: University of Minnesota, Institute for Research on Learning Disabilities.

SIPERSTEIN, G., & BAK, J. (1978). Students' and teachers' perceptions of the mentally retarded child. In J. Gottleib (Ed.), *Educating mentally retarded persons in the mainstream* (pp. 207–230). Baltimore: University Park.

SMITH, G. (1978). *Observer drift under monitored and unmonitored conditions.* Unpublished doctoral dissertation, The Pennsylvania State University, University Park, PA.

SNIEZEK, K. (1983). *Effects of presentation method and stimulus variation on the acquisition of generalization of color names.* Unpublished doctoral dissertation, The Pennsylvania State University, University Park, PA.

SOYSTER, H., & EHLY, S. (1986). Parent-rated adaptive behavior and in-school ratings of students referred for EMR evaluation. *American Journal of Mental Deficiency, 90,* 460–463.

SPACHE, G. (1981). *Diagnosing and correcting reading disabilities* (2d ed.). Boston: Allyn and Bacon.

SPACHE, G., & SPACHE, E. (1977). *Reading in the elementary school* (4th ed.). Boston: Allyn and Bacon.

SPARGO, E., & WILLISTON, G. (1980). *Timed readings.* Providence, RI: Jamestown.

SPRINGER, B., BROWN, T., & DUNCAN, P. (1981). Current measurement in applied behavior analysis. *The Behavior Analyst, 4*(1), 19–31.

STATE OF FLORIDA. (1983). *A resource manual for the development and evaluation of special programs for exceptional students (Vol 5-D): Techniques of precision teaching, part 3: Reading basic skills curriculum.* Tallahassee: Florida Department of Education.

STEPHENS, T. M., HARTMAN, A. C., & LUCAS, V. H. (1978). *Teaching children basic skills.* Columbus, OH: Merrill.

STEPHENS, T. M., HARTMAN, A. C., & LUCAS, V. H. (1982). *Teaching children basic skills: A curriculum handbook* (2d ed.). Columbus, OH: Merrill.

STEVENS, L. J. (1987). Cognition and metacognition: Teaching and learning strategies for mildly handicapped students. *PRISE Reporter, 18,* 1–3.

STEWART, M., & LEAMAN, H. (1983). Teachers' writing assignments across the high school curriculum. *Research in the Teaching of English, 17*(2), 113–125.

STOKES, T., BAER, D., & JACKSON, R. (1974). Programming generalization of a greeting response in four retarded children. *Journal of Applied Behavioral Analysis, 7,* 599–610.

SUGAI, G. (1986). Recording classroom events: Maintaining a critical incidents log. *Teaching Exceptional Children, 18*(2), 98–102.

SULZER-AZAROFF, B., & MAYER, G. (1977). *Applying behavior-analysis procedures with children and youth.* New York: Holt, Rinehart, & Winston.

STRUNCK, W., JR., & WHITE, E. B. (1959). *The elements of style.* New York: Macmillan.

THIBODEAU, G. (1974). Manipulation of numerical presentation in verbal problems and its effect on verbal problem solving among EMH children. *Education and Training of the Mentally Retarded, 9,* 9–14.

THOBURN, T. (1987). *Macmillan English: Thinking and writing processes.* New York: Macmillan.

THORNDIKE, R., & HAGEN, E. (1978). *Measurement and evaluation in psychology and education.* New York: Wiley.

TORGESEN, J. K. (1979). Factors related to poor performance on memory tasks in reading disabled children. *Learning Disabilities Quarterly, 2,* 17–23.

TRAVERS, R. (1982). *Essentials of learning: The new cognitive learning for students of education* (5th ed.). New York: Macmillan.

UNDERHILL, R. G., UPRICHARD, A. E., & HEDDENS, J. W. (1980). *Diagnosing mathematical difficulties.* Columbus, OH: Merrill.

UNDERWOOD, B. (1954). Speed of learning and amount retained: A consideration of methodology. *Psychological Bulletin, 51*(3), 276–279.

U.S.O.E. (1977). Assistance to states for education of handicapped children: Procedures for evaluating specific learning disabilities. *Federal Register, 42*(163), sec. 121 a.5, p. 42478.

VANRIPER, C. (1978). *Speech correction: Principles and methods* (6th ed.). Englewood Cliffs, NJ: Prentice-Hall.

VANRUSEN, A., BOS, C., SCHUMAKER, J., & DESHLER, D. (1987). *The education planning strategy.* Lawrence, KS: Excell Enterprises.

VIDEEN, J., DENO, S., & MARSTON, D. (1982). *Correct word sequences: A valid indicator of proficiency in written language* (Research Report No. 84). Minneapolis: University of Minnesota, Institute for Research on Learning Disabilities.

WALL, S., & PARADISE, L. (1981). A comparison of parent and teacher reports of selected adaptive behaviors of children. *Journal of School Psychology, 19,* 73–77.

WALLACE, G., & LARSEN, S. (1978). *Educational assessment of learning problems: Testing for teaching.* Boston: Allyn & Bacon.

WEIDERHOLT, L., & BRYANT, B. (1987). Assessment for instruction. In D. Hammill (Ed.), *Assessing the abilities and instructional needs of students* (pp. 237–316). Austin, TX: PRO-ED.

WESSON, C., SKIBA, R., KING, R., & DENO, S. (1984). The effects of technically adequate instructional data on achievement. *Remedial and Special Education, 5*(5), 17–22.

WESSON, C. (1989). *Curriculum-based measurement: Monitoring student progress and evaluating instructional effectiveness.* Paper presented at Conference on Curriculum-Based Assessment and Prereferral Interventions. Pennsylvania Resources and Information Center for Special Education, King of Prussia, PA

WESSON, C. (1987). Increasing efficiency. *Teaching Exceptional Children, 20*(1), 46–47.

WESSON, C., KING, R., & DENO, S. (1984). Direct and frequent measurement of student performance: If it's good for us, why don't we do it? *Learning Disability Quarterly, 7,* 45–48.

WHALEY, J. (1981). Story grammars and reading instruction. *The Reading Teacher, 34,* 762–771.

WHITAKER, K. K. (1982). *Development and field test of an assignment completion strategy for learning disabled adolescents.* Unpublished master's thesis. University of Kansas, Lawrence.

WHITE, O. R. (1986). Precision teaching-precision learning. *Exceptional Children, 52,* 522–534.

WHITE, O., & HARING, N. (1980). *Exceptional teaching* (2d ed.). Columbus, OH: Merrill.

WHITE, O. R., & LIBERTY, K. A. (1976). Behavioral assessment and precise educational measurement. In N. G. Haring & R. Schiefelbusch (Eds.), *Teaching special children* (pp. 31–71). New York: McGraw-Hill.

WILLOUGHBY-HERB, S., & NEISWORTH, J. (1983). *The HICOMP preschool curriculum.* New York: Psychological Corp.

WILSON, R., & CLELAND, C. (1985). *Diagnostic and remedial reading.* Columbus, OH: Merrill.

WIXSON, K. (1979). Miscue analysis: A critical review. *Journal of Reading Behavior, 11,* 163–175.

WOODCOCK, R. (1978). *Woodcock–Johnson psychoeducational battery.* Hingham, MA: Teaching Resources Corp.

WORRELL, J., & NELSON, C. (1974). *Managing instructional problems: A case study workbook.* New York: McGraw-Hill.

YSSELDYKE, J. E., THURLOW, M., GRADEN, J., WESSON, C., ALGOZZINE, B., & DENO, S. (1983). Generalizations from five years of research on assessment and decision making: The University of Minnesota Institute. *Exceptional Education Quarterly, 4*(1), 75–94.

Glossary

Abscissa. The horizontal (x) axis of the graph that is plotted near the bottom in relevant time intervals.

Abstract level. A task in which a learner manipulates symbols rather than concrete objects. For example, in mathematics a student required to solve problems only using numerals.

Achievement. What has been learned as a result of a specific course of instruction.

Active learner. A learner who, when presented with a task, will spontaneously use effective strategies in problem solving and task completion.

Adaptive behavior. An inclusive term for any action that increases people's likelihood of physical survival and ability to cope with social and physical demands of their environment.

Aid. In oral reading, a particular type of error in which a student asks for help or waits so long that a teacher must supply the word that cannot be read.

Aim. The level of achievement expected of a student; the criterion for acceptable performance.

Aimline. A line on a graph used to indicate the rate of progress or celeration a student must maintain in order to reach criteria by a certain time.

Algorithm. The sequence of steps or activities necessary to solve a problem.

Amplitude. A characteristic of behavior that describes the strength of response.

Application. The level of achievement at which a student is required to use previously learned skills in a context or problem in which they were not learned or previously practiced.

Atomistic scoring. In written language, a method of evaluating written language by noting each occurrence of an error in style, grammar, and so forth.

Attainment. What has been learned as a result of either systematic instruction or incidental acquisition.

Behavioral objective. A statement of what a student will learn in terms of the behavior that will be exhibited when learning occurs, the conditions under which the behavior will be exhibited, and the criteria to be used in evaluating the behavior.

Celeration. A numerical index of trend.

Classification. In special education, a process to establish eligibility for certain types of services.

Cloze procedure. In reading, a procedure to assess reading comprehension by examining the extent to which contextual clues are used to identify words that have been omitted from text.

Cognition. In psychology, the modern equivalent of thinking.

Component. In a curricular taxonomy, a subordinate set of skills or behavior to be learned.

Comprehension. The level of achievement at which a student is required to go beyond recognition or recall of information and to demonstrate understanding through translation, interpretation, and/or extrapolation of information.

Concrete level. A task in which a learner manipulates objects rather than symbols; for example, in mathematics a student required to solve problems using sticks to represent sets rather than numbers.

Consonant blends. Two or more consonants that are blended when pronounced in a word. Blends can occur at the beginning or end of a word. Students are taught to recognize these blends as units because if the consonants are pronounced separately, the pronounciation will be incorrect.

Content reliability. The extent to which one can generalize from a student's performance on a particular set of questions to performance on similar (but not identical) questions.

Content validity. The extent to which a set of items or behaviors represent all other items that might be included within the set in terms of the appropriateness of items included, the completeness of the item included, and the way in which each item assesses the content.

Criterion-referenced test. A test by which student performance is evaluated in comparison to an absolute standard of attainment.

Critical incident log. A written document in which a teacher describes important behavior demonstrated by students and notes potentially relevant factors associated with the behavior (e.g., its antecedents and consequences, dates and times of incidents).

Curriculum. All written or intended, academic and nonacademic instructional objectives for a student or group of students.

Curriculum-embedded assessment. A form of curriculum-based assessment in which assessment occurs as a part of instruction.

Curriculum-referenced assessment. A form of curriculum-based assessment used to assess the attainment of developmental milestones that are incorporated into preschool curricula but that are specific to no one curriculum.

Daily living skill. A skill required in managing the routine aspects of one's life (e.g., dressing, shopping, eating).

Data point. In general, a term used to describe a summarized performance; in graphing, the intersection of the level of performance (from the ordinate) and time when the performance occurred (on the abscissa).

Developmental age. The average chronological age at which a skill or set of skills is manifested.

Developmental curricula. Curricula sequenced according to the progression of skills evidenced by most students.

Developmental domain. Usually used in connection with preschool education, a term that refers both to content of instruction (i.e., skills that normally developing children demonstrate with little or no instruction in a variety of domains such language, fine and gross motor, social and emotional, etc.) and the sequence in which skills are acquired.

Developmental norms. Information, usually presented in tables, that quantifies the ages at which particular percentages of children acquire certain developmental skills (e.g., 10% of all children acquire skill X by age 2 years, 3 months; 25% by 2 years, 7 months; 50% by 2 years, 10 months; 75% by 3 years, 0 months; and 90% by 3 years, 6 months).

Developmental quotient. A test score that equals 100 times the ratio of developmental age divided by actual (chronological) age.

Diagnostic test. A test that has a sufficient number of items to allow correct inferences about the types of errors a pupil makes or about a pupil's mastery of particular skills or concepts.

Diction. The selection of words that convey precisely what the speaker or writer intends (also called word choice).

Digraph. A two-letter combination of either vowels (e.g., *ea* in wheat) or consonants (e.g., *ph*) that creates a single sound.

Diphthong. In phonics, two vowels that are both heard in making a compound sound (e.g., *oi* in boil).

Disregard of punctuation. In oral reading, an error in which a student does not pause for commas or periods, change inflection for questions and exclamations, and so forth.

Duration. A characteristic of behavior that refers to the length of time a behavior lasts once it has begun.

Duration recording. In systematic observation, a procedure used to record the time that a discrete event or behavior lasts, usually by noting the time at the start of the event and at its conclusion.

Equal-interval chart. A graph in which the vertical and horizontal axes are segmented equally and used to display an absolute rate of growth.

Evaluation of pupil progress. A purpose for assessment in which a student's acquisition, maintenance, and/or generalization is systematically assessed.

Event recording. In systematic observation, a procedure used to obtain the frequency with which a behavior occurs by tallying each occurrence as it happens throughout an entire period of observation.

Extinction. The cessation of a response as a result of withdrawal of a previously paired reinforcer.

Formative evaluation. The ongoing collection of data on pupil performance.

Frequency. The number of occurrences of a discrete event or behavior.

Functional curriculum. A sequence of instructional objectives designed to develop the application of skills necessary for daily living and work.

Functional range. The circumstances and extent of use of particular skills by an individual.

Goal component. Any of the important aspects (or subskills) of a generalized instructional intent.

Graded passages. A set of readings, evaluated and sequenced according to their level of grammatical and lexical difficulty, that can be used to assess word analysis skills, accuracy and fluency in word recognition, and comprehension.

Grammar. Refers to the sequencing and interrelationships among words that give meaning to written and oral expression.

Group-administered test. A test that can be given simultaneously to two or more test takers who usually write (or mark) their own responses.

Halo effect. The tendency for a person's characteristics, rather than intended criteria, to influence the evaluation of a performance.

Holistic scoring. A method of evaluating written language in which the overall quality of the writing is judged.

Individually administered test. A test that may be given to only one student at a time, usually because an examiner must read the questions and record the test taker's responses.

Insertion. In oral reading, the addition of words (or parts of words) not present in the text.

Instructional modification. A change in any aspect of a student's (or group of students') instructional program, including the demonstration, practice, sequence, pace, and contingencies for correct performance.

Instructional objective. A written statement describing what a student will learn.

Interscorer reliability. The consistency with which two or more scorers evaluate the same performance.

Interval recording. In systematic observation, a method of discontinuous observation in which specified times are chosen in which to observe behavior.

Inversion. An error in oral reading in which words are read in a sequence different from the sequence in which they are printed in the text.

Key. The answers to be credited as correct on a test or probe; a miskeyed item is one in which an incorrect answer is credited and a correct answer is not.

Knowledge. A level of achievement at which a student is required to recognize and produce factual information or demonstrate a behavior under the conditions in which it was taught.

Latency. The amount of time elapsed between the time a stimulus is presented and the onset of a response.

Learning picture. A visual record of performance shown when trend is apparent; three types of learning pictures are improving pictures, maintaining pictures, and worsening pictures.

Learning strategy. A sequence of steps intended to facilitate the acquisition, recall, and expression of learning.

Level of performance. A classification of the type of mastery expected of a learner (e.g., knowledge, comprehension, application).

Levels. The extent to which mastery occurs, including both cognitive (knowledge, comprehension, and application) and behavioral levels (acquisition, fluency, generalization, and maintenance).

Long-term objective. A statement of instructional intent about student performance several weeks in the future (e.g., by year-end).

Materials. The content on which mathematical operations are performed (for example, single-digit numbers, unlike fractions, or particular units of measurement).

Mechanics. In written language, the conventions to be followed in spelling, punctuation, and capitalization.

Metacognition. Awareness of one's own thinking and planning as they relate to learning or recall.

Miscue analysis. In oral reading, a process of inferring the underlying attributes of errors in word analysis and comprehension.

Mispronunciation. An error in oral reading in which the word said by the reader is improperly accented, has additional or omitted syllables, or is unrecognizable.

Mnemonic device. An artificial and intentional method of organizing material to facilitate its recall.

Momentary time sample. In systematic observation, a method of discontinuous sampling in which an observer notes the occurrence or nonoccurrence of a behavior at the instant the recording interval ends.

Nomination. In sociometry, a selection of a student by classmates on the basis of some predetermined criterion (e.g., "Who would you like to have on your softball team?").

Norm-referenced test. A test with which student performance is evaluated in terms of the performances of other comparable students (e.g., students in the same grade or of the same age) on the same materials.

Objective-referenced test. A test with which student performance is evaluated in terms of the specific objectives attained when the objectives are derived from individual test items.

Operations. In mathematics, the processes of addition, subtraction, multiplication, division, or exponential functions.

Ordinate. The verical (y) axis of the graph that is ordinarily plotted on the left and contains the number, frequency, or rate of performance.

Organization. In written language, organization refers to the logical and cohesive sequencing of ideas.

Paraphrasing. In reading, the restatement of the essential ideas and details of a passage.

Partial-interval recording. In systematic observation, a method of discontinuous sampling in which an event is recorded if it occurs within any part (or all) of the interval.

Penmanship. Usually referring to letters but occasionally to numbers, the production of both manuscript and cursive symbols that are correctly formed (i.e., of appropriate shape, size, orientation) and spaced.

Performance measure. A sample of behavior from which acquisition and fluency of the behavior can be assessed directly.

Phase change. In graphing, a change in educational programs, material, or criterion that is indicated graphically by a heavy vertical line.

Phonics. The regular relationship between symbols and sounds.

Phonogram. Vowels combined with r and groups of letters commonly used as word endings.

Placement. The assignment of a student who is eligible for special-education services to regular and/or special educators who have responsibility for providing instruction to that student.

Planning instruction. The selection and sequence of activities to facilitate learning.

Prereferral decision. A decision, usually related to the modification of instruction designed to enhance student learning, that takes place prior to assessment to determine eligibility for special educational services.

Probes. Measurement devices typically used for formative evaluations to assess single or multiple skills or objectives, and administered in brief (one- to three-minute) timed sessions. Probes can measure a variety of responses directly, including written and oral performance.

Problem solving. In mathematics, a component of most curricular strands in which students are required to analyze a question to ascertain the pertinent information and select appropriate operations to arrive at a numerical answer to a question.

Punctuation. In written language, the various symbols and rules governing their use for adding clarity and meaning to the communication.

Punishment. A consequence of behavior that has the effect of reducing the occurrence of that the behavior.

Quality. As a criterion in evaluating pupil performance, the extent to which a performance departs from perfect.

Quarter-intersect. In graphing, a method of determining a trend line.

Rating scale. An assessment device that solicits summary judgments about a person's performance that are usually based upon the rater's overall experience with the person.

Reading comprehension. Obtaining meaning from written material—individual words, phrases, sentences, paragraphs, and entire passages.

Referral. The process of seeking psychological and educational assessment to determine eligibility for special services.

Reinforcement. A consequence of behavior that has the effect of increasing the frequency, duration, or amplitude of that behavior.

Reliability. A generic term for the consistency with which a specific set of responses (e.g., answers to test questions) made at a specific time and evaluated by particular observer (e.g., tester) can be generalized to other similar responses, times, or observers.

Repetition. An error in oral reading in which a student repeats words or series of words.

Reversal. An error in oral reading in which a student reads all or part of a word from right to left.

Script-implicit questions. Questions used in reading comprehension that assume specific information and experiences on the part of the reader in order to be answered correctly.

Semiconcrete level. In mathematics, an intermediate level of abstraction between concrete objects and their representation by numbers; set values are represented in one-to-one correspondence with nonnumerical symbols such as slashes or number lines.

Semilogarithmic graph. A chart in which the horizontal axis is segmented equally and the vertical axis is segmented as a ratio scale in order to show proportional growth.

Sequential objectives. A series of teaching or learning objectives ordered with respect to some criterion (e.g., easy to hard, concrete to abstract).

Short-term objective. An instructional or learning goal to be accomplished in the near future.

Social behavior. An inclusive term for any action that affects another individual.

Sociogram. A method of displaying peer nominations so that mutual nominations are apparent; the nominations may be on any of several dimensions (e.g., "Who would you like to be on your spelling team?").

Spelling. The production of the correct sequence of letters to represent a word.

Split-middle method. In graphing, a method of determining a trend line that is used in conjunction with the quarter-intersect method.

Stability. Refers to the degree to which observations or test scores obtained at one time can be generalized to exactly the same behavior samples obtained at a later time.

Standard error of measurement. The standard deviation of error associated with any observation or score; the error implied is the failure of obtained scores or observations to estimate a person's true score exactly.

Strand. In curriculum development or analysis, a major subcomponent of a domain (e.g., within the domain of mathematics is the strand of operations).

Structural analysis. In reading and spelling, an approach to word attack in which words are decoded or encoded by subdividing them into meaningful parts or units (e.g., prefixes, suffixes, stems).

Study skill. Any one of a variety of skills necessary to learn and retain information (e.g., note taking, assignment completion).

Style. An aspect of written language that refers to grammar (i.e., parts of speech, sentence construction, pronoun case, agreement, and verb voice and mood), mechanics (i.e., punctuation, capitalization, font styles, abbreviations, number usage, referencing, and general format), and diction (i.e., word meaning, wordiness, and linguistic diversity).

Substitution. In oral reading, an error in which a reader replaces a word in the text with another meaningful word that may or may not be contextually appropriate.

Survey test. A test that contains a sufficient number of test items to make accurate discriminations among test takers but an insufficient number of items to assess mastery of particular skills or objectives.

Systematic observation. Observations that use a precise set of rules for defining the behavior or event to be observed, the conditions and times in which observations will be made, and the rules for recording instances of the target behavior.

Table of specifications. In curriculum or test development, a method of depicting instructional strands or components and the levels or types of learning required (e.g., knowledge, comprehension, application).

Test-retest reliability. See *Stability*.

Text-explicit question. A question that contains all of the information a student needs in order to answer.

Text-implicit question. A question that contains partial information and that a student is assumed to possess in order to answer.

Tool skill. A prerequisite academic skill necessary for demonstrating learning (i.e., writing or saying letters or numbers).

Transitional skill. A skill that has been partially acquired and occasionally demonstrated; an emerging skill is usually seen when a less advanced skill is used less frequently in favor of a more effective skill (e.g., walking replaces crawling).

Trend. The tendency for a performance to improve, to degrade, to remain stable, or to vary unpredictably over time; in graphing, a line that depicts this tendency.

T-unit. In language, a main clause plus whatever subordinate clauses or words are attached to or embedded within it.

Visual inspection. In graphing, a method of determining performance changes by looking for trends in performance data rather than quantifying them.

Whole-interval recording. In systematic observation, a method of discontinuous sampling in which the event must last for the entire interval in order to be considered an instance of occurrence.

Word recognition. In reading, the treatment of an entire sequence of letters as a single word that can be read without the need to apply word-attack skills.

Writing fluency. Usually in connected prose, the number of words correctly written or the rate at which words are written correctly.

APPENDIX: Computation of Basic Statistics

Variance and Standard Deviation

Definitions

Variance describes the relationship among scores and the mean of those scores. Variance is the average squared distance of each score from the mean. The standard deviation is the square root of the variance.

Commonly Used Symbols for Variance: S^2, σ^2, ν
Computation of Variance

Computational Formula: $\text{Variance} = \dfrac{\Sigma(X - \overline{X})^2}{N}$

Numerical Example:

Student	Raw scores (X)	Mean[1] (X̄)	Difference (raw score − mean)	Squared difference
1	3	12	−9	81
2	6	12	−6	36
3	9	12	−3	9
4	12	12	0	0
5	15	12	+3	9
6	18	12	+6	36
7	21	12	+9	81
Sums	84		0	252

$$\text{Variance} = \frac{\Sigma(X - \overline{X})^2}{N} = \frac{252}{7} = 36$$

Commonly Used Symbols for Standard Deviation: S, S^2, SD
Computation of Standard Deviation

$$\text{Standard Deviation} = \sqrt{\frac{\Sigma(X-\overline{X})^2}{N}} = \sqrt{\frac{252}{7}} = 6$$

[1]Mean = sum of raw scores divided by the number of scores
    = 84/7
    = 12

Pearson Product–Moment Correlation Coefficient

Definition

The Pearson Product–Moment correlation coefficient is a numerical index of the degree of relationship between two variables (e.g., X and Y). This coefficient fits a straight line so that the best fit is obtained. "Best fit line" is defined as the line that produces the smallest squared valued of each score pair (point) to that line.

Commonly Used Symbols for Correlation: r with various subscripts denoting the variables that are correlated; the same subscript (e.g., r_{xx}) indicates they are reliably coefficient.

Computation of Variance

Computational Formula:

$$r = \frac{N\Sigma XY - (\Sigma X)(\Sigma Y)}{\sqrt{N \cdot \Sigma X^2 - (\Sigma X)^2}\sqrt{N \cdot \Sigma Y^2 - (\Sigma Y)^2}}$$

Numerical Example:

Student	X	X²	Y	Y²	Product of X · Y
1	3	9	4	16	12
2	6	36	2	4	12
3	9	81	8	64	72
4	12	144	6	36	72
5	15	225	10	100	150
6	18	324	14	196	252
7	21	441	12	144	252
Sums	84	1,260	56	560	822

$$r = \frac{N \cdot \Sigma XY - (\Sigma X)(\Sigma Y)}{\sqrt{N \cdot \Sigma X^2 - (\Sigma X)^2}\sqrt{N \cdot \Sigma Y^2 - (\Sigma Y)^2}} = \frac{7 \cdot 822 - (84)(56)}{\sqrt{7 \cdot 1{,}260 - (84)^2}\ \sqrt{7 \cdot 560 - (56)^2}}$$

$$= \frac{5{,}754 - 4{,}704}{\sqrt{8{,}820 - 7{,}056}\ \sqrt{3{,}920 - 3{,}137}} = \frac{1{,}050}{\sqrt{1{,}764}\ \sqrt{784}}$$

$$= .89$$

Short-Cut Procedure for Item–Total Correlations

Definition

When items are scored dichotomously, means and variances can be computed differently (i.e., the mean is proportion of individuals getting the item correct and the variance is the proportion multiplied by one less than the proportion). The correlation between a dichotomously scored test item and the total score is a special form of the Pearson Product–Moment correlation, called a point biserial correlation, and takes advantage of the special properties of the dichotomously scored variable.

Symbol Used for Point Biserial Correlation: r_{ptbis}

Computation

Computational Formula: $r = \dfrac{M_p - M_x}{S_x} \cdot \sqrt{\dfrac{N_p}{N_q}}$

Definitions of Symbols in Formula:
M_x = mean of total scores
S_x = standard deviation of total scores
X_p = score for students passing the item
M_p = mean of students passing the dichotomously scored item
N_p = number of students passing the dichotomously scored item
N_q = number of students not passing the dichotomously scored item

Numerical Example:

Student	X	Y	$(X - M_x)$	$(X - M_x)^2$	X_p
1	3	0	-9	81	
3	9	0	-3	9	
5	15	0	3	9	
2	6	1	-6	36	6
4	12	1	0	0	12
6	18	1	6	36	18
7	21	1	9	81	21
Sums	84	4	0	252	57

$M_x = (3 + 9 + 15 + 6 + 12 + 18 + 21)/7 = 12.00$
$S_x = 252/7 = 6.00$
$M_p = (6 + 12 + 18 + 21)/4 = 14.25$
$N_p = 4$
$N_q = 3$

$$r = \dfrac{M_p - M_x}{S_x} \cdot \sqrt{\dfrac{N_p}{N_q}} = \dfrac{14.25 - 12.00}{6.00} \cdot \sqrt{\dfrac{4}{3}}$$
$$= (0.375)(1.155) = .43$$

Coefficient Alpha

Definition

Coefficient alpha is the mean of all possible split-half correlations[2] used to estimate the consistency (i.e., reliability) of test items.

[2]For dichotomous variables, alpha equals $KR - 20$, a formula developed by Kuder and Richardson.

Computation

Computation Formula: $\text{alpha} = k/(k - 1)(1 - \text{Sum } v_i/v_t)$

Definitions of Symbols in Formula:
k = number of test items
v_i = variance of test items
v_t = variance of the test

Numerical Example:

Ss	1	2	3	4	5	6	7	8	9	10	11	12	13	14	15	Total Test
1	1	0	1	0	1	0	1	0	1	0	1	0	1	1	0	8
2	1	1	0	0	1	1	0	1	1	0	1	1	0	1	1	10
3	0	1	0	1	0	1	0	1	0	1	0	1	0	1	1	8
4	0	0	1	0	1	0	0	1	0	1	0	0	1	0	0	5
5	0	1	1	0	0	1	1	0	1	1	0	1	1	0	1	9
6	1	1	1	0	1	1	1	0	0	1	1	1	0	0	0	9
7	0	1	1	0	0	1	1	0	1	1	0	1	1	0	1	9
8	0	0	0	1	0	1	0	0	1	0	1	0	0	1	0	5
9	1	1	1	0	1	1	1	1	1	1	0	1	1	1	0	12
10	1	1	0	1	1	1	1	1	1	0	1	1	1	0	1	12
11	1	1	1	0	1	1	1	0	0	1	1	0	1	1	0	10
12	0	0	1	1	1	0	1	1	1	0	0	1	1	0	0	8
13	0	1	1	1	0	1	1	1	1	1	1	0	1	1	1	12
14	0	1	1	1	0	1	1	1	0	0	1	1	1	1	0	10
15	1	1	1	1	0	1	1	1	1	1	1	0	1	1	1	13
Mean	.47	.73	.73	.47	.53	.80	.73	.73	.67	.67	.60	.53	.60	.47	.53	9.3
Variance	.25	.20	.20	.25	.25	.16	.20	.20	.22	.22	.24	.25	.24	.25	.25	19.40
$r_{pt\ bis}$	.46	.82	.17	−.03	−.06	.64	.58	.86	.94	.94	.91	.88	.91	.82	.51	

$$
\begin{aligned}
\text{alpha} &= k/(k - 1)(1 - \text{Sum } v_i/v_t) \\
&= (15/14)(1 - (.25 + .20 + .20 + .25 + .16 + .20 + .20 + \\
&\quad .22 + .22 + .24 + .25 + .24 + .25 + .25)/19.40 \\
&= (1.07)(1 - (3.36/19.40)) \\
&= .89
\end{aligned}
$$

Deleting Poor Items

The item total correlations from the preceding example are listed below. Three correlations are quite poor, although the remaining items correlate unusually well with total scores. If these items are dropped from the test, reliability should improve even though the test already is quite reliable.

$r_{pt\ bis}$ .46 .82 .17 −.003 −.06 .64 .58 .86 .94 .94 .91 .88 .91 .82 .51

Removal of the three items requires the recalculation of the total score for each student and the variance of the total scores. The variance of revised total scores is 19.45.

$$
\begin{aligned}
\text{alpha} &= k/(k-1)(1 - sum\ v_i/v_t) \\
&= (12/11)(1 - (.25 + .20 + .20 + .20 + .22 + .22 + .24 + \\
&\quad .25 + .24 + .25 + .25))19.45 \\
&= (1.09)(1 - (2.52/19.45)) \\
&= .95
\end{aligned}
$$

Author Index

Subject Index